CHANGING TRAINS

Changing Trains

Railway reform and the role of competition: The experience of six countries

Edited by
D. M. VAN DE VELDE
Department of Regional, Port and Transport Economics
Erasmus University Rotterdam
The Netherlands

Routledge
Taylor & Francis Group
LONDON AND NEW YORK

First published 1999 by Ashgate Publishing

Reissued 2018 by Routledge
2 Park Square, Milton Park, Abingdon, Oxon, OX14 4RN
711 Third Avenue, New York, NY 10017

Routledge is an imprint of the Taylor & Francis Group, an informa business

A Library of Congress record exists under LC control number: 99072240

ISBN 13: 978-1-138-61196-2 (hbk)
ISBN 13: 978-1-138-61198-6 (pbk)
ISBN 13: 978-0-429-46355-6 (ebk)

Contents

List of Contributors

Gunnar Alexandersson	Stockholm School of Economics
Olivier Domenach	Jonction / Université de la Méditerranée, Aix-en-Provence (CRET-LOG)
Staffan Hultén	Stockholm School of Economics
Carsten Lehmann	University of Münster (Institute for Transport Sciences)
Fumitoshi Mizutani	Kobe University (School of Business Administration) and Hertford College, Oxford (Regulatory Policy Institute)
John Preston	University of Oxford (Transport Studies Unit)
Amanda Root	University of Oxford (Transport Studies Unit)
Pierric Teurnier	Jonction / Université de la Méditerranée, Aix-en-Provence (CRET-LOG)
Didier van de Velde	Erasmus University Rotterdam (Department of Regional, Port and Transport Economics)
Peran van Reeven	Erasmus University Rotterdam (Department of Regional, Port and Transport Economics)

Foreword

JOHN PRESTON
Series Editor

The Oxford Studies in Transport series was established by Phil Goodwin in 1983, with nine volumes published by Gower and its successor Avebury. The aim of the series was to incorporate reports of research work undertaken at or in association with the Transport Studies Unit at the University of Oxford. Emphasis was placed on research in the fields of travel behaviour and transport operations and policy. It is with great pleasure that we announce the revival of this series under the editorship of the new Director of the Transport Studies Unit, Dr John Preston and published by Ashgate, the successor to Gower and Avebury. Our thanks are due to Kate Trew, of Ashgate, for enabling the series to be continued. The aims of the series remain as before but with a particular emphasis on international experience in addition to that of the United Kingdom.

This volume is particularly appropriate to mark the re-launch of the Oxford Studies in Transport. Its focus on railway reforms represents one of the main research interests of the Transport Studies Unit, namely that of regulatory studies, and builds on previous studies in the series on reforms in the British express coach[1] and local bus[2] industries. It focuses on an area of transport operations and policy that is of immense topical interest. It also is a truly international volume, incorporating the work not only of research at the University of Oxford, but also of researchers from France, Germany, Japan, the Netherlands and Sweden. Credit is particularly due to Didier van de Velde of Erasmus University Rotterdam, for putting together the research project from which this volume originates and for taking on the arduous task of editing this volume. We trust you, the reader, will agree with us that this volume represents an excellent start for the revived series.

[1] Kilvington, R.P. and Cross, A.K. (1986), *Deregulation of Express Coaches in Britain*, Gower, Aldershot.
[2] Pickup, L, Stokes, G., Meadowcroft, S., Goodwin, P.B., Tyson, B. and Kenny, F. (1990). *Bus Deregulation in the Metropolitan Areas*, Avebury, Aldershot.

Acknowledgements

This book is based on research work carried out in 1997 and financed by the Dutch Railways (NS) and the Dutch Ministry of Transport. The original research report titled *Railway reform and the role of competition: The experience of six countries* was finalised in January 1998 and included six country reports besides the main report.

The authors of this book wish to gratefully acknowledge the financial support given by the Dutch Railways (*NS Passengers*, Department of Strategic Planning and Business Intelligence) and the Dutch Ministry of Transport (Directorate-General for Passenger Transport) for the realisation of this report and for the opportunity given to use this work as a basis for this book. They also wish to thank the Transport Research Centre (AVV) of the Ministry of Transport and the other members of the research supervision group for their contributions and comments during the original study.

Furthermore the editor of this book wishes to thank all contributing authors for their commitment to making both the original research and this book happen. A special word of thanks goes to Peran van Reeven (Erasmus University Rotterdam) who was involved in the research work and who was also co-editor of the original report.

1 Introduction

DIDIER VAN DE VELDE
Erasmus University Rotterdam

The European railway sector is currently characterised in many countries by the development and implementation of important reforms. Keywords to these reforms are often 'regionalisation', 'contractualisation' and 'competition'. While these similarities appear out of a superficial comparison of the various regimes currently developed by several European countries, this masks a wide diversity in background and approach.

Reforms tend to be substantially more complex than can be perceived at first glance. Poorly informed people could for example think that the railways in Great Britain have simply been privatised and deregulated, while a further look learns that the sector is currently tightly regulated, perhaps even more than ever before. The European Directive 91/440 on the accounting separation of infrastructure and operations is often cited as a major impulse to railway reform, but other more specifically national railway problems play equally important roles. Various examples can be given. Local or regional government reform plays in some countries an important role creating a necessity to reform the control on passenger train services. The relative stagnation of the modal share of passenger railways in total mobility forms a focus of political interest in some countries. The accumulated railway debt problem plays a role in many countries but is tackled differently. On top of all of this, there is also the wide cultural and geographical diversity between European countries that is influencing the reform choices and the paths of implementation.

A thorny question in most reforms is what use to make of competition in a sector that has traditionally, at least in Europe, been dominated by authority-owned monopolies. Many options are thinkable and are being considered at one point or another by most authorities. Possible options are:

- direct competition on the tracks (on all services or only on a subset of services, such as long-distance services);
- a concessioning (franchising) system (e.g. splitting up the network in a number of areas or products to be tendered); and
- some form of monopoly for one operator on a core network (with a more or less detailed management contract and possibly some com-

petitive threat) and contracting (with or without tendering) on regional lines.

These are just a few of the possible options. Further combinations are possible with different choices in different regions of a same country or different choices on suburban markets and on long-distance markets.

This book is based on research work carried out in the second half of 1997 and financed by the Dutch Railways (NS) and the Dutch Ministry of Transport. The original research report titled *Railway reform and the role of competition: The experience of six countries* was finalised in January 1998 and included six country reports besides the main report. The first part of the research was dedicated to the collection of information on the organisation of the passenger railway sector in those areas that were characterised by a certain degree of competition and/or contracting. This was mainly based on existing literature. The second part of the research described examples of competition and contracting in greater detail and tried to trace the noticeable consequences of the introduction of competition and/or contracting on several dimensions, such as level of service and financial consequences for companies and authorities. This phase of the research focussed on dense and polycentric regional passenger networks and consisted mainly of interviews and consultation of additional sources.

The railway sector has proved to be highly dynamic in the months that followed the publication of the original report, at least in terms of legislation and regulation. Additional research work was therefore undertaken to enable the inclusion of most of these changes, up to the summer of 1998, into this book.

This book concentrates on the reforms being implemented in Europe and Japan with a special focus on the role played by competition and contracting in dense and polycentric passenger networks. The aim of the book is not to develop a policy statement but to enrich and stimulate the discussions on railway reform and on the use of competition therein. As such this book sticks to the aim of the original report which was to present 'facts' such as to allow the Dutch Ministry of Transport and NS to learn from experiences with various forms of competition in railway networks, and to determine their respective positions on competitive regimes.

Countries or areas with comparable levels of economic development and with dense and relatively intensively used networks were chosen to allow for a maximum of comparability. These are the United Kingdom, Sweden, Germany, Switzerland, Japan and France. Other countries in the world have chosen equally interesting organisational forms in the railway sector, such as the USA, or have implemented equally interesting reforms, such as Argentina, Australia or New Zealand. Another book ought to review these countries and reforms.

Each country study is, as much as possible and relevant, structured in a similar fashion to allow easy referencing and comparisons. A synthesis of the six country chapters is given in the last chapter of the book before drawing general lessons. Each chapter, covering one country, includes the following topics:

- presentation of the organisational framework for passenger transport by train (summary of the most relevant laws and regulations);
- description of the forms of competition that are present or planned and broad description of the functioning of the regime;
- presentation of the main arguments used in the country considered prior to the choices made, including the time path into which this should be placed; and
- presentation of relevant case studies focussing on the consequences of the reforms for the authorities, companies and/or passengers (Table 1.1 gives an overview of the selected case studies).

Table 1.1 Selected case studies

Great Britain	**Northern English conurbation:** A structure of several *franchises* in this region provides many similarities with other European polycentric urban areas, such as the Randstad in the Netherlands and the Ruhrgebied in Germany (dense and polycentric network with medium size cities). London is therefore left out on purpose.	
Sweden	**Jönköping region:** This region (lower density and longer regional distances) presents less similarities with other more densely populated European areas but was chosen because of the interesting experience related to the entry and exit of private operators during the past years.	
Germany	***VRR* (Verkehrsverbund Rhein-Ruhr):** This region shows many similarities with other dense polycentric conurbations where regional and national services overlap and where several regional authorities exist.	***VRS* (Verkehrsverbund Rhein-Sieg):** A further example of tendering was chosen in this area (Cologne/Bonn).
Switzerland	**The *Seelinie*:** This example was chosen as it is the first example of a transfer of a SBB-line to a private company in Switzerland. This case study focuses on the tendering and transfer process.	**Bern region:** This example focuses on the development of regional public transport legislation consequent upon the reform at the Federal level.
Japan	**Kyoto/Osaka/Kobe metropolitan area:** Several railway companies operate within this dense polycentric region. Most of these are private companies and do not require subsidisation. This model is characterised by vertical integration (infrastructure and operations) and extensive side-businesses (real estate developments).	
France	**No case studies:** France can be seen as a point of comparison with a rather traditional approach with, however, potentially interesting experiments with non-competitive regional contracts. The SCNF retains a long-term monopoly and competition is not expected in the near future.	

2 Great Britain

JOHN PRESTON and AMANDA ROOT
University of Oxford

2.1 Introduction

Railway services in Britain were nationalised in 1948 as a result of the 1947 Transport Act, which created the British Transport Commission. The 1962 Transport Act saw the creation of a separate British Railways Board (BRB) which remained in public ownership. Criticisms of BRB began to emerge in the 1970s (see for example, Pryke and Dodgson, 1975; Joy, 1973) highlighting low productivity, inappropriate investments, managerial inefficiency and spiralling subsidies. This resulted in a review of the railways finances (Serpell, 1983) which concluded that massive closures were needed if BRB was to be commercially viable. This was deemed to be politically unacceptable (Bagwell, 1984).

The commercialisation of BRB in the 1980s, as a result of sectorisation led to some marked improvements in productivity. However, the perceived success of privatisation in other sectors of the economy led to calls for this policy to be applied to BRB too (Redwood, 1988). However, there were delays as the Government attempted to determine an appropriate structure.

The search for an appropriate privatisation 'formula' intensified in the early 1990s as BRB's productivity and financial performance began to deteriorate again (partly as a result of a decline in the economy but also due to increased staffing, particularly in safety functions). The 1992 White Paper 'New Opportunities for the Railways' came up with a plan for reform which was largely implemented by the 1993 Railways Act and subsequent Government directives.

The aim of this chapter is to give some detailed information on how the rail reform process was implemented. In section 2.2, the reform of British Railways is described and the current organisation is detailed. In section 2.3, the franchising process is outlined and, in section 2.4, a general evaluation at the national level is undertaken and a case study of what we have called the Northern English conurbation is described. In section 2.5, future developments are examined. Lastly, in section 2.6, a set of conclusions is drawn. Root and Preston (1998) provide a more detailed version of this chapter.

2.2 Legal, regulatory and organisational framework

After presenting the reform of the British Railways, this section will present the various 'new' actors resulting from the reorganisation of British Rail and of its control by the various authorities. The presentation of the actors will be grouped according to 'authorities', 'inputs', 'operators', 'passenger representation' and 'others'.

2.2.1 The reform of British Railways

Introduction and overview

The reorganisation and privatisation of the railways in Britain in the 1990s is internationally recognised to be one of the most fundamental changes that have ever been implemented on a national railway company. It has resulted in the following:

- rail infrastructure has been separated from rail operations and has become the responsibility of Railtrack, initially a separate government-owned company but subsequently floated on the stock market in April 1996;
- the passenger rail business of BR has been split into 25 train operating units (TOUs), broadly corresponding to existing profit centres and operated by these units until franchising. These units were formally vested as BR subsidiaries and called trains operating companies (TOCs). These TOCs, have then been privatised in a franchising process conducted by the 'Director of Franchising' (head of the Office for Passenger Rail Franchising – OPRAF). The 25 passenger

franchises were sold to 11 different parent companies.[1] The sales were planned to be to private sector companies; to management-employee buy outs and, if the Franchising Director agreed, BR were to be allowed to bid for the franchises overseen by the Franchising Director. In the event, BR was not permitted to bid for any of the franchises;

- rights of access to the railway were made available to private freight operators without a franchise, but restricted for passenger services up to 2002;
- a Rail Regulator was appointed to grant licenses and to enforce compliance as well as regulating access to track, stations and depots and enforcing domestic law in relation to railway services;
- freight and parcels operations were privatised by direct sale;
- with certain restrictions, the right to purchase or lease stations was also given to the private sector;
- three Rolling stock Leasing Companies (ROSCOs) were created and also privatised; and
- over 50 ancillary businesses were created and privatised.

The current organisational structure is represented in Figure 2.1.

Aims and considerations leading to the model chosen

When railway privatisation was first seriously mooted in Britain in the late 1980s at least four options were discussed:

- privatising British Rail as a single unit;
- privatising British Rail as a series of geographical businesses; this would effectively be a reversal of the nationalisation (Gritten, 1988);
- privatising British Rail as a series of product-based businesses (the sector model); and
- separating infrastructure from operations (Irvine, 1987).

Options 1 to 3 were ultimately rejected on the basis that they did not permit full-scale competition. The option that was accepted had a unique structure, based largely on option 4 but with some elements of options 2 and 3. This structure provided for the privatisation of the formerly nation-

[1] As amalgamations and mergers take place, these numbers may change again.

alised British Rail, by sale of all parts of the business and the franchising of passenger services.

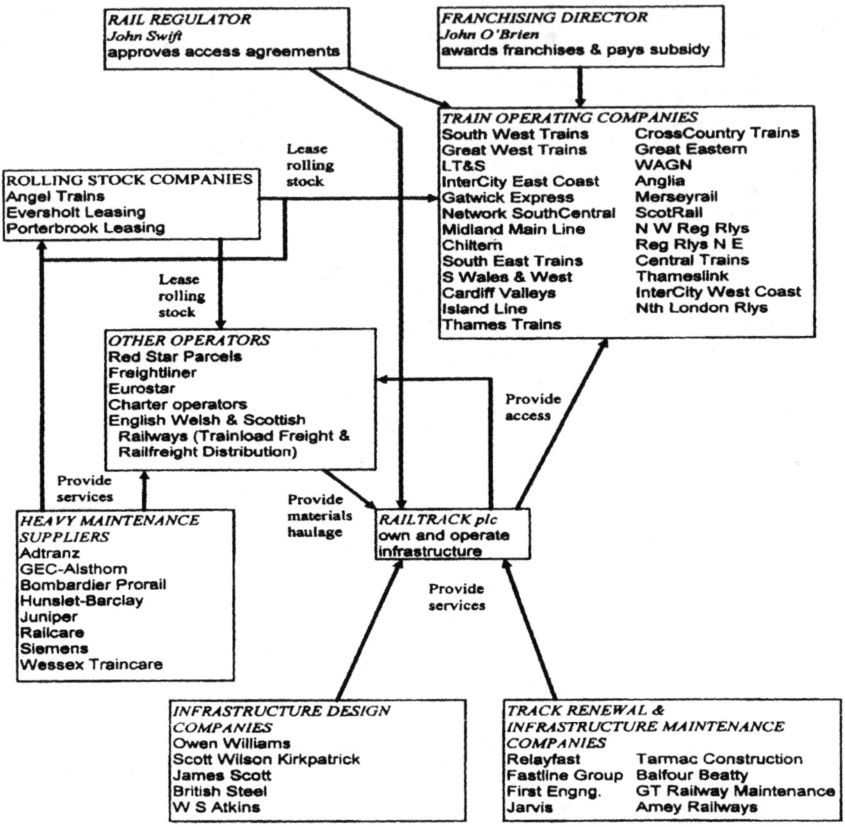

Figure 2.1 The Structure of the British Railway Industry after Privatisation

Source: Harris and Goodward, 1997, p. 85.

The 1992 White Paper on rail privatisation, titled *New Opportunities for Railways* (Cmnd 2012, 1992), set out six goals to be achieved before the end of the then Conservative Government's Parliamentary term, i.e. by April 1997. These were:

- to sell British Rail Freight and Parcels to the private sector;
- to establish a Franchising Authority and to franchise a substantial number of passenger services;
- to restructure British Rail to own and operate track and infrastructure separately from operations;
- to establish rights of access for new operators to the rail network;
- to establish an independent Regulator; and
- to provide opportunities for the sale or leasing of stations.

These goals were, by and large, achieved before the General Election held in May 1997, thus creating vertical separation of infrastructure and operations and a horizontal separation of rail services into 25 companies. The main exceptions were that open access was postponed until 2002 and that stations were not privatised separately but as part of Railtrack.

The White Paper was somewhat short (21 pages) and it did not contain any lengthy description of the aims or considerations that led to the choices behind the recommended legislative and organisational changes. The aims that lay behind these actions were simply described in the White Paper as to see a 'better railway system'. This included a determination to see 'better use made of railways in Great Britain, greater responsiveness to the customer, a higher quality of service and better value for money for the public who travel by rail'.

Legal framework

1993 Railways Act

The 1993 Railways Act laid the ground rules for the privatisation of British Rail: setting out the regulatory and statutory conditions under which this process could be undertaken. The main features of the Act included the regulations for the provision of services in which the structural foundations for the new UK railway system were established.

The first part of the Act (*Provision of Railway Services*) includes:

- selling out the role of the Rail Regulator with respect to granting operators railway licenses, approving access agreements, appointing consultative committees, promoting the network, and safeguarding the interests of those passengers who wish to use the service of more than one railway facility provider; and

- appointing the Director of Rail Franchising, who has the responsibility of submitting sections of the passenger rail network for franchising and of accepting bids.

The second part of the Act (*Reorganisation of the Railways*) addressed the economic conditions, namely:

- the disposal and transfer of British Rail's assets;
- employee's transfer of rights;
- government lending to companies owning or running parts of the railway;
- grants to British Rail; and
- powers given to the Secretary of State to sell BR to private companies.

The third part of the Act contained various miscellaneous, general and supplemental provisions concerning safety, national emergencies (such as terrorism); track access charges for freight and proceedings in Scotland.

UK legislation on restrictive agreements and anti-competitive behaviour

The Fair Trading Act subjects monopoly situations to investigation by the Director General of Fair Trading. The Director General can seek undertakings from any monopolist in lieu of a reference to the Monopolies and Mergers Commission (MMC) for investigation or can make such a reference. The Competition Act subjects anti-competitive practices to similar controls. The MMC can recommend, and the Secretary of State has wide powers to ensure, that monopoly abuses or anti-competitive practices are brought to an end. The Railways Act confers on the Rail Regulator these functions of the Director General of Fair Trading and provides that they are to be exercised by the Regulator concurrently with the Director General.

The Restrictive Trade Practices Act (RTPA) requires agreements between two or more persons carrying on business in the UK, and in which relevant restrictions as to the supply of goods or services are accepted by two or more parties, to be registered at the Office of Fair Trading (OFT). Certain information agreements must also be registered. Failure to do so renders the restrictions void and unenforceable and the parties may be subject to third party actions for damages. This is of importance for bus/rail integration.

Under the Fair Trading Act 1973, as amended, a merger qualifies for a reference to the Monopolies and Mergers Commission (MMC). The MMC investigates where two enterprises cease to be distinct, and as a result, either 25 per cent or more of goods or services (or a substantial part thereof) supplied in the UK are supplied to or by the same person. Or the value of the assets taken over exceeds £70 million. Following experience in the bus industry, even quite small areas of UK rail operations have been identified as a 'substantial part' for these purposes. The National Express Group's take over of the Midland Main Line franchise was investigated by the MMC, for example.

Safety legislation

The Safety Case regime is governed by the Railways (Safety Case) Regulations 1994 (the 'Regulations') which apply, with limited exceptions, to 'railway operators' (i.e. infrastructure controllers, train operators and station operators). Compliance with the Regulations is a pre-requisite to the granting of a licence by the Regulator to those operators. Failure to conform to the Safety Case may lead to the revocation of an operator's licence.

A new franchisee will not be able to commence passenger rail operations until it has had the Safety Case of its franchise operator revised where necessary and the revisions accepted by the Safety and Standards Directorate of Railtrack. Changes in those who ultimately control the franchise operation, its key management or employees, its rolling stock or most of its functions are all likely to require a revision of the Safety Case.

European Union laws and regulations

In 1991, the European Community adopted Council Directive 91/440 on the development of the Community's railways with the aim of adapting them to the needs of the Single Market and increasing their efficiency. The Directive requires accounting separation of the management of railway infrastructure from the provision of railway transport services and access to and transit rights over the networks of Member States for international groupings of railway undertakings and for railway undertakings engaged in the international combined transport of goods. The Directive was implemented in the UK by the Railway Regulations 1992 (as amended by the Railway Regulations 1994). Commercial agreements or arrangements to which an individual franchisee would be party are potentially subject to European Community governing agreements and arrangements which are restrictive of competition or the parties' commercial freedom (Art. 85 and

86, EC Treaty). The rail industry in Britain is also subject to EC Merger Regulation 4064/89.

2.2.2 Authorities

As explained above, two official authorities have been created at the national level: the *Franchising Director* and the *Rail Regulator*, each with its 'office' (Office of Passenger Rail Franchising and the Office of the Rail Regulator). Pre-existing regional/local transport authorities also have some influence on the railways (PTA/PTEs) and will also be examined here.

Office of Passenger Rail Franchising (OPRAF)

The Office of Passenger Rail Franchising (OPRAF) is a non-ministerial government department, with the Franchising Director as its head. OPRAF's role is to secure the provision of improved railway passenger services through franchise agreements. OPRAF invites bids in terms of the subsidy per annum that operators will require to run the services, usually on the basis of a 7 year franchise, but with the opportunity of a longer franchise if specific investments are incorporated. OPRAF sets minimum service standards (the PSR) in terms of frequency, speed and in some cases other criteria such as reliability and crowding, as well as controlling certain fares.

The Franchising Director's principal functions and duties are as follows:

- to designate passenger services eligible for franchising;
- to award franchises, normally on the basis of competitive tendering;
- to provide for the delivery of specified assets at the end of the franchise;
- to ensure that there is no disruption to services;
- to ensure that fares charged by a franchise operator are reasonable and that operators participate in approved discount schemes for the young, elderly and disabled;
- to receive and give notice of proposals to discontinue passenger services; to approve the designation of certain services as experimental (up to a maximum period of five years); and
- to secure compliance with the terms of franchise agreements.

Office of the Rail Regulator (ORR)

The Regulator's functions include three main areas of responsibility:

- *promotion of competition:* this involves using powers to prevent anti-competitive practises in the provision of railway services: including the investigation of monopolies;
- *dealing with line closures:* if an aggrieved person takes the case to the Secretary of State, the Regulator is responsible for deciding whether a closure should be allowed to take place; and
- *investigations and enforcement:* this involves the investigation of possible contravention of conditions attaching to licences and closure restrictions.

Under the Railways Act, licences are required for the operation of certain railway assets. There are four main types of license: train operator's licence (passenger or freight licence); station licence; depot licence and network licence. Franchise operators will not normally require network licences (these are only required by Railtrack). The basic position is that Railtrack awards safety certificates to train operators and ORR certifies Railtrack. The Regulator has also published a guidance document for each of the other three licences.

Section 4 of the Railways Act imposes on the Regulator a duty to exercise his functions in the manner he considers best calculated to protect the interests of those using the railways. In particular the Regulator must protect the interests of persons who are disabled and promote the use and development of the railway network, for passengers and goods, to the greatest extent that is considered economically practicable. The role also calls for the promotion of efficiency, economy and competition in the provision of railway services. The Regulator must also encourage measures designed to facilitate passenger journeys, which involve the services of more than one passenger service operator (e.g. mostly by the use of through-tickets).

Transport authorities at the regional/local level

A distinction should be made between a number of larger metropolitan areas (so-called PTA/PTE areas) where specific transport authorities and the rest of Great Britain. There are seven *Passenger Transport Executives* (PTEs) in the UK covering the main conurbations outside London. The

PTEs are controlled by their respective *Passenger Transport Authorities* (PTAs) which are responsible for drawing up local public transport policies for these seven metropolitan areas.[2] PTAs are policy-making bodies, consisting of elected political representatives, while PTEs are implementing bodies with as duty to secure, within their locality, the provision of such public passenger transport services as they consider appropriate in accordance with policies formulated by their PTA.

Central government provides support for the net cost of such services, which is channelled through the Revenue Support Grant (RSG) to the Metropolitan District Councils (MDCs). The PTAs levy their constituent MDCs for the funds they require. From these funds the PTEs pay for the passenger rail services for which they have contracted.

The other parts of Great Britain, which have either a two-tiered local authority structure of District Councils and County Councils, or have single-tier unitary authorities, have limited powers for direct public-sector based intervention in rail services. Counties and Unitary Councils[3] have overall responsibility for planning (including transport planning but not motorways or trunk roads which are dealt with at a national level) and some limited finance to subsidise bus and rail services they deem to be socially necessary but which are not commercially viable. District Councils are a less powerful tier of government with responsibility for matters such as parking policy.

2.2.3 Inputs

Railtrack

Railtrack was created by the 1993 Railways Act, and began trading in April 1994. Its key purpose is to own, maintain and develop Britain's mainline rail infrastructure. Railtrack owns and operates the track and associated infrastructure, such as signalling. Railtrack also owns most of the stations[4]

[2] PTAs are public sector but non-governmental bodies. Members are appointed by their constituent Metropolitan District Councils (MDCs) i.e. from already elected Councillors.

[3] These which combine both District and County functions, e.g. York.

[4] The stations were originally to be sold individually, but the Government backed away from this policy, on the grounds that separate ownership could have undesirable consequences for the whole network.

and depots, which will normally be leased to and operated by one of the TOCs. However, 14 large mainline stations are designated as Independent Stations and are owned and operated by Railtrack itself. Railtrack plans access to the network and manages the working timetable, ensuring central co-ordination of all train movements, and is responsible for planning and securing investment in infrastructure. It is licensed as a network operator and as an operator of stations.

The Government announced in November 1994 that it intended to privatise Railtrack and the sale was completed in 1996. The total sales price was £1 900m.

Railtrack is a commercial undertaking. It derives most of its revenue from charging for access to the infrastructure which it owns, particularly through charges for access to track and Independent Stations as well as lease rentals and access charges from other stations and lease rentals (including rent for plant and machinery) from depots. Table 2.1 sets out the early financial performance of Railtrack. The percentage change columns highlight the fact that, although revenues have increased, so has costs. Railtrack have stated that this is to clear the backlog of work, which had built up both during BR ownership and in Railtrack's period of state ownership.

Table 2.1 Railtrack plc: Financial Performance 1994-97

£m	1994-95 Total	1995-96 1st half	1995-96 2nd half	1995-96 Total	1996-97 1st half	%change 95/94	%change 96/95 1st half
INCOME							
• Pass. Franchise Revenue	1 955	1 001	1 002	2 003	1 046	+2.5	+4.4
• Freight Revenue	191	72	86	158	79	-17.3	+9.7
• Property Income	82	56	56	112	58	+3.6	+3.5
• Other income	47	10	17	27	21	-42.6	+110.0
Total income	**2 275**	**1 139**	**1 161**	**2 300**	**1 204**	**+1.1**	**+5.7**
COSTS							
• Production and Mngt	501	239	218	457	247	-8.8	+3.3
• Infrastructure Maintenance	696	348	377	725	371	+4.0	+6.6
Asset Maintenance Plan							
• Charge	483	253	250	503	259	+4.1	+2.3
• Joint Industry Cost	197	96	116	212	100	+7.6	+4.1
• Depreciation	93	52	55	107	58	+15.1	+11.5
Total Costs	**1 970**	**988**	**1 016**	**2 004**	**1 035**	**+1.7**	**+4.8**

Railtrack's income is derived by charging rail service operators fees for using its tracks. The most important segment of Railtrack's earnings are passenger services: around 90% of its income is from passenger operators (Table 2.1). As a monopoly, the prices that Railtrack can charge for access to its network are regulated by the Rail Regulator. As with other regulated industries (e.g. water, electricity) the Regulator can have a very significant impact upon the financial performance of a company. In 1995/6, Railtrack realised profits of around £300m on a turnover of £2,300m. Asset management plans have taken longer than anticipated to develop, and late in 1996 the Regulator issued an official warning about the increasing backlog of investment, then running at £333m.

As well as being a provider of infrastructure Railtrack is an important owner of property. The fragmentation of the industry saw much of the property portfolio transferred to Railtrack. The importance of property and its development on railway finances have long been recognised in railway business history. Although Railtrack's major land holdings had included many acres of derelict land that had formerly been sidings, yards and depots, it also possessed a great number of lucrative city centre sites. Railtrack has fallen short of what it terms 'internal' targets in relation to expenditure on stations and depots. It planned to commence a £760m property backlog programme immediately following its floatation on the stock exchange, but it took longer than expected to get his underway. Railtrack claims to be able to complete this work by 2001. Some property remained with the residual BRB, who have also been criticised for their development policy, leading to a moratorium on land sales (DETR1998b).

Expected demand for passenger and freight trains will be combined by Railtrack with objective measures of network capacity to determine points in the network where there may in future be capacity bottlenecks. The recent Transport White Paper (DETR, 1998a) has identified 15 such pinch-points.

In general, Railtrack has more flexibility in dealing with freight traffic because it works with freight operators to schedule trains outside peak periods. This is also true for the West Coast Main line, where detailed timetabling work has been carried out as part of the planning for the improvement in passenger services. Railtrack's work suggests that currently identified freight growth can be accommodated at least over the period of 1996-1997. This includes the potential incremental demand that would arise if that route were upgraded to accommodate higher cube intermodal freight and 'piggybacking' of road trailers.

Since 1996 the following new lines have been opened to passenger traffic:

- Crediton to Okehampton (29 km) opened in May 1997 and operated by South Wales and West Trains (but only on Sundays);
- Hedensford to Rugeley Town (6 km) opened in June 1997, operated by Central Trains; and
- Rugeley Town to Rugeley Trent Valley (2km), Walsall to Wolverhampton (10 km) and Mansfield Woodhouse to Worksop (21 km) opened in May 1998 and operated by Central Trains.

In addition, a number of new stations have been opened on existing lines including Ashchurch (Gloucestershire – opened May 1997), Euxton (Lancashire – opened December 1997) and Brunswick (Merseyside – opened March 1998) (Bevan, 1998).

The initiative to open new lines is now taken by Railtrack. It was normally the local authorities before privatisation. If new infrastructure is required, Railtrack is responsible. TOCs are responsible for new services on existing lines. With the exception of closures consequent upon investment schemes such as Thameslink 2000 scheme, Railtrack has no plans to close or limit the use of any line currently used by passenger or freight services.

Railtrack is currently split into seven zones (initially 10). Some TOCs fit the Railtrack zone quite closely. Others overlap several Railtrack zones (see Table 2.2). Where this happens the negotiations for track access have to take place with as many Railtrack zones as necessary.

Table 2.2 Railtrack zones and main TOCs

Railtrack zone	Main TOC
Scotland	Scotrail West Coast Main Line (part)
North West	Regional Railways North West, Merseyrail, WCML (part)
London North Eastern Zone	RRNE, GNER, WAGN (part)
East Anglia	LTS, GE, Anglia, WAGN (part)
Great Western	GW, SW and W, Thames, Cardiff Valley
Midlands	MML, Chiltern, North London Railways, Thameslink (part), Central WCML (part)
Southern	SWT, Connex SC, GE, Thameslink (part), Gatwick Express

Notes: Cross Country: all Railtrack zones except East Anglia.
Island Line is vertically integrated.

Railtrack determines the track access that TOCs can have. These 'slots' are determined mainly by 'Grandfather rights' i.e. if an operator already operates on a route he is allowed to continue to use it, but with some conditions to allow flexibility: operators can be moved by Railtrack a few minutes either side of their slot under 'flexing arrangements'.

Track access charging is based on route-specific (point-to-point) calculations and includes five elements:

- *a fixed annual charge.* These fixed costs were allocated in a three-stage process. First, the long-run incremental costs of each TOC were computed, on the assumption that the rest of the passenger railway was as now. Secondly, remaining Railtrack costs at the sub-zonal level were allocated by vehicle miles. Finally, cost incurred by zones and by Railtrack headquarters were allocated between TOCs according to budgeted receipts;
- *a variable track usage charge* based on the way maintenance costs vary with vehicle kilometres, speed and axle weight. Overall they only account for 3% of costs (ORR, 1994);
- *a variable traction electricity charge* (where electric traction is used) based on vehicle miles, train miles or gross tonne miles intended to reflect an estimate of the traction current used. Overall, they only account for 6% of costs;
- *an adjustment to reflect additional costs incurred and savings made by Railtrack as a result of a change of law,* this allows Railtrack to pass on to TOCs the results of certain changes in law, including directions by competent authorities which affect their business, e.g. new safety or environmental requirements; and
- *an adjustment to reflect the financial consequences for Railtrack of managing or dealing in property,* this is a mechanism for Railtrack to use for the sharing of profits from property, i.e. sales and purchases of land by the side of tracks and stations.

Originally the costs allocated included a target rate of return of 5.6% on a Modern Equivalent Asset Valuation of Railtrack's assets, to be gradually increased to 8% the next five years. Table 2.3 shows that assuming an interest rate of 5.6% and a capital valuation of £6.25 billion, a rate of return on capital of £350 million per annum is required.

Table 2.3 Track Access Charges 1994-95 (approx. breakdown in £m)

Operating Costs	1 500
Asset Renewals	560
Return on Capital	350
Total	**2 410**

Source: Nash, 1996.

There are besides track access charges also access charges for the use of stations and depots. Because these are leased to individual train operators, they cannot be treated in the same way as track. The operator to whom the station is leased is known as a *Station Facility Owner* (SFO). The SFO pays rent to Railtrack under the station lease ('Long-Term Charge'). This covers the cost of maintaining and repairing the station, and a return on capital based on the Modern Equivalent Asset value of the station. In most cases, other station users pay all of their station access charges to the SFO, who has leased the station from Railtrack. Similar arrangements also apply to passenger rolling stock maintenance depots, which are leased to a Depot Facility Owner (DFO).

Rolling Stock Leasing Companies (ROSCOs)

Three new rolling stock leasing companies (ROSCOs) have been established: Angel Trains, Eversholt Leasing and Porterbrook Leasing. The ROSCOs own and lease substantially all of the domestic passenger rolling stock previously owned or leased directly by British Rail. Each ROSCO owns between 3 000 and 4 200 vehicles comprising a mixed portfolio of different types and ages of stock. They are responsible for securing their own finance for any new rolling stock. When TOCs want to lease rolling stock, the ROSCOs can compete for the contract. ROSCOs are not required to renew rolling stock; the TOCs do this in consultation with the ROSCOs or directly with manufacturers. The ROSCOs have long-term contracts with the TOCs to supply specified rolling stock. These contracts are typically of up to 10 years duration, with the first contracts due for renewal early in the next millennium. Railtrack is responsible for the safety case.

The ROSCOs main obligations towards TOCs under a Master Lease (the lease that contains the standard terms and conditions for the leasing of rolling stock to TOCs, which each ROSCO has with those TOCs that are its customers) are as follows:

- delivery of a rolling stock to the TOC in an agreed condition;
- ensuring the TOC has trouble free use of the rolling stock;
- procurement (direct or indirect provision) of Heavy Maintenance and Heavy Repairs; and
- effecting and paying for any mandatory modifications (i.e. changes made compulsory by law). During the term of the initial leases, the Government will share in the cost of mandatory modifications above a threshold with up to ten per cent of the cost being payable by the affected TOCs.

A TOC is responsible for maintaining the safety and day-to-day operation of the rolling stock, except for heavy maintenance.

The Government announced in July 1994 that the ROSCOs were to be offered for sale. Invitations to tender for the ROSCOs were issued in early May 1995, and sales completed in 1996. The buyers were as follows: *Porterbrook Leasing Co.* was sold to *Charterhouse* (a management buy out for £528m in January 1996. *Angel Train Contracts* was sold to *GRS Holdings (Prideaux, Babcock and Nomura)* (venture capitalists) for £696m in January 1996 and *Eversholt Leasing* was sold to *Candover* (as a management buy out) in February 1996 for £518m plus an additional £80m dependent on the acceptance and satisfactory performance of the Class 365 fleet. All three have since been sold on: *Porterbrook* to *Stagecoach* for £826m in July 1996; *Eversholt* to *Forward Trust*, part of HSBC Holdings, for £726m in February 1997 and *Angel* to the *Royal Bank of Scotland* for £1 100m in December 1997 (National Audit Office, 1998).

In other words the ROSCOs were initially sold for around £1.82b. In a period of less than two years they have been sold on for around £2.65b. The reason is that these businesses are highly profitable. In 1994-5 these three businesses made pre-tax profits of £332m on turnover of £797m. Concern has been expressed at the transfer of these profits to the ROSCOs' new owners and the poor prices obtained at the time of sale. The National Audit Office estimates that these businesses were worth £2 200m to Government at the time of sale but they were sold for only £1 800m. They recommend that in future sales of Government assets valuations should be carried out well in advance of bidding. Detailed consideration should be given to the value for money achieved by sale and that the possibility of including in the sale terms provisions which allow Government to share in gains from resale should also be considered. There has been unease because of the failure of Angel and Eversholt to win new rolling stock deals signed in the recent past. The first five deals involving outside leasing finance have been won by Porterbrook. There have though also been a number of direct deals with the main manufacturers.

2.2.4 Operators

The 25 franchises are described in more detail in the next section ("The franchising process"). This paragraph will cover the Assocation of Transport Operating Companies, other passenger service operators than the TOCs and freight operators.

Association of Train Operating Companies (ATOC)

Association of Train Operating Companies (ATOC) was established to facilitate co-operation between the 11 train service operators running 25 franchises. ATOC aims to establish, provide administrative support for and run industry wide inter-operator schemes. These schemes (which are multi-party agreements) will cover areas of interaction between train operators such as ticket retailing, through-ticketing, inter-availability of tickets, revenue allocation and settlement, staff travel, telephone enquiry bureaux, London Travelcard and the various Railcard Schemes. For franchise operators participation in many of the ATOC Schemes is either a licence condition and/or a requirement of the franchise agreement. Accordingly, for such operators and for most other operators holding passenger licences, membership of ATOC is, in effect, compulsory. ATOC's remaining Schemes will be open to operators on a voluntary basis and ATOC itself is a voluntary association acting on behalf of the TOCs. It is a trade association and operates by consensus. Although it has mandatory functions (like running the national rail enquiry service) these have been jointly agreed. If something couldn't be agreed by consensus then ATOC could not coerce a TOC. It has no regulatory functions.

Three companies have been set up in connection with ATOC and the ATOC Schemes:

- *The Rail Settlement Plan Ltd. (RSP)* will be owned by the participants in the Ticketing and Settlement Scheme. Its functions include the clearance and settlement of revenue relating to passenger rail tickets and other products and the provision of services to the passenger operators to facilitate the creation and retailing of rail products.

- *Rail Staff Travel Ltd (RSTL)* is owned by the participants in the Staff Travel Scheme. Its functions will include procuring the provision of staff travel facilities for leisure and commuter use for past and present eligible British Railways Board (BRB) employees and their dependants.
- *ATOC Limited* will be owned by the members of ATOC and will be responsible for providing certain administrative services to participants in the Schemes. It will also employ the ATOC Secretariat.

Other passenger service operators

Other publicly owned railway passenger services, such as the 'Metro' operated by Tyne and Wear PTE and the Glasgow underground operated by Strathclyde PTE are, for the most part, only indirectly affected by rail privatisation.

London Underground requires access to some of the track and signalling owned and operated by Railtrack and certain stations leased by TOCs from Railtrack. In certain instances London Underground owns and operates track and stations used by British Rail. Under legislation predating the Railways Act, London Underground Ltd. (LUL) and British Railways Board each derived rights to use track and stations belonging to the other. In general, these rights are not documented. The rights of the British Railways Board (BRB) have, where appropriate, been transferred to Railtrack and the TOCs. The form of agreements between BRB, Railtrack, the TOCs and LUL was re-negotiated. LUL is obliged to participate in through-ticketing arrangements to be approved by the Regulator. In 1998 a partial privatisation of London Underground was announced in which the infrastructure is to be privatised as a series of long-term concessions but the operations are to remain in public ownership.

A number of other urban rail services in Britain are operated by private sector concessions including Manchester Metrolink, Sheffield Supertram (where Stagecoach is the operator) and the Docklands Light Rail system.

In addition, *European Passenger Services* (EPS) operates rail services between London, Paris and Brussels in conjunction with Société Nationale des Chemins de Fer Français and Société Nationale des Chemins de Fer Belges. EPS was owned by HM Government, it was transferred to *London and Continental Railways* (LCR), which initially included National Express Group and Virgin. LCR also won the right to build and operate the new

Channel Tunnel Rail Link. After financial difficulties, in June 1998 the consortium was restructured with British Airways replacing Virgin and Railtrack agreeing to purchase the Channel Tunnel Rail Link after its construction in two phases in 2003 and 2006.

Freight operators

Several freight operators were privatised:

- *Trainload Freight*, which specialises in the carriage of bulk raw materials, was divided into three geographically based companies. They were all sold during 1995 to English, Welsh and Scottish Railways (EWS), a subsidiary of *Wisconsin Central* which also owns *New Zealand Rail.*
- *Railfreight Distribution*, was privatised in two parts. Freightliner, its domestic container business, which transports containers to and from UK mainland ports and between other destinations with the UK mainland, has been offered for sale was sold to *MCB Ltd.* as a management buy-out (MBO) in May 1996. Railfreight Distribution's European intermodal and automotive freight business was also sold to EWS.
- *Red Star*, the express parcels service, was sold in 1995 as a MBO. Red Star has contracts with each of the TOCs which give Red Star the right to space on their train services.
- *Rail Express Systems Ltd.,* whose principal business is the carriage of mail for the Post Office was sold during 1995, also to EWS.

A number of own account railfreight operators have also emerged including National Power (who subsequently sold the business on to EWS), Mendip Rail (formed by two quarry companies) and British Nuclear Fuels Limited.

2.2.5 Rail users consultative committees

Under the 1993 Act, two tiers of passenger committees have been established:

- *Rail Users' Consultative Committees (RUCCs):* The RUCCs replace the former Area Transport Users' Consultative Committees and are divided into areas (up to a maximum of nine) covering the whole of Great Britain. Each RUCC consists of a chairman, appointed by the Secretary of State after consultation with the Regulator, and 10 to 20 members, appointed by the Regulator after consultation with the Secretary of State and with the Chairman.
- *Central Rail Users' Consultative Committee (CRUCC):* The CRUCC replaces the former Central Transport Consultative Committee for Great Britain. It consists of a chairman, appointed by the Secretary of State after consultation with the Regulator, the chairman of each RUCC or London Regional Passengers Committee and up to six other persons appointed by the Regulator after consultation with the Secretary of State and the chairman.

RUCCs and the Central Rail Users' Consultative Committee (CRUCC) have similar roles. They are under a duty to investigate any matter which relates to the provision of certain passenger or station services. After investigating the matter, they have the power to make representations to the relevant train or station operator. If the committee feels that those representations have not resolved the matter and that the taking of further steps will represent value for money, it can refer it to the Regulator. The committees also have the power to make a report on any matter which it investigates and to send it to the Secretary of State and the Regulator (in the case of the CRUCC), or to the CRUCC (in the case of a RUCC). Both types of committee may publish their reports, unless the matter in question was originally referred to it by the Regulator. Consultative committees must assist the Franchising Director (if he so requests, after consulting the Regulator) in ascertaining whether the service standards set for franchise operators are being met. Each of the committees must also make an annual report to the Regulator.

The consultative committees have an important role in the event of closure. They have the right to be consulted and a duty to make submissions to the Regulator. The Franchising Director must send details of the proposed closure to every RUCC affected by it. The Regulator must send to the committee a copy of every objection which he has duly received in relation to the closure. The RUCC must then consider what hardship (if any) the proposed closure will cause and identify any reasonable means of reducing any such hardship, taking into account value for money. A report of its conclusions must be sent to the Regulator and the CRUCC. It may also publish any such report. In carrying out these functions a consultative committee has the power to hold public hearings. However, The ultimate decision on whether or not the closure should take effect rests with the Regulator. He must send a copy of his decision, and any variation of closure conditions, to the relevant consultative committees. There has been some debate about whether the legislation will make closures more or less likely. On the one hand, the appeals process is now formalised. On the other hand, the commitment, stemming from the 1973 Railways Act, to maintain a network broadly comparable to that in existence, has been abandoned and the process has been de-politicised by making the Regulator rather than the Secretary of State responsible for the ultimate decision.

2.2.6 Other former BR businesses

A number of other British Railways Board subsidiary businesses were privatised and are listed below (Harris and Godward, 1997). Overall, privatisation led to £4.4 billion being raised through the sale of some 80 businesses (see Table 2.4).

Table 2.4 Former BR Businesses

Business	Purchaser	Date	Price £ m
Transmark	Halcrow	7/4/93	6.7
Meldon Quarry Ltd	ECC Construction Materials Ltd.	4/3/94	5.0
Special Trains Unit	Flying Scotsman Railways	31/3/95	1.3
Swindon Electronic Centre	ABB Customer Support Services Ltd.	5/6/95	
Chart Leacon Level 5 Depot	ABB Customer Support Services Ltd.	13/4/95	0.4
Doncaster BRML Depot	ABB Customer Support Services Ltd.	5/6/95	19.4
Ilford Level 5 Depot	ABB Customer Support Services Ltd.	5/6/95	
Springburn BRML Depot	Railcare	6/6/95	5.7
Wolverton BRML Depot	Railcare	6/6/95	
Eastleigh BRML Depot	Wessex Traincare Ltd (MBO)	7/6/95	7.1
Baileyfield S & C Works	VAE-Baileyfield Ltd	7/7/95	1.3
DCU Birmingham	Owen Williams Ltd	25/7/95	1.0
IDG Glasgow	Scott Wilson Kirkpatrick	18/8/95	0.6
Mainline Swindon	Scott Wilson Kirkpatrick	18/8/95	
Ditton Timber Treatment Works	The Phoenix Timber Group plc	1/9/95	0.5
Red Star Parcels	MBO Team	5/9/95	-0.3
Business Plant Engineering	James Scott Ltd. (AMEC Group)	15/9/95	0.2
CEDG York	British Steel plc	15/9/95	2.9
OBS Services Ltd.	MBO Team	3/10/95	11.6
Quality and Safety Services/QAS	Ingleby (805) Ltd. (MBO)	10/11/95	0.3
Rly Occupational Health Service	Occupational Health Care plc	30/11/95	0.7
Signalling Control UK Ltd.	BTR plc (Westinghouse Sigs Ltd)	1/12/95	39.9

Table 2.4 Former BR Businesses (continued)

Rail Express Systems	North and South Railways Ltd	9/12/95	16.0
Powertrack Engineering Co	W S Atkins	15/12/95	0.5
CEDAC Croydon	W S Atkins	15/12/95	
BR Telecommunications plc	Racal Electronics plc	21/12/95	132.8
Interlogic Control Engineering	Adtranz Ltd	4/1/96	17.5
Scotland Track Renewals Co	Relay Fast (MEBO)	8/2/96	10.7
Scotland Infrastructure Maint Co	First Engineering (MEBO)	14/2/96	27.5
Loadhaul	North and South Railways Ltd.	24/2/96	
Transrail Freight	North and South Railways Ltd.	24/2/96	225.1
Mainline Freight	North and South Railways Ltd.	24/2/96	
Central Track Renewals Co.	Tarmac Construction Ltd.	29/2/96	2.9
Castleton Works	British Steel plc	14/3/96	0.2
Eastern Track Renewals Co	Fastline Track Renewals (MEBO)	15/3/96	11.0
The Engineering Link	MBO Team	18/3/96	1.0
Interfleet Technology	MBO Team	22/3/96	0.5
Western Infrastructure Maint. Co	Amey Rlys Ltd (Amey/MBO)	25/3/96	15.0
College of Railway Technology	Advicepart Ltd (MBO)	29/3/96	0.6
Network Train Eng. Services	W S Atkins	1/4/96	0.8
Eastern Infrastructure Maint. Co	Balfour Beatty Ltd	2/4/96	29.7
Southern Track Renewals Co	Balfour Beatty Ltd	2/4/96	5.9
Sth East Infrastructure Maint Co	Balfour Beatty Ltd	2/4/96	14.4
Sth West Infrastructure Maint Co	AMEC plc	18/4/96	11.0
Central Infrastructure Maint Co	GT Railway Maintenance Ltd.	19/4/96	18.8
Northern Track Renewals Co	Fastline Group Ltd	24/5/96	4.6
Freightliner	MCB Ltd (MBO)	25/5/96	5.4
Nthn Infrastructure Maint Co	Jarvis plc	18/6/96	9.0
Western Track Renewals Co	Relayfast Ltd	23/6/96	8.5
BR Projects	MBO Team	26/6/96	1.3
BR Scientifics	Atesta Group Ltd	18/12/96	
BR Research	AEA	20/12/96	
BR QAS Ltd	MBO Team		
Railfreight Distribution	English Welsh & Scottish Rlys Ltd		100 (est)
BR Property Board			
BR International			
Business Systems	Sema Group plc		
Nat. Rail Supplies Ltd (incl. Collect. Corner)	MBO Team/Unipart		
Nationwide Fire Services	SERCo Ltd		
Rail Operational Research Ltd	BR Projects Ltd		
Opal Engineering	W. S. Atkins		
Raildata/RDDS			
Railpart (UK) Ltd			
Railtest	SERCo Ltd		
Rail Direct (was TRMC)			
GRAND TOTAL			**774.7**
of which	Freight	346.6	
	BRIS	168.9	
	BRT	132.8	
	all others	126.4	

Table 2.4 Former BR Businesses (continued)

Government Sales			
Porterbrook Leasing Co	MBO/Charterhouse	8/1/96	527
Angel Train Contracts	Prideaux/Babcock/Nomura	16/1/96	672.5
Eversholt Leasing	MBO/Candover	2/2/96	500*
Sparesco	Angel/Eversholt/Porterbrook	2/2/96	
Union Railways	London & Continental	1/6/96	
European Passenger Services	London and Continental	1/6/96	
Businesses Closed			
Rail News			
BR Savings Bank			
Taunton Concrete Works			
Engineering Development Unit			
Grove Management Training Centre			
Businesses Transferred to Joint Industry Ownership			
First Procurement			
Railpen Ltd			
Rail Settlement Plan Ltd.			
Rail Staff Travel Ltd			
Railway Trustees			

Remark: *plus an additional £80m dependent upon the acceptance and satisfactory performance of the class 365 fleet.

2.3 The franchising process

This chapter will briefly describe the franchising process. The franchising process and the contractual conditions to which franchisees are submitted are both very complex. It is not possible to present all details here. The reader interested in further details is referred to the report *Passenger Rail Industry Overview* (OPRAF, 1996) which describes at length all particularities of the franchising. This section will also give an overview of the results of the bidding process for the whole of the railway system.

2.3.1 Conditions under which the franchisees have to operate

Several obligations are imposed by the Director of Franchising upon the franchisee. These are described below.

Passenger Service Requirements

The purpose of the Passenger Service Requirement (PSR) is to ensure the provision of minimum level of services, without restricting more than is absolutely necessary the freedom of the franchise operator to adjust its timetable to passenger requirements and improve efficiency. Accordingly, the PSR for each TOC avoids specifying detailed timetables for each route and instead sets parameters within which the TOC must design a timetable compliant with the PSR. The PSR for each TOC is set out route by route and is broadly based on the current timetable. It specifies service characteristics which are important for passengers including: frequency of trains; stations to be served; maximum journey times; first and last trains; weekend services; through services; and load factors and/or peak train capacity, where appropriate.

Service levels close to current levels were asked for when unprofitable routes were being franchised. More freedom was given to operators where services were closer to commercial viability in order to give operators more freedom to tailor services over time to the needs of passengers whilst still retaining a core service. As the PSR typically impose qualitative restrictions on the services provided by the franchisees, they can not easily be translated into quantitative terms. However, it is estimated that they indirectly represent a percentage of the previous timetable varying from 70% to 100%.

Most current franchises have been let on the basis of preserving the status quo, largely because there was too little time in the first round to work out criteria on which to base the changing of service levels.

Fares

The Franchising Director decided that his duty should be exercised by constraining:

- unrestricted standard class return fares and certain single fares for short distance journeys;
- 'Saver'[5] fares (excluding 'Super Saver' fares) on other journeys; and
- certain standard class season ticket fares including all those tickets for weekly season tickets.

Various provisions were included in the franchise agreements to ensure compliance with these fare controls. Fares for children under 16 (whether the price is otherwise regulated or not) have to be available on terms which are no less favourable than would apply to the holder of a Young Person's Railcard.

For flows subject to the compulsory inter-availability requirement, only inter-available prices will be controlled and the lead operator will be obliged to create fares of specified type(s). When there is no compulsory inter-availability for any flow, and therefore no lead operator, the Franchising Director imposed equivalent obligations on one or more of any TOCs which provided direct train services on the flow(s) in question.

For three years from 1st January 1996, increases in capped fares are not permitted to rise more than the Retail Price Index (RPI) from the 1995 base price. For the four years from January 1st 1999, the price cap for such fares will be RPI minus one. Unless the Franchising Director decides otherwise, the price cap from 1st January 2003 will continue to be RPI minus one. There is some limited scope for individual fares to exceed the cap where these were balanced by other controlled fares being held below cap levels.

In the London, Edinburgh and Cardiff commuter markets, an extended approach was taken to regulating the prices of fares. Regulation was applied to an extended range of fares including all standard class season tickets and, within defined areas, unrestricted single and return standard class fares. Price control was exercised by reference to tariff baskets containing all relevant fares, weighted broadly according to income which a franchise operator derives from each. The overall weighted average of the prices of fares in tariff baskets was capped as for the individual fare controls described earlier. Within tariff baskets, the prices of individual fares may be increased by up to two per cent above the increase in the RPI in any year.

Table 2.5 gives an overview of the percentage of revenue subject to fares capping per franchise operator. OPRAF have said that the percentage

[5] Tickets valid one month off-peak (e.g. not between 0700-0900 and 1600-1830) on certain routes, mostly return.

of fares revenue which was regulated under BR was very small, estimated at less than 10%.

The Franchising Director wished to ensure that passengers are both compensated for poor performance and are made to pay for improved performance through fares. In consequence, the caps on the price of fares in the London, and, possibly other, area will be adjusted to reflect the quality of the franchise operator's performance. Quality of performance will be generally determined under the OPRAF performance regime. Improvements or deterioration in performance leads, under this regime, to the cap being adjusted by up to two percentage points up or down. Franchise operators are not permitted to benefit from both a fare increase and OPRAF incentive payments for the same quality improvement. The converse applies if performance deteriorates.

Table 2.5 Percentage of Revenue Subject to Fares Capping per Franchise operator

Anglia Railways	46	LTS	80
Cardiff Railway	44	*Merseyrail Electrics*	*100*
Central Trains	*45*	Midland Main Line	24
Chiltern	56	North London	58
Connex South Central	61	*North Western*	*(not spec.)*
Connex South Eastern	67	*RRNE*	*55*
Cross Country	*23*	Scotrail	57
Gatwick Express	5	South Wales and West	35
Great Eastern	73	South West Trains	47
Great North Eastern[(1)]	21	Thames Trains	44
Great Western	25	Thameslink	59
Intercity West Coast	22	WAGN	61
Island Line	40		

Source: OPRAF Press Releases. TOCs in the case study are listed in italics.

Franchises involving PTEs

For franchises which involved PTE areas, the commissioning and purchasing functions are handled by OPRAF and by the PTAs. OPRAF consults with the PTE to determine the PSR and fares and to award the contracts to support passenger rail services. Once the list of bids has been received, a short-list of bidders is drawn up with the PTEs (the confidentiality requirement meant that this did not involve the PTAs) and then a consultation phase followed, with the PTEs being given a chance to present their future development plans to each bidder on an individual basis.

Franchises involving PTEs were let fairly late in the overall timetable, with MerseyRail Electrics (ME) being the first of the five. Subsidy for PTE rail services is substantial. In 1994/5 this subsidy amounted to £259m out of total subsidy of £1 984m (Transport Statistics Great Britain, 1996).

The PTEs have some funding with which to subsidise services and all of them had some involvement in the franchise agreements of the operating companies. Despite the government restriction that extra service should not be incorporated in the PSR, every PTE achieved some limited enhancement to its service profile through the consultation phase during latter stages of bidding. However, the PTE enhancements are explicitly dissociated from the PSR as they are documented in the franchise plan produced by OPRAF as an auxiliary agreement. Although the franchisee has been required to sign this agreement as representing a commitment, there is some concern that the agreements in the franchise plan might represent a lower degree of obligation than the PSR. The details and the dates by which compliance should occur are in the future are still to be finalised, and they are sometimes phrased in terminology such as 'best endeavours'. Crucially, it is not clear whether the ultimate sanctions of terminating a franchise would be invoked in the absence of fulfilment, a response which seems more credible should a failing affect the fulfilment of the PSR.

The influence of the PTEs during the franchising process was also largely dependent upon whether or not they have taken on the revenue risk from the TOCs. If the PTE has retained revenue risk then it can determine the fares. If it has not retained the revenue risk, then the decision on levels of fares rests with the TOCs.

Operating performances

Every franchise operator is required to produce its own Passenger Charter, which must be at least as good as that formerly in place for British Rail. In addition, all franchise operators are required to conduct regular, independent customer satisfaction surveys. For each TOC, information is given in tables concerning their individual performance for Passenger Charter punctuality and reliability statistics. Bad performance results in some repayments to the passengers. The trigger levels for season ticket discounts are measured against a moving average for a whole year. This removes any normal seasonal variation from the figures. The statistics are compiled by the Train Operating Companies and are subject to annual independent audit.

The Franchise Agreement and the Railways Act 1993 provide the Franchising Director with a number of methods to enforce compliance. Many of these relate to operational performance. The Franchise Agreement provides for a special 'call in' meeting if operating performance in a four week period is unusually poor. A high number of cancellations or short formed trains will cause an operator to trigger this. Call in gives OPRAF the chance to investigate with the operator the causes of the problem and what is being done to correct it and prevent recurrence. The Franchising Director can deem three call ins within three years as a breach of the Franchise Agreement. During 1996-97 there were eight call-ins involving five separate operators (Chiltern Main Line, Midland Main Line, South West Trains (SWT), Connex South Central, and Regional Railways North East (RRNE)). Six call ins involved a high level of cancelled or diverted trains. Two call ins involved a high level of short formed trains.

Particularly poor operating performance can lead straight to a breach. Breaches can also occur in relation to other 'non-operational' obligations where operators do not meet their franchise plan or other commitments. The first three breaches of franchise agreements that led to 'notices on the register' were as follows:

- Chiltern Main Line failed on two occasions to provide the minimum number of seats on peak trains. In neither case was the breach serious. Chiltern placed an order for more carriages shortly afterwards.
- The Midland Main Line breaches involved only 27 seats; and the contract provision has now been changed so that small shortfalls of capacity lead to an automatic penalty payment rather than a breach.
- Finally SWT failed to deliver a number of Franchise Plan commitments on time – this was due to SWT making a number of drivers redundant and then finding it had staff shortages. A revised package was negotiated by OPRAF which contained significant additional commitments by South West Trains.

The Franchising Director can issue an enforcement order under Section 55 of the Act, setting out the action needed for compliance, or he may issue a public notice on the register, giving reasons why no further action is being taken. No enforcement orders were issued during 1996-97.

Exceptionally poor performance or other very serious failure can lead to a special kind of breach, an event of default. This gives the Franchising

Director the option to terminate the franchise. There were no such events in 1996-97.

Moderation of competition

While open access is in principle possible, the Rail Regulator has devised a regime of 'moderation of competition' for the passenger franchises. This regime determines in advance the degree of exposure to competition which each franchisee could face, ensuring that the adverse impact on the franchising process would be minimised (because bidders could allow for the risk). New entry was to be restricted through contractual control over Railtrack's ability to sell access rights to any operator in addition to those contained in their initial access agreements. The mechanism was intended to allow the market (i.e. the franchisees) to determine as far as possible where competitive entry should occur. The protection given was to be over the markets which operators serve rather than the track on which they operate. Markets were to be defined in terms of station to station flows (e.g. Paddington to Oxford).[6]

This mechanism operates in two stages. The first started when the last British Rail TOC has its long-term track access agreement approved and was originally planned to expire on 31st March 1999. The second was planned to expire on 31st March 2002. Substantial restrictions will remain in force until that moment when a further review will be conducted. The means of controlling competition for this period is the requirement to have the Regulator's approval for changes of terms and conditions of access agreements between Railtrack and the train operators.

The main way in which new entry of competitor franchisees is restricted is through the contractual limitation of Railtrack, limiting it to not being able to sell access rights to operators other than those named in the initial access agreements.

First stage of open access

In the first stage, franchisees can nominate a list of point-to-point flows on which no new entry for scheduled passenger services will be permitted without the franchisee's agreement. In general, a flow can be nominated if

[6] This ruling was later changed slightly to reflect that some stations in close proximity to major termini could effectively serve the same market.

it counts for more than 0.2 per cent of the franchisee's total fare revenue in a given year and the franchisee serves both origin and destination points. Franchise operators can nominate additional flows, not conforming to this rule, subject to the approval of the regulator. This is designed to allow passenger operators additional rights where there is no conflict with the protection given to other operators.

However, franchisees face the risk that an operator with initial access rights on the flow intensifies competition. The Franchising Director's policy is that existing operators with a significant share of the flow (generally 20 per cent or more) should be free to bid for additional timetable slots to serve that flow, but that existing operators without significant share and new entrants should not be permitted.

Second stage of open access

In the second stage, some new competition via open access is intended to be introduced. As with Stage 1, the key building block is the station to station flow and franchisees will be expected to re-nominate flows, but in Stage 2, franchisees will only be allowed a partial protection from new entrants. Up to a threshold level set by the Regulator, new entry can then occur, and compete for the operator's business.

In Stage 2 the competition mechanism is designed to limit the amount of the operator's passenger revenue that is open to competition to by another operator. In the second stage, franchisees will be able to nominate a revised list of flows. New entry will be permitted on nominated flows up to a threshold level, which was envisaged as 20% of those flows by revenue in a given year (OPRAF, 1995, p. 58). Flows which have pre-existing competition will count towards the threshold, but there will be no restrictions on entry for scheduled passenger services on such flows. New entry will be unrestricted, as in the first stage, on any unnominated flows.

The Regulator will change or add to this mechanism in individual cases where its strict application would produce undesirable results. The Regulator will review this competition regime and procedure in 2001 in parallel with his next review of access charges. Following consultation it was decided that the second stage of moderation would not commence until the introduction of the winter timetable in September 1999 (ORR, 1998).

Access to the inputs

Besides their personnel, the TOCs do not own many assets. They require access to tracks, stations and depots as well as rolling stock leases to be able to provide their services. This is obtained by agreements with, mainly, Railtrack and the ROSCOs. As will be seen in the following paragraphs, both the Franchising Director and the Rail Regulator play important roles in the determination of these agreements.

Right to use tracks, stations and depots

TOCs obtain the use of tracks by means of regulated access agreements with Railtrack. OPRAF negotiated with Railtrack and bought track access rights for the successful franchise bidder to enable them to provide train services as stipulated in the Franchise Agreement. This resulted in each TOC having a Track Access Agreement, which is a regulated legal contract between Railtrack (the facility owner) and the operator. This agreement, governed by Section 18 of the Railways Act, includes the provisions for operating certain stock on specific routes under a particular performance regime (i.e. track access sufficient to run the services specified under the PSR) and for the duration of the franchise.

The franchise operator determines how its PSR is to be met by its timetable within these specifications, although the exact timing of services must be agreed with Railtrack, which retains overall responsibility for the timetables of all TOCs and the interactions between them. If the TOC wants to start innovative services it has to negotiate with Railtrack for track access but there is no guarantee that such access will be provided. This is an uncertainty that the TOCs have to face. These amendments to track access agreements are entered into in a similar way as above, but are governed by Section 22 of the Railways Act. Both require the approval of the Rail Regulator, without which the agreements will be legally void.

ORR arbitrates on any disputes and difficulties concerning track access. Section 17 of the Railways Act gives the Regulator the power to direct a facility owner (in this instance Railtrack who owns the track) to enter contracts on specified terms with an operator for access to the network. Section 17 is a last resort for use when negotiation between the parties has failed. As yet this provision has not been used.

TOCs obtain the right to use stations and depots either by leasing such facilities from Railtrack (and so becoming the facility owner of those facilities) or by means of regulated access agreements with other TOCs which operate them or, in the case of independent stations, with Railtrack.

The TOCs may invest in the stations and the investment stays with the franchise, so it gets passed on to another TOC if they lose the franchise. This is seen as a disincentive to invest.

Rolling stock leasing agreements

Initially, the TOCs are obliged to lease rolling stock from the ROSCOs as a results of long term leases due to expire after seven years. There has been little competition between the ROSCOs. They are not leasing rolling stock for less than seven years, which is difficult if TOCs want more coaches for, say a busy summer season, and they are reluctant to purchase additional rolling stock. Various alternatives are being discussed to offer more competition to the ROSCOs, including supplying TOCs with trains directly from the manufacturers and regulation of the ROSCOs behaviour by ORR.

Personnel

The TOCs recruited from the former BR and local labour markets. Section 93 of the Railways Act applies the *Transfer of Undertakings (Protection of Employment) Regulations (TUPE) 1981* to all transfers made as a result of the Railways Act 1993. These regulations implement EC Directive 77/187, commonly known as the Acquired Rights Directive. TUPE provides that where there is a transfer of an undertaking (or part of one), the new employer takes over any employment liabilities and the responsibility for the employment contracts of the employees, who then transfer on their previous terms and conditions of service.

Under TUPE therefore, collective agreements would be expected to remain valid, for as long as employees' contracts continue. The typical legal position is that the franchisee will take over all of the existing TOC personnel with permanent or on-going contracts. The financial implications of this need to be reflected in the tender. Redundancy payments would, therefore, be borne by the Franchisee. However, in normal circumstances, a new franchisee would probably wish to retain a high proportion of existing staff and some staff would leave as a result of natural wastage (labour turnover in the industry is high) so a new franchisee would be unlikely to need to make a high proportion of the workforce redundant. Most redundancies are likely to be voluntary in nature.

The TOCs now conduct their own driver education. This means that drivers do not gain a network license. The only exception to this is English Welsh and Scottish (EWS) who provide training for driving freight trains on the whole the network. The issue of trained drivers may become a barrier to entry as it has been estimated that it takes £25,000 to train a driver (Nash and Preston, 1993) and thus the costs of training and the lack of availability of trained personnel could form a barrier to entry to the market by new franchisees. Virgin have, in conjunction with the union ASLEF, set up driver training centres in order to overcome some of these problems.

Franchise payments

The franchise payments paid by the Franchising Director to the TOC include the following headings:

- *fixed payments* - either the grant figure bid for BR or the contractual payment defined in the Franchise Agreement;
- *indexation charges* - franchise payments are adjusted annually to match the rate of inflation;
- *schedule 4, Schedule 8 and Level Crossings Supplements* - at the start of the franchising process, the track access charges were not known and some adjustments have been made for six of the early franchises (South West Trains, Great Western, Gatwick Express, GNER, Midland Main Line and Connex South Central); and
- *driver Restructuring* - a one off supplement paid to BR to cover the cost of restructuring deals made by BR TOCs with ASLEF where these were completed prior to the transfer of the TOC to the private sector.

Incentive regime: these are levied by OPRAF to operate a financial incentive regime which contains three critical elements:

- the *Punctuality Incentive Payment (PIP)* measures lateness and cancellations against the planned timetable. The results for each four week accounting period are compared with the benchmark figure established before franchising. If aggregate lateness is lower than the benchmark, OPRAF makes a payment to the operator; if higher, the operator pays OPRAF;
- the *Short Formations Incentive Payment (SFIP)* applies where the Passenger Service Requirement specifies a minimum capacity that the operator has to provide. This applies for peak services into London and some commuter flows to other major cities. Each operator

has to have a train plan showing how the capacity will be delivered. If the operator fails to meet the train plan, then an SFIP charge, based on a proportion of the cancellation charge, is made; and

- the *Timetable Change Incentive Payment (TCIP)* penalises operators who change the timetable from the printed version. But because it substitutes for a higher payment under PIP (if the operator had simply cancelled the trains without warning) TCIP gives operators an incentive to handle disruption in a planned way, and to give passengers advance notice of amended services.

The OPRAF performance regime applies regardless of cause. However, operators benefit from separate arrangements with Railtrack that incentivise Railtrack to improve its performance and provide compensation where there are delays caused by Railtrack.

If the operators had performed at the same level as the benchmarking period (normally 1994 to 1995), then the Punctuality Incentive Payment would have been nil. In the event OPRAF paid out £18.7 million which is a reflection of the improved performance as a result of the reform process and also the rather unambitious targets that have been set. The Short Formations Incentive Payment (SFIP) – which applies where the Passenger Service Requirement specifies a minimum capacity that the operator has to provide – meant, in this case, that the Operators paid £1.7m. OPRAF will be checking and recalculating the 1996-97 results during 1997-98, using the latest computer systems. This may result in some adjustment to the payments for franchised operators.

2.3.2 Sale of franchises and award criteria

The national procedure for selecting the successful franchise bidder began with a pre-qualification round. The Franchising Director has a statutory duty to satisfy himself as to the financial standing and management competence of potential franchisees before inviting them to tender. Successful qualifiers were then being asked to indicate how much subsidy would be required for a seven-year period. From the stage of establishing competence of Franchisees to the sale of the Franchise was planned to take about 6-9 months.

The Franchising Director had two key objectives with regard to sales (OPRAF, 1997): to secure value for money and to encourage the development of the railway.

The main consideration was price, the key variable in the tendering process. All bidders were required to name the subsidy they would require to operate the franchise, or the premium they would pay to OPRAF if the franchise was profitable, on the basis of a compliant franchise agreement for the stated term. As all bidders were bidding on a non-negotiable compliant basis, the price allowed a straightforward comparison. Bids were judged on the Net Present Value of the subsidy required over the term of the franchise (OPRAF, 1997).

The second consideration was that of additional investments (such as station refurbishments) and passenger improvements (such as commitment to additional services). Bidders were asked to include in their bids commitments to additional investment. They were guided that OPRAF's principal criterion remained that of price so they should generally only include investment that was self-financing over the term of the franchise, although in a number of cases they were required to address rolling stock replacement (OPRAF, 1997).

The principal factors the Franchising Director considered when awarding franchises were the level of subsidy required, the fare and service commitments proposed and the degree of risk accepted by the prospective franchisee.

In those cases where OPRAF believed there was a need for, or a bidder made a strong case for, making additional investment which could not be amortised within a single franchise term, then a different approach was adopted (such as for the upgrade of the West Coast Mainline). In these cases OPRAF invited tenderers to bid on two bases, with and without a commitment for an upgrade, for a 15 year term (OPRAF, 1997).

2.3.3 Results of the franchising process

Winning bids

The franchising process started with Great Western and South West Trains (which started operation in February 1996) and was completed in early 1997. Franchises were let for various periods, but most were let for about seven years. Some franchises were let for a longer period to reduce the risk of proposed investments (e.g. Inter-City Cross Country), but all franchises involving PTAs were around the seven-year period. The successful franchisees and the subsidies they are to receive are shown in Table 2.6.

Table 2.6 Franchises, franchisees, order, length, subsidy and start date

Franchise	Franchisee	Order	Years	Subsidy (£m) 1st y.	last y.	Private Service Commenced
Great Western	MBO	1	10*	59.9	31.6	4th February 1996
South West Trains	Stagecoach	1	7	60.1	40.3	4th February 1996
Intercity East Coast (GNER)	Sea Containers	3	7	64.6	0.0	28th April 1996
Midland Main Line	National Express	3	10*	16.5	-10.0	28th April 1996
Gatwick Express	National Express	3	15	-4.6	-22.6	28th April 1996
LTS Rail	Prism	6	15*	29.5	11.2	26th May 1996
South Central	Connex	6	7	85.3	34.6	26th May 1996
Chiltern Railways	MBO	8	7	16.5	2.9	21st July 1996
South East Trains	Connex	8	15	125.4	-2.8	13th October 1996
South Wales and West	Prism	8	7.5	70.9	38.1	13th October 1996
Cardiff Railways	Prism	8	7.5	19.9	13.3	13th October 1996
Thames Trains	MBO	8	7.5	33.2	0.0	13th October 1996
Island Railways	Stagecoach	8	5	2.0	1.75	13th October 1996
Cross Country	Virgin	14	15	112.9	-10.0	5th January 1997
Anglia	GB Railways	14	7 y 3 m	35.9	6.3	5th January 1997
Great Eastern	First Bus	14	7 y 3 m	29.0	-9.5	5th January 1997
West Anglia Great Northern	PRISM	14	7 y 3 m	52.9	-24.8	5th January 1997
MerseyRail	MTL	18	7 y 2 m	80.7	60.0	19th January 1997
North Western	G & W Holdings	19	10	191.9	125.5	2nd March 1997
Regional railways North East	MTL	19	7 y 1 m	223.2	145.6	2nd March 1997
North London Railways	NEG	19	7.5	54.8	16.9	2nd March 1997
Thameslink	GOVIA	19	7 y 1 m	-2.5	-28.4	2nd March 1997
Central	NEG	19	7 y 1 m	198.1	132.6	2nd March 1997
ICWC	Virgin	24	15	76.8	-220.3	9th March 1997
Scotrail	NEG	25	7	280.1	202.5	31st March 1997

Note: *Franchise length conditional on delivery of franchise plan commitments on rolling stock investment. Negative subsidy are forecast profits in the last year of the franchise (i.e. usually 2003 or 07)).

The franchise was always awarded to the lowest credible bid. Franchise bids are believed to have reflected expected rates of real revenue growth (or corresponding cost reductions) of between 2% and 7% per annum. Whilst the first two successful bids (from Great Western Holdings and Stagecoach) offered relatively low rates of reduction of subsidy, bids have become progressively more optimistic. This culminated in the InterCity West Cost franchise being won by Virgin Trains, promising to turn a £77m subsidy in the first year into a £220m premium payment to OPRAF in the last year of a 15 year franchise. Whilst the more ambitious bids clearly rely heavily on generating substantial increases in passenger revenue[7] it appears that substantial cost reductions are also anticipated.

[7] In the Virgin case as a result of introducing faster services operated by a new fleet of titling trains.

Operators agreed to certain service enhancements over and above the minimum Passenger Service Requirements (PSR). The main such enhancements are set out in Table 2.7. As the bidding developed it became more usual for successful bidders to bid for at least the current number of train miles and usually successful bidders offered more annual train miles than the PSR.

Table 2.7 Commitments made by Operators in relation to the PSR

Operator	Commitment
Anglia	• at least current mileage for 5 years, doubling of off-peak service on London-Norwich after September 2000.
Cardiff Railway	• at least the current train mileage
Central Trains	• at least the current train mileage
Chiltern	• at least the current mileage
Connex South Central	• 'plans' to maintain present level of services
Connex South Eastern	• at least the current train mileage for the first three years
Cross Country	• at least current train mileage. Increased by 14% for at least 4 years starting May 1998
Gatwick Express	• at least the present level of service
Great Eastern	• at least the current mileage for the first three years
Great North Eastern	• guaranteed to run the current train mileage for at least 2 years
Great Western	• at least the same number of trains as presently operated
InterCity West Coast	• services well in excess of the PSR and improved journey times
Island Line	• at least the current train mileage
LTS Line	• current mileage for 1st year, at least 95% for next 3 years
MerseyRail Electrics	• operate enhanced timetable set by PTE
Midland Main Line	• 'plans' for broadly current levels for 3 years, then enhancement
North London	• at least the current train mileage
RRNE	• at least the current train mileage
RRNW	• at least the current train mileage
Scotrail	• at least the current train mileage
South Wales and West	• at least the current train mileage
South West Trains	• 'plans' (but not committed) to maintain present level
Thames Trains	• at least the current train mileage for the first 2½ years
Thameslink	• at least the current train mileage
WAGN	• at least the current train mileage for the first three years

Source: OPRAF Press Releases.

The successful bidders

Although a relatively small number of organisations were involved in the bidding, it has the appearance of being very competitive (Nash, 1997, p. 3), with typically four serious bids per contract[8], one of which would be a Management Buy-Out (MBO). The main successful bidders were as follows:

Companies with British bus industry experience: this is the biggest group, accounting for at least 15 out of the 25 franchises:

- Stagecoach began as a coach operator after deregulation in 1980, and has grown to be the third largest bus operating group in the UK. Stagecoach was capitalised at £1.664b in December 1996. Stagecoach won two franchises, although it bid for all 25. It has subsequently linked up with the Virgin Group, which also won two franchises (see below).
- The National Express Group plc was privatised out of the National Bus Company, and is a major provider of inter-urban coach services in the UK. It won five franchises. It also operates local buses and airports.
- First Bus plc (a major bus operator with capitalisation of £622m in December 1996) won one franchise outright and two in conjunction with Great Western Holdings (the former management team of BR Great Western Trains) and the 3i Group plc (an Investment Company, full name: Investors in Industry). Subsequently these operations were merged as part of First Group plc.
- Go Ahead plc is a major bus company, which formed a joint venture with the BR management team of Thames Trains. Go Ahead also won a franchise for the Thameslink operation, with the French company Via GTI (a subsidiary of Banque Paribas).
- MTL Trust Holdings (a former PTE owned company) is a large bus operator with a turnover of £100 million, concentrated in Merseyside and Greater London and has won two franchises. In March 1998 MTL Trust holdings was put up for sale.
- Prism Rail plc was created specifically to tender for rail franchises, and, in this case, won four of them. Prism's founders had experience in the bus industry (running companies such as EYMS, Blazefield

[8] Although an interesting issue is whether bids got more serious over time.

Holdings, Lynton Travel and Q-Drive Management Ltd), and floated the company on the Alternative Investment Market (AIM) (this is set up as an environmentally-aware and ethical alternative to the main London Stock Exchange) in May 1996.

Management buy-outs (MBOs): this sector won four franchises (Great Western, Regional Railways North West, Thames and Chiltern) but required outside backers to do so (Firstbus/3i for the first two – which have already been sold on, Go-Ahead Group for the third - which has also been sold on, and John Laing, a construction and engineering group for the fourth). MBOs were noticably less successful in the privatisation of the rail industry than the privatisation of the bus industry and seem to be a short term phenomenon.

Consortia and companies founded in order to bid: this sector only won one franchise by GB Railways which was set up by entrepreneurs purely in order to bid in the franchising process. Like Prism, GB Railways are listed on the AIM. It is believed that a similar company, headed by a former BRB Manager, Railway Resurgence, were very close to winning the Great Western franchises but failed to deliver the financial guarantees required by OPRAF.

Transport Companies that were diversifying: this sector won five franchises:

- Virgin Trains was one of the private companies owned by Richard Branson, who has interests in a variety of areas including retailing, air flights and radio stations. Virgin won two franchises. It had been intended to launch Virgin Rail Group on the stock market but in June 1998 it was announced that Stagecoach will form a strategic partnership with a 49% share in the Virgin Rail Group at a cost of £158 million.
- Connex Rail is the UK subsidiary of a major French conglomerate (CGE), which operates in both the UK and France.
- Sea Containers is a transport conglomerate that was diversifying, extending its core interests from marine container leasing and port related transportation.

Unsuccessful bidders

Information about unsuccessful bids is limited as this is deemed commercially confidential and so not publicly available. The Government claimed that around 150 private sector companies were seriously interested in bidding for the franchises, but it is recognised that a number of enquiries came from banks which were collecting details for clients and were not potential bidders. Richard Tomkins, writing in the *Financial Times* of 21st July 1993, identified only 16 genuine potential bidders. The list is given in Table 2.8, with those that were successful identified with asterisks. It should be noted that seven successful bidders were *not* on this list, as bidders nor subsequently merged companies. They are: Management Buy Out (MBO) teams for Great Western, Chiltern Railways and Thames Trains; Prism; Connex; GB Railways; and Great Western Holdings.

Table 2.8 Potential bidders (successful bidders are marked by an *)

Company	Organisational development
*Badger Rail**	Became part of First Bus group
British Airways	
British Bus	Bidding with an MBO team for Thameslink
Burlington Northern	
Canadian Pacific	
*EYMS Group**	Management involved in the formation of Prism Rail
*Go-Ahead Northern**	Assisted MBO team for Thames Trains
*Grampian Regional Transport**	Became part of First Bus group
*MTL Trust Holdings**	
*National Express**	
*Rider Group**	Became part of First Bus group
*Sea Containers**	
Southern Vectis	Unsuccessful bid for Island line
*Stagecoach Rail**	
*West Midlands Travel**	Became part of National Express Group
*Virgin Group**	

Source: Tompkins, R., *Financial Times*, 21/7/93 and Harris and Godward, 1997.

Evaluation

The dominance of bus companies has raised concern about the lack of competition where the new railway franchise operator is also the major bus operator in particular districts (Nash, 1997). However, it should also be noted that this situation has opened up some opportunities for single companies to run interconnecting train and bus services where previously such routes were not provided (Willich, 1996). One of several example is in the Oxford area where the Go-Ahead Group operates Thames Train services and the main bus companies in the area.

It is interesting that the franchising and privatisation processes have resulted in a major concentration of ownership of amongst a few operators. By revenue, the largest operations after the first round were Connex, Virgin, National Express and Stagecoach, accounting for 54% of all revenue. A period of consolidation is expected with the industry re-agglomerating into about four groups (Preston et al., 1997). This has already begun with the alliance between Stagecoach and Virgin and the takeover of Great Western Holdings by First Group. The 'big four' (currently Stagecoach/Virgin, Connex, National Express and First Group) now account for around 70 percent of passenger revenue.

2.4 The experience so far

2.4.1 General evaluation of national statistics[9]

Investments in infrastructure and rolling stock

Table 2.9 shows the developments in infrastructure investments from 1990/91. These include track renewals, new routes and electrification, signalling, buildings, and plant and equipment. Track maintenance is not included nor are investments funded by PTE grants. After restructuring the industry in April 1994 some changes in accounting procedures were introduced. Therefore pre- and post-1994/1995 figures are not directly comparable.

During the years before privatisation investments in infrastructure can be considered low. BR could not even guarantee proper maintenance of the existing system. Much of the system was slowly wearing out (Save Our

[9] This section is based on a text written by the Transport Research Centre (AVV) of the Dutch Ministry of Transport for the original report on which this book is based.

Railways, 1997). The Rail Regulator had the same opinion: 'The backlog of expenditure which had accumulated by November 1996 was not acceptable to operators or to me' (ORR, 1997).

Railtrack has announced an extensive modernisation program, especially on signalling systems and control centres. From the planned investments as shown in Table 2.9 it seems that Railtrack is going to catch up with the backlog, with emphasis on the period up to the year 2000. In order to match as much as possible with the figures track maintenance costs have been excluded here. The differences for the years 1995/1996 and 1996/1997 between actual and planned investments is due to the fact that other private investors like the Eurostar operator are included actual investments.

Table 2.9 Investments in infrastructure and rolling stock

	National Rail infrastructure				Rolling stock		
	Actual mln £	Index current prices	Index constant prices	Plan Railtrack	mln £	Index current prices	Index constant prices
1990/91	693	100	100		329	100	100
1991/92	840	121	114		453	137	130
1992/93	939	135	123		537	163	148
1993/94	762	110	98		422	128	114
1994/95	890	128	112		360	109	96
1995/96	900	130	110	850	200	61	51
1996/97	1178*	170*	140*	950	46	14	12
1997/98				1050			
1998/99				1100			
1999/00				1425			
2000/01				1350			
2001/02				1050			
2002/03				900			

* estimate

Source: DETR (1997), Railtrack (1997).

Table 2.9 also shows that investments in rolling stock have decreased sharply since 1992/1993. Investments funded by PTE grants are not included in these figures. Some recovery may be expected here, however. DETR (1998a) reports that franchise commitments involve £1.6 billion investment in new or re-bodied stock, whilst voluntary commitments involve a further £0.26 billion in rolling stock investments.

Service levels

Table 2.10 shows the development in train kilometres. From a low of 349 million train kms in 1992/3, the quantity of service has increased by 3.2%.

Table 2.10 also shows development in punctuality (= number of trains running 'on time') and reliability (= number of trains that are not cancelled). The 1997/1998 figure applies to the months April – June 1997. The improvement of punctuality over the last couple of years seems to stagnate in 1997/98, while reliability is on a constantly high level.

Table 2.10 Loaded train-kilometres, punctuality and reliability

	Loaded train kilometres		Punctuality		Reliability	
	Mln	**Index**	**%**	**Index**	**%**	**Index**
1990/91	353.5	100				
1991/92	353.7	100				
1992/93	348.9	99	89.7	100	98.7	100
1993/94	350.2	99	90.3	101	98.8	100
1994/95	340.2	96	89.6	100	98.8	100
1995/96	353.5	100	89.5	100	98.8	100
1996/97	360.0	102	92.5	103	99.1	100
1997/98			91.7*	102*	99.0*	100*

* based on April - June 1997

Source: DETR (1997); OPRAF (1997)

The 25 TOCs are divided in to 63 Route Groups. Comparison of the performance in 1996/1997 with 1995/1996 shows that (OPRAF, Annual report 1996-97):

- punctuality: 59 groups are performing better, 2 the same, 2 worse: and
- reliability: 47 groups are performing better, 6 the same, 10 worse.

Following this initial improvement, a deterioration in performance has been noted. This can be seen by the latest data (The Independent, 1998a), which compares the year ending 27 June 1998 with the previous 12 months. The results are as follows:

- punctuality: 16 groups are performing better, 48 worse; and
- reliability: 21 groups are performing better, 9 the same, 33 worse.

Although many of the problems concerning punctuality coincide with known infrastructure problems, such as poor track and signalling quality (e.g. Virgin West Coast's Scottish and North West services), lack of track capacity (e.g. Connex South East's Kent services) and lack of terminal capacity (e.g. Great Western and Thames services into London Paddington), it is reported that the percentage of delays attributable to Railtrack has declined from 70 percent to 43 percent. ATOC believe a major cause is the expansion of the network (7 percent more passengers, 50,000 more trains and many new services) which has placed serious demands on rolling stock and staff.

Complaints to the passenger rail watchdog body, the Central Rail Users Consultative Committee are at record levels, having increased by 56 percent between 1996 and 1997 (CRUCC, 1997) but amounting to less than 10,000 complaints per annum. By contrast, press reports suggest that complaints to the train operating companies themselves are running at 650,000 per annum, mainly concerning punctuality, reliability and overcrowding (The Independent, 1998b); perhaps reflecting the higher level of expectation towards a privatised industry.

Innovations

The OPRAF (1997) annual report highlights around 113 key franchise commitments (over 4 per franchise), of which we estimate at the time of writing some 45 have been delivered. The commitments fall into five broad categories:

- 34 service commitments. 21 of these have been delivered, mainly related to maintaining the current timetable for a set period, whilst new and upgraded services have largely to be delivered;
- 22 commitments to new or refurbished trains. Not surprisingly, given the long lead times, only one of these has been delivered. The key commitments have been made by Virgin to introduce high speed tilting trains on the West Coast main line and high speed diesel multiple units on Cross Country services. It is likely that similar rolling stock will be deployed by other operators on a commercial basis;
- 20 commitments to improving stations. These were normally posited as a rolling programme so only two have been completed to date;

- 14 raising of Charter Standards, of which 4 have delivered. Typically this involves increasing punctuality and reliability targets, but not necessarily performance;
- 11 commitments to improving links with buses and other modes, the majority of which (9) have been delivered; and
- 12 other miscellaneous commitments, 8 of which have been delivered.

Over and above the franchise plan commitments there have been a number of commercial initiatives. These include:

- the development of a greater range of bargain fares. APEX are more prevalent and there have been a large number of initiatives in terms of group travel (two of which in franchise commitments). Customer loyalty schemes have been pioneered by Great North Eastern Railways. There is a general move towards airline style yield management techniques;
- improvement of distribution arrangements including on-station retailing (e.g. Connex South Central at Victoria) and the development of telesales facilities (e.g. by Great North Eastern Railways and Virgin Rail – the latter as part of the franchise agreement);
- development of integrated bus/rail ticketing in several areas, partly as part of franchise agreements; and
- upgrade of First Class and Standard-Plus services, including refurbishment of coaches and improved on-train services and at station facilities.

The impression is that the franchise plan commitments currently outweigh the commercial initiatives, but there are some indications that successful franchise plan initiatives will be copied commercially.

On the face of it there has been a significant injection of innovative entrepreneurship in the industry, epitomised by Brian Souter (Stagecoach), Richard Branson (Virgin) and James Sherwood (SeaContainers). However, in practice, much of the previous British Rail middle management is still in place. Moreover, the new institutional arrangements act to some extent as barriers to entrepreneurship.

Strategic decisions concerning overall transport policy and standards of accessibility are shared by the Ministry (DETR), ORR and OPRAF, although the proposed Strategic Rail Authority should streamline arrangements. Train operating companies do have some independence in determining their general aims, target groups and general product features and the process of moving from a producer led approach to a marketing led approach, which began with British Rail, appears to be continuing.

At the tactical level, many of the train operating companies decisions concerning routes, timetables and fares are constrained by OPRAF, whilst the development of new services has been limited by the ORR's moderation of competition and Railtrack's reluctance to provide new capacity. Arrangements between Railtrack and the train operating companies are also not conducive to improving station terminals. Choice of rolling stock is constrained in the medium term by the existing contracts with the ROSCOs. Between tracks competition has been limited to the few routes where this is geographically possible (such as London Birmingham). Between companies competition has mainly been for traffic along the same track, with the main example being the competition for Gatwick to London traffic. Competition in the train is mainly limited to First, Standard plus and Standard class, particularly on Intercity services.

At the operational level, the train operating companies are only responsible for less than 40% of their costs. The train operating companies' main responsibility is thus personnel scheduling and management. Arguably, it is here that entrepreneurial energies have initially been concentrated. In many respects, this is a re-run of events in the bus industry in the mid 1980s.

Our conclusion is that that although there has been an increase in entrepreneurial activity in the rail industry following the reforms, the main focus has been on cost-cutting. Greater emphasis may be placed on growing the market in the long run, with the development of new services and the ordering of new rolling stock. In other words in the future passenger rail companies may be expected to move from strategies based on cost leadership to strategies based on differentiation and focus.

In addition to the above, it is worth noting that the 25 franchisees, Eurostar and charter train operator Rail Express Systems, work together in ATOC to provide network benefits (such as through ticketing). The following has been realised by ATOC:

- T-12 project: establishment of a database to give notice of engineering work 12 weeks before the date of travel. Under BR, the standard of information about disruption by engineering works was often poor. Passengers would only find out about disruptions in their journey when they actually took place (European Railway Review, September 1997);

- National Rail Enquiry Service: instead of the 83 different telephone numbers in the BR-era, a single number for the whole country has been instituted, with local call charges (European Railway Review, September 1997). The target was to answer 90% of all calls. The performance figures since April 1997 have been: April 51%, May 65%, June 55%, July 71%, August 82%, September 85%, October 88%, November 97% (ORR, 1997c);
- Codes of Practice, which define the standards that the services delivered by the TOCs have to meet, including codes for handling customer correspondance, disabled persons' travel, handling of service disruption, lost property, connections and interchange (OPRAF, 1997); and
- Routeing Guide, which defines passengers' choice of routes for the first time (OPRAF, 1997).

ATOC plans for the future include:

- A new ticketing system which speeds up transaction times, improves productivity of ticket clerks and able to cope with a range of customer enquiries; and
- Real-time customer information, including information on whether or not a train will wait in case of delays (European Railway Review, September 1997).

Fares

Table 2.11 shows an increasing trend in the overall rail fares in current prices. However, after correction for inflation this trend stabilises since the privatisation process started. Overall fare trends have to be interpreted with caution since there is a large (and increasing) variety in fare types for different market segments with totally different developments.

Table 2.11 Rail fares, passenger-km and modal shares

	Rail Fares		Passenger kilometres		Modal shares (%)		
	Current prices	Constant prices	(bln)	Index	Car	Train	Other (bus, urban rail, bicycles, air)
1990/91	100	100	33.2	100	86	5	9
1991/92	110	104	32.5	98	86	5	9
1992/93	118	107	31.7	95	87	5	9
1993/94	127	113	30.4	92	87	4	9
1994/95	132	116	28.7	86	87	4	9
1995/96	138	117	30.0	90	87	4	9
1996/97	143	118	32.2	97	87	4	9
1997/98			34.2	103			

Source: DETR (1997). *Source*: Statistics Bulletin Quarter 4 1997, Government Statistical Service. *Source*: Transport Statistics Great Britain 1997 Edition.

Developments in travel demand

Table 2.11 shows the development in passenger kilometres on the national network. There has been a steady decrease in the 1990 - 1995 period. After this period demand started to rise again. The latest data for 1997/1998 shows an increase of over six percent compared to the previous year. Although rail travel demand is slowly increasing in recent years, its position in the total market is still very modest with a mere four percent mode share. Again, these are aggregate figures and give only an overall impression. At defined times and places, the picture will be very different.

Financial issues

Table 2.12 shows the development in passenger revenues and the revenues per passenger kilometre. It appears that revenues were increasing up to 1994 and are on the increase again after a small dip in 1994/1995. Although in the overall period 1990-1997 revenues lag behind compared to fare developments, in recent years they seem to exceed the fare trend (see Table 2.11), which is an indication of an improving performance. One of the main areas if improvement is believed to be in revenue collection and the elimination of fraud.

Table 2.12 Passenger revenues

	Total			Per passenger-km	
	(mln £)	Index current prices	Index constant prices	(pence) constant prices 1995/96	Index
1990/91	2056.7	100	100	7.42	100
1991/92	2116.9	103	97	7.36	99
1992/93	2153.5	105	95	7.36	99
1993/94	2192.6	107	95	7.58	102
1994/95	2171.0	106	93	7.84	106
1995/96	2379.4	116	98	7.93	107
1996/97	2581.7	126	104		
1997/98[1]	652	131[2]	106		

Notes: [1] Data available only for first quarter,
[2] First quarter 1997/1998 related to first quarter 1998/1999

Source: Transport Statistics Great Britain 1997 Edition.

Table 2.13 shows that franchise subsidies are forecast to decrease over the years. This reduction in franchise subsidies is partly due to the fact that access charges payable to Railtrack are reduced year by year. These charges are regulated by the Rail Regulator. For the whole franchise period of seven years, this reduction of access charge payments mounts to 20 percent. It is interesting to note that contracts which were franchised later (in 1997) needed less subsidies than franchises contracts that were signed earlier.

Table 2.13 Franchise Subsidies

1996/97	1997/98	1998/99	1999/00	2000/01	2001/02	2002/03
2,102	1,861	1,577	1,354	1,205	1,098	926

Note: in mln £, current prices as at February 1997.

Source: OPRAF 1997.

It would be interesting to compare the amount of subsidies payable to the private franchisees after 1996 with the amount of financial support to British Rail before its privatisation. In the last financial year before the privatisation reforms (1993/1994) subsidy to the passenger rail business was only around £0.5 billion. However, this comparison may lead to misleading conclusions due to accountancy changes (including making some hidden subsidies more explicit) and the deliberate policy of increasing capital costs (by using modern equivalent asset valuation techniques and requiring, eventually, an 8% rate of return). The subsidy reductions as a result of franchising are almost exactly offset by these changes. Besides, the TOCs have to pay access charges for the use of infrastructure and these charges are taken into account in the subsidy payments by the Franchise Director.

Data on costs are not available but from Table 2.12 and Table 2.13, it can be seen that in 1996/7 revenue was £2,582 million whilst subsidy was £2,102 million. This would suggest total costs for the passenger network of £4,684 million. However, this cost figure includes an element of profit. From Table 2.1, it is calculated that in the first half of 1996/7, Railtrack's profit was equivalent to over 16% of turnover. White (1998) estimates that the TOC's profits are in the range 1% to 4% of turnover, whilst for the ROSCOs the figure is 43-44% of turnover. From the case study data, we estimate that 33% of costs are attributed to TOCs, 50% to Railtrack and 17% to the ROSCOs. For the industry as a whole we thus estimate that profits constitute 16% of turnover. We thus estimate that in 1996/7 the industry's costs, net of profits, was £3,935 million, with profits estimated at £749 million. We thus estimate that almost half of the increase in subsidy between 1993/4 and 1996/7 is due to the increased profitability of the industry.

Commentators have claimed that the transitional costs of privatisation of British Rail have been as much as £5b (Harris and Godward, 1997). A Parliamentary reply quoted in Hansard of 15 November 1996 indicated that £450m had already been spent on management, legal and accountancy consultancy advice during the privatisation of the mainline rail businesses.

It would appear, writes Nash (1997), that the 'net outcome ... may be beneficial for the taxpayer, although not nearly so much as implied by a simple examination of trends in support of franchise agreements. White (1998) broadly concurs. This [also] presupposes that these reductions in support are actually achieved'. There is the problem of the counter-factual here – for it is impossible to tell what would have happened without privatisation.[10]

[10] The background is of cost reductions and productivity gains in the 1980s - but this was reversed in the early 1990s, possibly due to safety provisions after a major accident at Clapham and a fire at Kings Cross Station.

Employment

Table 2.14 shows the number of staff employed in the railway business. It appears that staff numbers already started to decrease during the pre-franchising period. This trend seems to have now stabilised.

Table 2.14 Employment in railways

	Thousands	Index	Thousands	Index
1990	137.6	100	137.6	100
1991	140.2	102	140.2	102
1992	141.7	103	141.7	103
1993	135.2	98	135.2	98
1994	127.7	93	133.5	97
1995	113.2	82	130.6	95
1996	92.3	67	122.1	89
1997	92.5	67	–	–
	Source: DETR, 1997.		*Source*: DETR, 1996.	

Concerning these employment statistics, it should be noted that in the 1996 edition of Transport Statistics Great Britain the figures differ markedly for the years 1994, 1995 and 1996 (see Table 2.14). There are no obvious reasons for the change given in the sources, except the change in methods of collection and classification of occupations. It has to be stressed that in this case many thousands of employees have been switched to railway related industries and are not lost to the industry altogether, even if the figures might make it appear that a massive employment reduction has taken place. The change, to some extent, is thus caused by the way in which the categories are constructed in the statistics and does not reflect such a huge loss of railway-related employment in reality. Altogether the DETR 1996 figures seem to reflect the employment trend in a more accurate way than the DETR 1997 figures.

A closer look at the most recent developments shows:

- in many cases elderly train drivers retire with redundancy pay. Several operators report a reduction in the number of drivers of the order of 30%;
- changes in working conditions such as greater flexibility in shift length; and
- higher pay in return for different working conditions. Great Western Trains, for instance, has eliminated the need for a second person in

> the cab of its trains when operating at above 177 km/h in return for higher pay (Briginshaw, 1997; Nash, 1997).

This can lead to substantial cost reductions. However, some operators like South West Trains, reduced operating staff numbers too abruptly, resulting in train cancellations and penalties imposed by OPRAF (Briginshaw, 1997).

The information in Table 2.14 does not seem to match the impression given by different other sources (as Briginshaw and Nash) that staff numbers are still on the decrease. It could be the case that the number of drivers is still decreasing with a simultaneous increase in staff at stations and management employees.

Nonetheless the data does indicates a large increase in productivity since the reforms. The number of passenger kilometres per member of staff has increased from an estimated from 225 thousand in 1993/94 to 371 thousand in 1996/97, an increase of 65%. Similarly, the number of train kilometres per member of staff increases from 2,590 in 1993/4 to 3,900 in 1996/97, an increase of 50%. However, these figures may be artificially inflated by a statistical rather than a real decline in employment. Table 2.14 indicates that employment in the rail industry, including contractors may be some 32% higher than the current statistics suggest. On this basis, the passenger kilometres per member of staff reduces to 280 thousand and the train kilometres per employee to 2,948 for 1996/97. The productivity increases are thus re-estimated as 24% and 14% respectively.

The deregulation and privatisation of the bus industry led to a significant drop in real wages. This is unlikely to happen in the railway sector, since the competition model is completely different with hardly any open access competition. Besides, it wouldn't be easy to replace railway operating staff by untrained newcomers (Save Our Railways, 1997b).

Table 2.13 showed that subsidies will decrease over the franchise period. In order to cope with this subsidy reduction the individual TOCs have to improve their business performance substantially. Some of the TOCs have to realise this improvement in performance in seven years while others need to accomplish this in fifteen years. Some of the cost efficiency improvements can be explained from the proposed reductions in Railtrack access charges (Harris 1997).

Developments outside the railway sector

In this paragraph an attempt is made to put the trends as described before in a broader perspective. This applies especially to the trend in travel demand. Some indicators can be identified which generally serve as determinants for travel demand. Apart from the level of service factors as described before distinction can be made between factors within the transport system like car ownership and fuel price and factors outside the transport system like GDP and employment rates.

Table 2.15 shows the developments in these indicators. Car ownership is still increasing and expected to go up by 2% yearly. This explains why the mode share of rail travel within the total market is quite modest and will not change spectacularly in the future. Concerning the fuel price, previous research shows that the relationship between this factor and rail travel demand is not very strong, unless major changes are involved. Though the fuel price is increasing slightly more since the new Labour Government took office, so far no significant influence on rail travel can be established.

Regarding the remaining key factors, GDP has grown substantially in recent years after the recession at the beginning of the 90's. In general, there is a strong relationship between such a development and travel demand, with elasticities reaching unity in certain circumstances. Employment rates are generally speaking a determinant for work-related travel and are particularly important in London.

Table 2.15 Determinants of travel demand

	1990	1991	1992	1993	1994	1995	1996	1997
Fuel price index (current prices)	**100**	**107**	**110**	**119**	**125**	**131**	**138**	-
Fuel price index (constant prices)	*100*	*101*	*100*	*106*	*110*	*111*	*114*	-
Cars per 1000 inhabitants	**393**	**395**	**398**	**403**	**409**	**416**	**432**	**440**
Index	*100*	*100*	*101*	*102*	*103*	*105*	*110*	*112*
GDP (bln £, constant prices)	**549**	**538**	**535**	**548**	**569**	**583**	**598**	**613**
Index	*100*	*98*	*97*	*100*	*104*	*106*	*109*	*112*
Employment (mln persons)	**27.2**	**26.3**	**25.7**	**25.3**	**25.5**	**25.7**	**25.8**	**25.9**
Index	*100*	*97*	*94*	*93*	*94*	*94*	*95*	*95*
Price Index	**100**	**106**	**110**	**112**	**114**	**118**	**121**	**121**

Sources: Prognos 1997; Transport Statistics 1997; International Auto Statistics 1996.

2.4.2 Case study: The Northern English Conurbation

This section contains an examination of five English TOCs. They are: Central, CrossCountry, MerseyRail, North Western and Regional Railways North East. They primarily serve a Northern English Conurbation, centred on a ring of cities that stretch from Manchester and Leeds in the north to Birmingham and Nottingham/Derby in the south. This area has been selected because of its relative similarities with the Netherlands in terms of polycentric structure and population density. After an initial presentation of the area, this section goes on to compare each of the franchises.

Case study selection

The case study area comprises a dense core network (served primarily by Cross Country and Inter City trains and Regional express services such as Transpennine), overlaid by commuter networks (focused on Birmingham, Liverpool, Manchester and Leeds) and a sparser peripheral network (served mainly by non-express Regional Railway trains). This distribution has many similarities with the geography of railways in the Netherlands with a Randstad-like rim city of Liverpool, Manchester, Leeds, Sheffield, Derby, Birmingham and Stoke, a peripheral network of services on rural branch lines complemented by long distance services (to Scotland and Wales, Newcastle, Brighton and Bristol and beyond) which could be compared to the international services of NS.

There are some similarities in train miles run by this group of companies, in comparison with NS. Table 2.16 shows that NS offers 12% more service than the five TOCs in our case study. However, the passenger mileage on NS is nearly three times greater than that on the selected UK railway networks – which may be partly due to lower fares and higher frequencies on NS services. Nonetheless, for the reasons of spatial and train mileage similarity, as well as the interesting divergence of passenger usage, these companies make a interesting and useful comparative case study.

Table 2.16 Train and passenger miles on selected UK Railway Franchises and NS

Franchise	Train miles (mln) 1993/4	Passenger miles (mln)
Central	15.8	656
Cross Country	9.6	1275
Merseyrail	3.4	280
North West Trains	14.6	455
Regional Railways North East	18.9	700
Total	**62.3**	**3 366**
Nederlandse Spoorwegen	(1994) **69.9**	(1994) **9 024**

Source: OPRAF, 1995; UIC, 1996.

Characteristics of the area

The area is also comparable to the Netherlands, as is the underlying population of the case study area, as can be seen by Table 2.17. The UK case study area is based on four Standard Economic Regions (the North West, Yorkshire and Humberside, the East Midlands and the West Midlands) with a population 28% greater and an area 17% greater than the Netherlands. Population density is 10% greater in the English case study area than in the Netherlands. This table also shows that in the UK dual car ownership is higher than in the Netherlands but that there are also a greater number of households without cars. Thus the situation is more polarised than in the Netherlands. There is both a higher mean percentage of UK households without car and a higher percentage of UK households with two or more cars.

The national transport statistics do not show the modal share for regional travel, except for journeys to work (see Table 2.18). It can be observed that the modal share of bus, coach and rail is higher for urbanised regions than for more rural regions. In the case study area, rail only has a 1% share of the journey to work market compared to a 5% share for Great Britain as a whole (including underground). The latter figure is clearly dominated by commuting into London.

Table 2.17 Area, population and car ownership of the UK case-study compared with the Netherlands

Regions/Counties	Counties	Km^2	Popul.	Density	% households no cars	% households 2+ cars
North West	Cheshire	2 331	940 887	403.6	26.8	28.9
	Greater Manchester	1 286	2 455 093	1 909.3	40.6	18.9
	Lancashire	3 070	1 383 998	450.8	33.3	21.6
	Merseyside	655	1 380 465	2 107.1	45.0	15.6
West Midlands	Shropshire	3 488	406 387	116.5	24.5	28.4
	Warwickshire	1 979	484 247	244.7	24.5	31.3
	H'ford and Worcs.	3 923	671 971	171.3	22.6	32.7
	Staffordshire	2 715	1 022 901	376.7	28.2	27.0
	West Midlands	899	2 511 007	2 793.9	39.8	19.2
East Midlands	Derbyshire	2 629	918 648	349.5	31.3	23.7
	Leicestershire	2 551	867 521	340.1	29.0	26.1
	Nottinghamshire	2 160	993 872	460.2	34.5	21.3
	Lincolnshire	5 921	580 114	98.0	25.1	25.3
Yorkshire and Humberside	North Yorkshire	7 022	830 948	118.3	27.6	25.0
	West Yorkshire	2 034	1 991 539	979.0	39.8	18.8
	South Yorkshire	1 559	1 253 959	804.1	41.6	16.3
	Humberside	3 508	847 987	241.7	36.2	18.9
Total		**47 729**	**19 541 544**	**409.4**	**35.1**	**21.7**
The Netherlands		**40 844**	**15 240 000**	**373.1**	**24.0**	**15.0**

Source: 1991 Census.

Table 2.18 Modal split for journeys to work, by region

Area of workplace	Car, van, minibus	Motor-cycle	Bicycle	Bus, coach	National Rail	Underground	Walk	Employment
	%							(1000)
South Yorkshire	69	-	2	13	-	-	12	476
West Yorkshire	70	-	1	13	2	-	13	879
Rest of Yorks & Humberside	71	-	8	5	-	-	13	659
East Midlands	74	1	5	7	-	-	12	1 711
West Midlands (Metr. Cty)	73	-	2	13	1	-	10	1 129
Rest of West Midlands	78	1	4	5	-	-	11	1 044
Greater Manchester	73	-	3	10	2	-	11	1 029
Merseyside	69	-	3	12	4	-	10	474
Rest of North West	77	-	4	5	-	-	12	1 006
Case Study Area	**73**	**-**	**4**	**9**	**1**	**-**	**12**	**8407**
Great Britain	**70**	**1**	**4**	**8**	**3**	**2**	**12**	**23 305**

Source: Department of the Environment, Transport and the Regions, *Transport Statistics Great Britain*, 1997 Edition, HMSO.

Details of the Five TOCs

In this section each of the five TOCs in the case study will be briefly described.

Central Trains Limited ('*Central*'), based in Birmingham, operates a variety of passenger services covering central England and extending into Wales and East Anglia. Commuter services are operated for West Midlands PTE ('Centro'). NEG (National Express Group) was confirmed as the preferred bidder on 11 February 1997 with a franchise for a seven years and one month term.

CrossCountry Trains Ltd. (*'CrossCountry'*), also based in Birmingham, operates InterCity/Express services linking over 130 stations across England, Scotland and Wales. The hub of CrossCountry's route network is Birmingham, with key services operating to Manchester, Sheffield, Reading and Bristol. Some trains also extend to Glasgow, Edinburgh, Aberdeen and Newcastle in the north, and to Brighton, Bournemouth, Swansea and Penzance in the south and west. Within its route network, CrossCountry operates a few long distance through trains, including services from Glasgow to Bournemouth, a distance of 470 miles, and from Dundee to Penzance, a distance of over 700 miles. Virgin Rail Group Limited was confirmed at the preferred bidder on 13th November 1996. The franchise has been let for a 15 year term. However, because of the need to complete outstanding legal and safety requirements, British Rail continued to operate trains until the official take-over, in January 1997.

Merseyrail Electrics, based in Liverpool, operates passenger rail services on two sets of lines comprising 75 route miles. The Wirral Lines, extending under the River Mersey, link Liverpool with West Kirby, Ellesmere Port, New Brighton and Chester. The Northern line links Liverpool with Ormskirk, Kirkby, Southport and Hunts Cross. The central part of the route network, covering some 6.5 miles, is underground, with four underground stations serving central Liverpool, a tunnel under the River Mersey and a further underground station in Birkenhead. There are passenger interchange facilities between the lines at two underground stations, Moorfields and Liverpool Central. Merseyrail Electrics is the sole provider of passenger services between stations on the rail network it uses and the Company has only limited interfaces with other TOCs. The greater part of Merseyrail Electrics services, accounting for approximately 85% of train miles and covering all but nine of the 65 stations served, is supported by, and operated to the specification of, Merseyside Passenger Transport Executive ('Merseytravel'). Merseyside PTE is a party to the Merseyrail Electrics franchise agreement. The approval of Merseyside Passenger Transport Authority was received before Merseyside PTE entered into the Merseyrail Electrics franchise agreement. MTL was confirmed as preferred bidder on 11th December 1996. The franchise has been let for a term of seven years and two months.

The *North Western Trains Ltd.* (NWT), based in Manchester, operates local and regional services in north western England and North Wales. In addition to inter urban services between some of the larger towns and cities in the region, North Western Trains Ltd. Provides urban services around Manchester and Liverpool Lime Street for Greater Manchester PTE and Merseytravel respectively and rural services in North Wales, Lancashire and Cumbria. The furthest points reached by its network are Carlisle in the north, Holyhead in the west, Birmingham International in the south and Sheffield in the east. Great Western Holdings was confirmed as the preferred bidder on 30th January 1997.

Regional Railways North East (RRNE) (recently renamed Northern Spirit), based in York, operates passenger services in northern England. Its services extend from the Scottish border in the north to south of the Humber, and from the east coast of England to Manchester, Liverpool and Blackpool in the west. RRNE services are concentrated around Leeds, Sheffield and Newcastle. The RRNE company provides a variety of passenger services to meet a range of journey purposes. Inter urban services operate between major cities such as Newcastle, Leeds, Manchester, Sheffield and Liverpool and serve largely leisure travellers (Transpennine services). Rural services operate principally in Northumberland, North Yorkshire and Cumbria providing transport links between local communities as well as serving leisure travellers. Urban services are provided mainly for Tyne and Wear PTE (Newcastle), West Yorkshire PTE (Leeds) and South Yorkshire PTE (Sheffield). The franchise was let to MTL Rail Ltd (MTL Holdings) on 2nd March 1997. The franchise has been let for a seven year and one month term.

Costs, revenues and subsidies

Figures for cost breakdown for the TOCs in the case study are given in Table 2.19. We calculate that the cost per train mile varies between £11.84

(for Merseyrail Electrics) to £4.55 (for North Western Trains). It is important to remember that, as far as the subsidy level is concerned, four out of seven PTEs have decided to retain the revenue risk on the urban/regional rail services which they support (see Table 2.20). In those cases, the franchise payment to the operator is higher than the net cost of the service to the public purse. However, as the areas of responsibility of the PTEs do not correspond exactly with the TOCs under study, an exact comparison of the two is difficult, therefore Table 2.21 is only an estimate of the net subsidy for the public purse.

Table 2.19 Cost breakdown per franchise (mln £) 1993/94

	Variable costs	Mainly fixed costs		Total Costs
	Operating costs	**Access charges**	**Train Leases**	
Central	61	123.3	23.84	208.14
CrossCountry	61	95.7	40.15	196.85
Merseyrail	45	38	20	103
North Western	61	41.2	41.2	143.4
RR North East	63	146.3	31.68	240.98
Total	**291**	**444.5**	**156.87**	**892.37**

Source: Harris and Godward, 1997, p. 94/95.

Table 2.20 Railway traffic revenue for PTEs 1996/97

	Revenue risk?	Revenue (mln £)
Centro (West Midlands PTE)	Yes	16.0
GMPTE (Greater Manchester PTE)	No	N/A
Merseytravel (Merseyside PTE)	Yes	MerseyRail 18.3 NWT 3.5 Total 21.8
Metro (West Yorkshire PTE)	No	N/A
Nexus (Tyne and Wear PTE)	Yes	2.5*
SPTE (Strathclyde PTE)	Yes	42.2
SYPTE (South Yorkshire PTE)	Yes	6

*estimate

Source: Personal communications with the PTEs

Figures related to passengers, fares and subsidies are included in Table 2.22. From this table it can be seen that the mean fare per passenger mile varies from 12.7 pence for Merseyrail Electrics to 9.9 pence for Cross Country. This reflects a tapered fare scale which gives discounts for longer journeys (the mean passenger journey on Cross Country is 103 miles, on Merseyrail it is seven miles).

Table 2.21 Estimation of net subsidy for the franchises in the case study

	Gross subsidy (£m)	Net subsidy (£m)
Central	213.9	197.9
CrossCountry	157.9	157.9
Merseyrail	110.1	91.8
North Western	193.1	189.5
RR North East	241.5	239.5
Total	**916.5**	**876.6**

Source: Based on Table 2.20 and OPRAF, 1997c.

Table 2.22 Passengers, fares and average support on the franchise period

	Franchise period	Passenger (1994/95)		Fares		Average support		
		Journeys	Miles	Revenue	Regulated	annual	/pass. jny	/pass. mile
		mln	mln	mln £	%	mln £	£	£
Central	7 y 1 m	37.0	601.0	65.6	45	152.9	4.13	0.25
Cross Country	15 y	11.0	1 128.0	108.0	23	36.4	3.31	0.03
MerseyRail	7 y 2 m	21.0	147.0	18.7	100	67.6	3.22	0.46
North Western	7 y 1 m	22.0	377.0	47.8	33[1]	148.3	6.74	0.39
RR NE	7 y 1 m	36.6	692.0	68.0	55	173.4	4.74	0.25

Note: [1] Greater Manchester PTE area only – estimate based on Kilburn (1994).

Source: Glover, J., *Modern Railways*, May 1997.

As can be seen from Table 2.22, the group of TOCs used in this case study receive considerable variation in levels of support. It ranges from CrossCountry which gets £0.03 per passenger mile to MerseyRail which gets £0.46 per passenger mile, over 15 times as much.

General conclusions from the case study

A large amount of data was collected concerning the 5 TOCs. The key data are presented in Table 2.23.

Table 2.23 Summary of key data collected for the case study TOCs

	Line Km	Train Km	Passenger Km	Passenger Revenue	Costs	Subsidy	Staff
Unit		Mln	Bln	£ Mln 1996/7 prices	£ Mln 1996/7 prices	£ Mln 1996/7 prices	
1993/4	5,923	62.3	3.366	334	956	622	10,751
1996/7	6,001	65.1	3.278	308	1,185	877	10,543

The case studies undertaken here reveal, in broad terms, that there is little evidence as yet of consistent industry-wide trends emerging in the UK rail industry. However, taken together we can say the following about the five TOCs studied:

- the five TOCs were the prime users on around 6,000 line km. This is around double the entire NS network (around 2,800 line km);
- in 1993/94, 62.3 million train miles were operated. By 1996/7, this figure was 65.1 million, an increase of 4.5%. Although franchising could have led to a decrease of around 5-10% in train miles (as the PSRs were set at a lower level than BR's timetable), franchise commitments and commercial innovations have prevented this happening;
- in 1993/94 3,366 million passenger miles were carried. The corresponding figure in 1996/7 was 3,278 million, a decrease of 2.5%. The main area of growth was in the Regional Railways North East TOC, related to successful marketing of its Transpennine Express Services. In 1993/94 129 million passengers were carried. In 1996/7 the figure was also around 129 million passengers. Patronage had decreased for NorthWest Trains and Merseyrail Electrics but had increased for the other TOCs;
- each TOC is committed to making improvements, typically by providing new services, improving existing services, improving station

facilities and introducing new or refurbished rolling stock. Most of these have been introduced as part of franchise plan agreements, but some have been introduced, above the franchise commitments, as commercial innovations, for example, certain fares promotions and telesales centres;

- in 1995/96 the average punctuality was 90.1% of trains arriving within 5 or 10 minutes (depending on service type). In 1996/97 this average had increased to 93.6%;
- in terms of reliability, in 1995/96 the average was for 98.7% of scheduled train miles to be operated. By 1996/97, this had increased to 99.3%;
- in terms of the labour issue, the main focus has been on drivers' pay and conditions. Basic pay has generally improved but at the expense of conditions. The number of drivers and administrative staff have been reduced, particularly by Regional Railways North East. The number of staff directly employed by the 5 TOCs has only decreased marginally (by 1.9%), although a number of redundancies are known to be in the pipeline; and
- the amount of gross subsidy received by the five TOCs in 1996/97 was £919.5 million. This is forecast to decrease to £503.9 million by 2003/4, a decrease of 45% or about 8% per annum. The study area covers six PTE areas of which 4 will bear the revenue risk, with an estimated traffic revenue of £40 million in 1996/97.

Our overall impression of the case study area is one of relatively poor commercial and financial performance. We find that in 1993/4 the mean train load was only 50 passengers, the mean revenue was high at 10 pence per passenger km (although this includes non fare revenue) and the cost recovery ratio was low, at only 35%. The mean density of track usage was only 10,848 train km per annum (although this excludes freight traffic). By contrast, Shires (1998 – although note the figures also include freight traffic) finds that the Dutch State Railways in 1994 had a mean load of 147 traffic units (≈passengers), a mean revenue of only 3.4 pence per traffic unit km and a cost recovery ratio of 54%. Moreover, the mean density of operations for the Dutch Railways was estimated at 39,458 train km per line km per annum. These results concur with recent work by Birch and Smyth (1998) that the rail network in Britain is relatively underutilised.

2.5 Possible future developments

The dynamics of the railways post privatisation are still evolving. Mergers of train operating companies and other parts of the industry are likely to continue and contract renegotiations are already taking place with OPRAF. A major issue is likely to be OPRAF's stance in the case of likely business failure. This will establish important precedents.

Labour Party policies on railways

The General Election of May 1997 ended 18 years of Conservative Government The Labour Party has, in the past, opposed railway privatisation. But in the General Election Manifesto (Labour Party, 1997) it took the position that privatisation was irreversible:

> the process of rail privatisation is now largely complete. It has made fortunes for a few, but has been a poor deal for the taxpayer. It has fragmented the network and now threatens services. Our task will be to improve the situation as we find it, not as we wish it to be. Our overriding goal must be to win more passengers and freight on to rail. The system must be run in the public interest with higher levels of investment and effective enforcement of train operator's service commitments. There must be convenient connections, through-ticketing and accurate travel information for the benefit of all passengers (Labour Party, 1997 p. 29).

John Prescott, the Deputy Prime Minister in the new Labour Government has responsibility for the newly merged Departments of the Environment and Transport and the newly created Department of the Regions (DETR). The Government has issued a Green Paper asking for contributions on the best ways to construct an integrated transport policy Developing an Integrated Transport Policy: an invitation to contribute (DETR, 1997).

The 1998 Transport White Paper

This process resulted in the White Paper 'A New Deal for Transport' (DETR, 1998a) and a daughter document on Railways Policy (DETR, 1998b) both published in July 1998. The White Paper acknowledges the need for a better railway and the potential for a rail renaissance. A number of positive developments are noted. These include the franchised passenger train operators plans to increase passenger mileage by 25% by 2002/3, EWS's aspirational target of doubling the tonne kms it carries in five years and tripling it over ten years and Freightliner's plan to increase the volume of containers carried by 50% over five years. A number of specific developments are also highlighted including LTS's 'Early Bird' scheme which offers 25% lower fares for commuters travelling before 7 am and the ten fold growth in the rail freight wagon load business as a result of the Enterprise service.

However, the Railways Policy document makes it clear that the Labour Government believes there are major flaws in the present situation. Problems highlighted include a lack of focus for long term planning, confusion in the roles of OPRAF and ORR, unwieldly sanctions, inadequate regulation of the ROSCOs, rail user views not being given enough prominence, public concern about safety and lack of investment. The TOCs' performance is considered to be mixed and in some cases unacceptable. The fragmented industry is not believed to be delivering the benefits of an integrated network, as witnessed by impartial retailing and complaints concerning rail enquiries and passenger compensation.

The main solution is seen to be the creation of a *Strategic Rail Authority* (SRA), which will provide a focus for the planning of passenger and freight railways with appropriate powers to influence the behaviour of key industry powers. It will support integrated transport initiatives and for the first time provide a clear focus for the promotion of rail freight. The SRA will take over OPRAF's functions (themselves revised in November 1997), the freight functions of the DETR, the role of residual operator from BRB and certain functions from ORR. In this last category are included powers concerning disabled passengers, complaints handling, consumer committees, environmental matters, policing, insurance, claims handling and rail closures. The SRA will have additional funds in the form of the Infrastructure Investment Fund, targeted at the elimination of pinch-points on the rail network, and the Rail Passenger Partnership programme, target at innovative schemes to increase rail use at the local and regional level. The SRA's main role is seen to be consumer protection at the franchise level. The ORR's main role will be the regulation of Railtrack, the ROSCOs and the implementation of competition policy. The Regulator's existing duties will be enhanced by having a new duty to have regard to statutory guidance from the Secretary of State on his broad policy objectives for the passenger and freight railway.

The SRA will thus:

- promote the use of rail within an integrated system:
- ensure it is planned as a coherent network;
- work with other agencies (Local Authorities, Regional Planning Conferences, Regional Development Agencies, transport operators and the Highway Agency);
- participate in regional and local land-use planning policies;
- ensure that rail options are assessed to achieve value for money and optimise social and environmental goals;
- take a view on the capacity of the railways, assess investment needs and identify priorities;
- promote accessible transport for the disabled;
- review the role of rail in sustainable transport; and
- produce criteria for competition between operators.

These proposals build on the Objectives, Instructions and Guidance (OIG) issued to the Franchising Director in November 1997. These require him to provide an assessment of Railtrack's investment plans, as set out in the Network Management Structure, as part of a wider review of the type and level of service the rail network should provide. The assessment is considering:

- whether the taxpayer is getting value for money from the track and station access charges already committed to Railtrack;
- whether Railtrack is doing enough to facilitate the progressive improvement in passenger services and facilities;
- evidence of bottlenecks on the rail network and the action Railtrack is proposing to tackle them; and
- the actions Railtrack proposes to take, with train operators, to improve overall levels of operating performance.

The SRA will expect to see in all new franchises – and in any that are renegotiated – more demanding performance standards for train operators and arrangements which enable passengers to hold operators to account for the services they run. An example of the kind of approach that might be expected is the 'passenger dividend' extracted from Thames Trains as a result of its complete takeover by the Go-Ahead Group (who had previously been in partnership with an MBO). This involved the introduction of a new service between Bristol and Oxford, station improvements and improved bus/rail integration.

With respect to the role of ORR, the Environment, Transport and Regional Affairs Committee (1998) drew attention to the importance of the Rail Regulator's forthcoming review of Railtrack's access charges from 2001 onwards. The White Paper expects the Regulator to review both the level and structure of charges, including the incentive mechanisms. This will build on the earlier review in 1995 which reduced Railtrack charges by 8% in 1995/6 and by 2% per annum up to 2000/2001 (ORR, 1995). The White Paper also notes that in 1997 the Regulator secured a licence modification which strengthens his powers to enforce the implementation of Railtrack's Network Management Statement. The Regulator noted at the time of Railtrack's publication of this statement (March 1998) that the statement provided passenger and freight customers with greater detail about Railtrack's plans but that the statement contained very few commitments to deliver significant improvements across the railway network. As a first step, he is therefore finding out from train operators and funders of the railway whether Railtrack's statements meets operators' reasonable needs, as required by the Railtrack licence. The White Paper proposes to strengthen section 55 of the 1993 Railways Act to provide the Rail Regulator with stronger and more timely sanctions to deal with Railtrack. Stronger enforcement powers will ensure that the modified Railtrack licence provides more effective and accountable regulation. Similar powers will enable the SRA to take effective action against operators who breach their contracts. In the future, it will be possible to impose penalties in respect of past breaches which have ceased, and to take quicker enforcement action.

In January 1998, the Government asked the Rail Regulator to report on the operation of the rolling stock leasing market. The resultant report, published in May 1998, rejected the previous Government's assumption that the ROSCOs do not have market power. The Competition Bill, being considered by Parliament at the time of writing, would provide substantial protection against abuse of that power. The Regulator recommended negotiation with the ROSCOs of rules of conduct to back up competition legislation. The White Paper agrees that a concordat between the Regulator and the ROSCOs is the minimum necessary to protect the public interest and the Regulator has been asked to enter into discussions with the ROSCOs.

2.6 General evaluation and conclusions

The experience of many reforms is that there is a mixture of expected and unexpected results. The privatisation of passenger railways in Britain is no exception. We present here some 20 lessons that we believe should be learnt from the British experience.

- The reform process is only at the half-way stage. The industry has been successfully privatised, with the main sell-offs and franchising occurring in 1996 and adjacent years. However, the second half will only get underway in around 2003 when the first round of tenders are due for renewal, the ROSCO contracts begin to expire and open access competition for passenger railways is possibly permitted. Those evaluations of privatisation that have been undertaken (e.g. Harris and Godward, 1997, White, 1998) have taken place at half-time rather than at the end of the match.
- On-the-track competition has been limited to where existing franchises overlap (e.g. London – Gatwick) or where railway geography permits route competition (e.g. London – Birmingham).
- Additional on-track competition is likely in the future with the introduction of the second stage of the moderation of competition in September 1999. The extent to which this competition will be beneficial will be largely determined by how innovative the new services provided are (Preston et al., 1997).
- Off-the-track competition (i.e. for franchises) has been substantial. There have been typically four serious bids per franchise: with one bid from a management buyout (MBO) team; two from bus companies and one from a company with other transport concerns. There have usually been a similar number of bids that were not deemed serious.
- The competition for franchises appears to have become more serious in later rounds, at least in terms of subsidy required. Those who entered the process early (e.g. Stagecoach) seem more likely to earn profits than those who entered late (e.g. Virgin). Similar trends of higher prices in later rounds have been noted in other privatisations e.g. of the National Bus Company. A phased approach to privatisation therefore seems sensible.
- 15 out of the 25 franchises have been won by bus companies. Off-the-track competition was highly dependent on the existence in Brit-

ain of a deregulated and privatised bus and coach industry. Elsewhere, rail reform may need to be preceded by bus and coach reform.

- MBOs only won four franchises, partly due to problems in accessing cheap capital. Moreover, they were a transitory phenomenon in that only one still survives. If, for socio-political reasons, management and employee buy-outs are to be encouraged then the incentives for re-sale need to be removed.
- Four alliances already account for 70% of the passenger rail business by income, whilst one operator dominated the freight market. There have thus been very strong tendencies towards re-agglomeration.
- Total subsidy for the first year of franchises is £1.9 billion. For the last year of franchises, it is forecast to be £0.5 billion (although given lesson 5 we believe there are substantial risks of business failures). In the first year, two franchises will not require subsidy. By the final year, this is forecast to increase to 10.
- It is difficult to judge the trend in total subsidy flowing to the railways in recent years because of accountancy changes, which made some hidden subsidies more explicit, and a deliberate policy of increasing capital costs by using modern equivalent asset valuation techniques and requiring an 8% rate of return. However, it is worth noting that subsidy in the last year before the reforms was £0.5 billion – that is about the same as forecast for the end of the first round of franchises.
- The lack of regulation of the ROSCOs was an oversight as was the lack of claw back provisions for future sales given that all three ROSCOs have been sold on for large profits.
- Railtrack's performance appears mixed. On the one hand, the incetive regime appears to have had a marked effect on performance. On the other hand, there have been severe problems in devising a transparent access and charging regime and in encouraging investment. The regulation of Railtrack remains a difficult problem with both the Rail Regulator and the Franchising Director (and in the future the Strategic Rail Authority) having a role to play.
- As far as passengers are concerned, the level of service in terms of train kms has increased between 1993/4 and 1996/7 by 3% and fares have increased in real terms by 4%. There was an increase in patronage in terms of passenger kms of 6% (this increase is 12.5% if 1997/8 data is used). For our case study area we estimate that train km also increased by 4% during this period but that fares (or at least revenue per passenger km) decreased in real terms by 5% and pa-

tronage by over 2%. This suggests that growth has been concentrated on the markets that we did not cover in the case study, mainly London based intercity and commuter traffic.

- Overall, rail demand has increased since privatisation. The widely agreed main reason for this is the ending of the UK recession, which has meant greater economic activity, including train journeys. Between 1994 and 1997 GDP grew in real terms by almost 8%. The growth in national rail demand is thus not out of line with conventional wisdom concerning GDP elasticities.
- Punctuality increased by 1.9 pecentage points and reliability by 0.3 of a percentage point between 1993/4 and 1996/7. There has since been some slippage so that in 1997/8 both punctuality and reliability are only 0.1 of a percentage point high than in 1993/4. The cause of this deterioration is thought to be due to the problems the TOCs have had in carrying extra passengers and running more services. Passenger complaints have gone up recently but this may partly be due to high public expectations of the advantages of the privatisation process.
- For staff, drivers have often seen their basic pay increase, but their conditions become less favourable and their numbers reduced by around 20%. There have been some examples of labour being made redundant too quickly contributing to reliability problems (South West Trains, Regional Railways North East).
- Labour productivity has improved dramatically since the reform process started. Assuming only a modest reduction in the overall workforce (and there are severe problems about the treatment of contractors etc), the number of passenger kilometres per employee has increased by 24% between 1993/4 and 1996/7, whilst the corresponding figure for train kilometres per employee is estimated at 14%.
- There have been some signs of increased innovation in the industry. In part, these are related to franchise commitments particularly to provide more service, new and refurbished rolling stock and improved stations. However, there have been important commercial initiatives particularly in the areas of ticketing (e.g. group travel, bonus schemes) and in retail and distribution (e.g. the creation of telesales centres).
- Although rail travel demand is increasing steadily, the competitive position of rail travel in Britain within the total passenger transport market is very low. The aspiration of the 1998 Transport White Pa-

per is for rail to play a greater role. The main mechanisms for achieving this are the creation of a Strategic Rail Authority and increases investment, although the precise details have still be worked out.

- The reform process has been incredibly complex and hence costly. The National Audit Office (1996) estimated the cost at greater than £1 billion. Nonetheless, the process has been made to work. A key issue remains whether alternative regimes such as vertically integrated concessions would have worked better.

As for the future, subsidies are expected to decrease for all franchises. Some of them are expected to turn into 'profits' within the current franchising period. If this is realised, the second half of the reform process may see the appearance of a two tier network. A substantial part of the network might then be operated commercially, under open access provisions, whilst the unprofitable services would be franchised. The passenger rail market would thus become like the local bus market.

The process of concentration of the passenger business into a few large alliances may continue in the future. This would provide a regulatory dilemma in that concentration may be desirable from a cost-efficiency viewpoint but may lead to franchising becoming less competitive in the future. To some extent these problems may be tempered by permitting a greater degree of on-the-track competition from September 1999.

The 1998 White Paper's proposals to create a Strategic Rail Authority and re-define the Rail Regulator's role will address some of the problems that have emerged. However, a legislative timetable has yet to be established and it is unlikely that the proposals will come into force before 2001. The effective regulation of Railtrack remains unresolved, despite the windfall tax imposed in the July 1997 budget. Moreover, although there are commitments to increase investment (the Comprehensive Spending Review proposes to increase expenditure on public transport by £1.7 billion over the period 1999 to 2002 – HM Treasury, 1998), it is unlikely to be sufficient to overcome the historic investment shortfall. Further reforms are inevitable.

References

Bagwell, P. S. (1984) *End of the Line?: The Fate of British Railways Under Thatcher*, Verso, London.

Bevan, A (Ed.) (1998) *A-Z of Rail Reopenings* Railway Development Society, Corby.

Birch, I. and Smyth, A. (1998) *Was the Structure Adopted for Passenger Rail Privatisation in the UK More Appropriate to Maintaining the Status Quo?* European Transport Forum, Loughborough University.

Briginshaw, D. (1997) 'Privatisation Proves Better Than Expected', *International Railway Journal*, September 1997.

Cmnd. 2012 (1992) *New Opportunities for the Railways*, HMSO, London.

Central Rail Users Consultative Committee (1997), *Quality Review 1997,* CRUCC, London.

Department of the Environment, Transport and the Regions (DETR) (1995), *Transport Statistics Great Britain, 1995 Edition*, HMSO, London.

Department of the Environment, Transport and the Regions, (DETR) (1996), *Transport Statistics Great Britain, 1996 Edition,* HMSO, London.

Department of the Environment, Transport and the Regions (DETR) (1997) *Developing an Integrated Transport Policy: an invitation to contribute*, DETR, London.

Department of the Environment, Transport and the Regions (DETR) (1997a), *Transport statistics Great Britain, 1997 Edition,* The Stationary Office, London

Department of the Environment, Transport and the Regions (DETR) (1997b), *Bulletin of Rail Statistics, Quarter 1 1997,* Government Statistical Office, London.

Department of the Environment, Transport and the Regions (DETR) (1997c), *Bulletin of Rail Statistics*, Quarter 2 1997 SB (97) 14, Government Statistical Office, London.

Department of the Environment, Transport and the Regions, (DETR) (1997d), *Transport report 1997/98 to 1999/00,* DETR, London.

Department of the Environment, Transport and the Regions (DETR) (1998a), *A New Deal for Transport: Better for Everyone* Cm3950. The Stationery Office, London.

Department of the Environment, Transport and the Regions (DETR) (1998b), *Railways Policy: a response to the third report of the Environment, Transport and Regional Affairs Committee on the proposed Strategic Rail Authority and railway regulation* Cm 4024. The Stationery Office, London.

Department of Transport (1992), *The Franchising of Passenger Rail Services: A Consultation Document*, Department of Transport, London.

Department of Transport (1994), *Britain's Railways: A New Era*, Department of Transport, London.

Department of Transport (1995), *Transport Statistics Report: National Travel Survey,* Department of Transport, HMSO, London.

Department of Transport (1996), *Transport Statistics Great Britain 1996 Edition,* HMSO, London.

EU (European Union) (1996), *Basic Statistics of the European Union, 33rd Edition,* EU, Brussels.

Foster, C. (1994) *The Economics of Rail Privatisation*, Chartered Institute of Public Finance and Accountancy, London.

European Railway Review (1997), A single voice for British train operators, September 1997.

Glover, J. (1997), 'The franchised railway', *Modern Railways*, May 1997.

Glover, J. (1997), 'Franchise performance', *Modern Railways*, September 1997.

Gritten, A. (1988), *Reviving the Railways - A Victorian Future*, Centre for Policy Studies, London.

Harris, N.G. (1997), 'Analysis of the Subsidies Bid for British Rail Passenger Franchises', PTRC European Transport Forum, Brunel University.

Harris, N.G. and Godward, E. (1997), *The Privatisation of British Rail*, The Railway Consultancy Press, London.

HM Treasury (1998), *Modern Public Services for Britain: Investing in Reform.* Cm 3798, The Stationery Office, London.

House of Commons (1993), *Railways Act*, HMSO, London.

International Auto Statistics (1996), *International Auto Statistics*,

International Railway Journal, various articles and years.

Irvine, K. (1987), *The Right Lines*, Adam Smith Institute, London.

Joy, S. (1973), *The Train that Ran Away,* Ian Allen, London.

Kilburn, D.J., (1994), *Urban Rail Transport: Cost and Productivity Comparisons*, Unpublished MSc Thesis, Institute of Transport Studies, University of Leeds, Leeds.

Labour Party (1997), *New Labour because Britain deserves better*, Labour Party, London.

Nash, C.A. (1995), 'Rail Privatisation: the Experience so Far', paper presented to the 4th International Conference on Competition and Ownership in Land Passenger Transport' Rotorua, New Zealand.

Nash, C.A. (1996), 'The separation of operations from infrastructure in the provision of railway services - the British experience', in: European Conference of Ministers of Transport, Round Table 103, *The separation of operations from infrastructure in the provision of railway services* ECMT, Paris.

Nash, C.A. (1997a), 'Rail Privatisation - How is it going?', Institute of Transport Studies Working Paper 497, University of Leeds, Leeds.

Nash, C.A., (1997b), 'Rail Privatisation in Great Britain', paper presented on the 5th International Conference on Competition and Ownership in Land passenger transport.

Nash, C.A., Preston, J. (1993), 'The Policy Debate in Great Britain' in: European Conference of Ministers of Transport, Round Table 90, *Privatisation of Railways*, ECMT, Paris.

National Audit Office (1996), *The Award of the First Three Passenger Rail Franchises*, Report HC 701, HMSO, London.

National Audit Office (1997), *Privatisation of the Rolling Stock Leasing Companies* HC 576 Session 1997-98, The Stationery Office, London.

Office for National Statistics (1997), *Annual Abstract of Statistics: 1997 Edition*, HMSO, London.

Office Passenger Rail Franchising (OPRAF) (1995), *Passenger Rail Industry Overview*, OPRAF, London.

Office of Passenger Rail Franchising (OPRAF) (1997a), *Bulletins*, (February; June; August; October; November), OPRAF, London.

Office of Passenger Rail Franchising (OPRAF) (1997b), *The Privatisation of Britain's Passenger Railway*, OPRAF, London.

Office of Passenger Rail Franchising (OPRAF) (1997c), *OPRAF 1996-97 Annual Report*, OPRAF, London.

Office of the Rail Regulator (ORR) (1994a), *Railtrack's Track Access Charges for Franchised Passenger Services: Developing the Structure of Charges*, Office of the Rail Regulator, London.

Office of the Rail Regulator (ORR) (1994b), *Competition for Railway Passenger Services*, ORR, London.

Office of the Rail Regulator (ORR) (1995), *Railtrack Access Charges for Franchised Passenger Services: The Future Level of Charges,* ORR, London.

Office of the Rail Regulator (ORR) (1997a), *New Service Opportunities for Passengers,* ORR, London.

Office of the Rail Regulator (ORR) (1997b), Press Notice 'Regulator Moves Towards Enforceable Standards for Accurate Retailing by train Operators', ORR, London.

Office of the Rail Regulator (ORR) (1997c), Press Notice 'National Rail Enquiry meets regulator's call answering targets' ORR, London.

Office of the Rail Regulator (ORR) (1997d), *Annual Report 1996/1997*, Regulator's Statement, ORR,London

Office of the Rail Regulator (ORR) (1998) *New Service Opportunites for Passengers: Criteria and Procedures for the Approval of Train Operators Proposals for Stagte II of Moderation of Competition.*

Preston, J.M., Nash, C.A., and Wardman, M.R. (Grantholders), Whelan, G.A., Clark, S.D., Cobbett, M.R., Siu, Y.L. and Shires, J.D. (Researchers) (1997), *The Privatisation of Passenger Rail Services: Analysis and Monitoring. End of Award Report,* Economic and Social Research Council Award ROOO234735, ESRC, Swindon.

Prognos (1996), *World Report '97, Industrial Countries 1995-2000-2005, 1996,* Basle.

Pryke, R. and Dodgson, J. (1975), *The Rail Problem,* Robertson, London.

Railtrack Group plc (1997a), *Railtrack Annual Report and Accountst 1996/97,* Railtrack, London.

Railtrack Group plc (1997b), *Railtrack Network Management Statement 1996/97*, Railtrack, London.

Railway Gazette International (1997), *Franchise operators confidential of growing revenue*, November 1997.

Redwood, J. (1988), *Signals from a Railway Conference*, Centre for Policy Studies, London.

Root, A. and Preston, J. (1998), Research on Railway Competition – National Report: Great Britain, in: Van de Velde, D.M. and P.A. van Reeven (eds.), *Railway Reform and the Role of Competition: The Experience of Six Countries*, Erasmus University Rotterdam.

Save Our Railways (1997a), *'The Prospects for the Franchised Railway: an analysis for Save Our Railways, prepared by Tim Powell, Transport Advisory Services,* Save Our Railways, London.

Save Our Railways (1997b), *Draft memorandum for house of commons transport select committee inquiry into the role of the proposed strategic rail authority*, London.

Serpell, D. (1983), *Railway Finances*, a Report of a Committee chaired by Sir David Serpell, KCB, CMG, OBE, HMSO, London.

Shires, J. (1998), *Appendix B: Railway Modelling Results,* SORT-IT Project Deliverable D4. April.

The Independent (1998a), 'Big Rise in Trains Failing to Run on Time', 13 August, p.5.

The Independent (1998b), 'Rail Firm Complaints Climb to 1,800 a Day', 1 June, p. 2.

Union Internationale des Chemins de Fer (UIC) (1996), *International Railway Statistics*, UIC, Paris.

White, P. (1998), *Financial Outcomes of Rail Privatisation in Britain* European Transport Forum, Loughborough University.

Willich, A. (1996), *Rail-links in Hampshire*, Unpublished MSc Thesis, University of Oxford, Oxford.

3 Sweden

GUNNAR ALEXANDERSSON and STAFFAN HULTÉN
Stockholm School of Economics

3.1 Introduction

Sweden's 1988 Transport Policy Act divided the state's rail assets between two state-owned organisations, *Statens Järnvägar* (SJ), the Swedish State Railways, and *Banverket*, the Swedish National Rail Administration. Since then, SJ has had the role of being a dominant railway operator, while Banverket has been the provider of the state's track infrastructure. In 1988, this vertical separation of infrastructure from operations was quite a unique event put in an international context. In recent years, other countries have followed similar paths, although choosing other border lines for the separation of railway assets.

Among many other things, the Act also implied a new classification of the state's railway network and thereby a transfer of responsibility for several lines to regional authorities - the County Public Transport Authorities (CPTAs). For these parts of the tracks, the possibility of competitive tendering for the track was introduced. Even if entries of other rail operators have been limited, one important feature of this arrangement was the fact that SJ to a greater extent than before became a contractor rather than a provider of services under its own flag.

During the 1990s several other steps towards more competition have been taken. In 1993 it became possible for the state's negotiator to put out to tendering those interregional lines that were non-commercial (but upheld for socio-economic reasons). In 1994 a private consortium was appointed to build a new airport link and the licence to operate the services. A decision implying on-the-track competition on the whole passenger network was taken by Parliament the same year, but was withdrawn shortly thereafter due to a shift of political power in Parliament. Instead, the powers of regional transport authorities were extended in 1996, making competitive tendering possible for a greater part of the network. Simultaneously, virtually open access for freight operators was introduced.

This chapter provides a description of the Swedish organisation of the railways and the reforms related to railway competition. Its structure is as follows: first, the evolution of transport policy issues and regulations related to the Swedish railway sector is described. This is a rather thorough exposition of how the system of today came into existence. Next, the resulting legislative and regulatory framework is presented. The actual current organisation of the railways is described at the national and regional levels, including descriptions of important events (i.e. entry of new operators) and effects caused by the reforms. In order to be able to go into more detail, one case study on regionalisation and the introduction of competitive tendering for regional railway services has been selected. The chapter ends with our overall findings and conclusions. Throughout, the focus will be on passenger services, but freight services are sometimes brought up in order to promote clarity.

3.2 The development of Swedish railway policies and regualtions

Ever since the 1950s, the Swedish State Railways (SJ) have been facing the problem of unprofitable railway lines. The closure of these lines has sometimes been the only possible solution, but frequently the discontinuation of train services has been a politically very difficult decision to take. In this conflict between commercial and political concerns, the importance of the latter lead to the introduction of subsidies aimed at upholding non-commercial services. In 1963, this practise became officially established by means of the division of the Swedish railway network into one commercial part and one subsidised part (Nilsson, 1995)

The purpose of this section will be to consider the transformations from 1979 to 1998 and the current movement towards further changes in the foreseeable future. The events are presented in a summarised form in Table 3.1 at the end of this section.

The Transport Policy Act of 1979

The Transport Policy Act of 1979 became something of a starting point for the step-wise reregulation[1] of the Swedish railway sector that has continued

[1] Our use of the word reregulation refers to (any) changes in a regulatory framework, rather than a situation where a deregulated industry is transformed into a more regulated state.

to this day. Over the years, the changes have primarily been motivated by the aims to reduce the long-term socio-economic deficits in the transport sector and to create a profitable railway operator. A prevailing notion has been that, in principle, railway operation, because of economies of scale, is a natural monopoly.

The Transport Policy Act of 1979 was aimed at adjusting the cost burden of competing modes of transportation so that the financial costs associated with infrastructure would reflect marginal costs. One implication of the Act was the creation of a new institutional structure for local and regional transport, with the formation of the County Public Transport Authorities (CPTAs) in Sweden's 24 counties (Nilsson, 1995). Foremost, the local and regional bus services were affected, but several CPTAs also became directly involved in the decisions concerning the future for some of the local and regional railway services threatened by closure. They were to look into alternative solutions for the passenger services on these lines. If they agreed on closing the lines, replacing them with bus services, they would receive state subsidies for that bus traffic for a period of five years. Therefore, this implied a first step towards decentralisation of the responsibility for non-commercial rail services, including the financing of these services. The majority of these lines were closed, but in a few cases, the regional authorities instead chose to take over the responsibility for providing these services by themselves, with SJ as the contractor.

The Railway Act of 1985

SJ's continued financial problems in the early 80s, resulted in the passing of a Railway Act in 1985, aimed at reducing SJ's deficits. The state accepted to expand its responsibility for infrastructure investments while SJ was instructed to separate the accounts for infrastructure from other parts of its business. The Passenger and Freight Division from now on were to pay internal fees for the use of railway infrastructure. SJ was also to divest the parts of its business that did not complement its core business: the railway services. This was a directive that SJ was very slow to observe, partly due to Parliament not being consistent in this demand over the following years. Another novelty in the Act was that SJ had to fund its investments in rolling stock through borrowings on commercial terms. Finally, the Act also made SJ more independent of the state, giving SJ the right to decide upon staffing and organising without the risk of intervention from Parliament.

The Transport Policy Act of 1988

Despite the efforts of 1985, SJ's financial position continued to deteriorate. When SJ in 1986 estimated that it needed 1 billion SEK in additional state aid, this resulted in a government plan for drastic changes (Nilsson, 1995). The outcome of this process was the 1988 Transport Policy Act, which may be viewed as an attempt to, once and for all, solve the problems with the unprofitable regional lines and the need for infrastructure investments, and turn SJ into a profitable train operator. The basic goal for Swedish transport policy, as it was set out by the Act of 1988, is to provide the citizens and the industry in the separate parts of the country with satisfactory, safe, and environmental-friendly transport services at the lowest possible cost to society as a whole (Proposition 1987/88:50). A strive for making the preconditions for the railways more similar with the ones for the roads was of major importance for the design of the reform.

The main feature of the 1988 Transport Policy Act was the vertical separation of the infrastructure organisation (Banverket) from railway operations (SJ) – a type of reform that Sweden was first in Europe to carry out. Through Banverket, the state was to have the main responsibility for infrastructure maintenance and renewal, to limited extent funded by infrastructure charges paid by train operators using the tracks. The charges were designed to reflect social marginal costs in order to induce optimal use of existing facilities. SJ committed itself to cut costs and increase revenues so that net profits would improve by 1 billion SEK within four years, while the state would continue to subsidise unprofitable services. A Railway Inspectorate, governing the safety issues of the railways, was to be established.

Possibly inspired by the experience from the early cases where some regional transport authorities had extended their responsibility into railway services, the Transport Policy Act of 1988 implied a more general policy step in that direction. The network was divided into main lines and county lines. SJ would continue to have the exclusive right to perform the services along the main lines, while the responsibility for the local and regional passenger services on the county lines was transferred from SJ to the CPTAs. This change came into effect in most counties in mid 1990. One goal behind this reform was to increase the co-ordination of bus services and railway traffic.

As a compensation for their thereby increased costs, the CPTAs were to receive, for a period of 10 years, an annual state-subsidy amounting to SJ's operating deficits on each line. This subsidy was not necessarily to be used for upholding train services. The CPTA could choose to replace the train services with bus services instead without being deprived of the subsidy. In addition to these direct subsidies, the vehicles used by SJ on the affected lines were given away by the state to the CPTAs under the condition that the regional railway services were to be continued.

With the rail infrastructure in the hands of a national authority (Banverket), SJ turned into a train operator, and the vehicles, money and responsibility for the regional passenger services in the hands of the CPTAs, the door was open for competitive tendering for the contracts of actually performing these services. The first tenders were carried out in 1989, although some of them were more like renegotiations between the CPTA and SJ.

Towards the 1994 Deregulation Bill

In February 1991, the Social Democrat government took a step towards further opening the rail service market, with the decision to look into the conditions for and consequences of increased competition on the state's railways. The primary reason behind this action was the general belief that competition fosters efficiency (Nilsson, 1995). Also of importance, was the perceived risk felt by many politicians that SJ's power on the market for transportation services could become too strong. Initiated by a Social Democrat government, the objective to open the railways to more competition was declared by the non-socialist government elected in September 1991.

In January 1992 the new Minister of Transport expressed the goal to put out the non-commercial interregional lines to tendering, instead of simply renegotiating the terms with SJ (TT-meddelande, 1992-01-01). A first round of tendering for these services was carried out in 1992. Even though some other companies apart from SJ placed bids for some of the services, SJ had the lowest bids in all cases. This tendering process came to be viewed as a test of whether competition for services on the main lines was actually possible, influencing the government's parallel investigation (begun in March 1992) into a suitable form for a more far-reaching deregulation. Two reports were published, one in February 1993 and one in the autumn the same year (SOU 1993:13 and Ds 1993:63, respectively). They differed in their approach towards deregulation and caused much debate until the government finally presented its bill on the matter in January 1994 (Proposition 1993/94:166). The bill argued for a far-reaching deregulation, where the dominant positions of SJ as well as of the CPTAs were to be discontinued as of January 1, 1995, opening up the entire network for new entrants. Any entrant with sound finances (not only railway operators), would be allowed to apply for track access on any part of the state's railways. A regulatory agency would be established, having the ultimate responsibility for track capacity allocation. During an interim period SJ would continue to manage the traffic control function and would also have the right to plan its railway services before any other actor could make its decisions. Rolling stock was to be made available (buying or leasing) to new operators from SJ's redundant rolling stock on "commercial grounds". Despite fierce opposition from Social Democrats and the left-wing party, this deregulation bill was accepted by Parliament in May 1994. However, when the Social Democrats regained power in Parliament through the election in September the same year, they quickly decided to postpone the deregulation of the railways (Proposition 1994/95:72).

During the non-socialist government, two other events related to railway competition occurred. Firstly, Banverket decided to grant the mining company LKAB the operating rights of ore transport on the Iron Ore Line. Secondly, the final stages of a special initiative aiming at increased private sector involvement in financing of railway investments and ownership of railways took place. It had since long been argued that the planned Arlanda Airport Link should, if any, constitute an attractive project for the private sector, in terms of building as well as operating the line. A competitive tender for the Arlanda Airport Link as a Build-Operate-Transfer project was completed in 1994, just before the Parliamentary election. The Social Democrats criticised the arrangement, saying that it directed private sector involvement only to the part of the line that was believed to be most profitable. When they had regained power they initially tried to break up the deal, but ended up adding some restrictions (Alexandersson and Hultén, 1997).

Heavy investments and a revised deregulation

In 1993-94 another important political decision was taken regarding the future development of the railway sector. This was a large-scale investment program in the Swedish railway infrastructure, going beyond the annual 1 billion SEK suggested in the Transport Policy Act of 1988. Instead, 32 billion SEK was to be invested in railway infrastructure over the years 1994-2003. The planning include massive investments in upgrading of the core network south of Sundsvall to allow for services with the X2000 - the tilting high speed trains (Banverket, 1994).

The Social Democrat Government launched a renewed investigation of the future organisation of the railway sector in late 1994. It resulted in a new report presented in June 1995, suggesting a less radical deregulation compared to the 1994 Deregulation Bill (Ds 1995:33). The functions of allocation of track capacity and train traffic control were to be transferred from SJ to Banverket, while other common facilities were to be available for other train operators under commercial but non-discriminating terms. Instead of promoting open access for new operators, it was suggested that each CPTA should get the right to run services also on the main lines within its respective county, a right that after special government decisions could be extended to services reaching into other counties. It was argued that this would promote the development of the local and regional services. For the freight services, however, the report suggested open access on the whole network, based upon the belief that these services would stand better chances against other modes of transportation if they were forced to adapt to what the market wanted. SJ's expressed fear that this could destroy its Freight Division's possibilities to gain from economies of scale had some influence on the bill that followed in October 1995 (Proposition 1995/96:92). A "Grandfather's right" rule was added, giving an operator the right of precedence to a timetable position it had used before. The bill was passed in December 1995, implying the deregulation of the freight services on these terms as of July 1, 1996, and also the extended rights for the CPTAs as proposed by the report. SJ's exclusive right to run the commercial interregional passenger services was maintained.

KOM-KOM and beyond

While SJ had been a profitable business administration for a couple of years in the 1990s, in principle fulfilling the obligations on this matter specified in the Transport Policy Act of 1988, it got into renewed financial difficulties in 1996. The year ended with losses reaching 477 million SEK (SJ, 1997). In particular, the Freight Division's performance was poor. This development formed the background to the final stages of the work of a special committee, "Kom-Kom", investigating the future of the transport sector. Its final report was presented in the spring of 1997 (SOU 1997:35). Among its suggestions were a new division of the railway network into a business network and an inter-regional basic network, and the abolishment of track fees for freight transport. The business network, consisting of SJ's profitable lines, was only to be accessed by SJ. This was motivated with the claim that railway operation in a country the size of Sweden is a natural monopoly due to economies of scale. The railway services on the interregional network were however to be purchased through competitive tenders, possibly carried out by a new national authority co-operating with the CPTAs.

Building upon these ideas, another committee presented a report taking a quite different view in late 1997 (SOU 1997:129). Probably inspired by the development in Great Britain, it suggested that profitable as well as non-profitable interregional passenger services should be subjected to competitive tendering, and that SJ should not enjoy any right of precedence to profitable passenger rail services. However, these ideas never made it to the government's transport policy bill presented in March 1998 (Proposition 1997/98:56). Instead, this bill (passed in Parliament in the beginning of June) stayed more close to the suggestions presented in the Kom-Kom report, with the addition of a proposed transfer of some of the fringe network from (primarily) SJ to Banverket, in order to make entry easier for competing freight operators.

A novelty in the Transport Policy Bill of 1998 is the suggestion to further deregulate the long-distance bus services. These services, almost solely run by private companies on commercial grounds, have been very restricted in the past. Since a reform in 1993, it has been up to SJ or any CPTA to prove that a suggested long-distance line would be harmful to their business, blocking new entrants (before, it was the task of the bus company to prove the opposite). Since then, a limited number of new connections have opened while several old ones have experienced an increase in the number of departures. Swebus has been a front runner in this development, having increased its supply substantially since the company was sold by SJ to Stagecoach in 1996. Coming into effect in January 1999, many of the remaining restrictions will be lifted, allowing full-scale competition between long-distance bus services and train services. Whether this action will primarily hurt SJ or increase total travelling has caused many debates in the past.

In late 1997 a new General Director for SJ was appointed. Recent statements from him suggest a change in SJ's view upon competition from other rail operators. Having traditionally argued that competition from other modes of transportation is enough, SJ's management now seems to view other train operators as necessary for the survival and well functioning of the railway transportation system. In this system, SJ will still be the dominant player, but perhaps with a market share of 75% rather than 98% (Dagens Industri, 1998-02-28).

Table 3.1 Summary of the evolution of transport policies for the Swedish Railways

Date	Decision or action	Part of railway service	Goals	Main effects
1979	• Transport Policy Act	• Local and regional railways	• Creating a new institutional structure for local and regional transport • Adjust cost burden of competing modes of transportation so that financial infrastructure costs would reflect marginal costs	• The County Public Transport Authorities (CPTAs) are established in Sweden's 24 counties, getting the formal responsibility for bus transportation and for some local and regional rail services • A first step in shifting the financial burden of commuter rail services to the counties and away from central government
1985	• Railway Act	• All railway traffic	• Improve SJ's financial situation • Let SJ's management act more like a normal market directed firm	• A separation of the accountings for infrastructure and operations • Increase of total investment allocations • Relax of centralised control of SJ's management

Table 3.1 Summary of the evolution of transport policies for the Swedish Railways (continued)

1988	• Transport Policy Act. Main features: • Separation of the infrastructure organisation (Banverket) from railway operation (SJ). • Division of railway network in national network and regional networks	• All railway traffic	• Safeguard the long-term survival of the railway, because of its advantages from an environmental and safety point of view • Safeguard balanced regional economic growth • Have an equal organisation for railway and road infrastructure • Improve the economic situation for SJ	• A large infrastructure investment program is launched • SJ starts to show profit • SJ starts to divest its non-railway activities (gradually)
1 July 1990	• The CPTAs become responsible for the regional railway services and can use tenders to purchase the traffic	• Local and regional passenger traffic	• Increase the co-ordination of bus services and railway traffic • Reduce the costs for local and regional passenger traffic	• SJ becomes a contractor • Private firms win some tenders • Increased co-ordination of bus and railway services • New local and regional services are launched • Reduced cost level
1 Jan 1991	• Railway Security Act • Permissions are required for all traffic	• All railway traffic	• Define the responsibilities concerning safety • Increase the safety of the railway network	• Highlights the large number of owners of the railway track
June 1991	• The CPTA of Jönköping county gets the permission to operate on part of the national network	• Railway passenger services Nässjö-Jönköping	• Increased number of departures	• On-the-track competition between BK Tåg and SJ

Table 3.1 Summary of the evolution of transport policies for the Swedish Railways (continued)

1992	• LKAB gets the permission to operate on the Iron Ore Line (Malmbanan)	• Freight transport on the Iron Ore line	• Reduce costs for the operation	• Reduced costs by cost savings and reduced profit margins for SJ and NSB • An important change is the use of the same personnel on the whole line
1992-93	• First competitive tenders for unprofitable railway operations on the national network	• Inter-regional passenger services on the national network	• Reduce costs • Test of possibilities for competition in advance of the upcoming deregulation	• Actual competition for 4 out of 12 lines. SJ wins all contracts but is forced to accept lower subsidy payments
1 July 1993	• New Competition law		• EU harmonisation	• Legal issue is raised • BK Tåg together with the Swedish Competition Authority claim that a winning bid from SJ did not cover all costs • SJ proved guilty in court in 1998. Sentenced to 8 mln SEK fine
May 1994	• Decision in Parliament on far-reaching deregulation from 1 January 1995, including on-the- track competition	• All passenger services on the national network	• Increase efficiency of railway operations	• Decision is turned over after Social Democratic election win 1994 • Instead new parliamentary investigations are initiated
Sep 1994	• Private consortium chosen as winner in tender for building and operating Arlanda Airport Link	• Passenger services on new line	• Increase private sector involvement in infrastructure investments	• New entrant A-Train will begin running passenger services on the line in 1999 • Its monopoly position restricted after Social Democratic election win

Table 3.1 Summary of the evolution of transport policies for the Swedish Railways (continued)

1 July 1996	• Banverket takes over the traffic control and capacity allocation functions from SJ • CPTAs are given extended rights to use the national network within their counties • Virtually open access for freight operators is introduced	• Freight transport on all lines • Passenger services on the regional parts of the national network	• Develop freight transport by rail • Facilitate for the CPTAs to co-ordinate and improve regional traffic	• Malmtrafik AB is founded • Several new freight operators enter the market, including BSM • Problems arise because of the fragmented ownership of the fringe railway tracks
Fall 1996	• The SJ-owned bus operator Swebus is sold to Stagecoach		• Forms part of SJ's goal to concentrate on railway operations	• Increased number of departures of already established long-distance bus services
March 1997	• KOM-KOM's final report. Suggests a new division of the railway network into a business network and an interregional basic network. Also suggests abolition of use-of-track charges for freight transport	• All railway traffic	• Enhance the competitiveness of the railway compared with other modes of transportation • All types of transportation shall cover their social costs	• New discussions and new studies are initiated

March 1998	• New Transport Policy Paper:
	  • Fringe network to be transferred to Banverket
	  • Lower track usage fees
	  • Deregulation of long-distance buses
		• All railway traffic	• Enhance the competitiveness of the railway compared with other modes of transportation	• Increased number of long-distance bus services competing with rail services
				• New study on co-ordination of tenders for all types of non-profitable transport services through new authority

3.3 Legal and regulatory framework

In this section we will present an overview of the laws and regulations of particular importance to the Swedish railways.[2] Before entering the description, something should be said about the relative status of laws and regulations. The Swedish National Parliament has the power to institute new laws and make changes in old ones, deciding upon bills proposed by (for the most part) the National Government. The Government has the power to produce additional regulations as long as they are in accordance with the laws and other decisions taken by Parliament. It is often the case that a specific regulation is closely related to a certain law. Some other national and local authorities have the powers to set up rules (or at least suggest such rules) for specific areas of business. We will refer to these as "regulations" as well.

Concerning the EU-directives related to the railways, Sweden has implemented them by means of introducing new laws or regulations and/or making revisions of old ones. Some of Sweden's early regulatory reforms preceded the directives with several years.[3]

Some special decisions taken by the Parliament, although not decisions upon laws, nevertheless constitute important building blocks in the overall legislative and regulatory framework. One striking example is the Parliament's decision of 1988 upon the transport policy of the 1990s. Due to its position as a guiding star for the subsequent laws and regulations, this Act will be described under the heading "legislative framework" despite not having the formal status as a "law". It also functions as an introduction to the more specified framework.

[2] Using their official reference key (year and number within brackets) in SFS (*Svensk Författningssamling*).

[3] Directive 91/440/EEC of July 29, 1991, on the need for separation of infrastructure and operations in terms of bookkeeping, is believed to have been implemented in Sweden by means of the regulations (1988:1379), (1988:707), (1988:626) and (1988:1378). Directive 95/18/EEC of June 19, 1995, on the licensing of railway undertakings, was implemented in Sweden by means of a law (1990:1157). Finally, directive 95/19/EEC of June 19, 1995, on the allocation of railway infrastructure capacity and the charging of infrastructure fees, has been implemented by means of several Swedish laws and regulations, the most important being the law (1997:756) and the regulations (1997:757) and (1988:1378).

Legal framework

Transport Policy Act of 1988

The Parliament's decision upon the transport policy for the 1990s (Proposition 1987/88:50) included the decision to split the state's rail assets of the Swedish State Railways, *Statens Järnvägar* (SJ) into one transport operator, "new SJ", and one national authority, *Banverket*, the National Rail Administration. In more detail, the decision set out the following guidelines for further legislation and decisions:

- through *Banverket*, the state has the main responsibility for the infrastructure of the railways. There shall be fees for using the track. The fees are to be calculated upon the principle of socio-economic marginal cost pricing;
- planning of infrastructure investments is to be based on socio-economic considerations;
- a special authority, *Järnvägsinspektionen*, the Railway Inspectorate, is to handle issues of safety;
- the state's railways are divided into three categories: 1) the main lines, 2) the county lines, and 3) the Iron Ore line;
- SJ enjoys the exclusive right to perform railway services on the main lines and freight services on all lines;[4]
- the County Public Transport Authorities (CPTAs) bear the responsibility for local and regional passenger services by train and hold the exclusive right to run passenger services on those county lines for which they accept financial responsibility;[5]
- on lines where either SJ or a CPTA has discontinued its services, *Banverket* is authorised to reassign rights to operate trains to third parties;
- the state will buy such interregional passenger services that are believed to be necessary for socio-economic reasons, but are not possible to run on a commercial basis;
- SJ is to concentrate on its core business: railway services;

[4] These exclusive rights have partly been offset by later decisions. The situation of today is defined by other laws and regulations presented below.

[5] These rights have later been extended, as defined by laws and regulations presented below.

- fair terms of competition between the transportation of freight by road and by rail are to be created;[6] and
- the state's interest in SJ, being the owner, is foremost a way to make sure railway services will be offered that are environmental-friendly and of high quality. SJ is to strive to reach as large a market share as possible for passenger and freight services by train, based upon sound business conditions.

Law on railway safety (1990:1157)

This law stipulates what is needed in order to get a permit to perform railway services or other types of operations related to railways.

Everyone (with the exception of SJ and Banverket) who wants to run railway services has to hold a licence for these operations. Permits are granted to those who are law-abiding, have the skills and fulfil the economic demands and other preconditions to be able to perform the services. The authority to handle the applications is the Railway Inspectorate. This authority prescribes what conditions the holder of the licence must fulfil to make sure that safety is promoted. It may adjust the rules to the applicant in question, taking into account the type and scale of the business. The rolling stock must get an approval from the Railway Inspectorate before use.

Law on commercial traffic (1988:263)

This law stipulates the demands for a person or company who wants to run any form of commercial traffic (for passengers or freight) with vehicles *other* than trains, scheduled or non-scheduled (like charter traffic).

Before any business of this kind may start, a permit is needed from the county administrative board in the applicant's county of origin. (For scheduled traffic crossing county borders the National Road Administration, is the relevant authority.) To get a permit the applicant must have the necessary skills, economic conditions, willingness and ability to perform his obligations towards society. Permits are not granted, if there is reason to believe that the suggested traffic services may harm the conditions for performing railway services or public transport in the area in question.

[6] The creation of an infrastructure provider (Banverket), being separate from the operators (SJ and others), makes the conditions for the railways as compared to the roads more similar. Since long ago the National Road Administration plays the infrastructure provider role for the roads. The channelling of subsidies through the infrastructure provider and the establishment of usage fees are other elements of this strive to create similar conditions.

Law on responsible authority for certain public transport (1978:438)

This law stipulates that in every Swedish county there shall be a transport authority responsible for planning and management of local and regional passenger services. The responsibility lies jointly at the municipalities and the county council in each county. They may agree upon forming a limited company for handling this responsibility as long as the responsible parties hold all shares.

Law on the right to operate certain scheduled traffic (1985:449)

This law stipulates that every county public transport authority (as created by the law above) has the right to perform scheduled passenger services within its county without the need for the kind of permits mentioned in the law (1988:263) above. This right may be extended, by means of decisions of The National Road Administration, to include services on certain lines crossing the borders of other counties. The traffic authorities also have the right to let other operators perform the services under contracts with the authorities.

Regulatory framework

Regulation on the state-owned railways (1996:734)

This regulation stipulates that the state-owned railways consists of 1) main lines, 2) county lines, and 3) the Iron Ore line, and contains some of the most important rules defining the possibilities for different actors in the industry.

- Banverket has the power to decide what parts of the network to be called county lines.
- Banverket may only cease to maintain a county line if the traffic along the line is very limited and not before affected parties have been able to bring forward their opinion. If Banverket plans not to maintain a part of the state-owned railways, it may give an operator the right to use the track as long as that operator takes over the responsibility to maintain the track.
- SJ holds the right to operate passenger services on the main lines and on the Iron Ore Line.

- Every regional traffic authority (CPTA) holds the right to perform passenger services on the county lines and local and regional passenger services on the main lines within its county. The Government may permit a regional traffic authority to perform services on the main lines in an adjacent county, if there are reasons to believe that the local and regional traffic services would gain from this.
- International joint ventures of railway companies have the right to perform through services between EES countries on the state's railways, as long as they fulfil the conditions stated in the law (1990:1157) above.
- If SJ or the regional traffic authorities during the process of track allocation do not apply for available train locations (in the timetable) for passenger services on a part of the state's railways, the Rail Traffic Administration may grant another operator the operating rights on this part.
- The state's railways shall be open for every freight operator located in Sweden. However, some types of services take precedence: passenger services tendered by the state and traffic using a train location being used by permission during the previous timetable period.
- The allocation of tracks is under the responsibility of the Rail Traffic Administration. This authority stipulates the timetable for the services along the state's railways, after having taken into account the suggestions from the operators and from Banverket.
- A train operator must not run train services without having reached an agreement with Banverket upon necessary administrative, technical and financial conditions for the traffic. Moreover, the conditions stated in the law (1990:1157) must be fulfilled.

Regulation on fees for usage of the state-owned railways (1988:1378)

This regulation sets out detailed rules for all the fees to be paid by operators on the state-owned tracks. The fees are based upon wear and tear caused by different types of vehicles.

The track usage fees consist of:

- *a fixed (annual) amount* which is calculated on the basis of a specified charge per unit of axletree or (for engines) per unit of driving shaft;
- *a variable amount* which consists of track fees, operating fees, energy fees and marshalling fees:

  - the track fees are calculated per ton of every vehicle's gross weight rolling 1 km of track;
  - operating fees are to be paid per km and train for trains running regular services. Electricity-powered trains are charged an additional charge per km and vehicle. Diesel fuel fees are to be paid for diesel-powered trains based upon the fuel consumption; and
  - marshalling fees are to be paid for freight cars when using certain marshalling yards; and
- *an additional fee to the Rail Traffic Administration* entity at Banverket which is supposed to cover the authority's annual costs for traffic control and allocation of tracks (the costs for passenger services along county lines not included), incurred by the train operating company. The charges are to be distributed in proportion to the amount of traffic performed.

Regulation with instructions to SJ (1988:626)

The regulation stipulates that SJ's main business is to run railway services. It also specifies the composition of the board (minimum five and maximum eight persons, plus the Director General and the persons representing the staff). The Director General and the chairman of the board are appointed by the Government. SJ decides upon all other staff.

Regulation with instructions to Banverket (1996:286)

This regulation states that Banverket is the central authority for handling issues related to the railways.

- Banverket's main duties are: 1) to promote the development of railways, 2) to run and administer the state's railway structures, 3) to be responsible for issues of safety related to railway operations and 4) to promote the railways as being an environmental friendly mode of transportation.
- The regulation specifies the composition of Banverket's board (minimum five and maximum nine persons, including the Director General and the chairman).
- *Delegationen för köp av viss kollektivtrafik*, the Committee for the purchase of certain public transport services, is linked to Banverket. It shall prepare and administer the state's procurement of passenger

services on the state's railways in accordance with the law (1978:438).

- The Railway Inspectorate and the Rail Traffic Administration are also entities within Banverket. The Railway Inspectorate is responsible for Banverket's task to handle rules of safety for railway operations and to supervise that they are followed. The same applies to permits to run railway services as defined and specified in the law (1990:1157). The Rail Traffic Administration is responsible for and decides upon matters related to track allocation and operating rights as described in the regulation (1996:734).

Regulation on plan for main lines (1989:67)

This regulation stipulates that Banverket must produce a 10-year investment plan forming the basis of the appropriations from the state's budget every fourth year. It also states that suggested improvements of railway infrastructure are to be co-ordinated with the objects covered by the county plans for regional transportation infrastructure. Furthermore, the plan must include estimations of the investments' effects upon people's health, the environment and the economising of land, water and other resources. SJ, regional authorities and others are to be consulted when the plan is being developed.

Regulation on safety of railway, underground and tramway (1990:1165)

This regulation contains rules for the application of the law (1990:1157). It states that the Railway Inspectorate has the right to produce additional rules for the application of the law and this regulation. It also contains rules of qualification and conduct for drivers.

3.4 Current organisation

This section provides an overview, as well as descriptions in more detail, of the actual organisation of the Swedish railways of today. The focus is to point at important changes that have followed from the changes in policies, laws and regulations related to the industry.

3.4.1 National overview

The current organisation of the Swedish railways draws heavily from the Transport policy Act of 1988 as presented in previous sections. The state's railways are divided into two main categories: 1) the main lines (6302 km of track in 1996) and 2) the county lines (3315 km of track). A third category is the Iron Ore line (446 km of tracks) serving Kiruna-Narvik (in Norway) and Kiruna-Boden/Luleå in the north (Banverket, 1997). Originally, 23 lines were categorised as being county lines in the Government Bill (Proposition 1987/88:50) preceding the Transport Policy Act of 1988. The actual transfer of responsibility to the CPTAs came about on May 27, 1990. After a special Government decision, the Blekinge Coast Line (Karlskrona-Kristianstad) also became a county line as of July 1 the same year, while the Haparanda line (Luleå-Haparanda) later became re-classified as a main line.

Another way of describing the Swedish railways is to look at the various passenger train services, categorised according to the forms of division of responsibility:

- the profitable inter-regional services (crossing one or several county borders) along main lines. These are run by SJ under its own flag, i.e. without contracts with other parties;
- the unprofitable interregional services procured by the state, contracting train operators (only SJ so far) to carry out the services,
- the local, regional and sometimes interregional services under the responsibility of the CPTAs, carried out by contractors along local lines, county lines and along parts of the main lines; and
- finally, there are some interregional services along main lines and/or county lines that are upheld by means of special agreements between several CPTAs, SJ and (sometimes) the state.

One important aspect of the Swedish railway network is the mix of passenger and freight services. During 1993, 92.7 million train km were operated over the network. Of this total, freight trains accounted for 37 percent and passenger trains for 63 percent (SIKA, 1996). Only a few lines support pre-dominantly single-purpose traffic.

3.4.2 Authorities

Swedish National Rail Administration *(Banverket)*

All the important national transport authorities are currently, in one way or another, linked to the state's provider of the infrastructure, Banverket, which therefore becomes the focus of this section.

Areas of responsibility

Banverket, The Swedish National Rail Administration, has been the national authority responsible for the major part of the state-owned track infrastructure since 1988-89. The actual division of responsibility between Banverket and SJ is a somewhat complicated matter. Banverket does not control *all* the infrastructure related to railways. Starting with the tracks, Banverket has in its hands the basic network of tracks, while SJ still owns the ground underneath the tracks. Moreover, side-tracks and a large part of other tracks referred to as the capillary or fringe network (totalling about 2300 km of tracks) are in the hands of SJ. Among other owners of these tracks are private companies and municipalities. These circumstances have recently become highlighted, as they seem to be an important obstacle for minor freight operators, eager to make use of the recently introduced right to open access for freight services.

Banverket is responsible for platforms, the larger marshalling yards and the signalling system, while SJ has kept the control of railway stations and minor marshalling yards. Until November 1996, SJ was, in practice, responsible for the allocation of tracks (timetable planning) and traffic control. A number of other "common facilities" are still controlled by SJ, but are to be available for other operators on non-discriminating, and competition neutral, terms.

Since July 1996, Banverket enjoys the extended status of being the principal authority responsible for all matters related to the railway sector. This is closely related to the transfer of the track allocation and train control functions from SJ to Banverket, and the incorporation of the unit responsible for procurement of non-commercial interregional services.

Legal form

In sharp contrast to SJ, Banverket is a state administration, depending on appropriations from the national budget. The track usage charges do not accrue to Banverket, but go directly to the state, and may therefore be seen as a form of taxation (Nordell, 1997). In 1996 they amounted to 846 million SEK. No institutionalised link exists between railway activity and the size of track expenditures. Since the fees are the same whether the traffic is run on county lines or main lines, they do not reflect the generally higher costs for maintenance and traffic control of the county lines.

Important to keep in mind is Banverket's close relation to the National Government. It implies for example a responsibility for the production of investment plans, supporting the Government with information and analyses used in the shaping of the future transport policy and other bills related to the railways.

Organisation

Due to the enlarged responsibility, Banverket has recently gone through a process of re-organisation, coming into effect as of January 1, 1998. The overall principle in the new organisation is to keep administrative functions related to the authority role separated from the parts of Banverket working as business units. The organigram for Banverket is useful as a reference to the further description and is given in Figure 3.1 (Banverket, 1998).

Banverket is organised as a central authority consisting of a head office managing an organisation consisting of one administrative branch and one business branch. The *administrative branch* consists of five regions, responsible for the shape, maintenance and renewal of the state's railways and adherent assets. They buy the work to be carried out from the five production units of Banverket's *operating branch* as well as from external contractors. These production units are managed like commercial profit centres. Making up an important part of the new railway sector responsibility of Banverket, there are four special administrative units linked to the authority, operating much like separate entities. They are Defence (responsible, jointly with SJ, for the functioning of railway transport during times of war), the Committee for the purchase of certain public transport services, the Rail Traffic Administration, and the Railway Inspectorate. The latter three are described separately below.

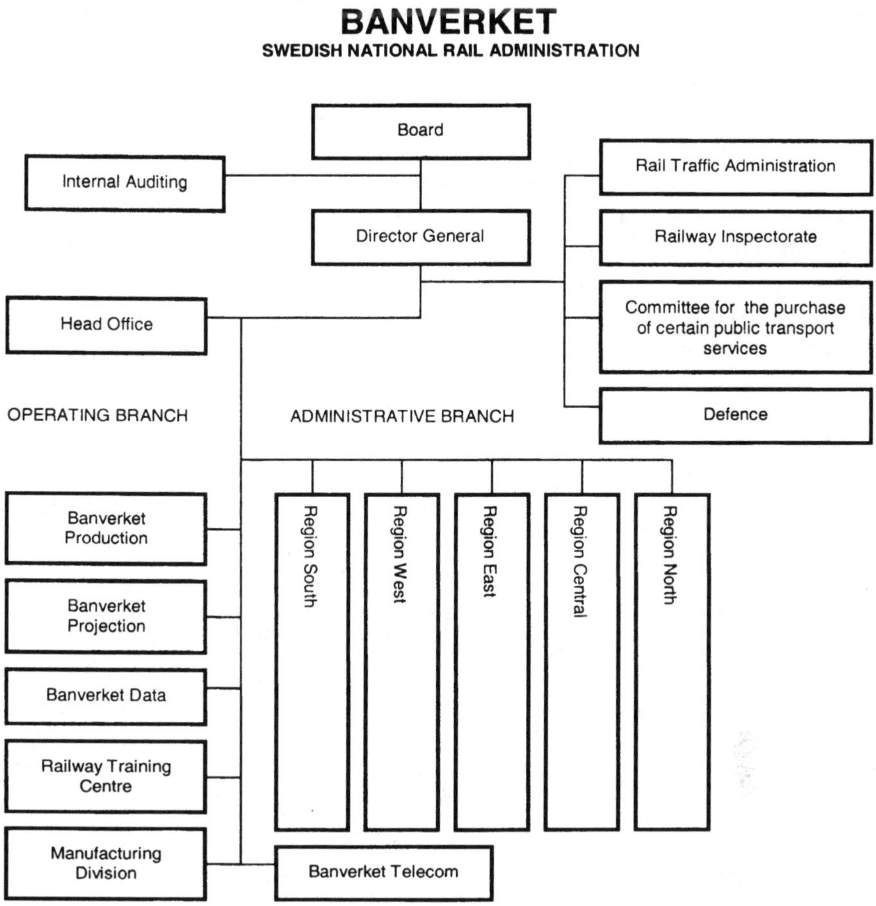

Figure 3.1 Organigram of Banverket

Source: Banverket (1994, 1998).

Railway Inspectorate

Companies wishing to apply for operating rights and permits to perform railway services are obliged to contact the Railway Inspectorate and the Rail Traffic Administration at Banverket. The Rail Traffic Administration will not grant operating rights (and is sometimes not even willing to consider it) unless the operator has first been approved by the Railway Inspectorate. Its role as an independent actor seems to have become increasingly strong in recent years.

The Inspectorate is responsible for the overall safety of the Swedish railway network, including all types of transportation on tracks. Its operations are based upon the law (1990:1157) and additional regulations issued by the Government and by the Inspectorate itself. In order to facilitate for the applicants to become familiar with the law and other regulations covering this area, the Inspectorate has issued a handbook and a paper of instructions along with the actual forms to be filled out by the applicant (Järnvägsinspektionen, 1997a and 1997b, respectively). This handbook is constantly revised and complemented with additional chapters, to keep pace with the new rules issued by the Inspectorate.

Rail Traffic Administration

The Rail Traffic Administration unit handles questions of capacity allocation for new operators, traffic control and traffic planning, as well as the granting of operating rights for train operators. The last function involves consideration of whether suggested passenger services oppose the current regulations governing the position of SJ and the CPTAs.

Committee for the purchase of certain public transport services - Competitive tendering of interregional services

Since January 1996, this unit has been responsible for the state's procurement of unprofitable interregional services, being upheld for social and political reasons. Although the organisation responsible for this purchasing function has changed over the years, the man in charge has been the same since 1992, when competitive tendering of these services became possible. Before that year, the state's negotiator could only negotiate with SJ on the amount of subsidy needed.

It should be noted that unless SJ provides the information that it considers a line to be unprofitable, no tender will take place. Only then will the Government have to decide whether the services are important enough to become subsidised (and thereby tendered) or not.[7] In the tenders, the overall principle for selecting the winning bid is to get the lowest price, as long as other conditions are fulfilled. The state's negotiator has some freedom to

[7] This makes it possible for SJ to keep an unprofitable line from being tendered, if it has reason to believe that the line will become profitable in the near future.

play the bidders off against each other. In contrast to the tenders for the regional services, ticket revenue accrue to the contractor and, most importantly, the state does not provide the contractor with the rolling stock. Therefore, in order to be able to present a complete bid, a bidder often has to close a deal with SJ on the price for renting vehicles. The same applies to other common functions held by SJ. Also, SJ provides the information on ticket revenues.

Since the competitive tendering of the unprofitable interregional services begun in 1992, several new train operators have tried to win such contracts, some of them coming very close. In the first round of tendering, SJ faced actual competition on all such lines, in the second on four out of 12 lines. But in the end SJ won all contracts and continued to do so until late 1998. That year, a special Government decision was taken, with the implication that the line between Göteborg and Malmö (Sweden's second and third largest cities) was to be tendered. Due to the bad shape of the tracks in the past, and heavy competition from cars, SJ had reported losses of 80 million SEK annually on this line, although rationalisations have taken that figure down to 30 million in recent years. Hoping to be able to make the line profitable in the near future, SJ has never asked for the line to be tendered. The Government's decision was caused by a wish to secure these railway services as new competition in the form of long-distance buses would emerge. In late December 1998, it was revealed that the surprising result of this tender is a preliminary deal, implying that BK Tåg, together with French VIA GTI and British Go Ahead Group will enter in January 2000, if only for a contract period of one year. Their winning bid demands no subsidies from the state whatsoever, i.e. revenues from ticket fares alone are expected to cover all costs, including the rent payed to SJ for the rolling stock. The Government has yet to acknowledge the committee's deal.

Despite the lack of new entrants until now[8], procurement of the unprofitable interregional services by competitive tendering has clearly forced SJ to accept lower subsidy levels. Costs have been reduced by 20-30% with roughly the same volumes of traffic (Hylén, 1997). Longer-terms contracts have also become more common. Initially, all contracts were let for only one year.

[8] The special case of the state's tender for the Arlanda Airport Link is presented in connection with the description of new operator A-Train.

Regional transport authorities (CPTAs)

Legal form, etc.

Since the late 1970s local and regional bus services in Sweden have been under the responsibility of the County Public Transport Authorities, contracting private and public bus operators for carrying out the services. The actual responsibility lies jointly at the county council and the municipalities in each county. However, apart from a few exceptions these have chosen to handle the responsibility by means of forming limited companies, the shares being owned by the county council and the municipalities. The boards of these companies are made up of local and regional politicians, representing the owners. Today, there are 25 such companies (or similar arrangements) spread over Sweden's 23 counties. Due to recent mergers of counties, some CPTAs are expected to merge as well in the near future.

The national legislation requires that the CPTA should provide good public transport services in the counties, but does not stipulate any minimum requirements or compulsory goals. The regional authorities may therefore define their own levels of ambition (which are often very high indeed) and pursue their own goals.[9] It is important to note that the services of the CPTAs are collectively running at a loss. This applies to bus services as well as train services. The deficits are covered by the shareholders of each CPTA using taxpayers' money (both the county council and the municipalities have taxation power) and subsidies from the state. For the bus services, the cost coverage amounts to 50-60 percent. Generally, the cost coverage for the regional train services is lower, about 30-40 percent.

The CPTAs are responsible for the planning of the traffic services. They decide upon ticket fees and collect all revenues from fares. Private and public companies under contract to the CPTAs carry out the actual transportation services. The situation for buses and trains differs in one important respect: the contractors normally own the buses used to perform the bus services, while they borrow the train vehicles from the CPTAs. There is generally little room for the operator to influence the passenger's perception of the services.

[9] An important overall feature of the municipalities in Sweden is that they have a very high degree of sovereignty when it comes to deciding on local goals and levels of ambition.

Enlarged responsibility

Having originally only held the responsibility for public transportation by bus, the CPTAs have gradually become involved also in other modes of transportation. A couple of CPTAs from the very start took over some responsibility for passenger services along local and regional railways threatened by termination. In the mid-1980s, the passenger services on about 15 regional railway lines were terminated, and transferred to bus services instead. In two counties, the CPTAs stepped in and overtook the full responsibility for the lines in question, in order to continue running the services by train. This was the case for two lines in the county of Jönköping and one line in the county of Kristianstad.

With the "creation" of the county lines, the responsibility of all CPTAs was extended to include the local and regional train services, and the services on the county lines in particular. 17 of the originally 23 county lines came to be included in a formal 10-year-agreement between the Government, the CPTAs and local municipalities, specifying the conditions for the transfer of responsibility and future subsidies to the CPTAs. Each CPTA is currently receiving an annual subsidy up to the year 2000, the size of which relates to SJ's operating deficit for the traffic in question at the time of the agreement. In total, these subsidies amount to 200 million SEK per annum. The money may be used either for the continuation of train services, or for replacing them with bus services. The CPTA that decided to continue operations by trains, however, gained control of the adequate rolling stock from the state for free. In all, these vehicles amounted to a total of 60 diesel-powered railcars and 16 electric train sets (Hylén, 1992). The CPTAs of Norrbotten, Västerbotten and Västernorrland counties (located in the northern part of Sweden) have replaced all or some of the county line passenger services by train with bus services, while all other CPTAs have chosen to continue to run the services by train.

In several counties, regional authorities have been very active to preserve and further develop and market the regional train services, once they got the responsibility for them. In some cases, the number of passengers have increased in remarkable ways, for instance on the Blekinge Coast Line and on the commuter line of Bergslagen (Hylén, 1995). Another example is the services of the commuter trains called *Pågatågen* in the county of Skåne. Since regional authorities decided to step in and develop these lines in 1983 (when SJ threatened to terminate them) they have experienced a remarkable growth in terms of passengers.

So far, there have been no obvious effects of the extended possibilities (as of July 1996) for the CPTAs to run passenger services on the main lines. A limited number of new connections have been opened. However, the services managed by CPTAs on the main lines have already for a long time been of a much greater magnitude than the services performed on the county lines. Partly, this is because the commuter lines near Stockholm, Göteborg and Malmö are of this type. Outside these metropolitan regions the CPTAs have also been busy trying to develop such services. Typically, two or more CPTAs have come to co-operate closely with SJ in order to develop already present or new connections and create more integrated regional networks of passenger services.

Co-ordination of services

Co-ordination of different types of public transport services has been an important feature of Swedish transport policy for a long time. This was an important factor behind the creation of the CPTAs in the late 1970s and their increased responsibility ever since. Closely related to this is the belief that tickets and fares should be co-ordinated (and subsidised) by the transport authorities in order to increase travelling. At the county level, integration between different types of public transportation tends to be complete. Since the CPTAs took over the responsibility for the county lines, they have generally strived to co-ordinate these services with their bus services, while the era of SJ's control was marked by a tradition of using these trains as feeders into the core network. In most counties, there are monthly travel cards for unlimited use on all of the CPTA-planned public transport modes.

Agreements across county borders have also become more common. Ten counties in the southern part of Sweden have agreed upon a common ticket system, taking the fare integration further. Since 1991, all the CPTAs and SJ co-operate at the national level within an organisation called *Samtrafiken*. Its aim is to co-ordinate the bus and train timetables, and make it possible for passengers to buy tickets valid for the whole journey from one locality to another, whether they go by bus or by train on separate parts of the trip.

Competitive tendering of CPTA-managed passenger train services

One important feature of the transfer of responsibility for the county lines to the CPTAs is the new relationship between SJ and the CPTAs, which has since become dominant for these services. Before the reform, SJ had run these services under its own flag, but has now become a contractor. Closely related to this is the fact that the CPTAs, by gaining the exclusive traffic licence for the traffic along these lines, became able to put these services out for tendering, thereby opening up this part of the railway market to competition from other operators. (Since July 1, 1989 this had been possible for the bus services under their responsibility.) The CPTAs have made use of this opportunity in different ways. No one has chosen to run the services under its own flag without the help of a contractor. In some cases, SJ has been entrusted (after renegotiations) with the task of running the services as a contractor without a prior tender. In other cases, the services were put out to tendering, with (typically) SJ, BK Tåg and Linjebuss bidding for the first contracts. In some counties these services have been put out to tendering several times since the CPTAs took over the responsibility. In contrast to the state's tenders, a couple of new train operators have entered the railway sector this way. They are presented in the next section. The price offered by the bidding train operators has become the single most important factor in the selection process, as long as conditions concerning quantity and quality characteristics of the services will be fulfilled. Detailed information on cost savings due to tenders for regional train services is somewhat scarce. Figures ranging between 20% and 30% have been reported.

In the next list, the train services for which the CPTAs currently bear a large part of the responsibility are presented. Included are also the services along county lines that have been replaced by other modes of transportation during the 1990s. The metro of Stockholm as well as some tram services have been excluded. For each connection, we indicate the type of service, in what way it has been procured by the CPTA since the transfer of responsibility, and the current train operator performing the services.

Table 3.2 CPTA-managed services: procurement procedures, etc.

County letter and CPTA	CPTA-managed passenger services[10] (partly or fully)	Type of service and line	Tenders or other events	Current operator
AB Storstockholms Lokaltrafik	Märsta-Stockholm-Södertälje(AB)-Gnesta(D)	Commuter on main lines	Tendered 1x	SJ[11]
	Kungsängen-Stockholm-Västerhaninge/Nynäshamn	Commuter on main/county lines	Tendered 1x	SJ
	Stockholm-Kårsta/Österskär/Näsbypark	Local on local line	Tendered 1x	Linjebuss
	Slussen-Saltsjöbaden/Solsidan	Local on local line	Tendered 1x	SL Tunnel-Banan[12]
	Ropsten-Gåshaga	Local on local line	Tendered 2x	SL Tunnel-banan
C Upplands Lokal-trafik	Uppsala-Tierp	Regional on main line	Negotiations	SJ
D Länstrafiken Sörmland	—			
E Östgötatrafiken	Norrköping(E)-Tranås(F)	Interregional on main line	Negotiations	SJ
	Linköping(E)-Västervik(H)	Interregional on county lines	Tendered 1x Negotiations	SJ
	Linköping(E)-Kalmar(H)	Interregional on county lines	Tendered 1x Negotiations	SJ

[10] For train services along lines crossing a county border, where the responsibility is shared between two CPTAs, the lines are only presented under one of the CPTAs. To indicate the shared responsibility, county letters are in these cases printed in brackets after each locality between which the services are running.

[11] A joint venture comprising of BK Tåg, VIA GTI and Go Ahead Group will take over all the commuter services in Stockholm in January 2000.

[12] SL Tunnelbanan is a subsidiary to the CPTA in Stockholm county. It also runs all the underground services in Stockholm.

Table 3.2 CPTA-managed services: procurement procedures, etc. (continued)

F	***Jönköpings Länstrafik***	Nässjö-Tranås	Regional on main line	Tendered 2x	BSM Järnväg
		Nässjö-Stockaryd	Regional on main line	Negotiations Tendered 1x	BSM Järnväg
		Jönköping-Värnamo	Regional on county line	Tendered 3x	BSM Järnväg
		Nässjö(F)-Hultsfred(H)-Oskarshamn(H)	Interregional on county lines	Tendered 3x	BSM/SJ[13]
		Nässjö(F)-Åseda(G)	Interregional on county line	Tendered 3x	BSM Järnväg
		Nässjö-Jönköping	Regional on main line	Tendered 3x	BSM Järnväg
G	***Länstrafiken Kronoberg***	see F above			
H	***Kalmar Läns Trafik***	see E & F above			
I	***Kollektivtrafiken Gotland***	—			
K	***Blekinge Länstrafik***	Karlskrona(K)-Kristianstad(L)	Interregional on county line	Tender / negotiations	SJ
LM (L)	***Länstrafiken Kristianstad***	Ystad(M)-Simrishamn(L)	(Inter)regional on county line	Tendered 2x	BK Tåg
LM (M)	***Länstrafiken Malmöhus***	Malmö-Ystad	Commuter on county line	Tender / negotiations	SJ
		Malmö-Höör	Commuter on main line	Negotiations	SJ
		Malmö-Helsingborg	Commuter on main line	Negotiations	SJ
		Helsingborg-Bjuv	Commuter on main line	Negotiations	SJ
		Malmö-Landskrona	Commuter on main/county lines	Negotiations	SJ
N	***Hallandstrafiken***	Halmstad(N)-Nässjö(F)	Interregional on county lines	Tendered 3x	BSM Järnväg
		Torup-Hyltebruk	Local on county line	Tendered 2x (bus since 96)	—

[13] BSM Järnväg works as a sub-contractor to SJ between Hultsfred and Oskarshamn.

Table 3.2 CPTA-managed services: procurement procedures, etc. (continued)

O	***Bohustrafiken***	Göteborg-Strömstad	Regional on county line	Tender / negotiations	SJ
N/O /P	***Göteborgs-regionens Lokal-trafik***	Göteborg-Alingsås	Commuter on main line	Negotiations	SJ
		Göteborg-Kungsbacka	Commuter on main line	Negotiations	SJ
P	***Älvsborgstrafiken***	Borås(P)-Varberg(N)	Interregional on county line	Tendered 1x Negotiations	SJ
R	***LänsTrafiken Skaraborg***	Hallsberg-Mariestad-Herrljunga	Interregional on county/main lines	Negotiations 1x Tendered 1x	SJ
S	***Värmlandstrafik***	Kil-Torsby	Regional on main/county lines	Tendered 2x New tender in progress	SJ
		Charlottenberg-Karlstad-Kristinehamn	Regional on main line	Tendered 2x New tender in progress	SJ
T	***Länstrafiken Örebro***	—			
U	***Västmanlands Lokaltrafik***	Västerås(U)-Ludvika(W)	Interregional on main/county lines	Negotiations	SJ
W	***Dalatrafik***	Borlänge-Malung	Regional on county line	Negotiations 1x Tendered 3x	BK Tåg
		Ludvika-Fagersta-Avesta	Regional on county/main lines	Tendered 1x	SJ
X	***X-Trafik***	Gävle-Ljusdal	Regional on main line	Negotiations Tendering due	SJ
Y	***Västernorrlands-läns Trafik***	(Sundsvall)-Härnösand-Långsele	Regional on county line	Negotiations	SJ
		Örnsköldsvik-Mellansel	Regional on county line	Replaced with taxi services 90	—
Z	***Länstrafiken i Jämtlands län***	—			

Table 3.2 CPTA-managed services: procurement procedures, etc. (continued)

AC Länstrafiken i Västerbotten	Bastuträsk-Skellefteå	Regional on county line	Replaced with bus services 90	—
	Storuman-Vännäs	Regional on county line	Negotiations (bus since 95)	—
	Jörn(AC)-Arvidsjaur(BD)	Interregional on county line	Replaced with bus services 90	—
BD Länstrafiken i Norrbotten	Boden-Haparanda	Regional on main line	Negotiations (bus since 92)	—

3.4.3 Train operators

SJ

Legal form, etc.

The "new" SJ that came out of the split of "old" SJ is referred to as being a state business administration. It differs from a state administration in the sense that it receives its resources in a different way. While a state administration is funded by appropriations, a state business administration is expected to generate its own revenues. SJ had been a state business administration even before the Act of 1988, but new in this respect was its instructions to operate as a *commercial firm,*[14] despite not being a state-owned limited liability corporation (Nilsson, 1995).

Organisation

The SJ Group is made up of the state business administration SJ and its subsidiaries (see the included organigram for details below). The Group's operations are divided into five business branches: passenger traffic, freight traffic, ferry traffic, maintenance of machines and vehicles and real estate administration, organised as separate divisions with control of different

[14] Although the restrictions had been loosened already in 1985, the Act of 1988 implied that the most important objective for SJ's management was to *improve profitability*. Thereby, it did not have to account for other things than just that, making it free to deny taking part in activities that could not be called profitable.

subsidiaries. Apart from the divisions, various staff functions and the service function SJ Cleaning are also incorporated within SJ. While the railway services are considered as the core business operations, the various subsidiaries dealing with other areas are supposed to support the core business.

The Act of 1988 instructed SJ to concentrate on its core business, the railway services, implying the divesting of subsidiaries not related to these services. In 1991 it was stipulated that SJ should instead follow a path of becoming something like a "department store of transport services". Later decisions pointed in the 1988 direction, and SJ has therefore sold several of its old subsidiaries. In 1995, ASG, one of Europe's leading truck transport forwarding agents was divested, and in 1996, Swebus, the largest bus operator in Sweden, was sold to Stagecoach. SJ is however still far from being solely a train operator, as is evident from the organigram (see Figure 3.2).

Through the subsidiary AB Swedecarrier, SJ also owns about 25% of Malmtrafik i Kiruna AB (MTAB), the company running ore freight services along the Iron Ore Line. Norway's NSB owns an equally large share, while the mining company LKAB is the majority stockholder.

Statistics

Table 3.3 presents some statistics on the Swedish railways between 1992 and 1997 for the parts involving SJ.

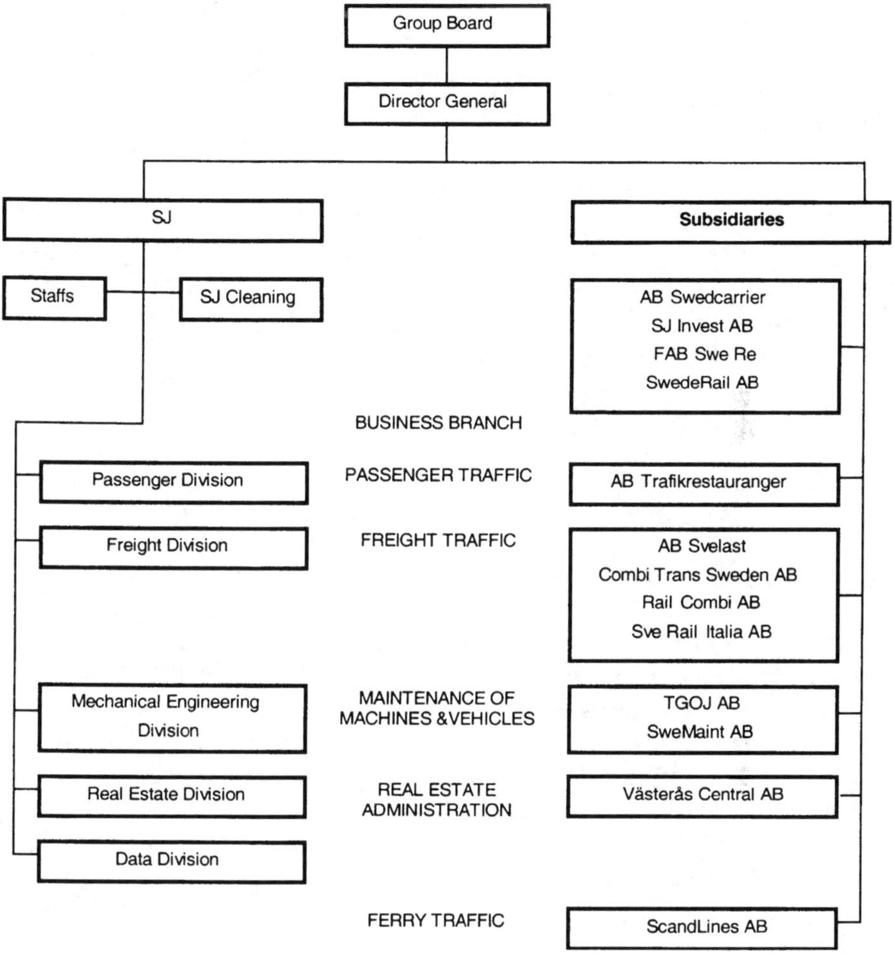

Figure 3.2 Organigram of SJ

Source: SJ (1998).

Table 3.3 Swedish railways statistics 1992-97 (SJ only)

	1992	1993	1994	1995	1996	1997[1]
Freight services (million)						
• Ton km	19 202	18 578	19 060	18 979	16 479	14 718
• Train km	34.0	34.1	37.3	39.1	35.2	32.2
Passenger services (million)						
• Trips, SJ own-flag	22.3	24.0	24.5	24.8	24.7	24.7
• Trips, SJ contractor	66.9	68.5	69.6	73.6	76.0	79.4
• Passenger km, SJ own-flag	4 114	4 410	4 482	4 674	4 611	4 592
• Passenger km, SJ contractor	1 330	1 420	1 424	1 545	1 607	1 694
• Train km	58.2	57.5	59.8	62.4	66.7	66.6

[1] Preliminary figures

Source: SJ (1997, 1998).

Other operators – the new entrants

Perhaps the most important effect of the Swedish railway reforms and the introduction of competitive tendering, are the increased possibilities for new entrants. Four companies have entered the passenger railway market in Sweden since it became possible by winning tenders in 1990: BK Tåg, Sydtåg, Linjebuss and BSM Järnväg. A fifth company, A-Train, will probably start running its services in 1999. In addition to the five operators described below, a handful of minor *freight* operators have also entered the market in recent years.

BK Tåg AB

BK Tåg, the sister company to a privately owned bus company called BK Buss, is the most well-known of the new train operators emerging in the wake of the introduction of competitive tendering for regional train services. The company was active as a bidder in most of the introductory round of tenders that took place in 1989-90, right after the reform. It resulted in four-year contracts with the CPTAs in the counties of Halland, Jönköping and Kalmar for a total of five routes, totalling about 450 km of tracks. These were, in fact, the only lines after the first round of tenders that were contracted to another operator than SJ. BK Tåg started to operate these lines in late May 1990. The second round of tendering for these lines resulted in a complete victory for SJ in 1993 and the further history of BK Tåg in this region will be presented in the case study later in the chapter.

In June 1992 BK Tåg started to run services on the county line between Borlänge and Malung in the county of Dalarna. SJ won the contract for these services after negotiations with the CPTA in 1989, but in the first real tender BK Tåg put in the best bid. In 1994 SJ won back the contract but again lost to BK Tåg three years later. This is the only case where BK Tåg and SJ have been taking turns in this way.

In spring 1997, another train operator, Sydtåg, went bankrupt (see below). In the auctioning of its assets, BK Tåg got hold of the contract for the passenger services between Ystad and Simrishamn. For the remaining two years of the contract-period, BK Tåg will run these services under contract to the CPTA of Kristianstad in Skåne county.

In the spring of 1998, BK Tåg closed a deal with French company VIA GTI and the British Go Ahead Group, in order to bid jointly in upcoming tenders for train services (Trafikforum, 1998). This marks a reawakening of the co-operation between BK Tåg and VIA GTI that resulted in a joint bid for one of the Stockholm metro lines in 1993. In mid December 1998, the result of the tender for the commuter services in Stockholm was made public. As of January 2000, BK Tåg together with its foreign partners will take over these services for a period of at least five years, implying the loss for SJ of its single most important contract. It is also possible that the same constellation of companies will be the first to enter the market for interregional passenger services, as a result of the state's tender for the line between Göteborg and Malmö. Apart from running passenger train services, BK Tåg is also very active in the rail freight sector.

Sydtåg AB

This private company experienced a brief period as an operator of passenger train services under contract to the CPTA of Kristianstad in Skåne county. In 1995 it won the tender for the traffic between Simrishamn and Ystad in the very south of Sweden. It was a four-year contract beginning in June 1995. Founded in 1991, Sydtåg had previously been busy in the railway sector as a freight operator, working as a sub-contractor to SJ. In early 1997, the company ran into financial difficulties. It seems as if its number of personnel had been growing too fast in response to expected future increases in freight volumes. When the freight volumes decreased instead, the company went bankrupt.

Linjebuss AB

This company is the second largest bus operator in Sweden, since January 1998 owned by the French transport conglomerate CGEA. Linjebuss has been taking part in several tenders for railway services since 1989 (some through a subsidiary called Linjetåg), including the tenders for the Stockholm metro lines. After eight years of placing bids in vain, Linjebuss finally won a contract, starting in January 1998 for five years onwards. The traffic in question is the services along Roslagsbanan, a network of three local lines in the Stockholm region under the responsibility of the CPTA of Stockholm county. Linjebuss won the tender in competition with the former operator SL Tåg (a subsidiary to the CPTA) and the British train operator Stagecoach Holdings among others.

BSM Järnväg AB

This company is the most recent new entrant on the passenger rail market in Sweden. In August 1998 it started running roughly the same services which BK Tåg once won in 1990, i.e. in the counties of Jönköping, Halland and Kalmar, after having won the third round of tendering for these services. BSM Järnväg is a subsidiary to the private company BSM, which started out as an engineering workshop near Borlänge (in Dalarna county) back in 1972. In 1993 BSM became involved in the renewing and building of railways, working as a contractor to Banverket, before turning mainly into a train freight operator in 1996. The BSM train division was transformed into the subsidiary BSM Järnväg on January 1, 1998.

A-Train

In 1993-94 the tender for the Arlanda Airport Link as a Build-Operate-Transfer project was carried out. In the final negotiations, two main competitors remained: Arlanda Link Consortium (ALC) including GEC Alsthom, Mowlem, NCC among others, and Arlanda Trafik AB (ATAB) where SJ, ABB, Skanska and Toumen were represented. In September 1994 ALC was chosen as the winning contractor. When the consortium has completed the building of the Arlanda Airport Link, it will transform into a train operating company, A-Train. A-Train is expected to start running these services in 1999. The company holds the licence to run the services and the control of ticket revenues until the year 2040. The Social Democrat Government, elected shortly after the completion of the tender, has worked to restrict the monopoly position of A-Train. Access for other train operators (paying fees to A-Train) will be easier, and a possibility to break the deal with A-Train in the year 2010 has been introduced (Alexandersson and Hultén, 1997).

More entrants to come?

Since the bus operator Swebus was sold to Stagecoach in late 1996, this company has evolved as a new and strong competitor in the tenders for passenger train services, primarily in the Stockholm region. Although it has yet to win a tender, it must be considered as a possible new entrant in the future.

A private company called Swedetrain Storuman AB has asked for a permit to run services between Göteborg and Mora, a connection not run by SJ today. The request was denied, partly on the grounds that SJ runs trains on parts of the line. However, in terms of regulations, it is unclear whether SJ automatically holds a total monopoly along a proposed connection only by having trains running on parts of the tracks. A similar question will arise if a new entrant would like to run night-trains (or day-time trains) between connections where SJ has stopped doing so. It is possible, although not likely, that this could be a new way of entry to the state's railways.

3.5 Case study: The county of Jönköping

The main focus in this section is on presenting the findings concerning the effects of the transfer of responsibility to regional authorities and the introduction of competitive tendering for regional railway services in the county of Jönköping and its surroundings. Hence, the practice of interest is the way in which regional railway services have been organised, with different forms of contractual arrangements, as opposed to the services run by SJ on its own merits. Special attention will be made to the contracts that are the results of some form of competitive tendering process. It should be noted that the form of competition used is best described as for the track. Some characteristics of on-the-track competition may sometimes become apparent, since different companies or authorities are responsible for different types of passenger services on the very same tracks.

3.5.1 Background and overview

Characteristics of the area

The county of Jönköping is located in the mid-south of Sweden, with its northern border along Sweden's second largest lake: Vättern. Some basic statistics of December 1995 are presented in Table 3.4. The national figures are also presented as reference. Roughly 80% of the county's population live in urban areas, but the only city of some scale is Jönköping, with about 80 000 inhabitants.

Table 3.4 Sweden and Jönköping county - some statistics

	Sweden	Jönköping	
		County	Urban core
Population	8 837 496	312 686	79 914
Area, km^2	410 934	9 944	44
Density, inh/km^2	22	31	1 810
Cars	3 630 760	133 147	
Cars, per 1000 inhabitants	411	426	

Road congestion problems are hardly severe in the county of Jönköping, at least not when compared to the situation in Stockholm or Göteborg. Some roads have been in bad shape in the past, but nowadays the important routes are modern highways. This makes it difficult for the railway services to compete with the car, especially since the highways follow the same routes as the railways. The presence of capacity problems on several railway lines is another obstacle.

Actors

The County Public Transport Authority (CPTA) of the county is formed as a limited company called Jönköpings Läns Trafik AB (JLT). The County Council owns 50% of the company's shares, while the county's municipalities own the rest in proportion to their population at the time when JLT was formed in 1980. JLT holds the responsibility for all scheduled local and regional bus services in the county as well as the regional train services. The bus services involved about 280 buses, producing a total of 13.5 million bus km in 1995/96, while the railway services needed 22 railcars to produce a total of 1.6 million train km in 1995/96. JLT's board of seven people is made up of local politicians. The company has a staff of about 15 people, including the C.E.O., working at the office in central Jönköping. One of them has the regional train services as his main responsibility.

An important regional goal is to keep the inhabitants interested in using the regional passenger train services. This stems to some extent from a proud tradition of train services in the region, but also from the belief that the railway services are important if the current structure of society is to survive.

Two passenger train operators are present in the county: the state-owned SJ and the privately owned BSM Järnväg. Both companies work as contractors to JLT. BK Tåg has its head office in the county but currently has no contract for passenger services in the region. Among the other relevant actors at the regional level one should mention the state's rail infrastructure owner Banverket, although its regional office is situated in Malmö (being responsible also for the counties of Skåne, Blekinge and Kalmar).

Brief description of the passenger train services in the county

About 512 km of railway tracks are currently used for passenger train services in the county, with Nässjö being the foremost hub of the network, despite the fact that the city itself has less than 17 000 inhabitants. A large part of the network consists of county lines, connecting not only the localities within the county with each other, but also the ones of the surrounding counties to the west, east and south of Jönköping county. The services on the county lines are divided into four separate connections (localities within brackets are located outside Jönköping county): 1) Nässjö-Vaggeryd-Värnamo-(Halmstad), 2) Jönköping-Vaggeryd-Värnamo, 3) Nässjö-Eksjö-(Hultsfred)-(Oskarshamn), and 4) Nässjö-Vetlanda-(Åseda).

The services on these lines are under the responsibility of the CPTA in the county (to some extent jointly with the CPTAs of the surrounding counties) and are marketed as *Länstågen* (the County Trains). In addition to this, the CPTA is responsible for some departures between Nässjö and Jönköping, Nässjö-Sävsjö-Stockaryd and Nässjö-Tranås on the main lines. All these additional services are included in the Länstågen-concept.

Running through from north to south and vice versa, are the SJ trains of the interregional services connecting Stockholm with Malmö (on the

Southern Main Line), with some trains stopping in Tranås, Nässjö and Sävsjö within the county. SJ has the full responsibility for these services.

The services of the Coast-to-Coast Line (Göteborg-Borås-Alvesta-Kalmar/Karlskrona) pass through the county's southern part, with trains stopping in Hestra, Gnosjö, Värnamo and Rydaholm within the county. These services are the result of an agreement between the CPTAs of the affected counties, SJ and the state. Finally, another main line, the Jönköping Line, runs from east to west (Nässjö-Jönköping-Falköping), with trains stopping mainly in Nässjö and Jönköping within the county. A similar agreement as the one for the Coast-to-Coast Line is in place here, with the services being marketed under the name *Vättertåg*.

Genesis/history

Krösatågen and Länstågen

In 1984, the passenger services along four lines in the county were facing the threat of closure from July 1, 1985. This was due to a parliamentary decision that determined that from that date these lines were no longer to be considered as being part of the national railway network. While the local and regional authorities considered two of them to be less important, they were determined to keep the services running on the two lines between Jönköping-Vaggeryd and Nässjö-Åseda, respectively. In October 1984 the board of JLT therefore decided to take the responsibility for the passenger services on these lines from July 1 1985. After negotiations, a 10-year contract with SJ as the operator was signed, including an agreement implying that SJ would invest 53 million SEK in restoration of the tracks. The passenger trains on these lines then came to be known as *Krösatågen* (JLT, 1986).

For Jönköping county, the county line reform following the Transport Policy Act of 1988, implied that four of the county's railways were defined as being county lines (see above), including the parts of the tracks for which JLT had already saved the services. Jointly with the other affected CPTAs it was decided that the train services on all these lines were to be continued at least for the next four years. The state was ready to hand over SJ's railcars, and to subsidise the passenger services with an amount equal to SJ's operating deficits for the services. However, due to the fact that JLT had already in 1985 taken over the responsibility for Jönköping-Vaggeryd and Nässjö-Åseda, the Government decided that no subsidies were to be paid for those parts of the lines. Moreover, SJ only had to give away 15 (of

20) railcars for free. JLT therefore had to reach a special agreement with SJ for the use of the remaining five railcars. In order to decide on a train operator for the services, JLT and the other affected CPTAs arranged a joint tender in 1989, in which BK Tåg came out as the winner (this and subsequent tenders will be described in more detail in a separate section). On the 27th of May 1990 the "new" services were launched.

In 1992 the CPTAs' passenger services on the county lines were evaluated in order to reach a decision on their future. It was decided that the passenger train services of the lines Jönköping-Vaggeryd-Värnamo and Nässjö-Hultsfred-Oskarshamn were to be further developed. A study of the Halmstad-Nässjö line lead to a similar decision in June 1995. For the line Nässjö-Vetlanda-Åseda, however, the train services were to be replaced with bus services, unless the affected municipalities decided to compensate JLT for the additional costs of keeping the train services. Since the municipalities were willing to do that, the services have continued.

On two occasions (1991 and 1995) SJ has reduced the number of departures on some of the main lines passing through the county. This has forced JLT to extend its involvement in regional services in order to maintain sufficient traffic volumes between certain localities.

Coast-to-coast and Vättertåg

The services between Göteborg-Borås-Värnamo-Kalmar/Karlskrona and Nässjö-Jönköping-Falköping-Skövde had been unprofitable for several years before a step to secure their future was taken, by means of a long-term agreement. In 1992-93, the state's tender for the unprofitable interregional services affected these lines and resulted in new agreements from June 1994, with the CPTAs along the lines co-operating with SJ and the state in renewal projects, the services now being marketed as Coast-to-Coast and Vättertåg, respectively.

3.5.2 Description and organisation of the contracting and tendering

Contracts and agreements for different services

Länstågen

The contracted train operator is paid a specified sum for every vehicle km produced, the production levels being decided upon by JLT. The sum is linked to the development of the Net Price Index, calculated by National Statistics Sweden. It is not sector-specific. The train operator bears the operation costs for running the services, including the costs for insurance, spare parts, minor repairs and regular maintenance. The operator pays the track usage fees but JLT compensates it with an equal amount of money after having received an invoice. For the parts of traffic performed on the main lines JLT pays an additional fee for traffic control. The vehicles needed for performing the services are provided by JLT and the costs for the renewal or rebuilding of vehicles are covered by JLT. No revenue risk is assigned to the contractor, and all the revenues from ticket sales are transferred to JLT (they are to some extent collected by the operator). The operator is responsible for having enough personnel to be able to operate the services and that these have the appropriate know-how. It is demanded by JLT that the trains run exactly on time (this is the only specified demand on quality) but so far, fines for late trains only have to be paid for trains being more than 30 minutes late.

The current contract with BSM Järnväg came into effect in August 1998, after the third round of tendering for Länstågen. The contract runs for 2 years, with an option for JLT to extend it with 1-2 years.

Vätterståg

SJ runs the Vätterståg trains Nässjö-Jönköping-Falköping-Skövde as part of an agreement with JLT and the CPTA of Skaraborg county. Roughly, each of the parties bears one third of the costs. SJ is responsible for providing the vehicles needed for the services (the state paid for the initial investment in new vehicles) and other operational costs, while the CPTAs guarantee a minimum amount of passengers. For example, JLT pays SJ a fixed sum as long as the number of passengers does not exceed 325 000. For each additional passenger, JLT pays some extra money (but less than the corresponding revenue). Both SJ's own tickets and JLT tickets are valid, JLT receiving the revenues from its own ticket sales. The contract period is for five years (1994-99).

Coast-to-coast

This agreement, concerning the services with X2-2-trains from Göteborg-Borås-Värnamo-Alvesta-Kalmar/Karlskrona is similar to the one for the Vätterståg trains, although involving more CPTAs: the CPTAs of Älvsborg, Jönköping, Kronoberg and Kalmar counties.

Tenders, entries and exits

Tender 1: BK Tåg enters (with some difficulties)

The first round of tendering in Jönköping county took place in 1989, preceding the transfer of responsibility for the county lines in May 1990. This tender was arranged jointly by the CPTAs of Jönköping, Halland and Kalmar counties, since the lines in question run through all these counties. Three train operators placed bids for all traffic (it was not possible to bid for minor parts only): SJ, Linjetåg and BK Tåg. After negotiations, it was decided that BK Tåg had won the 4-year contract, thereby breaking SJ's monopoly as a train operator.

BK Tåg had been created only months before. The private owner, KarlssonGruppen AB, had however been involved in the transport sector for a long time through the company BK Buss AB (founded in 1926). BK Buss had been operating bus services under contract to JLT since the early 80s. At the time of winning this contract, BK Tåg did not have the necessary knowledge to run the services and was not an approved train operator in the eyes of the Railway Inspectorate (it had not applied for such an approval yet). It was stipulated in the contract with JLT that this had to be taken care of before the services were to start.

Some people working as SJ-personnel had been in contact with BK Tåg at an early stage, showing interest in becoming employees. After having won the contract, some 135 people from all over Sweden expressed their willingness to work for BK Tåg. 35 were selected as drivers. Most of these were employed by SJ at the time or had previously worked for SJ. To qualify as an applicant for employment, BK Tåg demanded a willingness to accept changes in working conditions.

A building for maintenance and repair of vehicles had to be built in Vetlanda from scratch. This was because SJ initially had declared that BK Tåg could not count on having their trains maintained at the SJ repair shop in Nässjö. (SJ later changed its mind, but at that time BK Tåg had decided to complete its own building). In early May 1990, BK Tåg got the approval from the Railway Inspectorate and during the weeks preceding the transfer of the services on May 27, the new employees took part in an intensive educational programme.

The actual shift of the services did not take place without problems. Partly, these were caused by the great media interest and an introductory campaign from JLT to mark the occasion by inviting people to go by train for almost nothing. Of a more serious character were the problems caused on some stations by SJ personnel working at the traffic control and information functions. In Nässjö, the platforms for different departures had been changed without notice and the passengers were given no information from the loudspeakers, leading people to enter the wrong trains. Moreover, the local trains were sometimes given very low priority when approaching stations at the same time as SJ trains. This malpractice ended after BK Tåg as well as JLT had complained to SJ's central management.

Another issue was the transfer of vehicles. SJ was not willing to hand over the five railcars being used in the former Krösatåg-traffic. SJ demanded additional compensation since SJ had been running these vehicles under a 10-year contract that had been interrupted five years too early when the county line reform came about. For this reason, these railcars had been hidden at various places around the country, but BK Tåg somehow managed to get hold of them in time anyway. The conflict reached a climax in September 1990, when SJ stepped in and simply took the railcars away, making it impossible for BK Tåg to perform the services. For two weeks no trains were running between Jönköping and Värnamo. Then JLT and SJ closed a deal with the implication that JLT would lease the trains from SJ with an option to buy them after four years.

Tender 2: BK Tåg expands

In 1991 SJ announced its intention to reduce the number of departures on the main line between Nässjö and Jönköping. The CPTA of Jönköping then filed a request for a one-year-licence of its own to run those very departures that SJ would abort. It got the licence and could choose another operator - BK Tåg. In August 1991 BK Tåg thereby became the first private operator to run passenger services parallel to SJ's on a main line.

Tender 3: Exit BK Tåg, re-enter SJ

The second round of tendering for the county lines in Jönköping and bordering counties (now with only BK Tåg and SJ competing for the contract), took place in the autumn of 1993 and resulted in a complete victory for SJ. BK Tåg also lost the additional departures between Nässjö and Jönköping, since these were included in the tender. However, BK Tåg claimed that SJ's bid was way too low, suggesting that SJ placed a bid lower than its actual costs in order to win back the services from BK Tåg. In December 1993 BK Tåg filed an official request to *Konkurrensverket*, the Swedish Competition Authority, to investigate the matter, claiming that SJ had violated against §19 of the Competition Act of 1993 (abuse of dominant position).

The Swedish Competition Authority spent two years investigating the case before it came to the same conclusion as BK Tåg: Not all of SJ's costs had been accounted for in SJ's bid. The matter then became a legal issue when the authority sued SJ in early 1996 for this malpractice. SJ responded by claiming that a state-owned authority like the Swedish Competition Authority could not sue a state-owned company like SJ. That particular dispute was settled in December 1997, when a special court reached the conclusion that there are no legal obstacles for the Competition Authority to sue SJ. The actual trial finally begun in autumn 1998. In December, the court found SJ proven guilty and sentenced SJ to a 8 million SEK fine. This enables BK Tåg to sue SJ for damages, but SJ has appealed against the decision.

Of some importance in this case is the fact that SJ in late 1997 declared that it was not willing to continue running these train services for the additional optional year, claiming that it was not making any profits under the agreement. According to SJ this was due to a higher increase of costs in the railway sector in recent years that has not been compensated for under the terms of the contract (being linked to the NPI).

When SJ took over the services from BK Tåg in 1994, it initially had some difficulties to fulfil its obligations, with trains running late etc. This was probably caused by SJ having shrunk its local organisation too much during the intermediary years. Losing the services in 1994 (together with another contract in Dalarna) BK Tåg had to concentrate on other projects to survive. Due to its maintenance building in Vetlanda and its experiences as a train operator, it got plenty of contracts for rebuilding vehicles for JLT.

Tender 4: The state's tender

In 1993, when the state put out the so-called non-commercial services to tendering for the second time, they included the services of the Jönköping Main Line (Nässjö-Jönköping-Falköping-Skövde). Although SJ placed the lowest bid, the Minister of Transport expressed the view that it could be worth some extra taxpayers' money to get BK Tåg running on a main line and thereby introduce some real competition for SJ. He argued that it was too difficult for a competing operator to step in because of the high start-up costs. The politicians in power of the municipalities along the line were not happy with this suggestion, however. Apart from objections arguing that such an enforced entry was principally wrong, another reason for the criticism was apparently the fact that SJ threatened to lay off its personnel in Nässjö and would not let its X2000 trains stop there. After some weeks of lobbying, SJ came out as the winning contractor for what later came to be known as Vättertåg.

Tender 5: BK Tåg re-enters

In 1995 a minor tender took place for railcar services between Nässjö and Tranås on the Southern Main Line. JLT had got the traffic license for these departures since SJ had reduced its number of trains stopping at these localities. Competing only with SJ for these services, BK Tåg won the contract, resulting in it re-entering as a train operator under contract to JLT from January 1996.

Since SJ's comeback through tender 3, the relationship between SJ and BK Tåg has became friendlier. For the services run by BK Tåg, two railcars were in use. BK Tåg had no spare vehicle, but was now able to borrow one from SJ occasionally - something that would have been almost impossible a few years ago.

Tender 6: BSM Järnväg enters

In spring 1998 the third round of tendering for the county lines was completed, also including the Nässjö-Tranås and Nässjö-Stockaryd connections. In this tender three companies competed for the contract: SJ, BK Tåg and newcomer BSM Järnväg. The result was a victory for BSM Järnväg, which meant that this company started running these services in August 1998. Interestingly, BSM's bid was initially not the best one. The company had planned to set up its own maintenance and repair facilities if it won the tender, but during the process of tendering JLT declared that no additional maintenance buildings were needed in the county. BSM then had to negotiate with SJ and BK Tåg for the use of their facilities. This turned out to be crucial for winning the tender. After having closed an advantageous deal with SJ for the use of their maintenance and repair building, BSM Järnväg came out as the winner. Otherwise, BK Tåg would have won the contract.

For some connections between Hultsfred and Oskarshamn SJ still remained as the operator, under contract to the CPTA of Kalmar county. However, when it became clear that all its adjacent services had been lost to BSM Järnväg, SJ decided to let BSM run these services as well, working as a subcontractor to SJ. Once again, SJ thereby showed a friendly attitude towards a competitor, a far cry from its behaviour in the past.

Passenger interests

The most important ticket price reductions have emerged in connection with the shift of the services to the Länstågen-concept. Other important customer related issues have been slow to develop. A page of every timetable for JLT's train services may be used for comments and suggestions from passengers, to be sent to JLT for free. Passengers are also requested to call JLT if they have questions or suggestions concerning the traffic. Due to lack of time and personnel, JLT has not been able to perform market research as much or as regularly as it has wanted. In recent years, though, the passengers' feelings and attitudes towards the bus services as well as the train services are monitored by means of annual surveys called *Kundbarometern*.

3.5.3 Performance 'before' and 'after'

For Jönköping county, there are several different 'before' and 'after' years to be considered, depending on which services and what events that are to be considered. The autumn of 1982 has been chosen as suitable for looking at the status of the county's railway services at the time when SJ performed all services under its own flag. Autumn 1985 marks the first period of the CPTA's Krösatåg-services. Autumn 1989 and spring 1990 were the final timetable periods before JLT took over the responsibility for the services on all county lines. When describing the development in various aspects, it has not always been possible to obtain comparable data sets from every year.

Developments in production

Train km, departures, etc.

The development in production has been studied in several ways. Figure 3.3 shows the development in the total supply of train km per week (according to autumn timetables) in the county, distributed among different actors being responsible for the services, and (when relevant) the contracted operators. The recent entry of BSM Järnväg is not included.

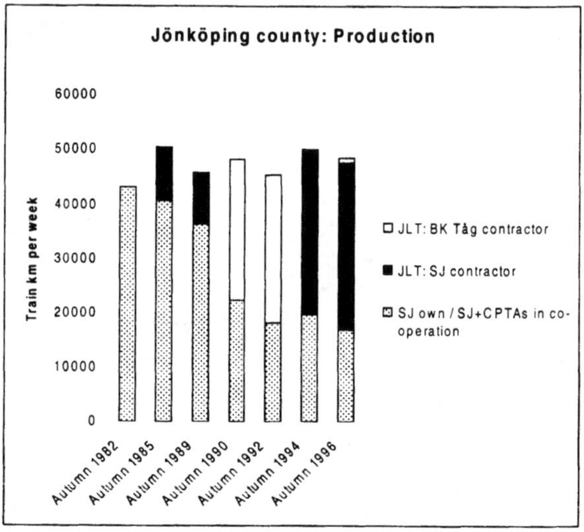

Figure 3.3 Jönköping county: production
Source: JLT (1992).

The most obvious observation to be made is the diminishing activity of SJ as a provider of its own traffic, even when the traffic supplied in co-operation with the CPTAs (Vättertåg and Coast-to-Coast) is added. This corresponds to an increasing supply of services provided by JLT. Put together, total supply has increased at both occasions when JLT was given substantially enhanced responsibility (1985 and 1990) but has tended to vary in the intermediate years. It should be noted that the unit train km underestimates the traffic volumes performed by SJ's own trains, since they consist of more units than the Länstågen trains.

Another aspect of production development is the increased number of stations served by Länstågen trains. In 1985 the railcars stopped at 46 stations within or close to the county border – in late 1997 the figure was 51. The explanation is twofold: the expansion of the network and the opening of new stations within the network.

Co-ordination within networks

JLT plans the connections within the regional railway network as well as the connections between regional train services and local bus services. Buses are not obliged to wait for late trains to arrive, however. The fares of buses and regional trains have been co-ordinated ever since the Krösatåg-years. This implies that the same fare applies to a journey between two localities, whether it is carried out by bus or by train.

Reliability

According to JLT, the capacity problems on some lines are behind most problems with late trains. This was not the case when SJ came back after the second tender in 1994. A period followed with severe problems of reliability. JLT then ordered SJ to provide a plausible explanation for every late train and to suggest ways to prevent such problems. After a while, reliability improved. Probably, the problems were to some extent caused by SJ having reduced its staff too much.

The rolling stock

Initially, JLT took over 15 Y1 railcars from the state when the county reform was implemented. Some railcars used in the previous Krösatåg-traffic were subsequently bought from SJ. Since then, a couple of railcars have also been bought from the northern counties of Västernorrland and Norrbotten, when they replaced their regional train services with bus services. In all, JLT controls 22 railcars, that have been re-built, modernised and painted with the JLT colours. Since 1995 JLT has been evaluating new vehicles, but the uncertainty concerning the county line subsidies expiring in 2000 makes it risky to make any investment decisions.

For the Vättertåg services, new X14-trains are in use since 1994. Similarly, the shorter model (X2-2) of SJ's X2000-train has been introduced for the Coast-to-Coast services.

Innovations

It is clear that the entry of BK Tåg meant a lot in terms of change and innovative practices for the railway services in Jönköping county. One important aspect was the reformation of the working conditions for train drivers, making them do more (fuel refilling, cleaning the railcars etc) than just driving trains. This had been impossible to implement before. The change did not only make it cheaper to run the services, but also made the drivers feel more important for the success of each trip.

Perhaps the most striking examples of innovative practices concern the vehicles. BK Tåg made use of its experience as a bus company, replacing many former train-specific (and expensive) parts with cheaper bus parts. The old Fiat engines, suffering from several problems in the Swedish climate and being expensive to maintain, were replaced with Volvo bus engines. The CPTA had suggested this to SJ earlier, but only received the answer that it was "impossible to do". The Volvo engines are more environmental friendly, need 10-15% less fuel and are cheaper to maintain.

The positive effects have not just stayed at BK Tåg or in Jönköping county. SJ has copied many of BK Tåg's practices, sometimes using "the threat of BK Tåg" to persuade people unwilling to change. Although the involvement of the driver continued to be strong with SJ as the contractor, SJ has not been able to keep the innovative spirit in recent years, according to JLT. The small scale of BK Tåg's operations meant that it no longer had the capacity to remain as involved as before.

Developments in demand

Länstågen

The available figures of demand refer in general to patronage measurements performed in October each year for a period of one week. These figures are presented by means of a diagram (see Figure 3.4).

The demand seems to have increased both when JLT created the Krösatåg services in the mid-80s and when Länstågen were created in 1990 (March 1990 marks the final period under SJ's regime). With the addition of new connections, total demand has continued to rise. The reduced fares on several connections when the traffic was incorporated with JLT's services, together with a modal shift - passengers streaming from bus to train services - explains a substantial part of the increasing number of passengers.

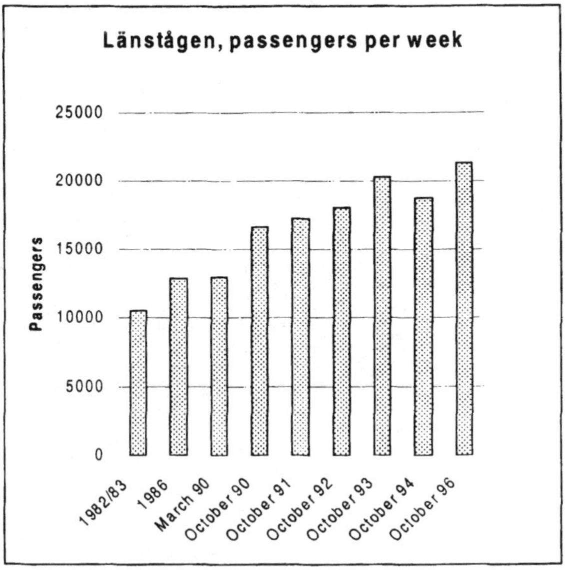

Figure 3.4 Länstågen, passenger per week
Source: JLT (1992).

In order to check whether patronage has increased more or less than supply, indices showing the development of patronage and supply have been put together in the same diagram (see Figure 3.5). From this, it is clear that demand has increased more than supply since JLT got the full responsibility for the services on the county lines in May 1990, implying reduced costs per train passenger.

Vätterståg

The only available figure for these services states that the demand (measured in passenger km) in 1995 had increased by almost 50% compared to the corresponding value of 1993 (one year before the new X-14 trains were introduced). According to JLT, the number of passengers is well above the "guaranteed level" by JLT in the agreement with SJ.

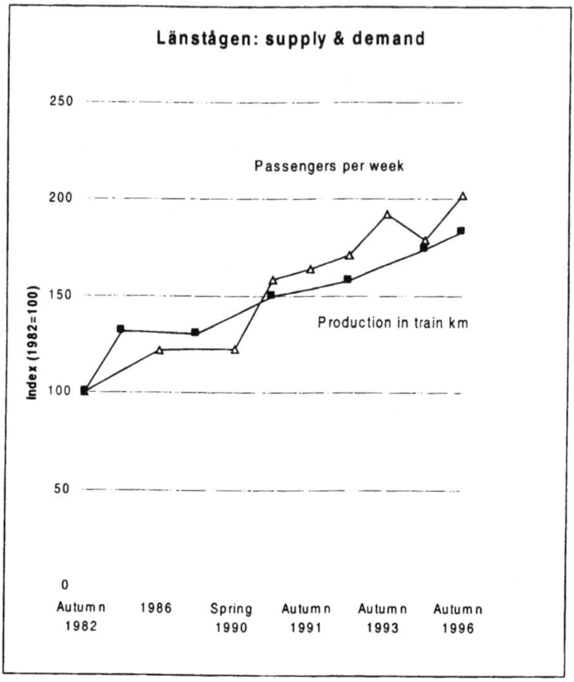

Figure 3.5 Länstågen, supply and demand

Developments in finance

JLT's finances

Unfortunately, JLT does not regularly produce official figures for its costs and revenues related to the Länstågen railway services. Most of the time, costs and revenues are presented collectively, thereby including the bus services and other cost- and revenue-sources. However, detailed figures from one year, 1991 (see Table 3.5), are available, and these may form a reference point when discussing earlier and later developments (JLT, 1992).

The corresponding figures may also be presented for the individual lines in a somewhat more condensed form, with or without state subsidies included (Table 3.6). This table shows that the state subsidy was very important in 1991 for JLT's ability to keep the train services.

Table 3.5 Länstågen in Jönköping county 1991

Costs (thousand SEK)	Traffic costs, BK Tåg AB	21 141
	Replacing traffic (taxi)	111
	Other CPTAs	210
	Track usage charges*	2 619
	5 railcars rented from SJ	3 250
	Maintenance	1 441
	Re-building of railcar (1)	439
	Train planner etc	240
	Part of JLT administration	300
	Total	**29 751**
Revenues (thousand SEK)	JLT travel cards etc	7 435
	Single tickets, drivers	1 561
	Samtrafiken-tickets	2 490
	Military tickets	210
	Other CPTA	520
	Total	**12 216**
Results (excl. state subsidies)		**- 17 535**
Cost Coverage		41%
State Subsidies		**9 154**
Results (incl. state subsidies)		**- 8 381**
Cost Coverage		72%

* JLT pays the track charges in 1991. Under the current contract, these are paid by the operator and ultimately paid by JLT.

What do we know about the cost effects from tenders in the county of Jönköping? According to JLT, the first tender for the Länstågen services corresponded to a reduction in JLT's total costs per train km with 21%, compared to the cost level for the Krösatåg-services. The second tender then resulted in a further 25% reduction. These comparisons are based upon the following included cost items (SOU 1994:109): traffic costs (contractor), track usage charges, maintenance and repairs, insurance and part of JLT's administration and marketing budget.

Table 3.6 Länstågen: Result per line 1991

Excluding state subsidies

Line	Costs	Revenues	Deficit	Cost coverage
• Jönköping-Värnamo	6 076	3 167	2 909	52.1%
• Nässjö-Åseda	5 002	1 931	3 071	38.6%
• Nässjö-Halmstad	11 891	3 853	8 038	32.4%
• Nässjö-Oskarshamn	5 747	2 394	3 353	41.7%
• Nässjö-Jönköping	1 035	871	164	84.2%
Total	**29 751**	**12 216**	**17 535**	**41.1%**

Including state subsidies

Line	Costs	Revenues	Deficit	Cost coverage
• Jönköping-Värnamo	6 076	5 104	972	84.0%
• Nässjö-Åseda	5 002	3 526	1 476	70.5%
• Nässjö-Halmstad	11 891	7 643	4 248	64.3%
• Nässjö-Oskarshamn	5 747	4 226	1 521	73.5%
• Nässjö-Jönköping	1 035	871	164	84.2%
Total	**29 751**	**21 370**	**8 381**	**71.8%**

When comparing the costs of 1990-93 and 1994-97 with those for Krösatågen (1985-89), it is important to note that the payments to SJ for the Krösatåg services included costs for vehicles and maintenance of the tracks. Likewise, the costs for upgrading the railcars have been excluded from the two later periods. Nevertheless, these tenders' impact on cost levels is evident. If BK Tåg's bid had won the second tender, that too had implied a reduction in JLT's costs, although a more moderate one. In contrast to the first two, the third tender for the Länstågen-services resulted in a slight increase of the costs for the CPTAs, indicating that the bottom level had been reached by means of the first two tenders.

Infrastructure investments

During the Krösatåg years, investments in the tracks were made in accordance with the agreement with SJ. About 53 million SEK were used, mainly for replacement of old parts of the tracks. From 1991 and onwards, about 22 million SEK per annum has been spent on infrastructure investments in the county, in accordance with the 10-year LTA-plan. Not much of this concerns the county lines however, since their future seemed uncertain at the time when the plan was developed.

3.6 General evaluation and conclusions

The county line reform of 1988, implying the transfer of the responsibility for the county lines to regional authorities from mid 1990, may be seen as an attempt by the state to once and for all bail out from the politically sensitive matter of the unprofitable regional passenger train services. The principal goal was to achieve decentralisation through a shift of responsibility and decision making to the regional level - the level where the arguments in favour of these lines had been so strong.

Our case study has shown some lines that were affected by this reform, as well as lines where local and regional authorities already in the early or mid 1980s had taken over the responsibility for providing local and regional train services. At these early occasions, the local authorities were forced to take this step without any support from state subsidies, if they wanted to keep the lines from being closed. In contrast to this, the later reform provided the CPTAs with the means (subsidies and vehicles) to manage the services.

Before the reform, once a regional line had become unprofitable to SJ, SJ had no real incentive to renew and develop the services, often leading to reinvestments in the tracks being neglected. Several county lines still suffer from this, resulting in the reinvestments of today becoming more similar to new investments.

It is clear that the change of responsibility for both the services and for the track infrastructure (Banverket) has resulted in local involvement and commitment to the services. The CPTAs have increased the number of departures, opening old and new stations, rebuilding the trains and integrating the services with the local and regional bus services. Taken together, this has had positive effects upon the image of the services and the number of passengers going by train. In several cases, the increase in the number of passengers has been higher than the increase in supply and costs, implying reduced costs per passenger. Although some passengers may have shifted from car to train, the shift from bus to train is more evident. The commitment to railway services has in some cases been so strong that even highly unprofitable services are being upheld by means of municipalities paying the extra amounts needed.

Most of the effects described above can be referred to the shift in responsibility and a higher propensity at the local level to develop the services. At the same time, the possibility of competition for the track has also been introduced, sometimes making it difficult to reach an agreement on the cause-and-effect relationships. Despite this, even the limited number of cases where SJ had come to face competition, in tenders being arranged by the transport authorities, provides evidence that cost reductions of about 20% have been possible to achieve with the help of this practice. The threat of competition also seem to have made SJ more willing to make far-reaching long-term agreements with the CPTAs on developing new train concepts like Kustpilen. The actual entry of BK Tåg clearly also introduced some innovative thinking into the sector (see below).

Since some of the very big contracts for regional train services (Pågatågen and the commuter lines in Göteborg) have yet to be tendered, the potential for cost savings should still be large in Sweden.

The innovative force of new entrants

Since only a few new train operators have entered the Swedish passenger services so far, almost all the gathered experience on this matter boils down to the experiences of one company: BK Tåg. It is clear however, that this company has meant a lot in terms of change and innovative practices. These have primarily concerned the maintenance of vehicles and the working conditions for train drivers, resulting in significant cost reductions.

The positive effects have not just stayed at BK Tåg or the CPTAs for which the company have been performing services. SJ has copied many of BK Tåg's practices, sometimes making use of "the threat of BK Tåg" to persuade people unwilling to change.

Entry and exit barriers

The scarcity of tendering

Since entry is currently only possible at occasions of tendering, some long-term agreements make up an important barrier to entry. However, several of the contracts for the regional services are due for tendering in the near future, some of them for the first time.

The common functions

Drawing from national experience, other important entry barriers are the common functions, most of them still in the hands of SJ. Since the transfer of the train traffic control function from SJ to the Rail Traffic Administration entity of Banverket, the railway stations, side-tracks and the facilities for repairs and maintenance of the rolling stock are among the most important of the common functions. Access to them is necessary for all railway operators. The politicians have stated that all of the common functions should be made available on equal terms for all railway operators, but they are currently not possible to buy on a normal market.

In a recent report from SIKA, looking into the effects of SJ's dominant position, it appears to be evident that the CPTAs and the new entrants on the one hand and SJ on the other hand have contradictory views on SJ's control of the common functions (SIKA, 1997). The CPTAs point out that they have to pay substantially more when they purchase railway services from other operators than SJ, due to the lack of a market for these functions. SJ claims that the common functions, and the railway stations in particular, are strategic assets for SJ's operations. It states that it aims to have a uniform price level for external and internal customers.

A recent report, commissioned by the Ministry of Transport, came to the conclusion that some of the common functions from an efficiency point of view are best provided by a single organisation (Nordell, 1997). The current policy seem to be that it may be an advantage to let SJ keep at least some of these functions, but to make the legal system intervene when needed.

The rolling stock

In the state's tenders, the demands upon a new entrant either to use vehicles of its own or rent them from SJ, functioned as an important entry barrier for several years. However, the recent outcome of the tender for the line Göteborg-Malmö shows that it is possible to overcome such obstacles.

The rolling stock is not an entry barrier for the regional services, since they are in the hands of the CPTAs and are provided for the contracted train operators. In some cases though, the scarcity of spare vehicles for other operators than SJ have caused some problems for new entrants. Overall, the lack of a well-functioning second-hand market for trains is a problem for CPTAs willing to increase their services. Buying new vehicles has in most cases not been a realistic option.

Know-how

The scarcity of railway know-how is considered to be a barrier to entry, but the BK Tåg case shows that it is possible to obtain the right personnel even within tight time limits. BK Tåg even had the advantage of being able to pick (from SJ) the people being most willing to change and to challenge "old SJ truths". It is doubtful whether future tenders will offer the same freedom when it comes to choosing employees.

The Railway Inspectorate

The Railway Inspectorate may be considered as an important barrier to entry, since its rules for granting a company the permission to perform train services are difficult to fulfil. Since these rules are based upon the goal to secure the safety on the railways, they are however believed to be appropriate by most actors. Perhaps more important is the fact that these rules may impede the propensity to innovate in the sector.

SJ's monopolistic behaviour

There are a couple of indications, most of them from the early days of BK Tåg's first entry, of SJ practising predatory monopolistic behaviour when facing competition. In most cases, these problems have been caused by a limited number of SJ employees at the local level. In these cases the malpractice has stopped after complaints from the CPTA. A more serious matter is the accusations that SJ has been placing bids lower than its actual costs. One such case is on its way to the court. In recent years, SJ has shown a more friendly attitude towards its competitors, trying to avoid conflicts.

The complicated matter of subsidies

The total amounts of state subsidies to the county lines have been kept stable at 200 million SEK in real value. Therefore it seems as if an important effect of the county line reform is that society gets more trains and more passengers travelling by train for the same amount of money. However, this is not telling the whole story, since most regional authorities have decided to spend more money of their own.

Generally, it has become increasingly difficult to get a clear picture of all the subsidies flowing to the railway sector, not only because of the county line reform, but also because of the creation of Banverket and the overall increase in the investments in railway infrastructure through several channels. The state controls Banverket's financial flows. The track charges go directly to the national budget and the capital to invest or reinvest in railway lines comes directly from the Ministry of Transport. The track charges amount to about 800 million SEK, while maintenance and investments amount to 8-10 billion SEK annually.

Other important issues

At present, many CPTAs are discussing the possibilities to buy new rolling stock in order to replace the Italian Y1's they got in 1990 and/or to make it possible to improve and develop old and new services. The problem of getting affordable rolling stock is widely known, but for the CPTAs there is an additional problem. If they openly show that they are committed to buy new rolling stock by themselves and are willing to continue to run trains on the county lines, the state may be less willing to direct new state subsidies for these operations in the future. The 10-year agreement of state subsidies is coming to an end in mid 2000. Several CPTAs are anxious to see what the future state policy towards these lines will look like.

Another issue is the need for automatic control of the traffic flows on the county lines. This would increase the capacity of the lines. Banverket is the relevant actor to pay for such projects, but has yet to recognise that this would reduce its costs for having personnel along the lines.

Some concluding lessons

Provision of shared functions on equal market negotiated terms are complicated because many of these functions are strategic assets for SJ and may also show strong economies of scale.

When the unified subsidy to the national railway operator is divided into a set of different subsidies – track maintenance, track construction, local and regional public transport subsidies, subsidies to loss making national lines etc – two problems appear: it becomes more difficult to monitor the total flow of subsidies to the railway sector, it gives the incumbent, former monopolist, an information advantage over the entrants.

The decentralisation of the railway organisation facilitates the co-ordination of railway services with other public transport systems, creating a more attractive regional public transport system.

By putting the control and the responsibility of the regional railways at the same geographical level as the railway services, the commitment of the regional transport authorities increases.

Competitive tendering decreases the total costs for the provision of regional railway operations.

The BK Tåg case shows that a new entrant may help to vitalise the regional railway system (and the former monopolist) through a willingness to try new ways of managing the train operations.

Our final observation concerns the path-dependent character of the deregulation process. Once the route of step-wise regulatory changes had been chosen, a change aiming at reaching a stable situation always lead to another change. The regulatory changes, despite resulting in positive effects, did not necessarily solve the envisaged problems – the unfulfilled promises of the railway sector and SJ's lack of profitability.

Acknowledgements

The authors are grateful to Henrik Schütz for his help with the research, and to KFB (The Swedish Transport & Communications Research Board) and Banverket for additional financial support.

References

Alexandersson, G. & Hultén, S. (1997), *Arlandabanan - järnvägsbygge med privata intressenter*, paper presented at the conference "Järnvägens organisation och finansiering i en avreglerad transportsektor", Borlänge, 25-26 November 1997.

Banverket (1994), *Investment plan 1994-2003 for Swedish Trunk Railways*, BV/P 1994:7, Borlänge.

Banverket (1997), Årsredovisning 1996.

Banverket (1998), Årsredovisning 1997.

Dagens Industri (1998-02-28).

Ds 1993:63: *En öppen järnvägsmarknad i Sverige*, Fritzes, Stockholm.

Ds 1995:33: *Nya möjligheter för järnvägstrafiken*, Fritzes, Stockholm.

Hylén, Bertil (1992), *Utvecklingen av persontrafiken på länsjärnvägarna*, VTI-meddelande 679, 1992.

Hylén, Bertil (1995), *Länsjärnvägarna och järnvägens avreglering - effekter på trafiken mm*, VTI 462/95-43.

Hylén, B. (1997), Sweden, in ECMT (1997), *The Separation of Operations from Infrastructure in the Provision of Railway Services*, Report of the 103rd Round Table on Transport Economics, Paris, 13-14 June 1996.

JLT (1986), *KrösaTåget - Utvärdering av Krösatågens inledande verksamhetsår*

JLT (1992), *Utvärdering av länsjärnvägar*, Rapport 1992-10-10.

Järnvägsinspektionen (1997a), *Handbok med regler för järnväg, tunnelbana och spårväg.*

Järnvägsinspektionen (1997b), *Vägledning för ansökan om tillstånd att driva spårtrafik, spåranläggning eller särskild trafikledningsverksamhet.*

Nilsson, J-E. (1995), Swedish Railways Case Study, CTS Working Paper 1995:2 (reprint of chapter 8 in Kopicki, R. & Thompson, L. S. (ed.) (1995), *Best Methods of Railway Reconstructuring*, CFS Discussion Paper Series, No. 111, The World Bank).

Nordell, O. (1997), *Organisation av myndighets- och sektorsuppgifter samt gemensamma funktioner inom järnvägssektorn*, Kommunikationsdepartementet K97/3944/2, 1997-10-07.
Proposition 1987/88:50: *Trafikpolitiken inför 90-talet*, Stockholm.
Proposition 1993/94:166: *Avreglering av järnvägstrafiken och riktlinjer m.m. för SJ:s verksamhet under åren 1994-1996*, Stockholm.
Proposition 1994/95:72: *Omprövning av beslutet om avreglering av järnvägstrafiken*, Stockholm.
Proposition 1995/96:92: *Nya förutsättningar för järnvägstrafiken*, Stockholm.
Proposition 1997/98:56: *Transportpolitik för en hållbar utveckling*, Stockholm.
SFS (1978:438).
SFS (1985:449).
SFS (1988:263).
SFS (1988:626).
SFS (1988:1378).
SFS (1989:67).
SFS (1990:1157).
SFS (1990:1165).
SFS (1996:286).
SFS (1996:734).
SIKA (1996), *Järnvägar 1993.*
SIKA (1997), *Järnvägens nya förutsättningar 1 juli 1996*, mimeo, 1997-08-15.
SJ (1997), *Annual report 1996.*
SJ (1998), *Årsredovisning 1997.*
SOU 1993:13: *Ökad konkurrens på järnvägen*, Fritzes, Stockholm.
SOU 1994:109: *Tåget kommer - Slutbetänkande av Tågutredningen*, Fritzes, Stockholm.
SOU 1997:35: *Ny kurs i trafikpolitiken - Slutbetänkande av Kommunikationskommittén*, chapter 6 (Järnvägstrafiken), Fritzes, Stockholm.
SOU 1997:129: *Kollektivtrafik i tid*, Fritzes, Stockholm.
Trafikforum (1998), no 6.
TT-meddelande (1992-01-01), *Ny olönsam järnvägslinje får statligt stöd.*

Interviews

- Adelöf, Thomas, Jönköpings Länstrafik.
- Danielsson, Lennart, SJ (Head Office), & Andersson, Magnus, SJ (Länstågen, Jönköpings län).
- Floresjö, Björn & Wärnfeldt, Sven, Dalatrafik.
- Hansson, Lars Göran & Carlsson, Kenny, Konkurrensverket.
- Hult, Tord, BK Tåg (Head Office).
- Johannesson, Eva, Banverket (Region South).
- Masgård, Johan, BSM Järnväg.
- Nordell, Olof, Vianord.
- Nordström, Ragnar & Åbrink, Kjell, Linjebuss.
- Prenler, Mikael, Delegationen för köp av viss kollektivtrafik, Banverket.
- Sundberg, Helena, Svenska Lokaltrafikföreningen.
- Wallenkurtz, Jan, Sydtåg.

4 Germany

CARSTEN LEHMANN
University of Münster

4.1 Introduction

In 1994 a new order for the railway system in Germany came into effect. The National German Railway company (*Deutsche Bundesbahn,* now called *Deutsche Bahn AG,* hereafter referred to as *old* and *new DB*) was restructured as a joint-stock company. Even though all shares will be owned by the state for the time being, this step was a symbol for the new belief that DB should operate profitably instead of having to follow diverse and conflicting public goals. In addition, open access to the track was introduced.

Aside from the developments on the European level, the main driving force behind railway reform was the dramatic financial situation of the old DB, which had become an unbearable financial burden for the state. In addition to annual support payments by the state in the order of DM 13 bln (constant level since 1978) DB's deficits had risen from DM 7.9 bln in 1963 to DM 63.2 bln in 1993. Further DM 15 bln of debt had to be taken over from former *Deutsche Reichsbahn* (DR) of East Germany after German reunification. Without change, forecasts had seen the deficit rising further, amounting to cumulated federal state payments for the period 1994-2000 of DM 329 bln. With reform, savings of DM 160 bln between 1991 and 2000 were estimated (see Regierungskommission Bundesbahn, 1991, p. 59).

In 1991, after 16 initiatives between 1949 until 1990 had failed, the reform finally came under way and was put into practice in 1993. The main elements of railway reform will be presented below along with the aims and considerations that shaped the new rules.

Since intramodal competition in railways until today is restricted to regional services, two case studies will be elaborated on in section 4.3 which are characterised by the introduction of tendering. Finally, an evaluation of the problems and chances of tendering as a form of competition within the current organisation of rail transport will follow in section 4.4.

4.2 Legal, regulatory and organisational framework

Passenger rail transport had been tightly regulated in Germany for a long time. The old DB was a state owned monopoly and subject to public service obligations. It had been structured like an administrative body unable to act as commercial entity. The rules for and organisation of rail transport in Germany changed with rail reform in 1994. The following topics will be covered below:

- the Structural Reform of DB,
- the new rules for operating the infrastructure and open access (including the current track pricing system)
- general principles for competition for transport operators,
- the special treatment of short-distance passenger rail transport (**S**chienen**p**ersonen**n**ah**v**erkehr, hereafter referred to as SPNV). This part of the reform is called Regionalisation.

4.2.1 Structural Reform of DB

In 1989, the Minister of Transport convened a governmental railway commission in order to evaluate reform options. The commission was staffed with representatives of transport science (2), business (3), politics (4) and of the employees (3) (see Deutsche Bahn, 1994, p. 11-14). The staffing reflected the political interests involved, as it had to be approved by the government (see Ewers, 1994, p. 205). In December of 1991, the governmental commission presented its report which in 64 pages lays out the basic structure of the current framework for railway operations (see Regierungskommission Bahn, 1991).

In the same year, the "deregulation commission", which was unanimously staffed with scientists, had produced more liberal suggestions to deregulate the railways in stressing how important it was for DB to be completely independent from political influence (see Deregulierungskommission, 1991, p. 42-46). This line of thinking did not prevail which may exemplify how the particular staffing of the governmental commission affected the outcome.

Both chambers of parliament passed the new laws in December 1993 almost unanimously. A widely accepted agreement had been necessary since the German constitution needed to be changed with a 2/3-majority in order to remove the states' organisational responsibility for its railways which had prohibited DB from being formally organised as a private company. The main aspects of structural reform can be divided into *organisational separation* and *transfer of financial obligations*.

Organisational separation

Legal Framework

In a first step, commercial and sovereign activities that had been combined under the roof of the old DB were separated. The "Law to found Deutsche Bahn AG" (*DBGrG*) established the new DB which is now responsible for all commercial activities. It received all properties adjacent to the railway business. Sovereign activities were transferred to the Federal Railway Agency (*Eisenbahnbundesamt*, referred to hereafter as *EBA*). It is supposed to act as a mediator between operators in cases of dispute over track access and it renders public services needed for the construction of new track. Residual properties not immediately needed for railway operations were transferred to the National Railway Fund (*Bundeseisenbahnvermögen*, hereafter referred to as *BEV*).

With the new law, DB is a joint-stock company (*Aktiengesellschaft*, in short: AG) owned by the government. DB is obliged to separate organisation and accounting of at least four business units: "track" (infrastructure), "freight", "passenger long distance" and "passenger short distance (SPNV)". Internal subsidisation is prohibited. Until January 1999, DB must establish a holding structure with these business units as independent companies. This holding may be dissolved later, requiring a separate law to be ratified by both chambers of government (The original intention to arrange for an automatic break up of the holding after 8 years was not adopted). The shares of the operating units *may* then be sold on the stock market (privatisation), except for the "track", which has to remain government-owned with at least 50.1% of equity (§2 DBGrG). Thus for the time being (until a new law has been passed) DB will remain a vertically integrated company.

Aims and considerations

DB has been given the formal structure of a private company. The advantages of turning an administrative body into a commercially operating entity - even if there is no change of ownership at first - are common knowledge in economics, and the commission adopted the reasoning: full responsibility for costs and revenues induces more entrepreneurship, the management is now free to make decisions without having to consult at length with politicians, and the flexibility of transferring staff to where it is most needed is improved.

The accounting separation between track, freight, passenger long-distance and passenger short-distance was regarded as a means to bring more transparency into the system and to enable the single units to operate as profit-centres close to the market. One special aim was to initiate a competitive process between passenger and freight transport for track capacity (See Albach, Schmitz and Pfannschmidt, 1991, p. 19).

The reason for separating long- and short-distance passenger transport stems from the logic of regionalisation which will be described in more detail below. In short it means the transfer of 'public service obligations' from DB to the federal states. Such public railway services are in fact those summarised as *SPNV*. The states are going to 'order' theses services in the future by chosing an efficient operator.

While discussing the reform in parliament the federal states realised that in practice they would mainly depend on DB for SPNV-services (until enough competitors have entered the market). The states were naturally interested in preventing DB from cross subsidising the long-distance traffic at the expense of the regional services. Consequently, the short-distance traffic was separated from the rest of passenger transport. The same logic applies to obliging DB to establish a holding structure until 1999. Legal accounting rules may make it harder for separate companies to hide undue cost-transfers, even though they will not remove completely the freedom to set internal prices.

The vertical separation of track and operating transport units is only an option, DB's transport units were not immediately privatised (not even partially) and, in the same context, the track shall always remain majority-owned by the state. The decision about true vertical separation of ownership between track and transport units was put off. Economic theory suggests that vertical integration of upstream and downstream activities in an industry can present an obstacle for effective competition. The German solution could imply then that intramodal competition in railway transport was not recognised as an important goal in itself and as a means to improve the efficiency of railway operations. Instead it was regarded more important to strengthen the railway business in *inter*modal competition and to make the monopolist DB more efficient. Also, as railway reform is considered a major public event and as long as federal government remains the single owner of DB, it was desirable politically to make the reform appear as a success. This success would have been in danger if DB's operating units had proved to be too inefficient when confronted with immediate competition, so some time was given to DB to adapt to the new situation instead.

It fits into this line of reasoning to assume that without the relevant EU-directives and with a more efficient DB in the past, probably nothing would have changed. The projected *Transrapid* between Hamburg and Berlin may serve as an example of how DB is still subject to political influence. DB is supposed to carry most of the operating risk in spite of the profitability of the Transrapid remaining quite uncertain, which is indicated by the fact that several large private companies involved in the technical development of the Transrapid were reluctant to take on this risk.

In addition, many left-wing politicians and interest groups in Germany are still pessimistic about the effects of free competition and privatisation. Providing infrastructure services in particular is still widely regarded as a natural duty of the state. The social democrats dominating the chamber of the federal states at first objected to give all responsibility for the track to DB, fearing that federal government might completely pull out of its obligations for the railway infrastructure some day, thereby unduly promoting road transport. The compromise found was that a formal task was laid down in the constitution for federal government to support railway infrastructure (financially) even though DB assumed ownership of the track in order to let track investments be guided by real management decisions.

However, it should also be mentioned that it is still a controversial debate among transport economists if considerable cost advantages exist due to economies of scope between track and transport operations. In this light, the German reform path can be interpreted as a careful approach towards privatisation and deregulation, as further steps should be guided by experience collected in the years following the reform.

Transfer of financial obligations

Legal framework

DB was alleviated from substantial financial obligations. These include the financial debt as shown in the balance sheet, payment duties linked to ecological pollution in the former GDR and investments deemed necessary to renew fixed assets of the former DR and to enhance its service and productivity level so that it could match the western standard (the federal government pays DM 33 bln. between 1994 and 2002, 30% of which has to go into SPNV). On the opposite side, the opening balance sheet of DB in 1994 showed a reduction of DM 73 bln. in capital assets (track capital and rolling stock).

Also, the burden of having been drastically "overstaffed" - especially due to the employment situation of the former DR - was lifted from DB. In particular the employment rules for the "public servants" (*Beamte*) could not be applied anymore to a privately organised company. The arrangement was that all *Beamte* were formally transferred to the BEV (which pays their salaries) and DB reimburses the BEV only for as much as this staff can be productively employed.

Aims and considerations

Since DB was to operate as a profitable commercial entity, especially in competition to other transport modes, it only seemed logical to relieve it from burdens of the past which it had been forced to take on for other than commercial reasons. This is true both for the immense financial obligations as well as the employment load, which had gained enormous weight due to the unification with DR. The "sell-and-lease-back" solution found for the former *Beamte* was probably the only possible solution in this respect, because this group could not have been laid off anyway due to its special public employment status.

It certainly was not necessary to relieve DB of *all* of its financial debt, especially since this might collide with the aim to guarantee fair conditions for intermodal competition (see Aberle and Brenner, 1996, p. 16). But it is naturally difficult to come up with just criteria to decide which part of the financial debt had originated from public service obligations and which part had to be attributed to DB's inefficiency of the past. The argument that instant success of railway reform was politically mandatory also applies here: with the debt taken away and depreciation cost for capital assets drastically reduced, DB was able to celebrate black numbers within the first year after restructuring.

4.2.2 Infrastructure and open access

Dividing line between infrastructure and operations

Legal framework

The organisational division of track and other operating units demanded a clear definition of the parts belonging to the infrastructure. The law defines "operation of infrastructure" to consist of the "construction and maintenance of railway track as well as the operation of guidance- and security systems." By enumerating the single parts of the infrastructure, the German law goes beyond the EC-directive 2598/70, as it also includes the "buildings for the administration of infrastructure and buildings that facilitate ticket-sales and the dispatching of passengers and goods" (§2 AEG).

Aims and considerations

The dividing line between operations and track was defined after having evaluated experiences with such divisions elsewhere in Europe. The German solution that has the track unit assume all responsibility for track investments, cost coverage and operation of the track (with the exception of expropriation powers and the coverage of interest duties by federal government) was regarded superior because:

- a responsibility for track investments by transport operating units (as e.g. in Italy, Switzerland and Austria) was thought to enable cross subsidising and technical foreclosure of competitors and
- if the track unit did not collect user charges itself (as in Sweden), it would be difficult to arrive at market prices for the track which is considered an efficient steering mechanism for allocating track capacity.

Open access and structure of charges

Legal framework

DB has to guarantee "non-discriminatory access to the railway infrastructure" to railway companies in Germany and to foreign railway companies that have opened access to their track as well. Open access also includes the right to construct a connection to the track of the infrastructure operator, if needed (§13 AEG).

The German law in general leaves it to the negotiating parties (track operator and transport operator) to agree on the level of the access charge, on the duration of the contract and on other operating conditions (safety requirements, punctuality rules, fines etc.). If no agreement can be reached, the EBA can be called upon to act as an intermediary. Apart from that, the general powers of the Federal Trade Commission ("Bundeskartellamt") remain untouched.

When deciding about the allocation of track-capacity, the operator of the infrastructure (division of DB) must "reasonably take into account" traffic that is part of a network or that is operated with a special frequency (*Taktverkehr*) (§14 AEG).

Beyond these general rules contained in the law, the following specific regulations apply: operators wishing to run a specific railway service (meaning a specific route and a specific time slot) have to register this service at least 8 months before a new timetable period starts. The infrastructure operator has to make an offer for reserving the slot for this service no later than 6 months before the start of the new period. If registered services collide, the infrastructure operator must act as an intermediary to come to a solution acceptable to the registrants. If that fails, the registrants are asked to bid for the service in a specific period of time, the right to operate the service will then be rendered to the highest bidder. Only frequent headway services in SPNV are exempted from this procedure. Services may not be resold to other service operators. Also, if a service is not being run within a month after it was supposed to be started the infrastructure operator may cancel the agreement instantly (§4 EIBV-E).

In general, the infrastructure operator is free to create a pricing system for the infrastructure (see chapter 2.2.3 for the solution found by DB track), but has to treat each registrant equally. Prices may vary with type of route, timing, duration and punctuality of the service, number of stops and overtaking, wear and tear of the track, working to capacity, and with the emissions of the traction engines used. The prices need to differentiate between the plain service carried out on the track and other inputs used such as stations and shunting facilities (§6). Special Rebates can be given on the basis of train-kilometres *on a specific route* within a year or a timetable period and on the basis of the duration of the contract. Train-km rebates are only allowed if the infrastructure operator can show that cost savings result from contracting with only one service operator or a group of operators (§7).

Since the track operator can act as a natural monopolist it is worth noting that principles on access charges only refer to the *structure* of charges. No regulation of price *levels* has been reserved for. This implies that a *rule of reason* was adopted for non-competitive behaviour in the track market, which would have to be tackled with general competition rules.

Aims and considerations

Open access had to be introduced to comply with EU-directive 440/91. The rules go beyond the scope of that directive as more than just "groups of international railway companies" are being guaranteed open access. This makes sense in Germany since many small railway companies already exist, mostly in freight transport.

The catalogue of criteria allowed for price-reductions and the duty for the operator of the infrastructure to publish price lists correspond to EU-directive 19/95 which obliged the member states to pass "rules for fixing track prices".

With a preference for network- and frequent headway-services, German law recognises that economic research has not come up yet with a theoretically sound allocation mechanism for track slots appropriately accounting for network effects.

The most effective obstacle for on-the-track-competition has already been mentioned: as long as DB is vertically integrated, DB still has the incentive, as well as some degree of discretion, for discriminatory actions. So it is not surprising that so far, no *on the track*-competition can be observed in Germany. Only in SPNV some degree of competition *for the market*, e.g. for specific routes or regional networks, is taking place (see *regionalisation* and *case studies*).

Cost coverage and infrastructure investments

Legal framework

In principle, DB shall independently decide which tracks to build and shall finance the track cost itself, but in fact, the planning procedure for track investments is more complicated (see §§8-10 BSchwAG). According to a specific "Law for the construction of federal railway track" track investments "for railway companies of the federal government" have to be included into a special "plan of demand" which has legal status and which is drawn up by the Ministry of Transport every five years. New construction is financed by federal government (20% of the funds have to be used for the SPNV). DB's track unit is responsible for the construction on the basis of special contracts with the EBA. These contracts regulate the cost contributions demanded of DB for the use of the track. DB has to recover full cost only for those investments that were included in the plan of demand on its own initiative. If DB can show for all other investment projects that operating the track is not or only partly in its own interest, DB only has to repay the corresponding part of the cost. A peculiarity exists in the fact that federal loans for these investments are free of interest duties, so that payments by DB will never surpass depreciation cost. (Note that these rules only apply to state-owned railway companies, an independent infrastructure operator - if he existed - would not profit from this public funding.)

If DB wants to shut down certain parts of its track because they can't be operated profitably, it has to *apply* for the closure to the EBA (§11 AEG). DB has to show that it would not be reasonable to demand of her to maintain the operation and that negotiations with third parties to take over the track were not successful. The authority can then take three months to decide. If it wishes for the operations to be continued it has to pay corresponding subsidies.

Cost coverage and infrastructure investments

Apart from politicians not willing to give up competencies it is difficult to find good reasons for the ministry of transport still drafting the "plan of demand" for rail infrastructure. The adopted planning procedure can have two negative effects: Either routes of commercial interest for DB are included in the plan of demand anyway, then the incentive for DB to reveal its true preference for certain routes or track qualities is diminished (see Schneider, 1996, p. 51-52). Or DB does not succeed in having its most favoured investments adopted by the plan, which would delay profitable investments.

The fact that no interest has to be paid for track investments and that certain track is paid for by the state is justified with concerns for intergenerational equity, with the intention to create fair conditions for intermodal competition and with the general duty of the state to provide public services (see Regierungskommission Bundesbahn, 1991, p. 17 and 25). The intermodal competition argument can easily be used in favour of rail, since equivalent pay back of rail and road construction cost is difficult to put into practice. Also, since no standard procedure for quantifying external effects exists and since road use is not equivalently financed by user charges, the degree to which both modes cover their social cost cannot be determined yet. Finally, cost coverage is affected by the large devaluation of capital assets. Since the current basis for calculating access charges is undervalued,[1] current global coverage of "true" track cost is estimated to be less than 57% (see DIW, 1997). If this figure is correct, the Federal government will probably have to pay for the rest when reinvestments become necessary.

The Track Pricing System

As a reaction of DB to the new legal and regulatory framework, DB is pricing its track by a special system, which was first introduced in 1994 and fundamentally revised in 1998. The main elements of both systems are presented below.

The first system was an attempt to find market prices for the usage of DB's track (see DB, 1995, p. 37). The system worked on the basis of three components:

- route categories,
- train categories,
- rebates on the prices derived by the first two criteria.

The *route category* depended on *traffic volume* and *quality of track*, resulting in 10 different route categories (see Table 4.1).

[1] At the start of the reform in 1994, DB showed capital assets in the order of DM 25 bln. compared to DM 98 bln. a year before, showing the devaluation of capital assets that took place. The track cost for "Inter-city express" services (ICE) alone amount to DM 18 bln., not including the value of 60 ICE-trains as well as subsequent modifications of train stations.

Table 4.1 Route Categories of the Track Pricing System

	Quality of track (the maximum speeds are listed)						
Potential of Traffic	**250**	**200**	**160**	**120**	**100**	**80**	**50**
A	A250	A200	A160	A120			
B			B160	B120			
C				C120	C100	C80	C50

Source: Rodi (1996), p. 80.

In addition, seven different *train categories* existed which were derived by the *wear and tear* of the train (defined by its weight) and the *quality of planning* (defined as the ratio of "preferred running time" and "operational possible running time", e.g. a quality of planning of 110% meant that the track unit of DB had a range of 10% to co-ordinate conflicting customer preferences). A *base price* was calculated from both route and train category. In a last step, rebates on the base price could be obtained: they referred to *annual volume of traffic* (train-km) and *duration of contract.* A peculiarity existed in SPNV: "additional" train-km (traffic that exceeds the service volume offered in 1993/94) cost DM 5,-. This was a reaction to the criticism DB encountered from politicians and regional authorities when it first published track prices, which were held to be too high, especially in comparison to track costs of small train companies in Germany.

Examples for the old prices (quoted are track prices per slot at the end of 1997, i.e. one trip one way):

- Fast intercity train (up to 200 km/h, e.g. EC and IC) from Hamburg to Berlin: DM 3.652,- (297 km)
- Fast train with regional stops (up to 160 km/h. e.g. IR) from Frankfurt to Dortmund: DM 2.840,- (280 km)
- S-Bahn from Cologne to Düsseldorf: DM 380,- (41 km).

The new system consists of two-part tariffs with a fixed charge (so-called "InfraCard") which applies to certain network parts (there are now 6 different route categories instead of 10) and a usage related part depending on train-km. In order to be eligible for the InfraCard, train companies must serve a minimum network length of 100 km in SPNV, 1000 km in long-distance passenger transport and 500 km in freight. If this condition is not met or the train-km offered are not high enough, the operator can choose to pay a "guest-tariff" which is presumably based on average cost (see DB, 1998).

Although the old system had already taken into account different costs of service (supply side), it had lacked some important demand-side criteria for differentiating prices. The new system represents an improvement in both respects, as:

- the two-part tariff attracts additional traffic;
- the degree of price discrimination between Freight, SPNV and long-distance passenger traffic is intended to become more adequate[2];
- in principle peak load pricing is intended by introducing 3 different categories of capacity usage; and as
- timetable flexibility is rewarded.

Rebates for long-term contracts remain (up to 10% for a 10-year period). In addition, DB Track will accept individual agreements on rebates or supplements according to the rules laid down in the general regulation of track prices mentioned in the former chapter, e.g. slots with a special speed or at a certain time-of-day can be priced differently. Also, ecological criteria of the rolling stock can influence track prices. It remains to be seen however, how this leeway in agreeing on individual prices will unduly favour DB's own transport units.

In addition to the track price, operators have to pay fees for the stations. Similar to track prices, 4 different train categories (groups of the above mentioned) and three different levels of "station attractiveness" exist, resulting in 12 different prices. A more detailed structure that includes the length of the train and certain quality elements of stations is being planned. The prices (as of 1997) range from DM 160,80 (IC and ICE at modern, large stations) to DM 0,94 (S-Bahn at small stations). A typical regional train pays DM 13,40 at a medium quality, regional station.

[2] According to estimates, only SPNV used to cover its full track costs when considering the federal subsidies as revenues, whereas long distance passenger transport covered 83% and freight transport only 25%; see DIW, 1997.

4.2.3 General principles for competition

Legal and regulatory framework

As a general rule, railway companies have to receive a permit from the EBA before they can operate an infrastructure or offer transport services. The registrant meets the requirements if he is considered to be *reliable*, *financially sound* and *competent* (§6 AEG).

The law contains some general rules as far as conditions and pricing of carrying passengers are concerned (§12 AEG), as it asks railway companies:

- to co-operate in enabling through-tariffing and –ticketing;
- to carry everyone "if it is possible within the carrying capacity regularly used";
- to establish and publish transparent pricing rules; and
- not to price-discriminate between passengers.

Since in practice no competition exists so far, it is not possible to tell which criteria the EBA will use to evaluate whether competitors comply with these rules (according to personal information from the EBA).

In spite of these rules, railway operations are not obstructed anymore by public service obligations. Where public authorities wish for conditions that are not in the private interest of a railway company, it can demand these obligations to be lifted in accordance with EU-directive 1191/69.

In inter-modal competition, railway operations are privileged by the fact that (except for Eurobuses) no intercity bus services exist. An existing railway operator would be free to run buses instead of continuing his railway business, but applications for a licence of potential competitors willing to run buses would be turned down due to the financial damage this would cause for the existing railway operator (§13 *PBefG*).

Aims and considerations

The reasoning for alleviating the company from public service obligations and thereby separating commercial from public goals is similar to what has been said in favour of giving DB a company structure. Efficiency can only be measured and subsequently controlled and improved in relation to a clearly stated goal. "Maximising profit" not only provides the managers with clear incentives, it also offers transparent indicators. This goal may be attributed to DB now because of its status as a limited company. Certainly, public ownership does not remove political influence altogether, yet the direction is clearly more market-oriented than before.

The obligation for transport companies to co-operate in tariffing and ticketing again reveals the uncertainty of how to deal with network effects. It seems inconsistent that this rule was not extended to publishing an integrated timetable, but it was argued that this must lie in the self-interest of the transport companies. The other rules recognise the de facto monopoly of DB as they are meant to prevent DB from price discriminating and from refusing to transport passengers.

Peculiar to the German framework is the coexistence of two authorities (EBA and federal trade commission) when it comes to settling disputes between the track operator and transport companies over track access charges. This might hinder the development of a clear line of judgement. The competence of EBA employees in technical matters (track and rolling stock compatibility and safety standards) could have been transferred to the federal trade commission.

As has been stated above, the political process of railway reform revealed a strong intention among many politicians to protect the railways from a volume cut as a possible method to increase efficiency. This is true for the continuing lack of inter-city bus competition but became especially apparent during the discussions about regionalisation.

4.2.4 Regionalisation

Legal framework

With the regionalisation law (RegG) the responsibility for the traditionally deficit producing public services (SPNV) was "regionalised". SPNV is defined as "commonly accessible transport services that are destined to satisfy demand for urban, suburban and regional transport. This is given when it takes the majority of travellers in one transport device no more than an hour or no farther than 50 km to reach their destination" (§2 RegG translated with some latitude).

With the reform, the federal states were put into the position to "order" SPNV according to their preferences. They were asked to pass their own laws in order to lay out the details of organising SPNV services. The states were free to keep this power on the state level or to delegate it further down to the municipal level, which only some states chose to do.

Due to the relevant EU-directives 50/92, 663/89 and 1191/69 the authorities in charge have to ensure that a transparent and fair contract-awarding procedure is used to find the solution which imposes the least cost on society. Tendering *may* be used to determine this but is not mandatory (§4 RegG).

The new institutional structure came into effect in 1996. Since time was needed to adjust to the new framework, DB continued to run all SPNV services in 1996 and 1997, while receiving a corresponding reimbursement from the states. From 1998 on, the federal states are free to chose different operators.

The Federal government pays out specific funds to the single states in the order of DM 12 bln. annually (§§5 and 8 RegG). These subsidies "shall be spent especially on SPNV" (§7 RegG). According to legal experts this grants the states some leeway in deciding which form of public transport to subsidise with this fund and whether the money should go into investments or into operating subsidies. The amount will rise annually in accordance with the growth rate of the receipts of German value added tax. Two audits were planned to evaluate if the sum and its growth rate are sufficient to keep up a certain base level of SPNV that is defined by the service volume offered in 1993/94. The first audit was finished in 1998 and resulted in only slightly lower payments to the states than first planned until 2001 when another audit will take place. Additional funds on the federal level are reserved for investments in new track for SPNV. Special funds for investments in new rolling stock also exist on the federal states' level.

The regional authorities were given the right to take over single parts of track (routes) from DB (§26 BENeuGlG, "Law to restructure the federal railways") if:

- the track in question is being used dominantly by SPNV
- no agreement was reached about the financing of the track (in other words: if the charges requested by the infrastructure division of DB were considered to be too high)
- the authority has guaranteed to operate SPNV for at least 15 years and to operate the track for at least 30 years. Apart from this, the authority would then be subject to the same rules as any other infrastructure operator.

The states chose different solutions as to at which level should assume the organisational powers for the SPNV. A first group (3 states) kept the responsibility at the state level. A second group (8 states) decided to organise SPNV at the state level only as an interim solution with the possibility of handing the powers down to the community level later. 5 states (including Northrhine-Westfalia with the Ruhr area) made full use of the principle of subsidiarity and gave the responsibility to the municipalities. Owing to the special network character of SPNV, neighbouring municipalities have established co-operations *(Zweckverbände,* 9 of them exist in Northrhine-Westfalia). So called "transport-integrating co-operations" *(Verkehrsverbünde)* usually assume the managerial tasks to integrate bus and rail services (co-ordinate timetables, tariffs and ticketing).

The different solutions selected by the states can partly be explained by the structures of settlement of the states: those with a distinct rural and disperse structure retained the responsibility for SPNV on the state level. An argument in favour of a higher level to be responsible rests on the divergence that often exists between the physical supply of SPNV and the demand for these transport services and which arises from the definition of SPNV: while the route length of a SPNV-train may be a lot longer than 50 km because it runs through a number of small towns, the majority of travellers may only travel short distances on this train.

Aims and considerations

Regionalisation is based on an idea of subsidiarity: combining the responsibility for organising and financing services at the lowest possible federal level is supposed to induce efficient behaviour. This was held to be particularly important in the section of rail operations that had been producing more than 50% of DB's deficits (see Allemeyer, 1997).

With its definition of SPNV the law is not very specific of how to divide between SPNV and long-distance services when either both services use the same track or travel demand for both services is satisfied with one train. In practice the dividing line is defined by the typical products DB has developed for regional transport such as "RegionalExpress", "RegionalBahn" or "StadtExpress". "InterRegio"-trains are currently listed as long-distance trains but might fit into the legal definition in some cases as well. This might become relevant now that DB considers to shut down unprofitable InterRegios if the states are not willing to pay the corresponding deficits.

Regionalisation does not necessarily imply that the state level will always be the actual initiator for a new design of services, as this will depend on the specific method used for selecting operators. Since tendering is no obligation, most services in the near future will be co-ordinated and contracted with the existing operator directly, so DB can certainly influence the outcome. If tendering is used, and the relevant characteristics of the service are specified beforehand, the initiator would indeed be the state planner. If, however, the tender is left open for new service suggestions, the initiative would at least partly be left to potential service providers. The fact that tendering was not made an instant obligation for the authorities is that an instant wave of tenders would have caused high transaction costs and might have overtaxed the market.

Due to the deficits of SPNV services, the states would not have accepted the responsibility without compensation. The sum and the portions each state receives are mainly based on the deficit DB incurred with its SPNV in 1993/94 (DM 7,79 billion). An additional billion was granted to the states for service improvements, while a further DM 3 billion results from a switch of subsidy funds (this sum was formerly used for subsidising roads and public transport in cities).

Instead of reducing subsidies, the states were able to convince the federal government to spend even more in the future. This should not be surprising since the federal states were needed to pass the constitutional amendments that rail reform required. The argument in favour of subsidies – apart from promoting rail transport as a second-best policy for tackling external effects from road transport – builds on the law itself: public transport is an element of some minimum standard of living which has to be guaranteed equally in Germany.

Since the source of payments is remote from the authority spending them, some of the incentive for the states to increase efficiency in SPNV via competition is naturally reduced. This is intensified by the missing guarantee that funds will remain at the level they are at today. The Federal Government will be tempted to reduce subsidies if the deficits went down.

Similar to long-distance passenger transport, where competition from bus is absent, a predominance of rail services is likely to develop in regional public transport. For one, the contestability of railway services is comparably low since buses will not be allowed to compete on the same routes (see Nash, 1985, p. 277), as this might hurt incumbents. The authority will naturally not want to weaken services for which it carries the financial responsibility itself (even if not the financial *burden* which lies with federal government). Secondly, regionalisation funds have to be spent especially on rail. This rule was adopted because it served several interests (see Allemeyer, 1997):

- the federal states were not interested in more road transport which they fear will develop with less regional rail services;

- federal government in line with the union of railway workers did not want drastic social consequences for DB and its employees;
- DB itself realised the strong position it will retain in SPNV in the future even with more competition to evolve and that public funds will turn the SPNV into a profitable business; and
- German railway industry profits from large orders for rolling stock.

The opportunity for the states to take over single routes or parts of track used predominantly by SPNV seems a logical option, considering that regional railway services are mainly offered in the public interest. Taking over track might also facilitate tendering, as track cost becomes more transparent.

4.2.5 Summary of legal framework and organisation

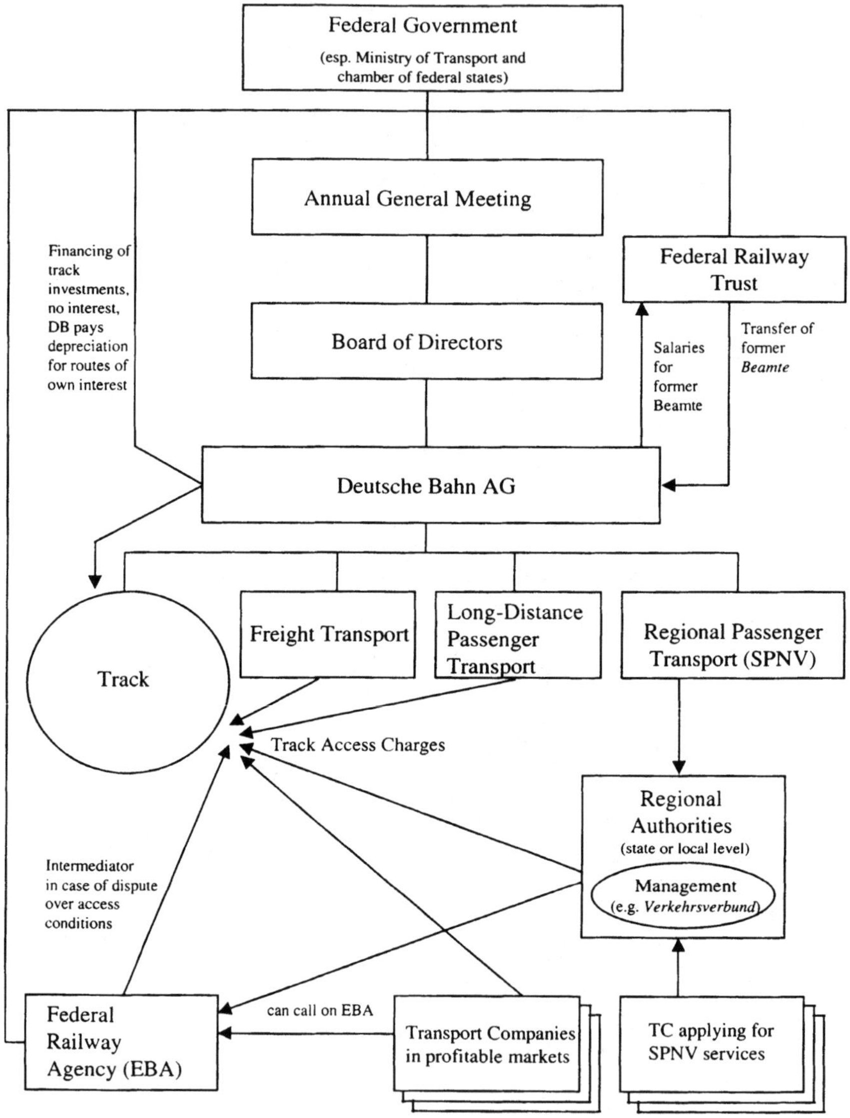

Figure 4.1 Overview of Organization of Railway Transport in Germany

Table 4.2 Summary of legal and expected regulatory framework

Regulation parameter	Type of regulation
Price	• No price-regulation in inter-city transport • Approval of prices in SPNV
Quantity	• No specific regulation
Quality	• Technical minimum standards
Entry	• Proof of reliability, financial soundness, competence
Exit	• Transport operator: only contractual rules in SPNV • Infrastructure operator: track shut down has to be approved
Relationships between track provider and operator	• Agreement between operators • Criteria for track access applied to each applicant on equal grounds • Access for highest bidder but priority for frequent headway services in SPNV • EBA acts as mediator in case of dispute
Horizontal	• Transport operators must co-operate in tarification and ticketing • Time-table to be published by the transport companies
Coverage of infrastructure cost	• Only depreciation on profitable routes, no interest payments • Grants/subsidies for unprofitable routes
Employment	• Transitory rules for former *Beamte*

To summarise the *organisational structure* of the German railway system, it is useful to distinguish between the strategic (setting of aims), tactical (deciding on the means) and operational ("production" of means) levels of decision-making (see Van de Velde, 1997). Because of the peculiarities of the German system these denominations have to be interpreted separately for SPNV and for the rest of transport operations (long-distance passenger and freight). For the latter, only the strategic level is divided among the federal government and the management of DB. The government follows general social aims and a particular transport policy by deciding on infrastructure investments. DB is responsible for running a profitable business which forces it to establish useful market strategies. Both the tactical and operational level are then left up to DB's transport units. In

SPNV on the other hand, regional authorities assume more competencies on the strategic and tactical level (which are usually divided between a political body on the top, e.g. representatives of local or state government, and some management body below that, e.g. the *Verkehrsverbund*). The activities of DB or other carriers are pretty much confined to the operational level. This will vary with the procedure the regions will use for coordinating the SPNV in the future as was discussed above. The activities currently under way suggest that planning includes the design of the product (quantity and quality), the tariff and even parts of the marketing.

4.3 Case studies

It has been pointed out above that competition in railway transport in Germany is still in an embryonic stage, and effects for the customer and the authorities are only gradually beginning to surface. So far, no autonomous market entry onto the rail network of DB has taken place. The only kind of competitive pressure that has been initiated stems from the activities of the regional authorities that have assumed the responsibility for regional passenger rail transport (SPNV). These services are known to be loss making but, by the same token, regarded as an undisputed element of public service.

Two case studies will be presented below. The first one deals with a tender for two routes organised by the *Verkehrsverbund Rhein-Ruhr (VRR)*, the first *Zweckverband* in Germany to experiment with tendering in SPNV. Since tender for one of the routes was stopped in due course, because no other operator than DB applied for the route, and since operations on the other successfully tendered route are not scheduled to start before May 1998, the text focuses on the conditions of tendering and the problems encountered by the authority and the operators. (performance effects are only of a prospective nature and based on contracts and expectations).

Due to the nature of the problem to be analysed, a comparison of the VRR tender with an additional case of tendering promises to add interesting findings to the report. The main differences of the procedure chosen for a tender of three routes in the Cologne-Bonn area as well as the differences in the outcome will be pointed out.

4.3.1 Tendering in the Ruhr area

General description

Area and routes considered

The Ruhr area, as defined by the borders of the VRR, has a size of 5 026 km^2 and a population of 7,35 million (1 463 inhabitants per km^2). Especially in its upper part, between the cities Dortmund and Duisburg, no clear borders of settlement exist. The train network is characterised by a large number of interconnections which enables long-distance passenger traffic to take different routes to cross the area. The number of trips per working day in regional rail services (SPNV) is 450 000.

The routes under consideration were (population numbers in brackets):

RB 52

- Length 57 km
- Dortmund (600 000) - Hagen (212 000) - Lüdenscheid (81 000)

S4

- Length 31 km
- Dortmund (600 000) - Unna (65 000).

Genesis and overview

Before regionalisation, DB carried out SPNV-services inside the Ruhr area according to a special "transport contract" with the VRR. Aside from DB's own fares, a special integrated ticket scheme for buses and trains (*Verbundtarif*) has existed in the VRR-area since 1980. For its services, DB received federal subsidies as well as payments by VRR in the order of DM 80m. annually on average. This subsidy has to be raised by the member municipalities of the VRR.

With regionalisation, the federal subsidies to DB were transferred into payments to the state of NRW which hands them down to the VRR (Allocation of these funds among the 9 co-operation areas in NRW is based on train-km offered in 1993/94). The VRR can independently decide where to order SPNV services. Since no other method than direct subsidisation[3] is used to achieve the social aims connected with the realisation of public transport, some form of tendering or franchising emerges as the only possibility to introduce entrepreneurial incentives into this segment of the transport market. Also, since no route-based costing method has existed in SPNV so far, tendering of single routes was intended to produce better information on this topic. In order to gain experience with tendering and to establish a study of reference for future practice, two routes were selected that exhibit some differences in terms of frequency, technical specification and network connection which will be given later on in this report.

The tendering documents were made available to the bidders in March 1996 and the bidders were asked to turn in their bids by August of that same year. While three different companies bid for the services of the RB 52, only one bid by DB was received for the S-Bahn route. Since the price demanded by DB was higher than what is being paid to DB today on the basis of the regionalisation funds, this tender was called off and the route included in the transport contract with DB, which was revised and settled with DB in September 1997 for all other SPNV-services in the Ruhr area.

Actors

The main actors involved are the regional authorities, the federal state of NRW and the bidders. Since both tendered routes leave the constituency of the VRR, another *Zweckverband* had to be consulted, but the VRR was the one to take the initiative in the tender and to specify all details of the tendering documents.

VRR The VRR is a complex organisation, supposed to solve the main problems adjacent to the joint production of public transport services by a number of transport operators: division of revenues between transport companies and allocation of deficit payments to the member municipalities. Strictly speaking, the VRR GmbH is the managing entity for the respective municipalities associated in the *Zweckverband VRR*. For simplicity, both are treated as one authority as all important decisions are taken by the board of the *Zweckverband*. While regular decisions are derived by a simple majority in the *Zweckverband*, important ones (e.g. changes of the code)

[3] The alternative being indirect subsidies by way of vouchers or subsidized fares for certain users (not to mention the possibility of direct transfers to the users, which is commonly regarded as superior from an economic point of view).

need 2/3 of the vote. Decisions that effect volume and shape of transport services of a particular municipality cannot be reached without the consent of that municipality.

The State of NRW The state level is involved in tendering for SPNV as financing of rolling stock is concerned. Investment grants are paid for 50% of the cost of new trains on the basis of the state-wide regionalisation law. These funds in NRW represent a subsidy on top of the federal regionalisation funds and are paid out of the current budget if certain conditions are met, the most important one requiring the subsidised rolling stock to be employed in public transport for at least 20 years. A transfer to a different route in the meantime has to be approved by the state.

An important exception to the otherwise exclusive organising and timetabling power of the VRR is an initiative by the federal state of Northrhine-Westfalia to introduce a new timetable with *Integraler Taktfahrplan (ITF)* (integral clockface timetable) throughout the state. This state initiative was triggered by DB's plans to change Intercity transport connections between the Ruhr area and Berlin. The ITF brings an increase in frequency on many SPNV routes on the basis of a special transport contract with DB. A concept for the ITF was drafted by a Swiss consultant specialised in transport planning. Several drafts of the ITF were discussed with all regional authorities in order to enable them to influence the outcome. The project is financed with supplementary funds from the state NRW. It is interesting to note that no maximum subsidy was fixed beforehand.

Operators Only three companies finally bid for the operation of the RB 52. Apart from DB and newly established, publicly owned DME (Dortmund-Märkische-Eisenbahn-Gesellschaft), which won the tender, the *Karstorfer Eisenbahngesellschaft* delivered a bid.

The latter is a private company owned by one individual and is active in freight transport as well as in regional passenger transport, especially in eastern Germany. Some of its activities are carried out in co-operation with DB. *Karstorfer* is also active in maintaining trains.

Several other companies had expressed interested in the tender at first but refrained from turning in a bid. This is probably due to certain conditions of the tender, a topic which will be addressed subsequently.

Organisation – Tendering conditions

Type of tender - risk allocation

The tender was published Europe-wide because it was intended to invite as many operators as possible to turn in a bid. The "negotiation method" of tendering was chosen.

The tender only applied to the gross cost of the service, that is the bidders were required to calculate the cost of producing services according to pre-determined characteristics (see further). Two important elements of the tender concerning cost calculation were that the bidder was to supply the rolling stock and that the duration of the contract was to be only 5 years.

At the outset, the authorities agreed to assume full revenue risk as all revenues that are collected should accrue to them. This creates a problem of revenue as well as cost division between the two *Zweckverbände* when determining the amounts to be paid by each constituency to DME. Since patronage on the route is not spread proportionally between the two regions as the majority of passenger travel inside the VRR area, revenues are going to remain in the area where they were collected and transfers will be paid according to passenger-km as observed by regular counts on the route. Regular counts will also be used to determine the division of revenues accruing from the sale of two different tickets, the DB fare and the "VRR-integrated fare". Cost partition between the VRR and the ZRL is based on train-km proportional to the distance travelled in each region.

Determination of service characteristics

Service characteristics in the call-for-tender Most service characteristics on both routes were specified beforehand in the tendering documents by the VRR and the ZRL. They were closely related to the current service characteristics.

Possibilities for changes in service RB 52 The details given below mostly refer to the RB 52, as it offered various possibilities for changes of service. This influenced the strategy of the bidders and proved to be decisive in the end for bidder selection.

The tender took part within a fixed framework that the bidders had to accept. Most importantly, the fares were not variable for the bidders since the route was to remain integrated in the SPNV network from the view of the customer (the regional authorities provide general information services about local public transport in their respective areas).

Additionally, all calculations were to be made on the basis of the existing timetable that is co-ordinated by the VRR with respect to connecting services especially in Hagen and Dortmund. The changes necessary in due course because of the recently introduced ITF did not affect the bidding process.

Table 4.3 Route characteristics

	RB 52 Dortmund-Hagen-Lüdenscheid	**S4* Dortmund-Unna**
Technical specification	One/two tracks non-electrified	Two tracks electrified
Length (km)	57	31
Stations	15	18
Platform height	15-96 cm	96 cm
Level of service (trip pairs per day)	16 (Mo-Fr) 15 (Sa) 10,5 (Su)	54 (Mo-Fr) 38 (Sa) 35 (Su)
Headway (min. between trains)	60 min.	20 min. (Mo-Fr. day) 30 min. (Sa,Su, So-Fr eve.)
Travel time	82/85 min.	49/50 min.
Av. speed km/h	42/40	49/50
Train/km p.a.	650 000	1 120 000
Fare (one trip/ whole route)	DM 9,80	DM 5,40
Passengers per day	3 800	19 241

* The tender for the S4 was stopped as no other operator than DB applied.

A calculation sheet was enclosed in the tendering documents, and the bidders were asked to fill in their calculations concerning the following service characteristics:

I. Regular Service

1. Operational services: personnel for regular service and substitutional for vacation times, safety personnel, fuel cost, track cost, other cost for guarantee of service.

The bidders were told that delays of more than 2 min. in the stations of Hagen and Dortmund were only acceptable for 5% of all trains. The maximum time of breakdown of the service was to be 120 min. with a substitutional bus service to be offered by the operator.

2. Train/rolling stock: trains for regular service and substitutional trains (calculated with reference to investment grants from the state as well as the residual value of the trains at termination of the contract), insurance, cleaning and maintenance cost (personnel, facility and material costs).

The VRR issues certain standards for cleanliness of the trains that have to be complied with.

3. Administration: personnel rostering, bookkeeping, purchases, traffic control.

4. Sales: personnel, material.

Information and other user-friendly services were regarded a key condition to be fulfilled by the operator. For example, the VRR issues standards for the design of timetable information and obliges the operator to make announcements by loudspeaker.

Apart from accepting the tickets sold by DB (especially in connection with long-distance travel), the bidders had to ensure the sale of the whole range of VRR-tickets. If no personnel is available as on smaller stations along the route, the installation and maintenance of a ticket-selling machine was mandatory.

II. Adjustments of Service

The authority retained the possibility to oblige the operator to accept adjustments of service. The bidders were asked to calculate per train/km the cost of the following alterations:

1. Increase of (seat) capacity (to be announced by the authority 2 weeks in advance).

2. Different departure times (2 months).

3. Increase/decrease of total service volume (by 10% max., 2 months).

4. Single additional trains (15 p.a. max., 1 week).

5. Periodic additional trains (e.g. on Saturdays before Christmas, 2 months).

III. Options

The following options could be bid for:

1. Train modifications: toilets, emergency phone, regular phone, bar/café.

2. Take-over of responsibility for the infrastructure: planning, track investments, maintenance, investments in stations.

3. Sales/marketing: personnel for ticket counters, selling machines within the train (with/without touch-screen), additional personnel on the train (for service, ticket sale and check), special marketing instruments.

4. Alternative operations: The bidders were informed about a plan that had been contemplated for some time by transport planners inside the VRR. Due to several disadvantages of the current service (slow speed, only one track at certain locations along the route and parallel operation of the S5 between the cities Dortmund and Hagen) a change of service was envisaged such that the RB 52 should be connected directly to the Stadtbahn (city train) in Dortmund (which runs partly underground). This would have implied for either the authority in co-ordination with DB or for the bidder to invest into the extension and electrification of the track between Dortmund and Hagen and the construction of additional stops.

These changes were considered to add immensely to the attractiveness of the route since speed and frequency could be increased and the accessibility of important locations inside and between the two cities improved. For example, the Stadtbahn today ends at the stadium of the popular football club Borussia Dortmund which of course attracts many passengers from the southern Ruhr area as well.

The rationale behind these ideas has meanwhile gained support by the success of a similar project in Karlsruhe. Here, the introduction of a new train-system that runs on DB track outside the city and on city-tram tracks inside the city was able to attract a substantial increase in patronage, which is claimed to be due to eliminating the need for the user to switch trains.

Apart from this fundamental change of service, additional possibilities to be considered were the construction or relocation of several stations along the route, an improvement of stations' surroundings, the removal of slow intervals due to unfavourable track characteristics and the elevation of the platform heights to a uniform 76 cm. Most of these measures would naturally have implied to co-operate closely with the infrastructure unit of DB.

The operator has to guarantee the quality of his service by some certified quality audit. If the operator does not comply with the contractually specified services, the fixed price will be reduced by 20% (for delays, damage and dirt in the trains) and by up to 100% for complete break downs of trains.

Passenger interests

Due to transaction costs and possible time delays passenger interests did not enter the procedure on an important scale, except for interested individuals having being allowed to attend the first information-meeting.

Rolling stock

A peculiar event took place after the decision about the winning bidder had been reached. The train to be used on the route is not the one first offered by DME. Instead, four trains of a different, more expensive type have been ordered. These offer 135 seats and 150 standing places each, a ticket-selling-machine on board and a toilet and are considered to be very attractive for the passenger (large windows, unrestricted view throughout the train and towards the front, view of the conductor's seat). At the same time, the federal state NRW raised its investment grant for the trains to 65% (instead of 50% as had been anticipated by the bidders) because - as is openly admitted - employment in NRW is supported by the train order as the manufacturer is located in Aachen near the Dutch border.

The increased investment grant by NRW may in fact have been the main reason for the change of train types although a specific explanation was not received. A different problem exists in the fact that the delivery of the new trains was delayed so that DME is forced to pay for the use of DB's material during the first months of the new operations.

As in many markets, the size of the order determines the final price for modern trains. By having ordered (or at least bought reservation rights for) a large volume of SPNV trains within the last two years, DB has moved into a privileged position when it comes to tenders for single routes. DB's strategy in this respect is clear: Firstly, the SPNV-market is only gradually opened by tenders so DB can rely on a stable demand by the authorities for quite a while. Secondly, by investing heavily in new rolling stock, DB enjoys cost advantages over potential competitors in forthcoming tenders while at the same time reducing the urge for the authorities to tender as they will be appeased by the improved service. While this strategy did not prove to be successful in this specific case, it is worth mentioning nevertheless, since the cost-advantages connected to the large order might have scared away other bidders.

Infrastructure

The track belongs to the respective unit of DB so that the regular track prices applied. Thus, the pricing of the track was not of particular concern to the authority or to the bidders. Apart from this status quo, the tendering documents contained the option for the bidders to calculate the specific cost of a take-over of the route's track (option 2). This would have implied for the authority to take over the track first and then have the winning bidder operate it. The significance of the track is mirrored by its high share of total cost, which is in the order of 40%.

A problem of the tender was the lack of transparency concerning the quality of the track, especially as it affects the service on the route (e.g. the profile of the route pre-determines the speed that can be run). The bidders apart from DB were not given any details in this respect that would have helped them to estimate the investments necessary to offer different speeds (including additional technical improvements) as they could only rely on their observation that the current services on the route were technically feasible. Also the future policy of the infrastructure unit of DB in respect to track and station's quality along the route was not known to bidders other than DB (which illustrates how the vertically integrated structure of DB acts as an effective barrier towards more entrepreneurship).

Another practical entry restriction can be seen in option Number 4 described above to alter the service on the route. The tendering documents described this option in some detail. However, on the same page, it was mentioned that planning on this option is still under way which was meant to explain the short duration of the tender (5 years). For example, the option would have implied for the train to be equipped with an electrical engine as well as the conventional diesel engine, since the route would have been electrified only half way. At the moment, only blueprints of such trains exist, which is the main reason why this option had no serious chance to be implemented right away. This shows that the VRR had probably not expected the competitors to turn in a serious bid on this option but at the same time signalled to them the future plans for the route. This signal may have scared away bidders who guessed that they would not be eligible to carry out such an altered service in the future, as it would have meant to intrude into the area of DSW.

To summarise the institutional structure, the strategic, tactical and operational level of service determination are listed in Table 4.4.

Table 4.4 Organisational form of the VRR tender

Actor	**Federal State**	**Zweckverband**	**DB Track**	**VRR/ZRL**	**Operators**
Type	Political council	Political council	Federal Co.	Zweckv. Co.	Priv. & pub. Co's
Relation	Democratic control	Indirect democratic control	Federal laws, control by EBA, FTC	Management contract with Zweckverband	Contract with VRR/ZRL after tendering
Strategic	Federal funds Empl. policy				
	Public service obligation	Effic. increase in SPNV		(suggestions)	
			Track prices		(option 2)
Tactical		(approval)		Route	(option 4)
		(approval)		Fares	
	ITF	(approval)	(Slot alloc.)	Timetable	
		(approval)		Risk allocation	
		(approval)		(Min. Std)	Train type (op. 1)
				Addit. services	
Operational					Train rostering
					Maintenance
				(Information)	Marketing
				(Min. Std)	Sales (op. 3)
					Pers. rostering
			Maint. of track and stations		(option 2)

Results

The bidders made use of the possibility to bid for all other options mentioned above.[4] While options 1 and 3 (1: optional train equipment and 3: sales/marketing) were priced specifically, the other two options (2: infra-

[4] The information received about the contents of the bids is not very substantial as both the authority and the bidders did not want details to become public that might harm them in some way later on.

structure operation and 4: change of service) were included only qualitatively as specific evaluations would have required more details. These are current quality of the track and technical specification for option 2 and exact conditions and framework for option 4. According to one of the bidders, the authority did not really expect to receive detailed calculations on these options. Nevertheless, this bidder was quite confident that operating the track would have led to lower track prices in the long run, but DB would probably have been reluctant to give away the infrastructure. In addition, the authority feared that the required take-over of the track from DB would have caused high transaction costs in the end (co-ordination of the municipalities involved, negotiations with DB and EBA) so that the option was probably mainly meant to supply the authority with more information on track costs.

Three rounds of negotiations took place between the VRR and the bidders. The decision on the winning bid (DME) was based on its cost advantage. Also, the marketing concept of DME was felt to be convincing as the company intends to stress the attractions of villages and cities along the route in order to draw more leisure travel. DME was willing to take on the full capacity risk of the rolling stock. This is especially significant because of the short 5-year duration of the contract. DB would have agreed to this as well, but the third bidder would have demanded a guaranteed price by the VRR to be paid for the rolling stock in case the transport contract would not have been renewed after 5 years.

As to the financial results of the tender, the only information made public is that the difference between the best and the most expensive offer was DM 1 mio. p.a. and that the cost advantage compared to average cost of all SPNV services per train-km is about 15%. A rough estimate of the total cost-price offered in the tender can be inferred from the interviews: DM 18,50 per train-km. With the new train, the cost will be somewhat higher. This amount should not be taken to cover the true cost of service since the bidders could expect to receive the regular investment grant by the state NRW (50% of train costs). When confronting this figure with the amount of federal regionalisation funds per train-km (DM 15,68) in NRW (in 1997), it becomes clear that these funds actually cover the majority of total cost. Consequently, the level of total cost coverage is quite low. And probably not more than 30%.[5] (See Table 4.5.) (Note, however, that this calculation takes DB's track prices as track costs that may be exaggerated.)

[5] Train funding by NRW per train-km was calculated on the basis of the following data: investment grant per train: DM 3.000.000; pay-back period: 20 years; interest-rate: 6% p.a. This gives an annuity (a) of DM 261.558,68. Since train-km per train and year on the route are 125.000, train funding per train-km is roughly DM 2,00.

Table 4.5 Selected financial data for the RB 52 (own estimations)

Est. total price p.a.	11,2m. – 13.9m.
Est. Bidded price per train-km	20,-
Regionalisation funds per train-km	15,68
Est. train funding per train-km	2,00
Revenues from ticket sales per train-km (average in VRR)	6,75
Est. Degree of total cost coverage	30%

Note: based on estimations by the author.

The administrative burden on the side of the authority and the bidders is difficult to assess. According to VRR officials, the preparation of the tender took about two years but no single person was busy with this job all of her time. At the final stage (March-December 1996), 2-3 persons were more frequently involved. An estimate of one bidder not involved in this particular tender is that between DM 200.000,- and 500.000,- in personnel cost are incurred in order to prepare for such bids, depending on the size of the order.

Evaluation of results

VRR officials regard the outcome of the tender as very successful. The cost reduction as well as the experience gained through the procedure are regarded valuable assets, and the fact that DME will operate the route is also seen as a convenient prerequisite for all eventual changes of the route and its service in the future.

What reasons can be given to explain the advantage that DME obviously had over its competitors? The main reason to be given rests on the special form of ownership of the company (note again that DME is a subsidiary of the *Dortmunder Stadtwerke,* the local energy supplier and public transport company for Dortmund and of the *Märkische Verkehrsgesellschaft* which is responsible for public transport around the city of Lüdenscheid at the other end of the route). Since the company is publicly owned, no risk of bankruptcy exists. By experience this leads to lower than market oriented risk valuations. Also, DSW is a "partner" of the VRR in bus transport and that the owner of DSW is at the same time share-holder of the VRR.

DME itself claims that reasonable economic estimations determined the final bid so that real cost advantages might in fact exist. DME's personnel on the management level is in fact only part-time active for DME, the managing director is at the same time second-level manager for DSW. Cost advantages of DME might rest on the fact that sales personnel inside Dortmund already exists which can easily sell this additional service as well. All personnel will be employed according to a regular contract with no social disadvantages compared to other DSW workers.

An additional circumstance is the above-mentioned idea to connect the service on the RB 52 route to the Stadtbahn in Dortmund. Since one of DME's mother companies carries out all local public transport within the Dortmund area and is responsible for route planning as well, it would encounter far lower transaction cost than any competitor when optimising the Dortmund network with a restructured and partly re-routed service on the RB 52 (according to the interviewed VRR official, DME was the only company able to manage the envisaged changes).

DME's attitude concerning the combination of capacity risk and short-term contract is a confident one, even if the transport contract would not be renewed after 5 years (which is not thought to be likely), DME could sell the rolling stock or would look for other opportunities in the vicinity to employ the material. Not only for this reason is DME prepared to compete in upcoming tenders, especially those that would extend the network towards the east and the north of Dortmund.

As a general conclusion is that other than pure commercial or transport-related goals seem to be an influential factor in public tendering as well. E.g., the aim to secure employment in Northrhine-Westfalia has led the state to pay a higher investment grant for the purchase of the new trains. It is especially peculiar that this was done after the bids had already been turned in, as well as the fact that the bidders had actually offered less expensive trains beforehand.

4.3.2 Tendering around Cologne and Bonn

General description

Around Cologne and Bonn, three routes were tendered which were selected by the fact that they are non-electrified routes and that they do not enter other transport areas (like for example the area of the VRR), thus not presenting any appreciable problems of administrative co-ordination. The routes connect the following cities (with corresponding population numbers):

- Bonn (310.000) - Euskirchen (52.000) - Bad Münstereifel (<20.000)
- Cologne (1.000.000) - Euskirchen - Jünkerath (<20.000)
- Cologne - Gummersbach (53.000).

Organisation – Tendering conditions

The procedure (cost, consultations in legal aspects) and the outcome (operator, duration of contract, risk sharing, etc.) show some distinct differences to tendering in the Ruhr area.

In order to reach a decision about the appropriate tendering procedure first, the organising authority, the *Zweckverband Verkehrsverbund Rhein Sieg* (VRS, similar structure to VRR) paid a substantial amount of money in order to have the legal implications of tendering evaluated by an expert. VRS officials feared the risk of being liable for legal mistakes they might make unconsciously during tendering.

The competitors were asked to bid for the standard timetable on all routes separately and - as an option - to bid for a package of all three routes. Other options to bid for were an increased frequency on certain parts of the routes, a direct connection of two formerly unconnected routes and an extension of service beyond one of the route's railheads. Quality standards were defined by the authority beforehand (e.g. the capacity of trains was to be planned such that only 50% of the standing places would be needed at the busiest times of day). All competitors were free to offer other options as well.

The duration of the contract was envisaged to be 10 years but the competitors could bid optionally for 15 years. A peculiar form of risk allocation was selected. Although the fares are determined by the authority the operator has to carry full revenue risk (respectively with full profit chance if revenues exceed the predefined base level which is calculated according to passenger counts in the recent past).

At the outset, eight companies had expressed interest to compete in the tender, but only three of them turned in a bid: DB, *SWB* (the electricity and public transport provider in the city of Bonn) and *DKB* (a small publicly owned company operating a SPNV route in the western part of NRW). Among the companies interested in the tender were *DEGV* (subsidiary of CGEA) and *HGK, Häfen- und Güterverkehr Köln AG* (harbour and freight transport Cologne). HGK had first planned to co-operate with SWB and to turn in a bid for all three routes but declined to take part in the end.

While DB and DKB bid for all three routes, SWB was only interested in the Bonn - Euskirchen route after the co-operation with HGK had been called off by HGK. The rationale of SWB's decision was to optimise an existing light-rail network inside the city of Bonn that SWB already operates. SWB had certain thoughts about improving the frequency on this route and building or relocating stops.

Results

The tender resulted in a 15-year contract for DB, the financial volume over this time-span being a total of DM 1 bln. DB not only bid the best price for the whole package but was also able to offer a better price for all single routes in the end. For the rest of SPNV, the VRS will settle a five-year contract with DB (just like the VRR) but does not intend to tender any further routes during this time.

After the bids had been turned in, negotiations took place with DB and SWB since DKB bid was not regarded to have a serious chance of winning. The SWB bid for the Bonn-Euskirchen route however was based on different service specifications than the DB bid and was therefore thought to deserve further attention. SWB and DB had quite different thoughts about the kind of frequency that should be offered in the Bonn area. SWB suggested having a 20-min. frequency on the Bonn route with an increase to 10-min. at demand peaks. DB on the contrary offered 30 and 15 minutes. In the end, DB took up the SWB idea and at the same time undercut their price so that the contract was allotted to DB.

VRS officials are very pleased with the outcome as they were able to reduce their combined costs for all routes by about 15% (with "costs" referring to the regionalisation funds the VRS receives from the state NRW which are DM 15,68 per train-km). They claim that this is a remarkable result considering the fact that DB is even willing to carry the revenue risk. At the same time, service improvements are going to be realised. Forty-five modern light-rail trains (the same type as the one ordered for the VRR route) have been ordered with air-conditioning, an on-board-ticket selling machine, toilet, emergency phones as well as first and second class compartments. The federal state NRW contributes a grant of DM 135 mln. to the financing of the trains which is 65% of total vehicle cost (which represents the same incentive to order trains manufactured in NRW as mentioned in the VRR tender). Higher service frequencies will be offered on two routes, especially on the Bonn-Euskirchen route where train-km are going to be increased by more than 20%. All routes taken together, about 3m. train-km will be run annually at first but by the year 2001, train-km will increase by about 10% in total.

The administrative cost on the part of the authority is difficult to estimate. The preparation of the tender took around half a year (from the beginning of 1996 until July) and the tender itself (negotiations) the same time-span again. In contrast to the VRR, a lot more meetings for negotiating the offers of the bidders were needed, around 20 in total. The direct cost for having the tender and the final contract prepared by legal experts was about DM 130.000,-.

Evaluation of results

Apart from having achieved its aims, the VRS is quite satisfied with the chosen tender procedure. In particular, it is seen as an advantage that three routes were tendered which are linked to one another as this could have theoretically enabled the bidders to arrive at cost reductions.

VRS officials also stress how important it is to have the contracts prepared for as many options (service characteristics, risk allocation) as possible. Otherwise it becomes difficult to compare bids if the bidders think that they will be able to alter certain contractual conditions to their advantage in the bargaining phase. This kind of behaviour was partly present in the VRS tender as DB demanded a more favourable risk allocation if all optional improvements it had offered were to be included in the contract. So, although the VRS had intended to keep supernormal revenues as its own profit, the authority conceded all chances for such profits to DB in the end. Also, the final negotiations were quite time-consuming as 6 all day meetings had to be held. However, since legal counsel had been involved in the VRS tender from the beginning, it is questionable to what extent such complete contracts can be drafted beforehand for all alternatives in regional passenger rail transport.

What reasons can be given for the success of DB? A first assumption is that DB put a strong effort into winning this tender after it had already lost in several tenders across Germany. A second factor is the absence of other more efficient bidders: they may have feared the consortium of SWB and HGK to be favoured by the VRS due to their public ownership (the fact that HGK resigned from the co-operation with SWB was probably due to its co-operation with DB in freight transport). Also, state politicians informally restricted market entry by letting the local manufacturer appear as the only acceptable supplier of rolling stock.

4.3.3 Comparison of the VRR tender and the VRS tender

Although quite different approaches were followed, both tenders resulted in some improvement of service accompanied by considerable cost reductions. The underlying reasons are difficult to observe, especially since the calculated cost reductions are based on some average level of route costs that may have been higher than former individual route costs.

Table 4.6 Differences between the VRR and the VRS tender

Topics	**VRR**	**VRS**
Routes tendered	2	3
Bidders	3 / 1	3 / 2 / 2
Contracts per routes	1 for 1	1 for 3
Form of contract	Gross-cost	Net-cost
Duration of contract	5 years	15 years (10 intended)
Administrative burden	Medium	High
Tactics defined by	Authority (winning bidder defines tactics on connecting services)	Authority
Cost reduction achieved	15% of regionalisation funds	15% of regionalisation funds
Increase in train-km	-	10% (by 2001)

Both tenders failed to attract a substantial number of bidders. This was probably only partly due to the different tendering conditions (duration, risk allocation). More importantly, "political circumstances" may have prevented more competitors from entering the procedure.

While the VRS tender applied to a small network of routes (all non-electrified) with the possibility of direct inter-linkage, the VRR tender had included two separate and technically different routes at first. The fact that one of them (S4) was withdrawn from the procedure subsequently was probably due to the difficulties arising from operating an electrified route when it is integrated in a network.

Despite the similarity of the results, important differences of the tenders are the duration of contract and the methods chosen for risk allocation. It is interesting in itself that such different approaches were followed and naturally, both versions (and their respective variations) of both parameters have their pros and cons.

- A longer duration of contract gives the operator more security to earn a return on his investment (and will thus normally invite more competitors) while at the same time increasing the dependency of the authority on the operator's performance and narrowing the scope for the authority to enhance dynamic efficiency by redefining service characteristics in the meantime since this would have to be contractually settled somehow (productive efficiency is easier to find incentives for as payments may be connected to certain performance measures).
- If the operator bears the revenue risk, the problem of ensuring dynamic efficiency becomes more severe as the operator will usually want to ensure that the authority cannot change any tactics during the contract that directly effect revenues (e.g. fares, parallel routes). In this respect, the solution in the VRS is peculiar as the authority keeps the power over fare policy and DB may theoretically suffer from lower fares. At the same time of course, the VRS does not profit from increased revenues due to increased fares. In such a situation, it should normally be expected that contractual specifications are agreed upon that entail financial consequences of fare changes for the authority.
- Making the operator bear the revenue risk may give him the right incentive, but (depending on how risk enters their utility function) may also induce the bidders to calculate prices on the basis of exaggerated risk supplements.

Administrative costs were probably somewhat higher in the VRS as a lot more time was spent on negotiating the bids than in the VRR. However, this is at least partially due to the different volumes of the two tenders.

4.4 General evaluation and conclusions

Tendering in SPNV in Germany is something new. From the specific cases presented above, but also from a general observation of the current state and framework of the SPNV market in Germany, some general conclusions can be drawn. These are associated with the following topics:

- determination of tendering parameters by the authority;
- market barriers for new companies; and
- problems of competition in SPNV due to rail reform

Determination of tendering parameters by the authority

How can tenders in SPNV lead to efficient outcomes in terms of the goals followed by society as a whole? When contemplating this question, it shall be assumed that the tendering authority does indeed have general welfare in mind

As a general recommendation, it is important to signal credibly to potential competitors that they will be treated fairly and equally and that the procedure will be managed in a transparent manner. From the observations made during the case studies presented here, it seems doubtful whether the VRR and the VRS always behaved in this manner. This also raises the question about appropriate institutional conditions. For example, private competitors easily feel fooled if some bidders are owned by municipalities that have a say in the association meeting of the tendering authority.

Then, the authority should avoid getting locked-in with a winning bidder in negotiations when important contractual clauses (e.g. risk allocation) are not clearly defined beforehand. This happened in the VRS tender, where the authority had intended to keep extra revenues for itself but ended up with DB profiting from such gains alone.

The observations made here do not allow a conclusion on the preferable method of risk allocation. Generally, private competitors are not reluctant to take on revenue risk since they welcome the incentive to increase their profits. However, the barrier of market knowledge which currently favours DB as well as municipally-owned local public transport companies carrying out some kind of rail transport may present a problem which the authority would have to remove. Strictly speaking, a decision about risk allocation does not have to be made beforehand. It could be left up to the competitors to reveal their risk premium by bidding for different risk allocation schemes. In case part of the revenue risk is assigned to the operator, the base level of revenues to be determined may be one of the past or even one of the future, only the second option naturally acts as a disincentive for the operator's sales activities in the base period.

From the view of the operators, the authorities should refrain from tendering single routes and should define more suitable regional networks instead, thus not having to co-ordinate all services themselves. This way, economies of scale as well as interrelating flows of demand enter the operators' valuation of their bid. The handling of these network advantages should be left up to the bidders as this enhances entrepreneurship and seems to be an important prerequisite for achieving considerable cost advantages as well as increases in demand. An important difference between these effects should be noted, however. While economies of scale on the *input side* can be realised by bidders directly if they are in charge of the *operational level*, the possible advantages resulting from economies of scope on the demand side may only be captured if the "right" *tactics* are chosen. That is, if fares, co-ordination of connecting services and marketing are conditioned to passengers' needs.

Who however defines these tactics? Tendering for socially desirable services implies that some of the tactics will always have to be determined beforehand, depending on the indicator used to measure that whatever is socially desirable has been reached. The main service qualities to be selected as such an indicator may be minimum standards of frequency and speed (the latter representing the time needed to get somewhere) and possibly maximum fare levels. This still leaves a considerable number of variables (timetable, vehicle type, marketing, fare structure, information services, routing, maybe even the definition of the network itself, if no constraints on property rights exist in this respect) to be determined on the tactical level and the question is, if tenders can be organised in such a way that competitors are given more entrepreneurial freedom and incentive to be creative on the tactical level. In order for potential competitors to feel this incentive, they need the security that their good ideas will be awarded in the end somehow (with "winning the tender" certainly being the most direct award but possibly not the only one to think of). Following this, the task for the authority would be to issue a consistent set of cost-benefit-indicators that enables transparent award decisions to be reached and would at the same time increase the scope for the competitors to offer a variety of options without the need to specify everything beforehand.

Whether the definition of "suitable networks" in tendering can be made a bidding parameter itself remains to be seen and would depend on how property rights of existing operators are defined. By selecting the exact size of the network to be tendered autonomously, the authority would run the danger of ending up with an inefficient decision if it does not know beforehand how network size actually relates to the potential for increases in efficiency. In this respect, private competitors should have the edge on the authority. Another point of consideration is, how the size of one tender influences the degree of competition over time inside the whole area under control of the authority. The market for the tendered services will be closed for the duration of the contract. A sound solution to the problem of market definition in tendering has yet to be found. For Germany, a cautious result is that the authorities would not go wrong if they moved to larger tenders in the future.

When comparing the resources (staff/costs) spent on tendering procedures with the benefit that is created by tendering, the balance is clearly positive, especially since the authorities will develop a routine in tendering which will lower the specific costs.

Finally, some operators are pressing for the duration of the tender to be long enough to write off the rolling stock completely. It remains doubtful, however, that investments in rolling stock really cause considerably higher sunk costs as the market for SPNV services is yet to be widened and the possibilities to transfer the trains to other markets should increase - both in terms of demand (more competitors) and of technological routines.

Market barriers for new companies

Some important market barriers for new companies can be identified. First, new companies need trained personnel in order to fulfil all requirements for approval as a railway company. This personnel is very scarce at the moment and exclusively employed in existing companies. Secondly, and even more important, an operating location from which the track can be accessed and where the trains can be maintained has to be found if existing locations of DB cannot be used co-operatively, which in turn may prove to be quite expensive. The location should also be near the route to be operated since empty trips are burdened with track prices. And thirdly, a certain amount of rolling stock is needed to sufficiently employ the capacity of maintenance facilities. Besides this, the market for modern rolling stock is yet unable to satisfy short-term demand of new rolling stock.

Problems of competition due to rail reform

The difficulties resulting from the vertical integration of track and operations underneath the roof of DB have been pointed out several times. It seems to be a common belief that the legal option for federal government to agree on a material vertical separation by privatising DB's operating units is not going to become reality in the near future. Since politics and DB have been interwoven for a long time and as it is DB's vital interest to keep the control over the track, the general arguments in favour of more transparent conditions for competition in the railway market will hardly be listened to. The lack of a strict time-path for material vertical separation is regarded a "congenital deformity" by many observers of rail reform in Germany. Similarly, the principle rule to cover track costs in the future is regarded to be an unfair burden for the rail system in respect to road transport.

The legal possibility given to the authorities to take over track from DB was unduly burdened with the obligation to continue the operation of that track for at least 30 years and to operate SPNV on the track for at least 15 years. This as well as transaction costs may have authorities refrain from making use of this option which would indeed remove some asymmetries in favour of DB today.

The institutional structure of rail reform has not succeeded in opening the market for long-distance passenger transport. Competitors believe that they will not receive any profitable track slots (the executive order concerning the use of the infrastructure has just removed this barrier, but it should have been passed along with rail reform four years ago). In addition, since DB had its capital written down by rail reform, no one really knows at the moment how profitable the Inter-City market is. This will only slowly surface when replacements will raise costs to their true level again.

A further obstacle is the polycentric structure of Germany since profitable operations would generally require *networks* to be operated (as opposed to France for example.) One route, which would normally have good chances of being profitable by itself even for competitors of DB, is the Hamburg - Berlin route. Here of course the political decision to operate the Transrapid immensely reduces the potential for market entry. These considerations as well as the volume of investments necessary for new competitors to enter the market for Inter-City transport make market success quite speculative.

Eisenbahnbundesamt (EBA) safety standards are regarded to put another barrier to market entry in railways in Germany. They are deemed to be exaggerated and to make track as well as rolling stock too expensive in multimodal competition (even if this may sound almost cynical after the tragic ICE catastrophe in Eschede). The informal connections between EBA and DB due to their former unity present another problem in that competitors may fear to be treated unfairly in future disputes over track access or when applying for operator licenses.

Coming back to SPNV, open questions remain as to how the competency structure within the federal states affects efficiency in SPNV. This includes the rules for funding. It is still open to discussion if the state level or a lower regional level should be in charge of tendering. The solutions selected in Germany are quite different in this respect. The advantages large tenders possibly exhibit (e.g. declining costs for large orders of rolling stock, network advantages, no co-ordination necessary between municipalities or *Zweckverbände*) have to be weighted with the advantages that lower levels have in acquiring subsidiary market know how and being closer to the customer.

Problems of capacity allocation between long-distance and regional trains have been solved inside DB so far. Problems are not expected to appear there were exclusive infrastructure exists for regional trains, but on routes used by both types of trains, with more competition developing, allocation of track slots might certainly become more of a problem. In practice, no clear mechanism for solving this has been developed so far. However, a certain priority for Intercity transport seems to exist with, e.g., the new ICE services between Berlin and the Ruhr area influencing the *ITF* (integrated timetable with frequent services) which was implemented in NRW. This also reveals that state-wide initiatives in SPNV (here the decision to introduce the ITF) will continue to interfere with regional responsibilities (e.g. those of the VRR and VRL), thereby increasing administrative costs. The fact that such schemes are pushed by the state and are not the result of a market process is at least questionable from an economic point of view. Also, frequent headway services are exempt from any form of bidding procedure for track slots. This situation is confusing to everybody involved in the business. The hope is obviously that a consensus over the use of the track can be reached (which is a somewhat typical attitude for German politics).

Finally, state funding (e.g. of trains) is another way of influencing the market outcome. The actual critique to be associated with these subsidies, however, is that their efficiency is in no way accounted for. This, of course, is not so much a problem of the institutional structure of rail reform but rather of the democratic system in Germany, lacking barriers for politicians to be uncontrolled masters of tax money.

References

Aberle, G.; Brenner, A. (1996), Bahnstrukturreform in Deutschland - Ziele und Umsetzungsprobleme (*Railway reform in Germany - Aims and practical problems*), Cologne.

Allemeyer, W. (1997), Idee und Umsetzung der Regionalisierung aus wissenschaftlicher Sicht, (*idea and practice of regionalisation from an economist's view*), paper presented to the Mannheim conference.

Albach, H.; Schmitz, R.; Pfannschmidt, A. (1991), Ein Dreistufen-Modell zur Privatisierung der Deutschen Bundesbahn (*a three-step-model to privatize the German railways*), 4. Ergebnisbericht, Bonn

Deregulierungskommission (1991), Marktöffnung und Wettbewerb (*opening markets and competition*), Stuttgart.

DB AG (1998), Mehr Verkehr auf die Schiene - Das neue Trassenpreissystem TPS '98, (*more traffic onto the track - the new track pricing system*), Frankfurt/Main.

DB AG (1997a), Annual Report 1996, Frankfurt/Main.

DB AG (1997b), Trassenpreise Personenverkehr (*track prices for passenger transport*), Frankfurt/Main.

DB AG (1996), Annual Report 1995, Frankfurt/Main.

DB AG (1995), Annual Report 1994, Frankfurt/Main.

DB AG (1994), Die Bahnreform (*rail reform*), Frankfurt/Main.

Deutsche Bundesbahn (1993), Annual Report 1992, Frankfurt/Main.

DIW (1997), Trassenpreise der Deutschen Bahn AG - diskriminierungsfrei und kostendeckend? (*track prices of DB - are they fair and do they cover costs?)*, in: Wochenbericht 26, Berlin.

Eiermann, R. (1997), Rechtsbeziehungen im SPNV zwischen Aufgabenträgern, Dienstleistungserbringern und Fahrwegbetreibern (*legal relationships in regional rail transport between authorities, transport operators and infrastructure operators*), in: Püttner, G. (ed.), Der regionalisierte Nahverkehr, Schriftenreihe der Gesellschaft für öffentliche Wirtschaft, Bd. 42, Baden-Baden.

Ewers, H.-J. (1994), Privatisierung und Deregulierung bei den Eisenbahnen, (*Privatization and Deregulation of the Railways*) in: Jahrbuch für Neue Politische Ökonomie, p. 178-208.

Faulhaber, G. R. (1975), Cross-Subsidization: Pricing in Public Enterprises, in: American Economic Review, Vol. 65, No. 5, p. 966-977.

Freise, R. (ed.) (1996), Taschenbuch der Eisenbahngesetze (*Handbook of Railway Laws*), 11. Auflage, Darmstadt.

Hedderich, A. (1996), Vertikale Desintegration im Schienenverkehr (*vertical desintegration in rail transport*), Hamburg.

Heimerl, G. (1995), Stadtentwicklung und Verkehr - Potentiale gegenseitiger Beeinflussung (*City development and Transport - potential for reciprocal impacts*), in: DVWG, B 187, Bergisch Gladbach.

Horn, C. (1993), Ordnungskonzept für die Einnahmeaufteilung und den Defizitausgleich bei Verkehrsverbünden des ÖPNV - unter besonderer Berücksichtigung des Verkehrsverbundes Rhein-Ruhr (*concept for dividing revenues and sharing deficits in transport integrating cooperations*), Bergisch Gladbach, p. 199ff.

Lehmann, C.; Rodi, H. (1998), ÖPNV in der Marktwirtschaft - Ein Ordnungsentwurf mit kritischer Würdigung der jüngsten Reformen, (*Public Transport in market systems - a normative concept with critical evaluation of recent reforms*), in: ZögU, No. 2, p. 167-188.

Link, H. (1998), The German railway market in transition - is there a need for regulation? Paper presented at the 8th Worl Conference on Transport Research, Antwerp.

Ludwig, D. (1995), Die Trassenpreise aus der Sicht eines regionalen Anbieters und Nachfragers (*track prices from the view of regional supplier and customer*), in: VDV (Hrsg.), Die Umsetzung der Regionalisierung in die Praxis, Schriftenreihe der DVWG, B 181, S. 67-69.

Ludwig, D. (1994), Die Regionalisierung des SPNV am Beispiel des Raumes Karlsruhe, in: VDV (Hrsg.), Die Anforderungen an einen regionalisierten ÖPNV, Schriftenreihe der DVWG, B 168, S. 141-150.

Montada, M. (1994), Neue Bedienungsformen für den regionalen Personen- und Güterverkehr, in: VDV (Hrsg.), Die Anforderungen an einen regionalisierten ÖPNV, Schriftenreihe der DVWG, B 168, S. 122-129.

Nash, C. (1985), Policies towards suburban rail services in Britain and the Federal Republic of Germany - a comparison, in: Transport Reviews, p. 269-282.

Regierungskommission Bundesbahn (1991), Bericht der Regierungskommission Bundesbahn (*Report of the governmental comission on the railways*).

Rodi, H. (1996), Effizienz im Schienenverkehr, Eine mikroökonomische Analyse unter besonderer Berücksichtigung der institutionellen Ausgestaltung des Trassenmarktes (*efficiency in rail transport - a microeconomic analysis with special reference to the institutional structure of the market for track access*), Göttingen.

Schneider, J. (1995), Die Privatisierung der Deutschen Bundes- und Reichsbahn: Institutioneller Rahmen - Wertkettenorientiertes Synergiekonzept - Analyse der Infrastrukturgesellschaft (*Privatization of the German Railways - institutional framework - value chain-oriented concept for synergies - analysis of the infratsructure company*), Wiesbaden.

Van de Velde, D.M. (1997), Entrepreneurship and tendering in local public transport services, paper presented at the 5th International Conference on Competition and Ownership in Land Passenger Transport, Leeds May 1997.

VDV (1996), Statistik '95, Köln.

VRR GmbH (1996), Verbundbericht 1995, Gelsenkirchen.

Wachinger, L.; Wittemann, M. (1996), Regionalisierung des ÖPNV - Der rechtliche Rahmen in Bund und Ländern nach der Bahnreform (*Regionalisation of Public Transport - the legal framework after rail reform*), Bielefeld.

Zeller, R.; Emmerich, K. (1997), RailService-Gesellschaften (*rail service companies*), in: Nahverkehrspraxis, No. 6, p. 15-19.

"Die Neuordnung der Deutschen Bahn ist sozialverträglich verlaufen" (*Restructuring of DB has been socially fair*), FAZ v. 2.8.97, S. 14.

"Kostendeckung für Schiene fraglich (*Cost Coverage for the Track is questionable*)", Handelsblatt of June 26th, 1997, p. 20.

Relevant Laws taken from Freise (1996):

AEG, Allgemeines Eisenbahngesetz (*general railway law*) from Dec. 27th, 1993.

BENeuGlG, Gesetz zur Zusammenführung und Neugliederung der Bundeseisenbahnen (*Law to merge and restructure the federal railways*) from Dec. 27th, 1993.

DBGrG, Gesetz über die Gründung einer Deutschen Bahn Aktiengesellschaft (*Law to found Deutsche Bahn AG*), from Dec. 27th, 1993.

PBefG, Personenbeförderungsgesetz (*Public Transport Law*), from Aug. 8th, 1990, last amended Dec. 27th, 1993.

RegG, Regionalisierungsgesetz (*Regionalisation Law*), from Dec. 27th, 1993.

Abbreviations

- bln. Billion
- DB Deutsche Bahn AG
- DEGV Deutsche Eisenbahn Gesellschaft Verkehrs GmbH
- DKB Dürener Kreisbahn
- DME Dortmund-Märkische-Eisenbahngesellschaft
- DSW Dortmunder Stadtwerke
- EBA Eisenbahnbundesamt
- HGK Hafen- und Güterverkehr Köln
- ITF Integraler Taktfahrplan (i.e. integral clockface timetable)
- mln. Million
- NE-Bahn Railway company not owned by the federal government
- NRW Nordrhein Westfalen
- RB 52 Tendered route in VRR
- SPNV Schienenpersonennahverkehr
- SWB Stadtwerke Bonn
- VRR Verkehrsverbund Rhein-Ruhr
- VRS Verkehrsverbund Rhein-Sieg
- ZRL Zweckverband SPNV Ruhr-Lippe

5 Switzerland

DIDIER VAN DE VELDE
Erasmus University Rotterdam

5.1 Introduction

Switzerland counts a large number of railway companies. These have co-operated for a long period of time and have established a system reputed for its co-ordination. Shared use of infrastructures (tracks and stations) exists for many years, as well as through-ticketing arrangements and integrated information systems.

Even if the Swiss railways do not yet know much competition, the features mentioned above make the study of the Swiss example interesting as it illustrates the co-ordination requirements in the presence of many railway companies.

Concerns about the efficiency of the Swiss passenger transport system have recently triggered a reform of the legal and regulatory framework (1996 reform). This has resulted in a total reorganisation of the subsidisation of regional passenger services (all transport modes). As far as the railways are concerned, it has also opened the door to competition *for* the track to some degree, even if little can be observed up till now.

Further reforms were adopted in 1998, concentrating on the (national) long-distance services and on the further introduction of some form of open-access, especially in freight transport. While the national passenger market is likely to remain regulated for the time being, this does not mean that competition is to be totally excluded.

This report on Switzerland will present the legal and regulatory framework and the considerations which led to the current situation. Two case studies will be described. The one illustrating the tendering of a line which was owned and operated by the Federal railways and the other illustrating the implementation of Cantonal legislation as a consequence of the regionalisation of the subsidisation of the regional railway services in the Canton of Bern.

5.2 Legal and regulatory framework

The current legal and regulatory framework for the Swiss railways is based on several laws. The main ones are:

- *Federal Railway Law*: This law (dating back to 1957 and subsequently modified) is applicable to railway construction and operation, and to their relationships with the other transport companies, the authorities and thirds.
- *Federal Law on Passenger Transport*: This law is applicable to the granting of concessions for passenger transport.
- *Federal Law on the Federal Railways (SBB)*[1]: This law organises the Federal Railways known under the name *SBB CFF FFS* and determines that an service agreement will be established to define their specific tasks.
- *Federal Law on Public Transport*: This law regulates the operations of the transport services. It is applicable to the transport of passengers, freight and luggage by public transport companies, but not to air transport and pipelines.
- *Cantonal legislation*: The Swiss Cantons can develop their own additional legislation on public transport on the basis of the rights and duties given to them by the federal constitution and federal laws.

These laws and regulations have been subject to important reforms in 1996 and 1998. This was the result of reforms which find their origin in the *Message on the revision of the Railway Law (compensations and financial aids for the regional traffic)* adopted by the Government on 17 December 1993 and the *Message on Railway Reform (ref. 96.090)* adopted by the Government on 13 November 1996. Based on these reforms, the following legal and regulatory framework has emerged.

[1] The *Federal Railway Law* should not be confused with the *Law on the Federal Railways*. The former being the general railway legislation while the latter is specific to SBB/CFF/FFS.

5.2.1 Current legal and regulatory framework

The main features of the current legal and regulatory framework will be summarised hereafter.[2]

Federal Railway Law

This law is applicable to railway construction and operation, and to the relationships of railway companies with other transport companies, authorities and thirds.

The law stipulates that a concession from the Confederation is necessary to build and operate a railway. The infrastructure concession given by this law gives a company the right to build and operate railway infrastructure.[3] The concessions are given for a maximum of 50 year and can be modified or renewed. When public interest justifies it, it is possible to terminate a concession before its normal expiry date, this against payment of a compensation.

An accounting separation between infrastructure[4] and the other activities of the companies is required. An organisational separation between infrastructure and other activities is also required but the Federal Office of Transport is allowed to free the narrow gauge railways and the small railway companies from this requirement.

A company can, without exclusivity, operate all services on its own infrastructure but several conditions (authorisation procedure) have to be fulfilled for a company to be granted access to the infrastructure of another company. The conditions are related to the personnel (qualification and respect of usual working conditions in the sector), organisational safety, rolling stock safety, insurance, solvability, etc. The authorisation is given for a maximum of 10 years and can be renewed.

A concessionary company has to grant non-discriminatory access to its network to all authorised companies. The law, however, stipulates that

[2] Further details can be found in Van de Velde (1998).

[3] For particular cases, such as railway infrastructure where open access is not feasible (cable cars, rack-railways, unusual gauge railways), the authority giving the concession is allowed to regulate both the infrastructure and the transport services part in one and the same concession.

[4] Switzerland counts: (i) *under infrastructure*: the tracks and all installations giving access to the railway network; (ii) *under operations*: the transport activities themselves (incl. traction and personnel on board of trains), marketing, sales, rolling stock and maintenance.

clockface timetabled passenger transport services have priority over other services and that connections within a co-ordinated transport chain may not be jeopardised.

Infrastructure operators and train service operators have to conclude agreements on track access and an access fee has to be paid respecting specific regulations on the calculation of these fees. The prices to be paid by the track user have to be clear and non-discriminatory (this is subject to an arbitration committee). The law determines that the fee should be at least equal to the marginal costs for an equivalent piece of modern infrastructure, as calculated by the Office. The fee has to take account of the various network related costs, the environmental costs of the vehicles used and demand. Operators of scheduled passenger transport also have to pay a share of their passenger revenues to the infrastructure operator, besides the marginal costs calculated by the Office. This share is to be determined by the authority that has issued the concession for these services.

All companies have to help the technical and practical realisation of connections between railways to ensure the easy transfer of passengers, rolling stock, etc. between the railways. When a common utilisation of the installations and equipment is not strictly necessary (as for ticket selling), the companies have contract freedom. In the other cases (e.g. usage of the same station), a non-discriminatory access charge has to be established according to the same principles as for track access.[5]

The law determines that the Confederation (or the Confederation and the Cantons jointly) have to compensate financially the railway companies for the deficits resulting from the services they have ordered. The Railway Law requires the company to have separate accounting at least for regional passenger transport and infrastructure as a condition to receive such payments and determines that the payments have to be determined beforehand on the basis of the provisional accounts of the companies concerned. The service proposals to be provided by the companies have to be based upon demand, an appropriate level of basic supply, regional policy issues (such as the development of underprivileged regions), land-use planning aims,

[5] According to Swiss practice, most private companies do not own the main stations where their services terminate, these stations are in most cases SBB stations and the services were considered to be SBB services as soon as SBB tracks were used (costs and revenues for that portion accrue to SBB). The companies were free to conclude different agreements (to be approved by the Department). In practice companies often agreed to co-operate in the production of the services such as to avoid payments (production by each company of a number of services on the tracks of the other company proportional to the track length used, and revenue sharing according to the tracks).

environmental aims and the needs of handicapped people. The Confederation, the Cantons and even the municipalities can, under specific rules and conditions, participate in the payments.

Ordinance on indemnities, loans and financial aids according to the railway law[6]

The *Ordinance on indemnities, loans and financial aids according to the railway law* (18 December 1995) further regulates the payment of indemnities paid for the deficit incurred on the transport services ordered by the Confederation or the Confederation together with the Cantons.

This ordinance gives the definition of what is regional (passenger and freight traffic and infrastructure predominantly used for regional transport) and defines a basic level of service to be provided.[7] The fares have to be broadly similar throughout the country for similar services. Rebates can be offered to the local population.

This ordinance also regulates the ordering procedure that has to be carried out every year (normal procedure at the beginning of each timetable period lasting two years, simplified procedure for the other years).

> 1. *The transport companies can exercise no right to ordered services.*
>
> 2. *The Confederation determines the budget for regional transport for the coming four years.* These means are transferred to the Cantons who are allowed to re-allocate them to other public transport services. The Cantons inform the companies on their wishes concerning the services and on the funds available and the Federal Office of Transport declares how much long-distance traffic it plans to order. Before starting the ordering procedure, SBB provides its plans for the long-distance traffic. The Confederation, the Cantons and the transport companies have to create an adequate organisation to co-ordinate the regional

[6] To elaborate ordinances the Federal Office for Transport (*Bundesamt für Verkehr* – BAV), as part of the Federal Ministry of Transport, usually creates working groups composed of concessionary transport companies, SBB and representants of BAV. The members of the working groups are selected on the basis of their expertise and not as representants of their companies. This approach is meant to gather the necessary expertise to find the best solution for all and to check the ideas developed by the ministry. The companies are welcome to make comments but have no right of objection, the government takes the final decision, after receiving the proposals made by BAV together with the possible comments by interested parties.

[7] Minimum hourly frequency when on average more than 500 persons are transported on the heaviest section of the route. A minimal level of service of 4 pairs per day is to be guaranteed if the weakest section of the route transports at least 32 persons per day on average.

supplies and their integration into the higher level networks and to discuss other problems linked to the ordering procedure. The Ordinance requires that permanent contacts be maintained here, besides the ordering procedure.

3. The Confederation or a Canton can invite a transport company to present an offer and several variants:[8] if the first offer is not satisfying, others can be asked. All transport companies also have the possibility to present an offer spontaneously. Some services can be subject to call-for-tenders when large changes influencing several routes are planned or when the offers by a specific company are deemed to be non-satisfying. Transport services can also be generally subject to call-for-tender when the Canton concerned so decides. A company is only allowed to refuse to make an offer when its infrastructure is open to other operators.

4. The offer has to include a presentation of the project, information on the fares system and level, a provisional accounting for the first timetable year, a provisional accounting for the medium term, including investment planning[9,10,11] and information on the working conditions for the personnel. The presentation of the project should include:

- For passenger traffic (and accompanied transport of motor vehicles): the supply of services (number of daily services, spreading during the day, stops served, seats offered), the quality of the services (guaranteed connections, means of transport used, additional services such as on-board staffing, safety services, handicapped transport, bicycle transport, catering services, sales and information) and the resulting production (total vehicle-km, service-km, gross-ton-km, hours of service).
- For freight traffic: the type, density and timing of the services.
- For infrastructure services: building norms, hours of operation, maximum capacity, foreseen use and main maintenance work.

5. The analysis of the offer: if an offer differs significantly from other offers in similar conditions, the ordering authority can request the Federal Office for Transport to proceed to a control. If the Office can not justify the differences,

[8] A request which would lead to a fundamental change in the operations has to be formulated at least three years before the start of the new service pattern.
[9] The Federal Office for Transport delivers the planned inflation and interest rates for these calculations.
[10] When an offer results from a call-for-tender, the companies do not have to indicate the reasons for the yearly changes in the accounts.
[11] If large changes to the long-distance traffic is planned, the regional transport operator will have to formulate its proposal (taking the new frequencies, connections, etc.) taking into account at least two years of the introduction of the new services.

after hearing the Cantons and companies concerned, the unit costs are reduced to those of similar companies.

6. *Agreement on the offer*: when the ordering authorities accept an offer, an agreement is established for one timetable year.[12]

7. *Transfer to a different company*: This can only be allowed, against the will of the incumbent, when the authority thinks to be able to realise long-term gains by doing so. The new operator is then obliged to take over the installations and rolling stock (and loans) of the incumbent for the services concerned for an amount equivalent to the accounting value, this if the existing company requires so and if the acquisition of these goods had been agreed by the authorities in the first place. When possible under the new operational regime, the new operator has to take over the existing personnel according to the usual working conditions. No new agreement can be concluded if the existing company declares to be able to maintain the existing supply without subsidy.

8. *Simplified procedure*: within a timetable period (two years), the operator has to transmit to the ordering authorities all information concerning the changes to be implemented at least one year before implementation. A new agreement can then be signed.

The transport companies receiving subsidies are required to provide the ordering authorities access to their accounting and statistical information. The ordinance contains detailed requirements concerning the accounting conventions to follow to be entitled to benefit from subsidisation. These include the following sectoral split in the accounting:

- infrastructure;
- long-distance passenger transport (incl. car-trains);
- regional passenger transport;
- local traffic;
- excursion traffic;
- accompanied motor-vehicle traffic;
- wagon-load traffic;
- combined traffic; and
- various.

All services that receive some form of subsidies will have to take an infrastructure fee into account. In regional normal gauge passenger traffic, an

[12] Changes in the international timetable can lead to renegotiations.

amount of 3,50 CHF/train-km has to be charged and an amount of 0,01 CHF/gross-ton-km has to be added.[13] For all new offers, lower amounts can be used if it can be shown that the corresponding infrastructure costs are lower than these amounts. In the other cases the Federal Office for Transport will determine the fee depending upon the market circumstances and after hearing the companies and Cantons concerned.

The Confederation is entitled to supply financial investment aid when investments can not be financed by the amortisation funds. The Canton is required to participate. Such aid is in principle limited to investments necessary for services ordered by authorities. The aid is given only if the company can prove that this will improve profitability, capacity, safety or handicapped-persons' requirements and if all other possibilities for rationalisation have already been implemented (such as mergers, groupings, etc.) Loans with conditional reimbursement are given for the infrastructure, reimbursable loans for the other sectors. The Confederation is also allowed to take participation in the capital of the company.

Law on passenger transport

Since March 1998, this law, which was until then only valid for road passenger transport, has become valid for all passenger transport, thus including rail passenger transport.

Regular passenger transport concessions give an exclusive right to scheduled transport passengers on a specific route. Such concessions are meant to give to the authorities an instrument to guarantee efficient public transport in the whole of Switzerland. The concessions are also meant to prevent existing non-profitable services, that have been ordered and subsidised by the authorities, to be cream-skimmed by competitors. Such cream-skimming is considered to be undesirable as it would lead to an increase in the need for subsidisation. It is thinkable that several concessions are given for the same route (e.g. regional passenger transport and long-distance passenger transport).

Concessions can be given for a maximum length of 25 years (based in general on the amortisation period of vehicles) and can be modified or renewed. The company requesting a concession will have to show that it owns the necessary concessions and authorisations to use the required infrastructure (road or rail). It will also have to show that it can do so

[13] These were based on averages.

adequately and economically and that existing services offered by other transport companies will not be influenced negatively seen from the point of view of society as a whole, or that an important new transport link for the region is created. The Department will have the possibility to terminate a concession (against appropriate compensation) if this is deemed to be in the public interest, e.g. to achieve the transport needs in a more adequate and economical way.

Law on the Federal Railways (SBB)[14] and Federal Arrest on the Refinancing of the Federal Railways

The old Federal Railway law dating back to 1944 has been replaced in 1998 by a new version re-creating the Federal Railway Company (*SBB CFF FFS*) as a *société anonyme de droit public.*

Every four years, the Federal Government defines the objectives of SBB jointly with SBB. These are fixed in an agreement, after hearing the Cantons, and submitted to Parliament. The Parliament then fixes a maximum budget available to SBB.

The *Federal Arrest on the Refinancing of the Federal Railways* (20 March 1998) removes a substantial part of the debt burden from SBB. The 1997 balance deficit (153 mln CHF) is amortised, the Confederation takes over the loans from the railway retirement fund (5 560 mln CHF). The long-term loans granted by the Confederation are converted into own capital (8 000 mln CHF) and the remaining loans (3 647 mln CHF) are converted into loans with variable interest rates. These loans reimbursable under conditions.

Federal Law and Ordinance on Public Transport

This law regulates the operation of transport services and also contains important prescriptions concerning fares. The law states clearly that the *direct service*[15] is of special importance and that additional regulations can be developed to organise it, especially if the companies do not organise it themselves in due time. In practice the ticketing system developed by SBB is used by most railway companies against the payment of specific fees; in

[14] See footnote 1.

[15] Possibility to buy a single transport ticket or pass even if the user has to use several transport companies.

return commissions are paid for all tickets sold. The *Ordinance on Public Transport* adds a number of additional obligations related to passenger rights.

Other relevant ordinances

The Ordinance on the timetables (1995), resulting from the Law on Public Transport, regulates the procedure to establish, publish and for early modifications to public transport timetables. The procedure counts the following steps:[16]

- *definition of long-distance traffic project by the companies*: this is presented to the Office, Customs and Cantons; the Cantons can request changes which are then included if this is economically feasible and respects the regional integration of services;
- *definition of a timetable pre-project*, followed by further discussions between the regional and long-distance transport companies to ensure all connections;
- *definition of a timetable project*, after this all other companies insure adequate connections and the project is presented to the Office, Customs and Cantons which can require further changes;
- *definition of the final timetable*; and
- *publication of the timetable* by the Office, through SBB.

The *Ordinance on the Cantonal shares in the indemnities and financial aids for the regional traffic (1995)* is based on the Railway Law and determines the share paid by each Canton. This share depends on a rather complex calculation which is based on the financial capacity and structural conditions (population density, length of private railway network) of the Canton.

The *Ordinance on the accounting of concessionary companies (1995)* specifies the requirements for the accounting of the concessionary companies. It includes the principles of the analytical accounting that has to be implemented by the companies.

[16] Only the main points are presented here.

Cantonal legislation

The additional Cantonal legislation varies from Canton to Canton. As no overview of this legislation is available an example will be given as a case study (see section 5.4).

5.2.2 Aims and considerations leading to the current situation

Two documents are determinant to understand the reasoning that has led to the current situation in terms of railway regulation. These are the report from the so-called *Groupe de Réflexion*, the *Message on the Revision of the Railway Law (regional traffic)* from 1993 that resulted in the new legislation by 1996 and the *Message on Railway Reform* from 1996 that resulted in new legislation in 1998. The main considerations included in these documents will be presented hereafter.

Report from the *Groupe de Réflexion*

As some of the objectives of the *mandates* for SBB, which had been adopted by the Swiss Parliament in 1982 and in 1987, had not been reached due to various reasons,[17] a larger growth of debts and interest charges than expected had resulted. In this context, the Department of Transport, Communications and Energy created on 20 March 1992 a *Groupe de Réflexion* on the future of the Federal Railways. This expert group was asked to propose to the Parliament broad guidelines and proposals for service agreements and also to suggest how the Federal Railways should be managed and operated in the future. The final report of the *Groupe de Réflexion,* produced in April 1993, contains the following recommendations (ref. 96-090, p. 7):

- create free market conditions in the transport sector;
- internalise external costs;

[17] Such as changes in the economic environment, political interventions in the company management.

- regroup management, marketing and financing of regional public transport by enlarging the field of action of the operators and by integrating the cantons and thirds to the financing of the public transport (while transferring adequate resources to them for this purpose);
- review the scale of supply, investment and timing of the Federal Rail2000 investment project in order to take into account the expected costs for the Confederation;
- transform the SBB into a 'lighter' federal company with more management freedoms and submit it to market-led incentives;
- separate clearly the accounting of operations and infrastructure;
- allow infrastructure access by thirds against appropriate payments for as much as this does not damage the transport system as a whole;
- transfer specific tasks to more specialised companies;
- review the supply of freight transport by rail and continue to subsidise only those relations where some public interest is involved;
- create broad guidelines to serve as a basis for the reform of the Federal Railways; and
- introduce a management contract as a political management tool towards the Federal Railways.

This report was accepted by the government on 1 June 1993 and the Department was subsequently charged with the initiation of the necessary reforms. The *Message on the revision of the Railway Law* was then published on 17 November 1993.

Message on the revision of the Railway Law (regional traffic) (1993)[18]

This law revision was to be implemented on 1 January 1996 and focused on the financial aids to regional traffic. It introduced the transparency of the financing of regional traffic and the principle of the *ordering of services* in regional traffic to replace the five previous legal basis that were used to finance the deficit of those services. Since this reform all companies (SBB, 'private' railways and Postal buses) are treated equally and the *ex post* financing of the deficits has been replaced by financial contributions that are determined in advance.

This reform was based, amongst others, on the report from the *Groupe de Réflexion*, on the opinions of the Cantons and on the request by the

[18] This section is largely based on the *Message on Railway Reform* (ref. 93.091).

Parliament to eliminate the inequalities resulting from the previous system (especially between Federal companies and the private railways).

Until 1996 the subsidies[19] for regional transport had five legal bases:

- *subsidies according to the Federal Railway Law*: According to the Federal Railway Law, these subsidies, which excluded local traffic and tourist routes,[20] could be paid as compensation for public service obligations (by the Confederation) or as financial aid (deficit coverage where the Canton participates according to specific apportionment rules, investment aids and federal aid for repairs due to natural forces).
- *equalisation of fares*: Considerations of regional policy has also led to the introduction of the fares equalisation scheme in 1959.[21] According to these, the Confederation compensated transport companies the difference between their 1959 fare scale and reduced fare scale based on lower SBB fares. While inflation had been taken into account in the meantime, it had not been possible to review fundamentally the system since 1959 to adapt it to new circumstances (such as innovations in the SBB fare system and the growing usage of fare integration in several regions).
- *federal subsidies to SBB*: these are, since 1982, agreed upon beforehand and paid according to specific performance agreements (1982 and 1987) between the Confederation and SBB. These agreements distinguish between a market-based sector (which is supposed to cover at least its operating costs and to contribute to the infrastructure costs),[22] a public service sector (670 mln CHF for regional traffic and 88 mln CHF for combined traffic in 1992) and infrastructure (since 1987, 1 215 mln CHF in 1992).

[19] The Swiss legislation makes a distinction between *indemnités* (compensations) and *aides financières* (financial aids), where both have to be linked to the realisation of some public purpose. They have therefore to be seen as a *price* for the realisation of a specific task and not as a support to a transport company. The word *subsidisation*, which we will use here, is therefore formally speaking not the right word.

[20] All services which serve settlements where people live the whole year are not considered to be tourist routes.

[21] This was essentially meant to reduce the relatively high fares of the private railways, bus companies and cable cars in the Alps, Jura and Tessin due to lower potential demand and higher costs.

[22] Since 1992 this contribution has not been feasible anymore, which is the reason why the Government considers the 1987 agreement to be a failure (ref. 93.091, p. 7).

- *deficit financing for Postal Buses*: The PTT Law determined that the PTT is an autonomous federal public company which benefits from a monopoly on postal services (up to 5 kg) and regular passenger transport. Up till the reform, the profits, mainly from telecommunication, were used to cross-subsidise the deficits of the other sectors, in particular the Postal Bus network, such that the Confederation did not have to pay compensations for those services.[23] The Government considered (ref. 93.091, p. 8) this situation as not acceptable anymore in the context of a further liberalisation of the European telecommunication market.
- *investment subsidies for regional transport*:

  - According to the Law on Public Transport, authorities (Confederation, Cantons and/or municipalities) have the possibility to agree with transport companies on the production of additional services or reduction of fares against payment of compensation when this is considered to be the only or most efficient way to reach some cultural, social, ecological, energy, economic or defence objective. This has resulted in considerable subsidisation for local transport services; this is not influenced by the 1993 reform proposals.
  - The investments of SBB were made with Federal funds, unless they were requested by thirds.[24] While it was considered desirable to involve the Cantons in the financing of specific regional infrastructure investments of SBB, the accounting mechanisms were not yet available and it was decided to limit the Cantonal involvement to operational subsidies.
  - The investments required for the Postal Buses were either financed by the PTT (vehicles) or co-financed with the municipalities (stops).
  - The investments of concessionary companies were divided into four categories with varying shares paid by the companies, the Confederation and the Cantons: (i) financing by own means or

[23] All routes existing before 1972 are functioning according to this system. The routes established since then are, partially, compensated by the Cantons (20 millions CHF in 1992), while the cross-subsidy within PTT amounts to 182 millions CHF in 1992.

[24] E.g. in the case of the investments needed to realise the regional train services around Zürich (S-Bahn) the Canton Zürich had to provide financial means.

third-party long-term capital,[25] (ii) technical improvement investments in the form of conditionally reimbursable subsidies when this improves the profitability or the safety of the operations,[26] (iii) aids for the adoption of an other mode of transport when this improves profitability while maintaining quality and (iv) aids for repairing damages caused by natural forces.

According to the revised law, the authorities now 'order' the transport services and under specific conditions tendering procedures can also be initiated. The solution chosen was a division in sectors (national passenger transport, regional passenger transport, local transport, excursion, piggy-back, car alp-crossings, infrastructure) as this was thought to be more flexible and oriented towards the future. The alternative, being a division between profitable services and non-profitable (public) services with special status for the infrastructure account, was thought to be less desirable.

The main aim of the reform was to achieve a greater transparency while allowing to choose the best offer. This was to be reached by the implementation of two main changes. On the one hand, the barriers created by the company-based and transport mode related financing (SBB, PTT, concessionary companies) which were seen to hamper the establishment of an attractive regional public transport supply had to be suppressed. This resulted for instance in the Cantons and municipalities preferring to require additional services from SBB and PTT as the deficit of those services would have to be paid by the Confederation, even though it would have been more efficient to require a local concessionary to modify its services.[27] It was expected that the new model would allow SBB to focus more on the national level, for which it was considered to have more feeling, than for the regional level. The concessionary companies would then possibly grow by becoming responsible for the whole of the regional transport (ref. 93.091, p. 19). On the other hand, *ex post* deficit compensation had to be

[25] Amortisation funds were usually not even sufficient to cover installations replacement and only touristic companies were still able to finance themselves by redeemable bonds.

[26] Contributions for vehicle purchasing have to be reimbursed by amortisation.

[27] Up till 1996 the Cantons were paying relatively more for the concessionary companies than for SBB and PTT. In order to introduce a similar treatment for all companies, the Confederation considered that it was necessary to reshuffle the financing without increasing the total share that had to be paid by the Cantons (between 5 and 50%). Therefore the reform led to a reduction of the share paid by the Cantons in return for a payment by the Cantons of the same share for *all* transport companies. This operation had therefore no influence on the total subsidisation given by the Canton to the regional public transport system, but it clarified and harmonised the subsidisation mechanism.

replaced by an *ex ante* determination of the subsidy budget in order to allow for more managerial freedom for the companies.

As a total harmonisation of the infrastructure accounting was deemed to be impossible in a first step, the harmonisation of the financing was to be limited to the subsidisation of the operations by this reform. This would require the private railways to create a separate infrastructure account. Also it would require from SBB to move away from the market/public service split that had been imposed on her by the 1982 and 1987 agreements and separate regional passenger transport from the rest. The Government considered that the success of the reform was dependent upon the implementation of an analytical accounting system at the concessionary companies; the law now requires this.[28] This regime allows to evaluate and compare the proposals of several companies.

There were fears that the new sectoral model would reduce the managerial dynamism of the transport companies as it gives the impression that the whole sector is subsidised. However, the Government considered (ref. 93.091, p. 11) that this disadvantage would be more than counterbalanced by providing clearly stated conditions (*ordering of services* by the authority, statement of the goals, etc.).

Provisions were made to compensate for the lack of direct competition in the sector. The Government created the possibility to reduce payments made to companies when these were deemed to behave in an uneconomical way. This is to be based on comparisons with similar companies using analytical accounting. The possibility is also given to require a different company to provide an offer for similar services (ref. 93.091, p. 38). It was also suggested that it might be desirable to transfer some routes from SBB or PTT to locally-run (or new) concessionary companies such as to improve the efficiency. Proposals by the *Groupe de Réflexion* already went in this direction by suggesting to transfer whole SBB-routes, or only regional passenger transport services to concessionary companies. The infrastructure and freight transport would remain at SBB as long as no further reform of SBB could be implemented. The Government considered it to be necessary to wait for the results of pilots-experiments before adopting a definitive solution in this respect (ref. 93.091, p. 31).

[28] Art. 50 of the revised Railway Law requires the company to have separate accounting at least for regional passenger transport and infrastructure as a condition to receive the subsidy.

Message on Railway Reform (1996)[29]

A further reform of the regulation of the Swiss railways has been adopted in 1998 on the basis of proposals included in the *Message on Railway Reform* (ref. 96.090) (13 November 1996).

Guiding principles

The reform to the Railway Law which was implemented in 1996 resulted from the *Message on the revision of the Railway Law* issued in 1993, itself partly inspired by the report from the *Groupe de Réflexion.* It was only a first reform step and concentrated on regional passenger traffic. This first step resulted in 'guiding principles' given by the Department in May 1994 for the further reform of the Federal railways which themselves formed the inspiration for the *Message on Railway Reform* issued in 1996, being a second step in the reform of the Swiss railways to be implemented in 1998. These 'guiding principles' were meant, amongst other, to delineate the legal and regulatory changes that had to be implemented when the new management contract with the Federal Railways was to be enforced. These principles, submitted to discussion by the Federal Government in May 1994 (i.e. before the implementation of the reform of the railway law) included: the objectives of the transport policy and the position of the companies in this context; the tasks and structure of SBB; the services to produce and the fares to adopt and the accounting system to adopt by SBB.

The political response to this focussed on the protection of the existing basic level of public transport service, while confirming the necessity of public financing. A systematic implementation of the principle of *ordering services* in public transport was asked for. The necessity of the financial 'cleaning' of SBB was recognised and a further orientation towards the client was welcomed. However, a lack of a more global strategy towards the whole of the public transport sector was identified. This forced the Department to broaden the content and scope of the proposals.

Reasons for further railway reform

This second message considered that the existing public transport structures did not correspond anymore to the needs for a modern public transport system, and that they resulted in a lack of efficiency in the production of

[29] This section is largely based on the *Message on Railway Reform* (ref. 96.090).

the transport services. The two main aims of the reform proposals were to improve the effectiveness of railways (both the SBB and the other railway companies) by improving their competitiveness and to improve the cost-benefit ratio of the intervention by the authorities. Additional aims were formulated, such as adapting public transport, in particular the railways, to the new environment; introducing a clearer separation between public policy and company management; increasing the performances of public transport by increasing its effectiveness, client-mindedness and profitability; introducing some elements of competition into the railways; solving the debt problem of the SBB and improving the transparency of the processes of authority intervention through new ways of financing public transport.

The message considered that the subsidisation of public transport will remain necessary but that to control the level of expenses the principle of the *ordering* of services by the authorities had to be generalised. Therefore the authorities would have to indicate what public transport supply they require and how much they are prepared to pay for it. The control by Parliament would be exerted by the discussion and approval of four-year service agreements with SBB, fixing the available budget. Under this regime the only services to be produced would be those (profitable) that respond to market demand and those (unprofitable) that have been ordered by the various authorities.

The message stressed that the railway reform is only one part of a co-ordinated transport policy.[30] It also stated that the measures suggested are to be seen as a first step in a 'permanent reform' process (ref. 96.090, p. 62). The Government considered that a dynamic and pragmatic approach, allowing to learn from the experiences of the reforms carried out so far in order to re-direct the stream and timing of further reforms, is the only effective way to go. In that respect, the regionalisation implemented by the 1996 law and following ordinances can be seen as broadly similar in its principles with the further reform suggested by the 1996 Message, this latter reform has therefore little or no additional influence on regional railway traffic.

The response to the proposals were broadly speaking favourable to the orientations chosen (ref. 96.090, p. 14). Except for divergences of opinion concerning the speed and scope of the reforms, there seemed to be a broad consensus on the necessity to achieve more efficiency and competitiveness under a process of 'permanent reform'. It is interesting to note that both

[30] New financing of the rest of public transport, a new proportional lorry taxation, the realisation of the new Alps transit corridors and further negotiation with the EU.

SBB and the other operators (e.g. the private railways) were favourable to the reform and to the abolition of the inequalities that still exist between them.

Separation of infrastructure and operations and introduction of open access

With the introduction of open access, Switzerland aims at giving a clear and non-discriminatory base to the access of operators to the infrastructure of the various companies. The general aim being to improve the competitiveness, cost-effectiveness and market share of the railways by introducing incentives which reward the most efficient companies. Switzerland considers that it is more or less obliged to implement the 91/440 EU directive on open access and considers the non-uniform way in which its neighbouring EU countries have implemented the directive to be an advantage. This situation is considered to give Switzerland some leeway in the exact way to implement the directive (ref. 96.090, p. 16). It will also only allow access of foreign companies if a specific agreement exists between Switzerland and that country.

The accounting separation between infrastructure and operations is seen as an essential condition for the access of thirds to the network. Until 1998, according to the Railway Law, the *concession* included both the building and the operation of railways, with the principle that the vertically integrated company was given an exclusive right to operate services on its own infrastructure. All exceptions to these were voluntary and regulated by contract. This exclusivity was considered to be extinct as the principle of *ordering of services* had been introduced in 1996 by the legislator for regional traffic, whereby other operators could in principle get the right to operate on existing infrastructures, and as open access further infringes upon exclusivity rights. Therefore it was considered necessary to adapt the *concession* system towards a split between a *concession* for the infrastructure (given according to the Federal Railway Law) and a *concession* for the operation of services (given according to the Federal Law on Passenger Transport). The concessions thus continue to exist under the open access regime, except for freight transport and non-regular passenger transport which are completely liberalised. This means that the regulations pertaining to open access are only valid for regional and for long-distance passenger rail transport when a route is transferred to another company either by *ordering of service* or by *concession*.

Non-discriminatory principles (technical and economic conditions, but also booking time) have to be developed for the new open access system to work properly. As Switzerland attaches much importance to the supply of integrated and harmonised regional and long-distance passenger rail services (number of trains, stops, travelling times, connections, etc.), priority is given to these integrated services in the utilisation of the network. Cream-skimming, such as the supply by thirds of new profitable trains at peak hours only, is explicitly rejected. Some wagon-load trains are likewise considered to have this priority. In the message detailed proposals were made concerning the priorities in track access but these were subsequently amended in Parliament. It is now stated that clockface traffic must have priority on other traffics and that connections between services forming a public transport chain may not be jeopardised. The infrastructure operator is the one to decide in principle on track allocation (co-ordination of the slots and the optimal utilisation of the network) but an independent committee is charged with checking that no discrimination takes place and that the priority order is followed. The concessioned train operator is responsible for the timetabling procedure.

Infrastructure access charges

The aims suggested in the Message for the track access charges are to charge a part of the infrastructure costs, to influence demand in order to reach an optimal utilisation of the network, to encourage an environmentally friendly behaviour and to create efficiency incentives for the operators of infrastructure and train services. An additional aim is to establish a system that is as simple, transparent and market-based as possible. This requires non-discrimination and an arbitration committee to control this. Three systems were suggested in the report on railway reform (ref. 96.090, p. 21):

- *cost-based system*: The advantage of this system was considered to be that subsidies are required for the transport services only; which would currently mean that all services would have to be subsidised. The disadvantage of this system was considered to be that it leads to widely different outcomes, dependent on the cost-allocation method;
- *demand-based system*: The total infrastructure costs would not be covered by this system where the track access charge would be determined by demand and competition (fees would then vary according to the track and to the time of the day). This would allow the rail to remain competitive compared to the road but it would require subsidisation of both the services and the infrastructure; and

- *mixed system*: This third system was recommended by the report in order to take the advantages and inconveniences of the two first systems into account. It is demand-based as it aims at reaching a payment which is as high as possible for the most profitable traffics. The minimum price should thus cover at least the short-term average marginal infrastructure costs (i.e. the direct costs resulting from an additional train: energy, share of the maintenance costs, costs of planning and management of the capacity).

The model chosen is based upon the principle that the capacity of each service operator to pay has to be exploited and that the marginal costs have, at least, to be covered. As marginal costs vary widely from route to route, there would be a danger that the most unattractive route where less replacement investments are carried out would generate the highest marginal costs. This situation is deemed to be undesirable (ref. 96.090, p. 45) and that is why the Federal Office of Transport determines standard marginal costs for all routes on the basis of modern costs.

For passenger services resulting from a *concession* the authority giving the concession has to determine the share of the passenger revenues that will have to be transferred to the infrastructure operator. The reason for this choice is the lack of competitive pressure on these services. The additional payment, which is meant to cover part of fixed costs of the infrastructure operator, should give him an incentive to maximise the number of passengers using his infrastructure.

Financing of public transport

The various sources of financing existing in the present regime were considered to lack transparency and to lead to varying degrees of financial burdens.

As far as SBB is concerned, a first step in the harmonisation of the rules for the financing of investments had to be accomplished by 1 January 1997 and led to the following new financing methods:

- reimbursable loans with normal interest rate for rolling stock, garages and other profitable investments which are not necessary for the operations (such as shopping malls);
- loans with varying interest rate levels and varying reimbursement conditions (according to the financial result of the railway) for the

pieces of infrastructure which are necessary for the operations (such as tracks, platforms, safety installations, stations, etc.);
- loans *à fonds perdu* (i.e. subsidies) for keeping the existing infrastructure at the level of the amortisation funds; and
- special financing for the large projects (such as the new Alps crossing and Rail2000).

Further steps to harmonise the financing of SBB and the private railways have not yet been finalised but have to be discussed with the Cantons within 3 years, according to a motion in Parliament.

Further reform of SBB

Until 1998, SBB was submitted to a regime of 'mandates' established to define their specific tasks. Such a mandate has been determined by Federal Arrest for a period staring in 1982 and a second one starting in 1987 (determined in 1986). The *general mandate* of 1987 determined that the Federal Railways had to adapt supply and investments to market needs, balance their accounts according to the principles of a sound economy (within the limits of the existing regulations) and supply *public services* inasmuch as the mandate or other Federal arrest requires them to do so and that an indemnity is paid. If the Cantons, municipalities or thirds required additional services, they had to provide these according to a fair indemnity. The services considered as *public service* were regional passenger transport and piggy-back services. By contrast the services falling under *market economy* were passenger transport on long-distances (and their luggage), wagon-load freight transport and container transport. The Confederation paid the deficit on the infrastructure (interest, amortisation and maintenance) but the Arrest determined that the Government decides for a three-year period how much the Federal Railways had to participate in the covering of infrastructure costs.

The status of SBB until 1998 (no *personnalité juridique*) was considered to be badly adapted to the current requirements. Two alternatives were considered: *établissement de droit public doté de la personnalité juridique* and *société anonyme de droit public*. The Government marked its preference for the second form as it allows, in the long run to associate other shareholders to the capital of the company (Cantons, municipalities and, possibly, private shareholders). Furthermore this company form, being more akin to that of the private and foreign railways is considered to contribute to the equality of treatment between companies. The railway reform adopted in 1998, and re-creating SBB, aims at giving a clear task division between the Confederation and SBB, the Confederation being responsible for the policy and financial objectives, SBB being responsible for the company management. SBB and the Confederation will therefore fix the aims of SBB every four years and this will form an agreement to be submitted to the Parliament. This also requires reinforcing the Board of SBB, which will be responsible for strategic management, in analogy with the law on commercial companies. Also the Government considers that the interests of the Confederation, as owner, will have to be better represented on the Board. In short, the management instruments in the hands of the Confederation should become mainly strategic:

- maximum budget (to be decided in Parliament);
- agreement on the aims and services (every four year, to be established by the Government and agreed in Parliament); and
- election of the members of the Board by the Government (incl. modification to the composition of the Board).

A new agreement between SBB and the Confederation for the period 1999-2002 has to be presented in Parliament in 1998 and will include the medium term aims for the company, the size of the service supply in the various sectors, the infrastructure development and the financial consequences. It is expected (ref. 96.090, p. 33) that the agreement will give to SBB the aim to produce market-based infrastructure and transport services. Non-profitable services will have to be ordered by authorities that will have to pay a financial compensation for these services. As the minimisation of the burden for the public purse should be taken as an objective both co-operation and competition with other transport companies (even outside the railway field, e.g. in order to improve the utilisation of infrastructure) should be initiated. In terms of passenger transport, the agreement is expected to give strategic orientations, to order the production of specific services, to give additional objectives in terms of service and to delineate the principles of the fares policy.

Main external changes that influence directly the competitiveness of the railways would lead to a revision of the agreement (e.g. major changes in the road freight policy). Other circumstances in which the agreement would be revised would be if the Parliament decides to reduce the level of expenses suggested in which case the Government would be charged with a re-negotiation of the agreement with SBB. Also if the (compulsory) reporting from SBB to the Department on the achievement of the aims shows the impossibility to remain under the agreed level of expense then the Government might ask the Parliament to amend this level.

The civil servants status of the personnel will remain valid for the personnel of SBB after the reform. However, the new law on the personnel of the Confederation will allow an autonomous status for the personnel of the federal companies (*régies*). This regime will be applicable to SBB after the year 2000 and will provide for more flexibility in terms of hiring and firing of personnel, payments, litigation, etc. It will become possible to conclude own agreements on working conditions (*conventions collectives de travail*). The retirement funds of the railwaymen may be merged in due course, or remain independent. Several technical problems have prevented the realisation of this merger up till now and further action is considered to be needed with as aim to achieve equality of treatment between SBB and the private railways.

The report on the railway reform mentions that the long-term obligations of SBB are currently four times as high as the own capital such that SBB is currently neither in a position to pay interests nor to reimburse infrastructure investments. The interest charges represented in 1996 about 10% of the total expenses of SBB. Therefore both SBB and the Government think that it is necessary to reduce the SBB debts. The Government has therefore decided to amortise the cumulated deficit up till the end of 1996. The 1997 deficit will be taken care of in the context of the railway reform. For the most, former infrastructure loans will be converted into own capital and loans with varying level of interest.

SBB itself is currently reforming the company aiming at reinforcing the capacity of action by implementing new structure closer to market requirements and simplifying the decision processes. The general aim being to give stronger incentives to all parts of the company. The reform should be ready by 1998. Besides the 'General Direction', the company will be composed of two main sectors, each with its own accounting and each composed of several units. The 'Transport sector' will include passenger transport, freight transport, real estate, traction, rolling Stock, Rail2000 and supply co-ordination. The 'Infrastructure sector' will include infrastructure management (planning, capacity utilisation, global timetable) and operations,[31] building, safety, materials and purchasing, traction energy and AlpTransit. SBB has also reorganised its passenger network into six regions since the introduction of the *ordering of services* in regional passen-

[31] Infrastructure management and its operations are now organised into three regional units.

ger transport. Each one has a regional representative charged with the contacts with the local authorities.

It is not excluded that a formal splitting of SBB into an infrastructure company and a transport service company (possibly under a holding company) will be carried out in the future. But for the time being the following reasons have led to the reform of SBB as a single company with accounting and organisational separation (ref. 96.090, p. 62):

- seen from the point of view of the transport company, the splitting in two companies would result in a loss of synergy because of the high level of utilisation of capacity in Switzerland and the narrow collaboration between the infrastructure and transport sectors;
- the accounting separation already constitutes a major step forward; and
- it will remain possible, at a later date, to split company while learning from the experience of the accounting and organisational separation.

The relationships between SBB and the private railways have developed in the course of history. They are essentially based on co-operation while the railway reform will lead to more competition. It is therefore necessary to guarantee the equality of treatment between the various companies involved. Up till now, SBB has also played a major role as general manager of the whole railway system with or without payment (determination of general fares, ticketing and apportionment system, etc.) The Government therefore suggests that some of these general functions might have to be transferred to new forms of co-operation in order to have a better complementarity in the new regime between competition and co-operation. The revision of the relationship between SBB and the private railways will be carried step by step, beginning with the most urgent points, such as the status of common stations. Further talks with SBB and the private railways should lead to further steps.

It is expected that SBB will keep its leadership and responsibilities in long-distance passenger transport, even after the reform, with its own network planning leading to a co-ordinated transport system at the national level. The SBB will therefore be expected to listen to the specific needs of the various regions in terms of integration of the regional traffic in the national system. SBB will be required to provide a clockface (hourly or two-hourly) timetable on the main lines and to realise the first phase of the Rail2000 plan in the new agreement (*Impulsion 1997*). It is expected that

SBB keeps its market share in international transport, even under the development of competition.

5.3 Authorities and railways in Switzerland

5.3.1 Authorities

The Department of Transport, Communications and Energy is the federal authority in terms of transport for Switzerland. Its action concerning public transport (all modes) takes place through a specific section of the Department called the 'Federal Office for Transport'(*Bundesamt für Verkehr*). From the analysis of the legislation and regulation presented earlier in this report, it can be observed that in many instances the Federal Office for Transport has a function of 'regulator' of the public transport market. It should however be noted that this function is not formalised by an independence status as that the British industry regulators. The links between the Department and the Office are therefore quite direct.

As federal country, Switzerland has own legislation in each of the Cantons. This is also the case for public transport where the Cantons have the right to establish their own additional legislation within, however, the framework given by the federal legislations and regulations. It is not possible to give here the full overview of the cantonal legislation and regulation in terms of public transport as such overview does not exist. The case study on the Canton of Bern (see chapter 5.4) gives an example of the type of legislation that can exist at the cantonal level.

5.3.2 Operators

Switzerland counts 56 so-called 'private' railway companies besides the Federal Railways (SBB). Besides this 180 bus companies, 16 regional transport companies and 280 mountain railways and cable-cars are licensed for regular passenger transport.

SBB – Swiss Federal Railways

Much of what has been presented in the chapter on the planned reform of the railways concerns the reorganisation of SBB (Swiss Federal Railways) and the specific law on the Federal railways. That information will not be repeated here. Table 5.1 provides some general statistical information on the network length, the personnel and the performances of SBB in terms of train-km and passenger-km.

The regionalisation of the control on the regional railway lines has led SBB to restructure its passenger transport division into 6 regional divisions on 1 January 1996. Each division is responsible for the regional passenger transport in its region. SBB gives the following missions to its regional divisions:

- function as a 'hinge' between SBB and the Cantons;
- exert the leading function of SBB in terms of public transport and confirm this function under competitive conditions;
- take care of the total 'system' (connections with long-distance traffic); and
- reach synergies with regional partners (total public transport system).

The regional passenger divisions of SBB are thus supposed to plan the regional passenger transport supply and establish a regional marketing of those services, they are entitled to negotiate the supply with the relevant Cantons and play a role of general entrepreneur for their services towards the rest of SBB, this means that they order the production of relevant services at the various SBB departments, control their realisation according to the requested specifications and take the necessary measures to ensure the realisation of the standards established. If needed they establish alliances with other regional transport companies.

Private railways

The 56 Swiss 'private' railways are only private in name and in company form. Both the normal and narrow gauge private railways have in general a minority participation from the private sector (around 10% on average with however a wide variance between 0% up till about 50%). This means that the public sector has the majority of the votes at the general assembly of these companies. It is to be noted that the Federal, Cantonal and municipal authorities are usually simultaneously shareholders of most of these companies. Their relative shares in the capital vary widely from company to company such that no typical picture can be given. The exceptions to this picture are the cable cars where the ownership is in most cases private (up to 100%), but here too, participation from the municipalities is current. General statistics on the inputs and outputs of the private railways can be found in Table 5.1.

Table 5.1 General statistics on the Swiss railways (1975-1996)

	1975	1980	1985	1990	1995	1996
Passenger train-km (millions)						
• *SBB*	-	66.9	80.1	94.7	90.4	89.8
• *Private railways*	-	31.9	34.8	40.2	42.5	-
Passenger-km (millions)						
• *SBB*	-	8 680	8 793	11 001	11 711	11 662
• *Private railways*	-	1 281	1 373	1 673	*(1994) 1 751*	-
Modal share (%)	-	12.5	-	13.2	-	-
Network length (km)						
• *SBB*	2 933	2 943	2 986	2 998	2 999	2 989
• *Private railways*	2 043	2 039	2 031	2 032	2 031	-
Personnel (incl. freight)						
• *SBB*	40 867	38 367	37 109	37 694	33 529	32 581
• *Private railways*	8 214	7 916	8 117	8 443	*(1994) 8 207*	-
SBB[1]						
Revenues (mln CHF)						
• *Passenger traffic*	-	-	1 191	1 423	1 578	1 575
• *Freight traffic*	-	-	1 179	1 286	1 033	933
• *Compensations (subsidy)*	-	-	604	592	818	816
Costs (mln CHF)	-	-	4 151	5 364	6 740	7 060
Federal infra. subsidy	-	-	0	1 053	1 450	1 497
Result (after subsidies)	-	-	-281	3	-496	-293
Punctuality (%)[2]	-	-	90	92	95	92

Notes: [1] For simplification, not all data on costs and revenues are presented here.
[2] Defined as "less than 5 minutes of delay (4 minutes since 1996) at 9 main stations in the country".

Source: SBB, BFS, LITRA.

5.3.3 General statistics

Table 5.2 gives an historical perspective of the modal shares in passenger transport. It can be observed that public transport globally has maintained a relatively high modal share of 18% (in terms of passenger-km). This should of course be interpreted with care as bicycling, e.g., represents a rather low modal share in Switzerland. It is also interesting to note that the mobility by public transport has more than doubled since the 1950s.

Table 5.2 Switzerland – Transport Statistics 1996

Year	Public Transport			Private transport	Other	Total
	Rail*	Bus	Total			
			Passengers (millions)			
1950	593	130	723	410	8	1 141
1960	650	279	929	1 237	12	2 178
1970	669	468	1 137	3 412	16	4 565
1980	666	555	1 221	4 992	21	6 234
1990	834	766	1 600	5 927	29	7 556
*1995***	924	770	1 694	5 940	32	7 666
			Passengers (Modal shares)			
1950	52,0%	11,4%	63,4%	35,9%	0,7%	100,0%
1960	29,8%	12,8%	42,7%	56,8%	0,6%	100,0%
1970	14,7%	10,3%	24,9%	74,7%	0,4%	100,0%
1980	10,7%	8,9%	19,6%	80,1%	0,3%	100,0%
1990	11,0%	10,1%	21,2%	78,4%	0,4%	100,0%
*1995***	12,1%	10,0%	22,1%	77,5%	0,4%	100,0%
			Passengers –km (millions)			
1950	7 703	550	8 253	6 400	145	14 798
1960	9 156	874	10 030	18 590	366	28 986
1970	10 625	1 885	12 510	45 882	904	59 296
1980	11 290	2 486	13 776	67 041	1 365	82 182
1990	14 356	3 318	17 674	78 579	2 010	98 263
*1995***	14 700	3 364	18 064	80 180	2 297	100 541
			Passengers –km (Modal shares)			
1950	52,1%	3,7%	55,8%	43,2%	1,0%	100,0%
1960	31,6%	3,0%	34,6%	64,1%	1,3%	100,0%
1970	17,9%	3,2%	21,1%	77,4%	1,5%	100,0%
1980	13,7%	3,0%	16,8%	81,6%	1,7%	100,0%
1990	14,6%	3,4%	18,0%	80,0%	2,0%	100,0%
*1995***	14,6%	3,3%	18,0%	79,7%	2,3%	100,0%

Notes: *Trains, trams & cable-cars
** Partially provisional

Source: LITRA (1996).

As can be seen in Table 5.3, the price index of rail fares follows broadly the consumption price index, whereas the petrol price has been submitted to much lower price increases.

Table 5.3 Selected Swiss Price Indexes

	1977	1980	1990	1995
Train fares*	100,0	102,6	141,1	192,6
Consumption prices	100,0	108,6	148,6	173,5
Petrol price**	100,0	121,1	107,4	116,4

Notes: *Increase in 1995 due to the introduction of VAT
**Until 1977 normal, from 1978 unleaded, from March 1993 all types

Source: LITRA (1996).

Due to the many authorities involved in various ways in public transport subsidisation, indemnities and aids, it is not simple to give a total overview of public transport subsidisation in Switzerland. Table 5.4 makes an approximation of the subsidisation given by the Cantons and the Confederation and level of passenger revenues for the current situation. Municipal subsidies are not included.

Table 5.4 Estimated revenues and subsidisation by Confederation and Cantons for 1996

(millions CHF)		Revenues	Compensations
Confederation	Long-distance	1 000	1 500
Confederation + Cantons	Regional transport	1 200	1 200 + 400
Cantons	Local transport	700	600
(Cantons)	Excursions	900	10

Source: Personal communication with BAV.

5.4 Case study: public transport legislation in the Canton of Bern

The first railway reform, enlarging the powers of the Canton on railway services has changed the way in which the Canton can co-ordinate the supply of public transport services by road and rail. The implementation of this reform into the Cantonal public transport legislation and regulations will form the focus of this case study, as an illustration of the consequences of the national reform at the Cantonal level.

5.4.1 Implementation of the regionalisation in the Canton of Bern[32]

The transport policy of the Canton of Bern (1990/94) aimed at expanding public transport and reduce the usage of private cars. Two measures were initiated to this effect: the introduction of the Bernese S-Bahn[33] and the rebuilding of Bern Central Station to function as central transit point in the region. Summarising the aims of both Confederation and Canton, the main objectives for the S-Bahn concept were to reduce the difference in attraction between private car and public transport by improving supply, timetables, services and comfort; to increase public transport usage in order reduce the effects of private car use; and to increase operational performances of the transport modes by co-ordinating traffic planning.

The development of this process is influenced by the implementation of the 'regionalisation' as the Canton gets more comprehensive powers on the public transport system. The Confederation and the Cantons now order together the public transport services, pay the desired levels of regional public transport,[34] agreements are made concerning the minimum level of services to be provided and subsidies are now paid *ex ante*. To implement this system the transport companies have to introduce substantial changes to their accounting information in order to be able to answer detailed questions by the Cantons who become active and well-informed authorities.

The Canton of Bern has developed its own Public Transport Law to implement in the Canton the regionalisation decided at the Federal level. The main features of this legislation will be presented hereafter.

[32] Most of the description of this implementation is based on documents established by the Bernese Office for Public Transport (1996).

[33] The name is copied from the German *S-Bahn* railway network which provide urban/regional services according to fixed patterns (numbered lines) and frequencies.

[34] The Cantons used to order only those services offered by private transport operators, while the Confederation took care of the services offered by the Federal companies.

New Cantonal legislation

The new Cantonal Law on Public Transport in the Canton of Bern (16 September 1993), aims (Art. 1) at guaranteeing a satisfying level of public transport supply, taking into account the general economic interest and the social policy, while aiming at the highest possible efficiency. Additional aims are the reduction of pollution and an ordered land usage.

The means to these aims are the periodic definition of a Cantonal transport policy (Art. 2), the subsidisation of (or loans to) transport companies (both infrastructure and operations), measures to allow the Canton to influence the management of transport companies, the creation of fares associations, etc. Art. 3 of the Cantonal law gives to the Canton the right to determine the principles of public transport supply (i.e. a public transport plan), including levels of service, fares, minimum passenger numbers to supply services and minimum level of cost coverage. Since 1 January 1996, the law prescribes the approval by the Cantonal Parliament of this medium term plan for public transport supply which has to be founded on a knowledge of the wishes of the users and on an appraisal of the financial consequences of this supply.

The new Cantonal law on public transport has created 'Regional Transport Conferences – RTCs' charged with the planning of public transport (art. 16). Six RTCs were created and had to organise themselves (5 to 9 members) based on the representation of the municipalities they cover. For 1997-2001, these RTCs are charged to establish regional public transport plans (which form the basis for the medium term supply planning by the Canton), to co-operate in the investment planning by the Canton, to develop and support the creation of tariff associations (*Tarifverbünde*), to prepare the definition of additional regional transport services requested by municipalities in the RTC, to co-ordinate individual and public transport in the region and to participate in the implementation of the transport plan (see further for more details on the public transport plan).

The Cantonal government then decides, within the limits of the framework agreed by the Cantonal parliament, and after hearing the RTCs, on the realisation of the supply of public transport services. The Canton is then entitled to establish service contracts with the transport companies to realise the plan and specific compensations can be paid. The Canton can also pay specific investments (such as new vehicles, safety improvements at road crossings and environmental measures). The Canton (art. 7) can only grant subsidies when the operations are efficient and can even request from the companies the disclosure of specific line accounts to check the profitability of the services. The municipalities in the Canton have to pay 1/3 of the investment grants and operational subsidies given by the Canton to the operators.[35] The municipalities of the Canton are entitled to establish additional service contracts if they also cover the additional financial needs of those services.

The Cantonal government (art. 13) has to report regularly to the Cantonal parliament on the evolution of supply and demand in public transport (including the investments). The planned modifications to the supply for the coming timetable periods have to be joined and links have to be made with the evolution of private transport and land-use. On the basis of this report, the Cantonal parliament then agrees (art. 14) on the supply of public transport services and on the financial means necessary for its realisation (investments and operations).

The Cantonal government is also entitled to choose the representatives of the Canton in the transport companies in which it detains shares. The Canton also has the right to conclude contracts with the transport companies to force them to create tariff associations, the Canton will then compensate the losses and additional costs.

Cantonal public transport plan

The Canton adopted in November 1996 the public transport plan for 1997-2001. The principles adopted in the plan are the following:

- guarantee in the whole Canton a minimum level of service (in depopulated area guarantee a minimum mobility);
- individual and public transport are to be complementary in rural areas and regional centres, public transport is the main mode of transport in the agglomerations;
- supply and demand have to correspond, a 'supply directive' will be issued to this effect;
- regular clockface timetables should be realised, with good connections and an efficient usage of the vehicles;
- services have to be co-ordinated with land-use planning, environment protection and road planning; and
- transport policy has to aim at an improvement of the level of cost coverage of both individual and public transport.

[35] Municipalities and Cantons have taxation powers in Switzerland.

The plan further determines the framework within which the supply of public transport services will have to fit. It determines the public transport network by indicating the settlements that have to be linked, it determines four categories of level of supply and mode (rail or bus) used to classify each line to be served and it determines the principles for the fares. The plan counts six regional maps indicating the level of supply to be provided on the various lines, as decided by the RTCs under a number of conditions, e.g. a zero growth of subsidy requirements (in real term).

Detailed supply requirements

In fulfilment of the public transport plan, the Cantonal government issued an *Ordinance on the Supply of Public Transport Services* (10 September 1997). This ordinance is meant to concretise the public transport plan, to create the framework within which the contracts with the transport companies (all modes) will be established and to determine the minimum level of usage and cost coverage allowed to supply services.[36]

The ordinance establishes principles for the level of service that has to be realised. This includes requirements concerning the settlements to be served (depending on the population level norms), distances to public transport stops, levels of supply (e.g. frequencies and mode), hours of operation, service integration requirements, usage of clockface timetables, avoidance of excessive interchanges, environmental requirements, service provision (e.g. on-board, catering, information, puntuality), etc.

The Cantonal administration will then establish yearly service contracts with the transport companies, following the procedures established in the Federal *Ordinance on the Indemnities, Loans and Financial Aids according to the Railway Law*, by negotiating with the transport companies.

The transport companies have to provide the services as established by the transport plan in such a way as to reach the aims of occupancy and cost coverage indicated in Table 5.5. The transport companies have, during the ordering procedure, to suggest measures to reach those aims if these are not yet achieved. The Cantonal administration discusses the proposals with the RTCs and municipalities concerned and can make other suggestions. If the minimum levels stated in the table are not reached, a detailed analysis on

[36] The supply of fast trains services (national and international long distance services) fall under the national public transport system and are not concerned by the action of the Canton at this level.

the usefulness of the service has to be carried out. If the service has to be maintained, the transport companies have to suggest ways to reach the minimum levels (changes in the lines, vehicles and operational modes are permitted). After further discussions, the service can still be kept if it fulfils some specific criteria stated in the Federal Ordinance. Services are still supplied for one year when deemed not useful. Alternative forms of services can be introduced if more efficient (call-a-ride, etc.) Additional services not in the transport plan can also be supplied when they are compatible with the aims of the transport plan and detailed service requirements and do not compete with existing services.

Table 5.5 Service passenger occupancy: aims and requirements

	Passenger occupancy per mode										Cost coverage	
	Small bus		Midi- and std. bus		Articulated bus		Tram, etc.		Regional train			
Level of supply	Aim	Min.	Aim	Min.	Aim	Min.	Aim	Min.	Aim	Min.	Aim	Min.
1 (4-15 pairs per day)	3	2	6	4	8	5	20	12	25	15	35%	20%
2 (16-25 pairs per day)	5	3	10	6	15	9	25	15	35	20	40%	20%
3 (26-39 pairs per day)	6	4	13	8	20	12	30	20	50	30	45%	25%
4 (40+ pairs per day)	8	5	16	10	25	15	40	25	60	40	50%	30%

Note: Occupancy measured as average number of passengers per service on the heaviest point of the line.

Service requests

The Canton has for the first time issued service requests to the transport companies for the timetable period 1997/98. The procedure determined in the Federal law was used and the proposals by the transport companies had to include: costs (personnel, amortisation, financial costs, other costs), revenues (transport and others), estimated passenger numbers and passenger-km per year, vehicle-km supplied, fares systems and levels, selling systems (including opening hours), working conditions for the personnel and vehicles that will be used. The following calendar was been established:

- 11 June 1997: publication of the request for proposals;
- 8 August 1997: submission of proposals by the transport companies;
- July to October 1997: negotiations on the proposals;

- July to November 1997: provisional ordering of services; and
- End of January 1998: final ordering of services.

A multi-criteria analysis taking qualitative aspects into account and weighing the various aspects is being developed by the Canton to evaluate proposals (Beglinger and Gugger, 1997). Recognising that such methodology is not implementable in a mechanistic way to all proposals because of specificities of each line, the methodology is rather meant to be used for call-for-tenders in true competition. The methodology uses two types of criteria: necessary service aspects (related, e.g., to legal requirements of rolling stock and safety of passengers) and desired service aspects containing all other types of measurable aspects which are then valued and weighed. These include the quality and the price of the bid, the service supply concepts, the ability of the company to provide the services, the rolling stock, the personnel, user friendliness aspects and comfort, distribution and marketing and past experience with the company.

5.4.2 Appraisal and conclusion

The implementation of the 'regionalisation' by the development of a specific Cantonal legislation in the Canton of Bern illustrates the very comprehensive way in which the Canton has developed its influence on public transport. The advantage of the new regime is that the aims of the intervention are made more explicit and that the deficit subsidisation has been replaced by specific lump sum contracting.

The relations and division of tasks established by the new regime provides an interesting combination of 'ordering of services' by the authority and 'entrepreneurial responsibility' by the transport operators. To realise the public transport plan, the Canton has not (yet) decided to introduce full scale call-for-tenders for all services.[37] Some degree of protection for incumbents still exists. Incumbents are first asked to react to the requests

[37] It has to be remembered that the Swiss railways have for many years been characterised by co-operation between existing companies. The change of attitude necessary for the introduction of competition is difficult to envisage for many of them, together with the shift from the position as competitor during the tendering period to that of partners once the contract is won. A trial in the past to stimulate companies to make bids for an existing line had, e.g., not resulted in any concrete proposal. Further trials should however be expected as the Canton hopes to stimulate innovation on specific parts of the railway network.

for proposals made by the Canton (except for the creation of new services) and, clearly, the system aims at achieving long-term relationships between authorities and operators with, however, a stricter division of tasks compared to the previous regime. In this process, the Canton has felt the need to formulate clearer frameworks for the judgement of the proposals made by transport operators and it is to be expected that this will, in due course, develop towards more tendering of services. In the meantime, the threat of tendering, in case of unsatisfactory services, is expected to discipline the actors. Local commentators indeed state that this threat has already made the companies – especially SBB – more flexible, accepting that other companies can do things better and starting to think that they could reach the same points too.

With the regionalisation, the situation of the regional railway traffic is changing. The Canton hopes that this will encourage new forms of organisation, and possibly competition, leading to more efficiency. As stated in documents related to the establishment of the public transport plan, the Canton is broadly speaking satisfied with the current public transport services in terms of quality, possibly less in terms of efficiency.

5.5 Case study: the *Seelinie*

This case study describes the transfer of a railway line, called *Seelinie*, from the Swiss Federal Railway (SBB) to a different railway company called Mittelthurgaubahn (MThB). This case is unique in character as it is the first time in the recent Swiss's history that a SBB line has been transferred to another operator, in this case an existing regional railway.

The purpose of this case study is to give an overview of this transfer, how it was initiated and formally organised. As this experiment took place before the implementation of the regionalisation, it should not be seen as an example of the functioning of the current legislation but only as illustrative for the possible implementation of tendering in the Swiss context.

5.5.1 The area: the Canton Thurgau

The area considered lies in the north-eastern part of Switzerland, alongside a lake (*Bodensee*) which forms the border with Germany. The main cities in the area are Schaffhausen and Konstanz and, further away, St. Gallen and Winterthur. The closest major city is Zürich. The area has a touristic character due to the Bodensee. Table 5.6 gives some statistics on the area.

The line considered in this study, the *Seelinie*, stretches a line between Schaffhausen and Romanshorn (and further to Rorschach) and covers mainly the Canton of Thurgau. At Kreuzlingen, about halfway, the *Seelinie* crosses the services of the core line of the *Mittelthurgau Bahn* (MThB) from Wil and Weinfelden to Konstanz in Germany (see Figure 5.1).

Table 5.6 Statistics Canton Thurgau (1994)

Characteristics of the Canton of Thurgau	
• Population	222 202
• Number of passenger vehicles	100 901
Kilometres of track in Thurgau	
• SBB	147.3
• Private Companies	61.7
Total	*209.0*
Kilometres of road in Thurgau	
• National	38.5
• Cantonal	816.8
• Municipal	2 320.0
Total	*3 175.3*

Source: Bundesamt für Statistik (Bern).

5.5.2 The actors

The authorities: *Bundesamt für Verkehr* (BAV) and the Cantons

The Federal Office for Transport (*Bundesamt für Verkehr* BAV), which is a part of the Federal Department of Transport, played a major role in the experimental transfer of the *Seelinie* to a different operator. It has to be remembered that this experiment took place before the introduction of the so-called 'regionalisation' which gave to the Cantons the powers to 'order' passenger transport services. The role played by BAV was therefore more significant than what its role would be under the present regime if a Canton decided to tender one of the regional routes.

The Cantons involved in the process were the Cantons of Thurgau, Zürich, Schaffhausen and St. Gallen.

The regional private railway: *Mittelthurgau Bahn* MThB[38]

The *Mittelthurgau Bahn* (MThB) is a so-called 'private' railway company operating mainly in the Canton of Thurgau in Switzerland. Specific company statistics are given in Table 5.7. The company was founded in 1911. The shareholders are mostly public (with the Confederation, the Cantons (Thurgau and St. Gallen) and municipalities each having about 1/3 of the shares, private shareholders have a small proportion of the shares). It has to be noted that the present director of the company has worked for 15 years at the BAV where he was responsible for the control of the private railway companies.

MThB transports both passengers and freight on their core line (42 km) in Switzerland: Wil-Weinfelden-Konstanz (see Figure 5.1). The main part of the freight transport are oil trains. The train-km operated by MThB tripled between 1993 and 1996. From a regional Swiss operation a few years ago, the company currently produces two thirds of its train-km in neighbouring German areas.[39] MThB has several subsidiaries. The *Reisebüro Mittelthurgau AG* is a successful travel agency, owned for 71% by MThB, active in the organisation of train and fluvial travel around the world. MThB, together with *Reisebüro Mittelthurgau* and *Schweizerische Südostbahn* (SOB), also created in May 1994 a new common subsidiary called *LOKOOP AG*. The aim if this company is to acquire and rent rolling stock and to intensify the co-operation of the shareholders in this domain. The long-term aim is to improve the capacity utilisation and reduce the need for spare rolling stock for all shareholders. A first action of the company was to acquire locomotives from the former Deutsche Reichsbahn (DR) and to adapt them to the Swiss requirements. These are essentially meant to be used in freight transport by MThB in the framework of the European 'open access'. MThB owns 100% of *Mittelthurgau Bahn*

[38] Much of the information concerning MThB comes from the MThB yearly reports of 1994, 1995 and 1996.

[39] Interestingly, MThB now operates under three different regimes in Germany: between Konstanz and Engen (*Seehas*) as sub-contractor to DB who formally supports the risks; between Radolfzell and Stahringen (*Seehäsle*) as open-access operator paying track access charges to DB Track; between Stahringen and Stockach (*Seehäsle*) as operator and infrastructure manager for the regional authority (this infrastructure is open to others too).

Deutschland (GmbH), a subsidiary set up in Germany to operate the *Seehäsle* service. This was needed as this service operates only on German territory. By owning a EU railway company, MThB is now allowed to enter the total EU rail market.

Table 5.7 Main statistics Mittelthurgau Bahn (MThB) 1996

	(1995)		(x1000)
Network length (km)	39.1	Pass. train-km**	1 854
Stations and stops	16	Passengers***	1 371
Electric Locomotives	2	Passenger-km***	22 556
Diesel Locomotives	2	Freight train-km	68
EMUs	10	Freight tonnes	631
Pass. carriages	30	Ton-kilometres	14 763
Freight wagons	0		
Employees 1996*	115		

	(x1000 CHF)
Total Costs	**24 885**
Transport revenues	*8 005*
Federal compensations	*7 300*
*Other revenues*****	*9 677*
Total revenue	**24 981**
Operational result	96
Cost coverage ratio	100.4
w/o fed. compensations	*71.0*

Notes: * Without other transport companies and side activities.
** Incl. services in Germany on behalf of local authority (681 on MThB, 1 173 in Germany)
*** Excl. passengers in Germany.
**** Mainly service production for others (i.e. services in Germany).

Source: MThB Yearly Report 1996

The Swiss Federal Railways (SBB)

SBB, as national carrier, operates 60% of the Swiss railway network (with 86% of the railway passenger-km). SBB was the operator of the line known as *Seelinie* up till the transfer to MThB, which will be described in this case study. The services were provided mainly on a hourly basis with an additional fast train once a day.

5.5.3 Organisation of transfer of the *Seelinie*

The tendering procedure and its design, the bids, the choice made and the contractual arrangements and their design will be presented in chronological order.

Origins of the experiment

The *Seelinie* was operated by SBB as a simple regional route with a rather simple timetable. The process which led to the organisation of an experimental transfer of the route from SBB to a different operator appeared in a rather informal way in 1992. Persons involved say that SBB had shown a lack of interest for the line and that there was political discontent with SBB's performance. A, perhaps unthought, statement by the SBB management that others could take over the line if they wanted triggered a reaction by the management of MThB, which operates in the region. MThB indicated an interest to take over the *Seelinie* and was confident to be able to operate it in a more profitable way. This is said to have prompted a defensive reaction by SBB who suddenly was less enthusiast in giving up the line.

According to the Swiss railway legislation at that time it was not yet possible to organise any form of competition for the operation of a line. BAV was however quite interested in the possibility of having some form of competition among railway companies, as this fitted in the trend towards more competition and in the introduction of open access in the European Union. BAV then required from SBB to find a solution to the situation. SBB and MThB came up in September 1993 with the suggestion to organise a competition between SBB and MThB in the form of a tendering procedure. The agreement also suggested the way to evaluate the bids. This was accepted by BAV who then organised a restricted tendering procedure where only SBB and MThB were invited to bid. Due to the experimental character of the process, the Government did not consider to start an open tendering.

The bids and their evaluation

Some amount of basic information on the accounts of the line was available to the contenders. Line-level accounting has been available at SBB since 1987 but the accounting base for the *Seelinie* was split into two different services, which made the calculation for the whole line more complex. This information was not total, however, and it is believed that the estimations made – especially by MThB in the process of bidding – were based more on their professional experience as regional railway company (in particular for the infrastructural part) than on the given information.

Both concepts of SBB and MThB for the Seelinie were given to BAV on 6 September 1994. As it appeared that the concepts were not comparable in several points further details had to be delivered. This was achieved by mid December 1994.

Both concepts differed quite significantly from each other.

The SBB bid

The SBB concept was essentially based on the existing level of service with trains operating from one end of the line to the other and connections to the rest of the network at both ends. Minor improvements were suggested (such as new colours and some ideas which could be realised if certain pre-requisites were to be fulfilled).

The bid was based on the concept of the so-called 'lean infrastructure' (*schlanken Infrastruktur*), which meant that all unnecessary infrastructure (switches and tracks) would be removed to cut on infrastructure maintenance costs.

The MThB bid[40]

The MThB concept was based on a consequent rationalisation and a substantial increase in usage of the track, resulting in short in 50% more train-km for the same amount of subsidy. The four main elements of the bid were (see also Figure 5.1):

- a basic supply of one train per hour and additional train services in the rush hours;
- better connections to neighbouring lines by dividing the end-to-end local train service into two different services terminating at Stein-am-Rhein and through local trains offering services from end-to-end and circulating only in the peak hours in the morning and in the evening but additional regional fast trains circulating every two hours

[40] The information concerning the procedure and MThB's bid was taken over from the yearly reports of MThB (1994, 1995, 1996).

from end-to-end offered as compensation outside these hours. Furthermore, supply of additional touristic trains to increase the attractivity of the route (using the available carriages from MThB's subsidiary *Reisebüro Mittelthurgau*);

- introduction of new light-weighted trains to meet the requirements of the passengers and to allow them to identify themselves with the route but also to save energy; and
- transformation of the Seelinie into an essential link between the services of MThB and BT (Bodensee-Toggenburg Bahn; a neighbouring railway company). This is the reason for the inclusion in the bid of an hourly train service to be supplied by BT from St. Gallen via Romanshorn, Konstanz (D) and Singen (D) to Engen (D). These additional trains are offered both to realise a long-standing wish from the local communities to realise this direct connection between St. Gallen (CH) and Singen (D), but also to double the frequency on the Romanshorn-Kreuzlingen section of the Seelinie. Allowing the connection between MThB and BT, the Seelinie allow both private railways to have more co-operation (technical know-how and maintenance of both rolling stock and infrastructure).

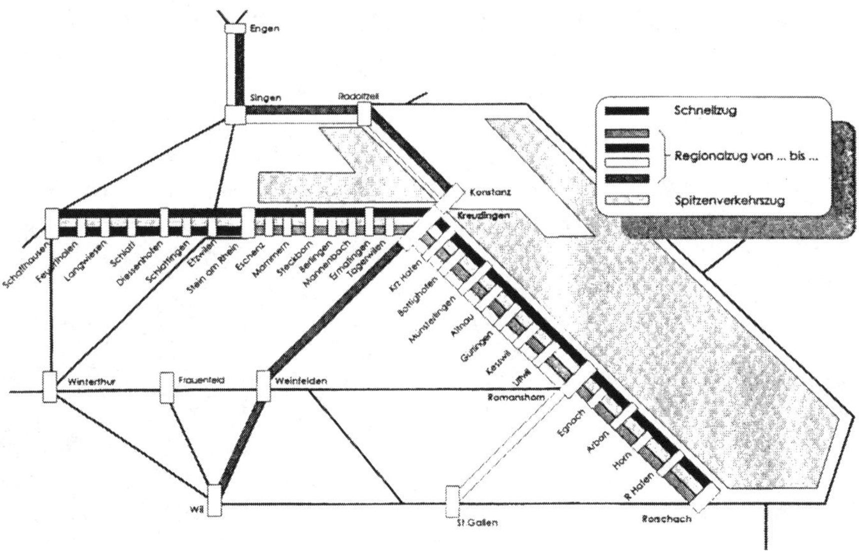

Figure 5.1 The 'Seelinie' concept (first version)

Source: MThB.

Due to the fact that the above elements would not substantially contribute to a better financial position, the MThB had to develop new revenue carrying activities. They suggested offering new touristic products. New touristic trains were suggested to enhance the attraction of the Seelinie. Besides this, MThB suggested to expand freight traffic. Due to the position of Konstanz at the border between Germany and Switzerland, the Seelinie would give to MThB the strategically important possibility to develop a second north-south international freight connection besides Basel which was controlled by SBB.

To realise its concept, MThB needed specific investments to be realised. Both in terms of infrastructure and rolling stock:

- the signalling and control system of the track dated back to the beginning of the century and had to be fundamentally renewed in order to save about half of all station staff along the route, the new system would then allow to control the route with only one or two persons from a central control post at Kreuzlingen to replace about 40 persons. The required investments for this purpose amounted to 45 million CHF; and
- in terms of rolling stock, MThB requested a starting capital aid to finance the purchasing of 9 new trains.[41] This amounted to 35 million CHF.

The interests and the amortisation of these investments were to be included in the bid such as to be neutral with other bids. MThB considered that these investments were necessary to realise substantial economies in terms of operations and to allow substantial increases in revenues, especially in freight transport but that these revenues would allow to repay for the additional investments.

Evaluation of the offers and 'decision of principle'

The final bids were given to BAV by December 1994. The subsidy requirement was the main criteria used to evaluate the bids, the services offered counted as additional criteria. The criteria suggested by SBB and

[41] The director of MThB considers that it is no problem to require from the operator to own the rolling stock, even if its amortization period is longer than the contract as it is better to be out of contract with than without rolling stock. This position is however influenced by the fact that Swiss rolling stock can relatively easily be utilised in Germany and Austria.

MThB at the beginning of the process were used by the ministry to choose its own weights.[42]

In January 1995, BAV presented its comparative study on the bids to the Cantons of Thurgau, St. Gallen, Schaffhausen and Zürich, and to both railway companies. It suggested a choice for the MThB bid as MThB offered more services and expected more earnings on the line by an expansion of the services than SBB for the existing subsidy requirement (for the year 2001 SBB was expected to have a cost level of 36 million CHF and revenues amounting to 14 million CHF, while MThB was expected to have a cost level of 34 million CHF and revenues amounting to 18 million CHF). This led to a further phase of clarification which ended in March 1995 with discussions between the Ministry, both railways and representatives of the Cantons in August 1995.

The final decision of principle by the Government had however to be postponed as a change at the head of the Ministry required to allow some time for the newcomer to learn get acquainted with the file. The final decision of principle to transfer the Seelinie to MThB, as an experiment, could therefore not be reached before 24 February 1996. The governmental 'decision of principle' gave order to the BAV to arrange all details of the transfer together with MThB and SBB by contract and to report to the Ministry by the end of 1996 to allow the final approval of the agreements.

Negotiations

Intensive negotiations had to be organised to realise the transfer of the Seelinie to MThB. These were organised at two levels: between BAV, SBB, MThB and the Cantons to clarify the conditions of the experiment, and bilateral discussions were organised between SBB and MThB which focussed on all personnel and operational aspects of the experiment.

Discussion between BAV, SBB, MThB and the Cantons

Discussion in different groupings between BAV, SBB, MThB and, partially, the Cantons were needed to clarify the conditions of the experiment. The main discussion were conducted in a committee called '*Leitorgan Seelinie*' composed of BAV, SBB, MThB and a number of neutral experts.

[42] Marketing instruments to be used were also included, but could hardly be evaluated and weighed, because of the vagueness of such criteria.

This committee based its discussions on the results of two working groups that had studied detailed financial and legal aspects. The discussions focussed on the updating and clarification of the bid and on the modalities and conditions for the transfer of the line and for the termination of the experiment. This resulted in a concept-concession, a leasing agreement between the Confederation and MThB for the track, the modalities for the transfer of the line, for the experimentation and, possibly, the transfer back and the assorted criteria. These negotiations are said to have been tough but constructive. A group led by BAV discussed with the Cantons all questions related to the 'ordering' of services. A group led by BAV took care of the relations with third parties, such as the trade unions and the other Ministries. Besides this, the same partners discussed together with the neighbouring railway BT (Bodensee-Toggenburg-Bahn) the supply on the lines Romanshorn-Rorschach and Romanshorn-St. Gallen. These lines fell out of the experiment area but it was felt that co-ordination was needed both from a point of view of operation and from a commercial point of view.

Bilateral discussion between SBB and MThB

Bilateral discussions between SBB and MThB were needed to focus on all personnel and operational aspects of the experiment. Besides numerous details, this included:

- the transitional phase between the take-over of the line on 1 June 1997 and the beginning of the new operational concept in 1999;
- the working conditions of the personnel transferring from SBB to MThB and the detaching of SBB personnel and the service delivery by SBB during the 1997/98 period and during the rest of the experiment;[43]
- the payments for the common usage of some stations (Schaffhausen and Romanshorn owned by SBB and Etzwilen owned by MThB); and
- the possible return of the line to SBB at the end of the experiment.

[43] The trade unions also indicated to prefer the civil servant status given by SBB compared to that of MThB but the director of MThB (*Bund*, 15 July 1995) regrets this position which he considers to be a false security. According to him, further personnel cuts are to be expected by SBB, while the private railways have already reached a higher efficiency due to rationalisations which started in the 1970s.

Results of the negotiations

The results of these negotiations can be summarised into four points:

- firstly, MThB takes over the Seelinie already on 1 June 1997, i.e. before being able to provide its new concept for the services. In a transitional period of one year MThB will then provide the services according to the SBB timetable with the means of production of SBB. This transitional period is meant to facilitate the conversion of the line as it is considered that the co-ordination of the infrastructure works will be easier if the same company both conducts the infrastructure works and the operations of the services;
- secondly, the Government gives to MThB a concession for the experimental period;
- thirdly, a leasing agreement between the Confederation and MThB will settle all issues related to the assets. This agreement gives entrepreneurial freedom to MThB during the experimental period for the realisation of its concept and its operation, but it requires MThB to take account of a possible return of the line at the end of the experiment. The lease concerns the *Seelinie* between the stations of Romanshorn and Schaffhausen (both stations excluded), the connecting lines from Kreuzlingen Port and Kreuzlingen to Konstanz and all other pieces of land required for the operations. The leasing agreement determines that MThB will pay to SBB an amount equivalent to the yearly amortization and interest of the installations that are transferred. The agreement determines that MThB will also replace SBB for all other agreements linked to the Seelinie; and
- finally, in terms of investments the Confederation gives to MThB an amount of 34 million CHF for the realisation of the new signalling and remote control of the line.[44] Furthermore, as a result of the negotiations with the Cantons, the Confederation agrees to finance the conversion of all platforms along the line to a minimum height of 35 cm. MThB finances itself (by loan or leasing) the purchasing of the new rolling stock, the interests and amortization have to be paid by the subsidies received for the line (as for all SBB lines).

[44] This decision was neutral in terms of comparison of the bids. An amount equivalent to the interests and amortization was included in the bid of MThB to make both bids comparable.

After these intensive negotiations, the 'decision of principle' was confirmed on 8 December 1996.

The final service concept

The service concept proposed by MThB dated back to 1994. MThB considered it necessary to actualise the concept to take account of new insights. Furthermore, the proposed timetable had become impossible because of timetable changes at Schaffhausen, something which could not have been taken into account when the proposal was made. This led to the question of the legitimacy of such change in service concept in the context of this tendering procedure. After discussions, the *Leitorgan* decided that the requested changes were well founded and did not fundamentally alter the competitive process.

The experiment has a length of 10 years (up till the year 2007). 8 out of those 10 years will be operated according to the new service concept developed by MThB. The final evaluation will then take place according to the criteria developed by the *Leitorgan*. These are mainly based on the subsidy needed to operate the services and the comparison of this amount to what SBB would have required before the introduction of the new concept.

The final service concept aims at: regional passenger transport (9 mln CHF expected by 2001), additional revenue carrying activities (6 mln CHF in freight and 2.5 mln CHF other revenues expected by 2001) and rationalisation investments (as explained earlier). All combined lead to about 50% more services for a similar subsidy requirement as the current services (in 1997/98: 12.2 mln CHF for regional passenger transport subsidies and 6.5 mln CHF for infrastructure), which leads to a level of cost-coverage (excl. all compensations) of about 50%.[45]

The three main aims of the final service concept for the Seelinie are:

- *to give good connections and to create new through services*: the line must provide connections to the hierarchically higher services at Schaffhausen, Etzwilen/Stein am Rhein, Kreuzlingen, Romanshorn and Rorschach. This can only be implemented by providing a higher frequency and new through services compared to the current SBB services. The final service concept results in a half-hourly service

[45] This percentage depends heavily on the definition used, such as way to include the infrastructure costs, and the place given to additional freight and other revenues!

between Schaffhausen and Stein am Rhein and between Kreuzlingen and Romanshorn throughout the day and on the rest of the line at peak hours only (see Figure 5.2);

- *to create new stops*: the line does currently not serve a number of market needs. Four additional stations are suggested, amongst others by request from the region. All requests were evaluated by MThB which will link the realisation of the additional stops to the co-operation of the local authorities (negotiations in 1997); and
- *to stop on request*: to compensate for the creation of additional stops, other stops will be converted to 'stops on request'. This requires additional installations both at the stations and in the vehicles.

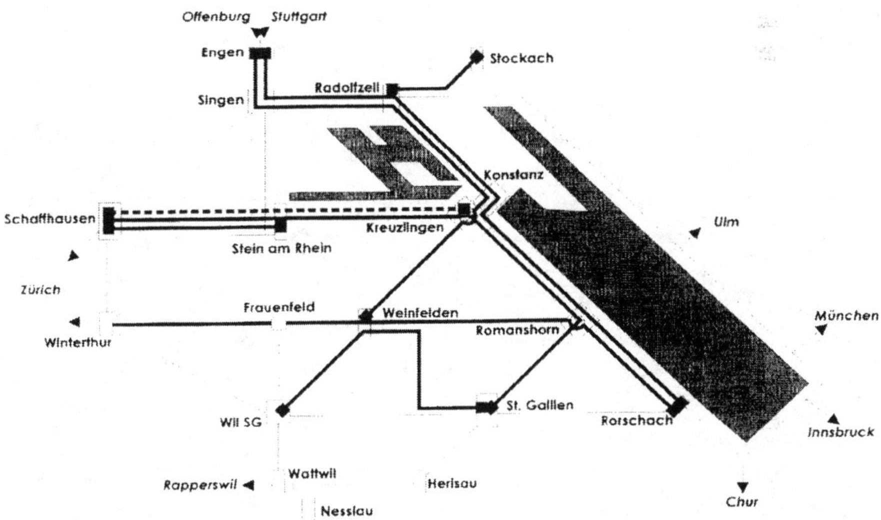

Figure 5.2 The 'Seelinie' final service concept
Source: MThB.

The fares used on the *Seelinie* are taken over from SBB in first instance. New fares will be introduced with the realisation of the concept but will still be integrated in the national fare system.

MThB considers that regional passenger transport is a service to the region and that it can not, in the long term, be profitable. Therefore MThB chooses to provide additional services which are more profitable. Two main types of services are envisaged:

- *touristic transport*: MThB considers that the Seelinie has a high touristic potential which was underdeveloped until now. The final service concept therefore plans to develop touristics services together with the other touristic activities in the area. Nostalgic trains, owned by Reisebüro Mittelthurgau, will, e.g., be used to provide touristic fast trains; and
- *freight transport*: To the example of the current practice of MThB on its core line, the development of freight transport is planned to generate additional revenues. This will however only come to full development when the open access for freight transport will have been implemented by the second Swiss railway reform.

To allow a more intensive utilisation of the line, specific investments need to be realised:

- *signalling and remore control*: the investment in new signalling and remote control of the whole line from Kreuzlingen allows to reduce drastically station staffing to commercial functions only. The realisation of this investment has been submitted to a European tender and this has resulted in attractive prices;[46]
- *stations and stops*: The experience of MThB in efficient rebuilding of stops and stations between Radolfzell and Stockach (Seehäsle) will serve as a basis for the rebuilding work on the Seelinie. Additional modifications to the existing stations and stops are discussed with the municipalities in 1997; and
- *vehicles*: low floor electric train sets built by Stadler-Fahrzeuge AG, ADtranz and SIG will be used on the Seelinie. These are akin to the diesel train sets used by MThB for the Seehäsle. These trains cost about half the price of usual regional trains and weigh only about a third, which reduces the energy consumption in the same order of magnitude. Furthermore these trains require less maintenance than usual trains.

[46] The new track control system proposed by MThB in their first concept appeared to be more expensive than the more traditional system used in Switzerland. This led to a final choice for this traditional system which had as additional advantage to fit better in the SBB system, in the event of a return of the *Seelinie* to SBB at the end of the experiment.

5.5.4 Evaluation and conclusion

As one of the few procedures in Europe where creativity by the bidders has actually been stimulated, the experiment of the transfer of the *Seelinie* from SBB to MThB is probably one of the most interesting experiments to follow in the coming years.

The transfer of an SBB line to a different operator is unique in Switzerland. This case study is perhaps crucial for the rest of Switzerland. With this experiment, the Federal ministry (in particular BAV) aimed at providing an answer to two questions: is it possible with the same amount of subsidy to achieve better performances on the *Seelinie*, or is it possible to achieve the same performances at lower costs? If it proves to be worthwhile, the Confederation or the Cantons are likely to put more lines into tendering. This could lead to a fundamental change in the position of SBB. It is expected that the combination of the regionalisation, railway reform and the results of the *Seelinie* experiment will already lead to a more entrepreneurial attitude by SBB as it will realise that its position is no longer guaranteed and that more attention has to be paid towards more market driven and commercial activities.[47]

The outcome of the tendering process between MThB and SBB has shown that more services (50% more train kilometres, new rolling stock, more efficient production and modified service patterns) are promised for the same amount of subsidy but that a substantial part of those subsidies had to go into infrastructure investments. As the experiment is currently in a transitional phase (the necessary investments for the realisation of the new service concept are not yet fully realised), little can yet be said about the performance of the new service concept by MThB in terms of ridership. The evaluation of the case study has therefore to focus on the tendering process itself and it will be necessary to wait several years before being able to evaluate the true consequences of the transfer.

Two observations can however be made. Firstly, the Swiss authorities have recognised that a 10 year trial period is needed before being able to evaluate the experiment. Secondly, a substantial amount of time is needed before being able to implement the new service patterns: about 2 years

[47] In an interview with the newspaper *Bund* (15 July 1995), the director of MThB states, comparing its experience in Germany and Switzerland, that the national railway companies have become defensive and afraid of the smaller regional railways who could appear to be able to do things better in the regions than themselves.

will be needed for the new operator to realise all investments needed to upgrade the services.[48]

SBB is said to have tried everything to stop the experiment, possibly afraid of what it had, inadvertently, started itself. In the end, SBB had however to accept the strong Federal wish to try something different at the regional level. MThB took the opportunity with much enthusiasm and tries to establish, with its new concept for the line, the advantages of the regionalisation of the regional passenger traffic in contrast to more centralist service concepts by SBB.

In terms of service innovation, MThB has suggested fundamental changes in the service patterns to be offered. In this respect a few remarks can be made. The services proposed are imbedded into a broader network. Even if the tendering concerned only one line, the service concept offered includes several connecting lines operated by MThB both in Switzerland and Germany, but also by other companies on MThB tracks, such as BT and even SBB. A stricter tendering procedure which would not have taken this broader scope into account would surely have resulted into poorer proposals. Interestingly too, the possibilities given to the Swiss companies to organise such services on their own initiative depend for a large extent on the current organisational form which is not based on tendering.

This experiment, which took place before the implementation of the new legal and regulatory framework, is based on a vertically integrated concept (infrastructure and operations are run by the same company). The tendering process itself illustrated the co-ordination needs between both: infrastructure investments required to provide the new passenger transport services, co-ordination of operations and building works during the transitional period.

Related to this is the fact that revenues from other activites (freight traffic, touristic activities) could be taken as revenue when formulating the bid. As the further reform of the railways at the Federal level, implemented in the meantime, will mean that open access will be introduced in freight

[48] Pushed by the impatience of its passengers, MThB decided to introduce its new timetable in May 1998, even before the realisation of all necessary investments and delivery of the new rolling stock. This choice was also based on the fact that most necessary investments will be realised by the Autumn 1998 and that a postponement of the new timetable for one more year would prevent the passengers from benefiting from the improvements for more than half a year. While this choice has led to substantial increases in service, it has however proved to be impossible to guarantee punctuality. The main factors being the lacking infrastructure and the inadequate rolling stock. It is expected that the situation will normalise in the next months.

transport, this may have its influence on the *Seelinie* too. SBB, e.g., could operate services on that route and it is not yet clear which influence this would have on the viability of the experiment as it has been designed. This situation is of course related to the vertical integration model chosen here, where a total line is transferred.

The whole process required substantial time for negotiations. Of course, this is probably due to the fact that there was no experience with such process, but it is unlikely that, with more experience, a straightforward mechanistic awarding procedure could have been followed.

Furthermore, the service concept formulated by MThB at the time of tendering appeared to need some fundamental rethinking at the time of the final agreement due, amongst others, to changes which were external to the *Seelinie*, such as changes in services at connecting stations. It can be observed from a comparison of the first and second version of the service concept that the changes were not minimal. Such changes may have been required by new market insights too, but it is the external influence which is interesting here as it illustrates the difficulty residing in choosing a 'service concept' not knowing what will happen in the rest of the network. Fortunately, the choice between both the first and second version of MThB's bid and that of SBB was easy. It is however interesting to think of the problem that would have appeared if the bid had been much closer to each other in terms of expected service quality, of if there had been more bids (only two were invited in this case).

Finally, one could ask why the new operator has had to take a lease on the infrastructure and not on the specific rolling stock of the line. But as it appears here, SBB was not prepared to sell its rolling-stock. This illustrates problems related to what is called 'level-playing field'. In the new Federal procedures implemented in the meantime for cases of transfer of a line to a different operator, specific provisions have been made to solve this problem. A deeper problem is probably an inadequate amortisation or valuation of the existing rolling stock at SBB.

5.6 General evaluation and conclusions

To conclude, a general evaluation of the legal and regulatory framework in which the Swiss railways have to operate will be made. This evaluation is based on the elements presented above and a number of insight gathered in the literature and during interviews.

An integrated public transport system

The Swiss public transport system is known for the focus placed on the integration of services. Punctuality, good connections, clockface timetables, through ticketing between railway companies and regional bus services, fares association at the urban or regional level are all well known features. Interestingly, many of the persons interviewed in Switzerland cite the Netherlands as their example in terms of service integration (national fares integration, clockface timetable, connections, etc.)

Both the authorities, at all levels, and the railway companies (SBB and privates) share the belief in the integrated public transport 'system'. All refer to their experience to prove the advantages of this system. However, a total economic proof of the advantage of this integrated system, which avoids all competition between services, does not seem to exist.[49]

The planning freedom of the companies is therefore always subordinated to the preservation of the integrated timetable and the regulation developed by the Federal and Cantonal authorities indeed takes great care to prescribe various forms of integration.

Many 'private' railways

Switzerland features a substantial number of railway companies, amongst which many so-called 'private' railways established in the form of private companies. It has however to be observed that authorities detain in most cases a large majority of the shares. The Confederation, the Cantons and the municipalities detain the shares in varied proportions and the influence of private capital in the Swiss railways is very minimal.

Opinions on the usefulness of this large number of railways vary. Some consider that many of them are too small and that mergers could substantially reduce their production costs (Berger, 1997). Others believe that these companies are in many respects more efficient than the Federal railways (SBB). This is based on comparisons of specific costs when co-operations between SBB and private operators are set up. Both opinions are probably

[49] In this respect it can be noted that the question of the punctual connection between services is in many cases very relevant as the general frequency of the railway services in Switzerland is hourly. The current Rail2000 project in Switzerland aims at increasing the frequency of a number of train services to 2 per hour. As a point of comparison: the Dutch railways have a general frequency of 2 trains per hour and have increased this to 4 trains per hour on several routes.

correct and movements towards more co-operation and, e.g., the creation of common subsidiaries between private railways can now be observed (e.g., SOB and MThB). It should be noted that differences in cost are only partially the result of differences in wages between SBB and the 'private' railways.

National railway reform

Fagagnini (1996), as director of SBB, complained that the existing regime was not clear enough about the goals given to the company. Incompatible goals of welfare maximisation and normal business economics decision-making caused trouble here. It is to be expected that the new regime for the national railway services will clarify this situation.

The exact future of the regulatory regime for the national railway services is not yet fully decided as discussions continue in Parliament. The way chosen is one parallel to that of the regional railway services. The situation will however be different as the long-distance railway services are supposed to be self-sufficient, at least from an operational point of view. The level of involvement of the authorities in the determination of the service level will thus probably be much lower and SBB is expected, at least for the foreseeable future, to retain its de facto monopoly.

SBB is a Federal company and, in the current situation, the Federal government could actually prescribe almost anything to the SBB management. There are however no instances where that has happened; the experiment with the *Seelinie* being an exception. So, even if the new status of the company will reduce the direct powers of the government on the management of SBB, this is not expected to have much influence on the day-to-day practice.

The greater ability of the private railways to respond adequately to regional needs, by being less bureaucratic (less overhead) and closer to their markets, is one of the arguments often heard to favour their further involvement in the regional passenger services in Switzerland. Many welcome in this respect the decision of SBB to reorganise its regional services on the basis of regional management units, themselves subdivided into groups of a few lines. This move away from central bureaucracy is considered by many as essential for the ability of SBB to respond to the regional needs. But SBB's conviction that they are better than the others still irritates many.

Separation of infrastructure and operations

Several opinions exist in Switzerland concerning the separation between infrastructure and operations and, most importantly, the degree to which this should be realised: accounting, organisational or institutional separation. Some are favourable to radical solutions if the necessary requirements to make them work can be realised (see, e.g., Liechti, 1996 and Basler Handelskammer, 1995).

The external institutional separation is almost unanimously rejected by the companies, both by SBB (see Fagagnini, 1996) and by the 'privates' (see Boos and Scheidegger, 1996). The accounting separation, which is in any case legally required, does not seem to cause too much resistance and is even welcomed by at least some railways (see, e.g., Boos and Scheidegger, 1996) that expect this possibility to lead to more efficiency in the network as a whole. The internal organisational separation also seems to be accepted by the larger railways (as SBB and BLS) in spite of the expected increase in co-ordination costs (Fagagnini, 1996).

The arguments used by Fagagnini (1996), as general director of SBB, mainly relate to the higher costs of co-ordination and losses in synergy caused by such a separation. The optimisation between supply, track equipment and rolling stock is given to exemplify the synergy. The example of the *Seelinie* could also be given in this respect and this is also given as an example by Boos and Scheidegger (1996).

Boos and Scheidegger (1996), both directors of sizeable 'private' railways (SOB and RBS), stress the strong need for co-ordination due to the high level of capacity utilisation and strong interrelationships between services in Switzerland compared to other countries. On the basis of this observation, they consider that the separation would create new 'cuts' in the organisations and that their current ability to realise a high level of capacity utilisation would be reduced. Due to this, more infrastructure investments would then be required to realise the same level of traffic.

Open access

Most seem to agree that some form of open access is desirable, especially in the case of freight transport. Some even point to the fact that it is economically interesting for a railway company to grant access to others as this delivers additional revenues due to the infrastructure charges paid by the user. However, a limit to the possibilities of open access is set by current capacity utilisation which is said to be high at essential facilities, such as main stations, while tracks could allow more traffic. Furthermore, the additional capacity that is currently being realised is designed to be in accordance with the requirements of the Rail2000 programme of improvement in the passenger railway services by SBB. Observators consequently point to the fact that there will be only very limited capacity available and that a complex 'slot allocation' mechanism would need to be designed to really make open access possible. Problems, e.g. for passenger services, could indeed already appear if the railfreight sector suddenly became more successful.

Even if some, possibly a growing minority at this moment, would like to envisage more possibilities for entry in the passenger services, the general belief is that this should not endanger the integrated clockface timetable and that new entries on the infrastructure would only be desirable for (international) long-distance services which complement or fit into the existing national services. The main point here is that it is not open-access in itself which is questionned but the possibility to engage into 'cherry-picking' activities upon existing concessions.

The present and the future of competition

There is in Switzerland a will to introduce 'some' competition in the public transport system, but only if it allows to keep the present quality, which is considered to be good, and also if it does not jeopardise all existing co-operation between the providers. The aim of competition should therefore be, mainly, more efficiency but also some innovation within the existing integrating framework.

The idea of free competition is simply rejected by most and is furthermore considered to be unrealistic because of capacity problems at stations, where often many lines converge, and because of the optimisation between planned infrastructure capacity improvements and planned service improvements according to the Rail2000 service concept in the national network.

A systematic introduction of competition *for* the track is not yet seriously envisaged, neither at the Federal not at the Cantonal level, but most interviewed persons would not reject the possibility of using this form of competition to a greater extent in the future. The UK experience is followed with great interest, but most are afraid that the co-ordination problems translate into substantial transaction costs.

The possibility of giving additional concessions for services using the same tracks, but which would not compete directly with existing services, is however not rejected, yet it is not expected to take place at a large scale, if at all. This leads several observers to conclude that the only practical way for entry and changes in services to occur is to be allowed to 'take over' an existing line from the early morning to the late evening with all associated co-ordination requirements. There is no clear view yet on the way to organise such transfers (yet the Seelinie may serve as an example), but these thoughts nevertheless illustrate the wish to change 'something' to the current protected positions. The 'continuous reform' planned by the Government will no doubt bring further changes to the current situation.

Joss (1997), director of MThB and former vice-director at the Federal Office for Transport, compares a number of scenarios for the future of the railways and favours a scenario based on co-operation between the railways rather than simple competition. He stresses however that this needs to be a different form of co-operation compared to the existing one. He considers that the current form of co-operation is more based on regulation and protection and that a new form of co-operation should rather be based on voluntary partnerships based on the strenghts and weaknesses of the partners (to the example of the US freight railways). He regrets however that especially the larger Swiss railway companies are not yet ready to accept this vision and that stronger forms of competition may be required in the short term to realise co-operation in the longer term.

An interesting possibility opened up by the new Swiss regulatory regime is the possibility given to transport companies to present service proposals spontaneously at the regional level. It is not yet clear whether this will have much effect. It will all depend on the further implementation measures which will be taken by the Cantons. As far as systematic competition is concerned, there does not yet seem to be a tendency towards the compulsory usage of competitive tendering procedures at the Cantonal level. However, it is expected that tendering will gain in importance if the financial difficulties of the Cantons further worsen.

Apparently, other forms of competition than that between SBB and the regionally established 'private' railway companies are not expected by most observers, at least not in the foreseeable future, but this will depend on future agreements with the EU. Some say that it is still necessary to be on the spot to be competitive (relating this to the necessity of knowing the local market and needs and – most importantly – knowing the local authorities). For the same reason, the appearance of management competition for the 'private' railways is not expected either.

Continuous reform

An important feature of the action of the Federal government on the organisational framework in which the railways and the rest of the public transport system has to operate is the principle of the 'continuous reform'. This entails a step-by-step approach, in which the most urgent problems are tackled first (equalisation of the conditions at the regional level to favour efficiency, open access for freight, reform of SBB and solution for the debt problem). The possibilities for further reforms that would lead to more competition are not rejected but are not considered to be top priority. The approach chosen is based on the desire to learn from experience. The experiment with the transfer of the *Seelinie* has, in this perspective, to be seen as a first step. The possible introduction of some form of yardstick competition with a threat of tendering a second a step.

A regulator?

An essential actor in the Swiss public transport system (all modes) is the Federal Office for Transport (as part of the Ministry of Transport and Energy). Its importance will remain and maybe even increase in the future. This actor has many functions akin to that of a 'regulator' in the British case. Its functions are however not formalised into the same independence. The Swiss model is more based on discussions and consensus. This consensus approach is similar to that in the Netherlands. A major difference, however, is that the basic principles and goals are clear at the start of the discussions; such as the idea of system integration, which requires clear action (legal and regulatory) towards service, fares and information integration, without however taking all freedoms of the companies, and by indicating to them their responsibilities and threatening to take action if adequate integration is not realised.

An interesting aspect of the action of the Federal Office for Transport is the (planned) development of a kind of yardstick competition system. This tool of analysis of service proposals made by regional operators will be developed to assist the Cantons in the evaluation of the proposals and in the making of their choice (a substantial part of the subsidisation for regional transport is paid by the Confederation).

Boos and Scheidegger (1996), as directors of private railways, would actually welcome the idea of introducing this model, known as 'virtual competition'. This model is actually a form of 'threat' of competition where the authorities would only decide to organise competitive tendering procedures when the performance of a company has proved to be insufficient after a peer performance comparison. The possibility of introducing such a model has also been mentioned by several interviewed persons as a way to avoid some of the stiffening features of the introduction of systematic competitive tendering while still allowing for indirect competition. It has to be observed that a similar regulatory system is also used and further developed in Japan, albeit without the threat of competitive tendering, on the basis of the regulation of fares which is made possible by the general profitability of the services.

Regionalisation

One of the main aims of the regionalisation was to treat all suppliers equally. A second aim was to achieve more efficiency in regional transport (it is said, e.g., that the regionalisation has already resulted in an easier replacement of trains by buses there were this is efficient).

The regionalisation has indeed already led to significant changes. The first movements can be observed even if the introduction of a more distant, transparent and formalised way to regulate companies to replace more direct but diffuse forms of intervention has not yet come to total fruition. SBB has reorganised the management of its regional services into a number of regions responsible for the negotiations with the 26 Cantons who, themselves, have started to develop new legislation (see the Bern case study).

Berger (1997) mentions that the new organisational framework required a clearer cut between company management and political involvement and that, for many companies, this meant more professional and smaller boards. The federal government itself is currently reviewing its involvement in the numerous companies in which shares are held by the Confederation. Fewer people will represent the Confederation as co-owner but these people will receive clearer instructions. The government also recommends that the local interests be represented on the political side rather than in the boards of the transport companies.

The split between national (long-distance IC and fast trains) and regional (local trains) services did not cause much discussion. There is however a fear, especially at SBB, that a loss of feedering between long-distance and local services may lead to the disappearance of local trains. Regional 'private' operators, however, have more confidence in their ability to deliver the same services at lower costs, thereby neutralising the effect. It is then quite likely that the remaining operational 'profits' at the national level will flow towards a repayment of the deficits of the infrastructure.

The *Seelinie* experiment (started before the regionalisation but in a similar spirit and using some of the features of the new regime), that resulted in the transfer of the line from SBB to a regional 'private' railway, can serve as an illustration of what may happen in the near future in several Swiss areas. While it is still too early to judge the true consequences of the experiment, the new service concept for the area plans to deliver a substantial improvement in the level of service without requiring additional subsidisation.

As can be seen in the description of the legal and regulatory framework, much care has now been taken to ensure that the possible transfer of a line to a different operator takes place without transitional problems. The creation of the new regime was assorted with some care for the creation of a level playing field. The issue of the infrastructure and rolling stock is apparently settled, but practice only will reveal the adequacy of the chosen procedures. The issue of the personnel might prove to be somewhat more contentious but problems and strikes are commonly not expected; the cultural difference of Switzerland may play an important role here, together with the traditional existence of private railway companies.

The results of the new organisational form will only become apparent after 1999 when the next Swiss timetable period starts. Yet, without having introduced any systematic form of competition in the regional railways, many observers state that only the 'threat' of competition has already resulted in a much more open position by SBB towards new ideas suggested by the Cantons than was the case before the reform. One has, however, to be careful about such statements. If a more responsive attitude to regional needs is positive, the situation still requires the Canton to have 'good' ideas. This requires the Canton to be expert in the exercise of its new tasks as 'orderer' of public transport services. In this respect, many observers consider it to be essential that the Cantons and municipalities provide a substantial amount of public transport subsidies on the basis of their own taxation as this improves democratic accountability. Others state that the current reforms at the Cantonal level, besides the possible effect on the efficiency of the transport companies, are also beneficial in a different dimension, namely that of forcing the political and administrative level to clarify their thoughts and reasons for intervention.

The example of the Canton of Bern has also shown that the development of the new organisational framework requires clarity by the Canton in its (political) aims and decisions related to public transport. Very detailed public transport plans have been developed and steps towards the establishment of multi-criteria evaluation methods have been made and it is to be expected that this will have a growing influence in the future. One could question whether such extensive regulation will be adequate in the longer run in order to develop the responsiveness of the transport companies.

It would thus be wrong to think that the regulatory reform of the railways and of the rest of the public transport system in Switzerland has reduced the authority intervention in absolute terms. As for many other countries, it would be more appropriate to talk of a 'reform' of the regulation rather than to talk of a 'deregulation', even if the consequence of the reform is that competition, as a 'regulatory instrument', will, in due course, get a more important function.

References

Basler Handelskammer (1995), *Marktöffnung im Schienenverkehr durch freien Zugang zum Netz*, Schriftenreihe der Basler Handelskammer, 29 Oktober 1995.

Beglinger, C. and H. Gugger (1997), *Beurteilungsverfahren für Angebotsofferten im öffentlichen Verkehr*, Canton Bern, Bern.

Berger, H.-U. (1997), "Die 'kleine öV-Reform' 1995", *Swiss Traffic*, Bundesamt für Verkehr, 3, 1-2.

Boos, E. and P. Scheidegger (1996), "Bahninfrastruktur und Betrieb gehören zusammen, auch wenn der 'third party access' für weitere Effizienzsteigerung nötig ist", *Jahrbuch des Schweizerischen Verkehrswirstschaft*, 1995/96, 1-11.

Bund (1995), *Am Bodensee fällt der erste Dominostein*, 15 July 1995.

Bundesamt für Statistik (1994), *Schweizerische Verkehrsstatistik*, Bern.

Fagagnigi, H.P. (1996), "Spannungsfelder einer Schweizerischen Bahnreform", *Jahrbuch des Schweizerischen Verkehrswirstschaft*, 1995/96, 13-23.

Joss, P. (1997), "Die Privatbahnen im Jahr 2015", in: Nachhaltige Spitzenleistungen der Bahnen (modul 8), Internationaler Bahnkongress Schweiz, 26-28 May 1997, Luzern.

Liechti, M. (1996), "Free access zur Schieneninfrastruktur: Mehr Effizienz durch intramodalen Wettbewerb", *Jahrbuch des Schweizerischen Verkehrswirstschaft*, 1995/96, 64-73.

LITRA (1996), *Verkehrszahlen '96*, Informationsdienst für den Öffentlichen Verkehr, LITRA, Bern.

Merz, P. (1997), "Rail2000: le train du prochain millénaire", *Revue Technique Suisse*, Dossier spécial 1997: "150 ans des chemins de fer en Suisse", p. 12-15.

Mittelthurgaubahn (1994), *87. Bericht des Verwaltungrats über die Geschäftsführung im Jahre 1994*, Weinfelden.

Mittelthurgaubahn (1995), *88. Bericht des Verwaltungrats über die Geschäftsführung im Jahre 1994*, Weinfelden.

Mittelthurgaubahn (1996), *89. Bericht des Verwaltungrats über die Geschäftsführung im Jahre 1994*, Weinfelden.

Office des Transports Publics (1996), *Schéma d'offre 1997-2001 transports publics régionaux*, Direction des travaux publics, des transports et de l'énergie, Berne.

SBB (1997), *Rapport de Gestion 1996 SBB CFF FFS*, Bern.

Van de Velde, D.M. (1998), *Switzerland – Research on Railway Competition: National Report*, Department of Transport Economics, Erasmus University, Rotterdam.

And various documents provided by the railway companies.

Legal texts

Arrêté fédéral fixant les principes du mandat 1987 des Chemins de fer fédéraux et l'indemnisation de leurs prestations de service public, ref. 742.37, 9/10/1986 (1/1/1996).

Loi fédérale sur les chemins de fer, ref. 742.101, 20/12/1957 (1/1/1996).

Loi fédérale sur les chemins de fer fédéraux, ref. 742.31, 23/6/1944 (1/7/1994).

Loi fédérale sur le transport public, ref. 742.40, 4/10/1985 (1/1/1996).

Message sur la réforme des chemins de fer: indemnités et aides financières pour le trafic régional, ref. 93.091, 17/11/1993.

Message sur la réforme des chemins de fer, ref. 96.090, 13/11/1996.

Ordonnance du DFTCE concernant la comptabilité des entreprises de transport concessionaires, ref. 742.221, 18/12/1995.

Ordonnance sur les chemins de fer fédéraux, ref. 742.311, 29/6/1988 (1/7/1994).

Ordonnance sur les horaires, ref. 742.151.4, 18/12/1995.

Ordonnance sur les indemnités, les prêts et les aides financières selon la loi sur les chemins de fer, ref. 742.101.1, 18/12/1995 (1/4/1996).

Ordonnance sur les parts cantonales dans les indemnités et les aides financières pour le traffic régional, ref. 742.101.2, 18/12/1995.

Ordonnance sur le transport public, ref. 742.401, 5/11/1986 (1/1/1995).

Interviews

- BAV Federal Office for Transport (Mr. Giger).[50]
- EVED Ministry of Transport and Energy (Mr. Oetterli).
- Canton of Bern (Mrs. Beglinger).
- BLS Lötschbergbahn Regionalverkehr (Mr. Luginbühl).
- MThB Mittelthurgaubahn (Mr. Joss).
- RM Regionalverkehr Mittelland (Mr. Selz).
- RBS Regionalverkehr Bern-Solothurn (Mr. Scheidegger).
- SBB Passenger (Mr. Grossenbacher), SBB Infrastructure (Mr. Geyer), SBB Bahn2000 (Mr. Perin), SBB Regionalverkehr Mittelland-Jura (Mr. Heiz).
- SOB Südostbahn (Mr. Boos).
- SZU Sihlthal-Zürich-Uetlibergbahn (Mrs. Weibel).

[50] With many thanks for the extensive help and discussions.

6 Japan

FUMITOSHI MIZUTANI
Kobe University and Hertford College, Oxford

6.1 Introduction

The Japanese rail industry can be described by three main characteristics. First, the Railway Enterprise Law requires potential entrants to have a railway license. Entry regulations seem to avoid creating rail competition but yardstick competition, as well as the full cost principle in fare regulation, may induce indirect competition among rail operators. Second, privately owned railways play a crucial role in the Japanese railway industry. Most private railways run on a commercial basis and major private railways are considered efficient. Furthermore, these major private railways behave in an entrepreneurial way, engaging in non-rail business to enhance rail services. Third, rail operation and infrastructure are integrated in the same organisation. There are cases of organisations whose business is limited to rail operation only or to the provision of rail infrastructure only, but these cases are very rare.

This chapter gives an overview of regulatory and competition policy in the Japanese railway industry and includes case studies of privatisation effects and private railways' performance. In the case studies, the behaviour of private operators will be discussed. Using a diagram of ownership-competitive environment, the competitive situation in the Japanese rail industry will be presented. Second, the area selected for case studies (the Kinki region and the Osaka metropolis) is described before focusing on the private railways and JRs in the area, their general regulation and business diversification. Then, JNR's privatisation and a private-public comparison are presented as case studies, with several performance factors being assessed. Furthermore, competition factors such as real estate development and accessibility are also discussed.

6.2 Legal and regulatory framework

6.2.1 Description

The Railway Enterprise Law (*Tetsudo Jigyoho*) has been in effect to regulate all railway companies since April 1, 1987, when the Japan National Railway (JNR) was privatised.[1] Before the privatisation, there were two main laws in the industry: the Japan National Railway Law (*Nihon Kokuyu Tetsudoho*) for the Japan National Railway, and the Local Railway Law (*Chiho Tetsudoho*) for private railways and public subway systems. The Ministry of Transport regulates the industry based upon the Railway Enterprise Law. In addition to this regulation, there are approximately 128 laws directed at the industry and enforced by the Ministry of Transport.

Entry and exit

Entry regulation stipulates that a railway license is necessary for the railway service. This license must be approved by the Minister of Transport according to the Railway Enterprise Law (Article 3). The Railway Enterprise Law (Article 2) classifies railway licenses into the following categories:

- class 1: enterprises that provide rail passenger and/or freight services while holding their own rail infrastructure;
- class 2: enterprises that provide rail passenger and/or freight services using rail infrastructure owned by another organisation; and
- class 3: enterprises that build rail infrastructure for sale to a class 1 enterprise, or an enterprise which owns infrastructure and rents it to a class 2 enterprise.

Most railways are class 1 enterprises. A typical example of a class 2 enterprise is JR Freight, which provides rail services by using rail tracks

[1]Strictly speaking, it cannot be said that the Japan National Railway was 'privatised,' because the ownership of JRs was still in the public sector. However, I use the word 'privatisation' conventionally, because JRs are on the way to full privatisation. See more details in Mizutani and Nakamura (1997a).

owned by six JR passenger companies. A typical example of a class 3 enterprise is Kobe Kosoku Tetsudo, which owns rail track and rents it to four private operators. There is no one-to-one relationship between each rail enterprise and type of license. Since a license is given to each line, it is possible for an enterprise to have different kinds of licenses. For example, Hankyu, a private railway, has two kinds of rail license (class 1 and class 2). On most of its lines, it provides services as a class 1 operator. However, for the Kobe Kosoku line, Hankyu becomes a class 2 enterprise because this line's tracks are owned by the Kobe Kosoku company.

The Railway Enterprise Law (Article 5) also describes the criteria for evaluating those applying to provide rail services (potential entrants). There are five criteria to be met in order for the Ministry of Transport to grant a rail service license:

- it must be determined that demand for railway service is sufficient;
- there should be no imbalance between supply and demand for rail service when a potential entrant enters the market;
- a potential entrant takes on liability for providing service safely;
- a potential entrant takes on financial and technological liability; and
- rail services by a potential entrant are in the public's interest.

The Ministry of Transport assesses a potential entrant based on these five criteria (Saito, 1993). This assessment is considered to be very strict and many documents are required. It is said that since the new Railway Enterprise Law was enacted, the number of required documents has decreased. There are, however, still several criticisms of the criteria. For example, there is no description of the specific conditions necessary to get a rail license such as the minimum demand level, the degree of demand-supply imbalance, and the required level of safety provision.

There is no limit to the duration of a rail license. Once a rail operator obtains the license, then it is fully responsible for providing rail services, except in cases where a license is lost due to negligence, and where the operator requests and is granted permission for exit by the Ministry. The Railway Enterprise Law (Article 28) states that in order for an operator to cease supplying service, approval by the Minister of Transport is necessary. This law allows exit of rail service provided such closure does not damage public interest. This vague description seems to allow an easy exit for railway service providers, but in fact it is very difficult for railways to go out of business (Saito, 1993).

Determination of service characteristics

Service characteristics are regulated by the Railway Business Law (*Tetsudo Eigyo-ho*) and the Regulation for Railway Transport (*Tetsudo Unyu Kitei*). In general, train schedules can be determined by a railway operator. Rail operators are required to publish their time and fare schedules. Every station has information on train schedules and rail users can easily obtain information. This information is also easily available through commercial booklets such as 'Timetable (*Jikokuhyo*)', published by JR and the travel agency JTB. These sources include nationwide timetables and fares, are issued every month for about 1000 yen (US$ 8), and are easily obtainable at station kiosks or bookstores.

Fares

There are five important points in fare regulation based on the Railway Enterprise Law (Article 16). First, rail fare must be approved by the Minister of Transport.[2] Second, the Japanese railway industry is based upon the full cost principle. The rail fare should cover rail costs including the operator's profits. Rail enterprises are expected not to receive subsidies. Third, rail fare should not discriminate against any special group. Fourth, the fare level should not be so high that users cannot enjoy service. Last, rail fare should not cause unfair competition with other railways. The Ministry of Transport must approve basic rates such as price per travel length and price per travel zone, which applies for regular ticket and pass uses. On the other hand, many kinds of other tickets such as serial tickets, group discount tickets, express charges, and entrance fees are decided by the rail companies, although the companies have to report to the Ministry of Transport.

In the railway industry, the full cost principle is used to calculate fair price. Furthermore, two different systems, the cost accumulating method for small private railways and the rate-base method for major private railways, are used to calculate the rail fare. These methods have disadvantages

[2] This is an important point to remember when we compare the present situation with the fare approval of the Japan National Railway (JNR) before privatisation, when JNR's fare had to be approved by the Diet (parliament). The problem with the former fare approval system was that fare revision, often used for political deals, damaged management's efforts to manage their own business. From this point of view, the new approval system by the Transport Ministry posed less threat of political intervention.

because they are both cost-plus systems so that there is no incentive for a rail operator to decrease rail cost. To avoid inefficiency, the Ministry of Transport has used the yardstick competition scheme in the assessment of the rail fare. The Ministry of Transport sets up three evaluation criteria, namely: improvement rate in operating cost; improvement rate in productivity; and improvement rate in revenue.

Rail track fee regulation

The Rail Enterprise Law (Article 15) describes the rail track fee. The law does not regulate how much the rail operator pays to the track holding organisation, but does require that track fee and conditions of usage must be approved by the Ministry of Transport.

The general procedure is as follows:

- the infrastructure provider decides the rail track fee;
- the provider negotiates with the operator and makes a mutually agreed upon decision;
- the provider applies for approval of the track fee; and
- the Transport Ministry assesses the reasonableness of the fee.

There are no specific criteria for the assessment of the rail track fee. The Enforcement Regulation of Railway Enterprise Law (*Tetsudo Jigyo Shiko Kisoku*) (Article 30), however, requires the provider to submit the documents detailing how the rail track fee is calculated. The Ministry of Transport evaluates the documents. In general, because rail track fee is set up to cover the provider's cost, the Ministry of Transport assesses whether or not the cost is reasonable.

Regulation of non-rail business

Japanese private railways have long been allowed to operate non-rail business as well as rail business. However, railway business and non-rail business are strictly separated by Railway Accounting Regulations (*Tetsudo Kaikei Kisoku*). A railway company is forbidden to allocate rail and non-rail cost at its own discretion, but must follow regulations which describe in detail how to allocate the costs of common facilities and administration. Therefore, an intentional cross-subsidy strategy is avoided, whereby a rail company charges high rail fares and transfers costs from the non-rail service, and vice versa.

6.2.2 Aims and considerations

License system and entry competition

The Japanese railway regulation for entry is based upon the licensing system. The license system seems based on the concept of traditional monopoly regulation. The authority gives a license for monopolistic rail service to a railway enterprise while regulating rail fare and service standards to protect rail users from the hazards of a real monopoly. One advantage of this system is a that a rail enterprise can concentrate on providing better services in the long run, because this system protects incumbent rail enterprises from potential entrants as long as incumbents' services are not terribly bad. Conversely, the efficiency of incumbents may suffer due to the less competitive situation. Although it is true that since the Railway Enterprise Law was introduced in 1987 a rail enterprise can choose more flexible forms of rail operation to enter the market, there is not much competition to enter markets.

Yardstick competition

The Ministry of Transport uses a yardstick competition scheme to increase efficiency among existing railway companies. Shleifer (1985) originally proposed the conceptual framework of yardstick competition. Yardstick competition is considered as competition among rail operators operating in different markets. In this scheme a regulator sets up several performance measures such as operating cost and productivity and evaluates rail operators' performance.

In Japan this scheme has been applied to fare revision in fifteen large private railways. For example, if a rail operator is inferior to other operators, then as a penalty the Ministry does not approve the fare level desired by the operator. On the other hand, if an operator's performance is relatively better than that of others, then the fare level is approved without revision. Thus any monopolistic behaviour due to the licensing system can be counterbalanced to some degree by this scheme.

However, there are two issues related to yardstick competition. First, how much the yardstick competition scheme is effective. Although the scheme does not bring about a situation of perfect competition, some kind of competition seems to exist. In fact, Mizutani's (1997) results, based upon Japanese railways' data set, have shown that yardstick competition among large private railways works to some degree. The second issue is related to the number of rail operators involved. The yardstick competition scheme had not been applied to public railways and small private railways. However, quite recently, the Ministry of Transport has decided to employ this scheme with public subway systems and passenger JRs in addition to major private railways (Okabe, 1997). If the competition effect can be detected in these operators, then the scheme will be considered effective.

Open access and new entrants

There is almost no literature discussing the possibility of open access as a Japanese railway policy. There are several possible explanations:

- first, historically, Japanese rail operation has been dependent on private railways. Aggressive competition policies such as open access could not be adopted because stable management might be threatened;
- second, existing private railways have been performing well. On the other hand, publicly owned railways' performance has not been good: a typical case was the JNR. Therefore, the ownership matter was a priority in railway reform;
- third, it becomes necessary to separate operation from rail infrastructure to introduce competition, but most railways in Japan are integrated. It is not easy to separate the ownership of infrastructure from operation because the infrastructure is a private company's property. Furthermore, most railway companies believe that integration is more cost advantageous; and
- fourth, because of non-rail businesses such as real estate development, companies are unlikely to want to sell tracks and adjacent land in which they have already invested a great deal (through business development) in order to increase rail ridership and stimulate the operations side of their railway companies.

Public purpose and social policy

Japanese public transportation is based on the full cost principle, with few subsidies available. However, if some areas suffer from insufficient public transportation, then facilities may be obtained through subsidy, though the level of demand would determine whether the transportation would be train or bus. Areas with existing rail systems for which demand is shown to be insufficient may be converted to bus transportation.

Most rail subsidies in Japan are for public subway systems. Furthermore, the amount of subsidy is limited compared with other countries. As for private railways, compared to the international standard, there are almost no subsidies. Even the former Japan National Railway before privatisation had fewer subsidies than those for other countries' national railways. According to the Japan Society of Civil Engineers (1990), the percentage of subsidies to total revenues in 1988 was 54.6 per cent for British Rail, 59.9 per cent for DB Railway, 87.5 per cent for SNCF but only 18.1 per cent for the Japan National Railway. Thus, subsidy programs for public transportation, especially railways, are limited.

There are several reasons why there are so few subsidies for railways:

- Japanese cities are highly dense so that traffic demand is sufficient for public transportation. As long as railways operate efficiently, they manage to operate without deficits;
- in Japan there are many private rail operators to which the national government hesitates to supply public money; and
- assistance programmes are available for specific target groups from local governments. For example, many local governments provide public transportation passes free or cheaply to the old and the disabled so that they can access public transportation.

However, in some rural areas with financially struggling local governments, where there is insufficient demand for maintaining private railways, quasi-private railways have emerged, supported and managed by both the private and public sectors. Since the privatisation of JNR, many branch lines in rural areas have been operated by this method.

6.3 Current organisation

6.3.1 Authorities

In the current Japanese railway market, the most important authority is the Ministry of Transport, which is responsible for regulating the transportation industry, not only railway but also bus, taxi, air, and maritime transportation. As for railway transportation, the Ministry of Transport's main responsibilities are: approval of railway licenses to rail service entrants; approval of rail fare; auditing and investigation of rail services; approval of rail service exits; and assessment of subsidy schemes. These administrative powers are authorised by laws and regulations. The Ministry of Transport regulates all railway transportation regardless of whether the operators are national or regional.

There are three other authorities related to rail industry. First, the Ministry of Finance is concerned with public finance and the national budget in railway projects such as the construction of the Shinkansen networks. The Ministry does not intervene in the management of a railway but it does assess national railway investment projects. Second, although the Ministry of Construction is not involved in railway projects, the road projects approved by the Ministry of Construction could conflict with the railway network. Furthermore, when railway operators provide services by using regular roads, these projects are regulated by the Ministry of Construction. Last, local governments may become involved in some areas of the rail industry such as the subsidy program and the network planning of public subway systems. Such unprofitable but socially necessary lines might be helped through subsidy by local governments. Local governments in large metropolitan areas get involved in the planning of public subway networks.

6.3.2 Operators

As of September 1, 1996, there were 188 organisations defined as rail operators. Of these operators, heavy and light rail operators account for 160 operators and others such as monorails, automated guideway transit, and cable cars account for 28 operators (see Figure 6.1).

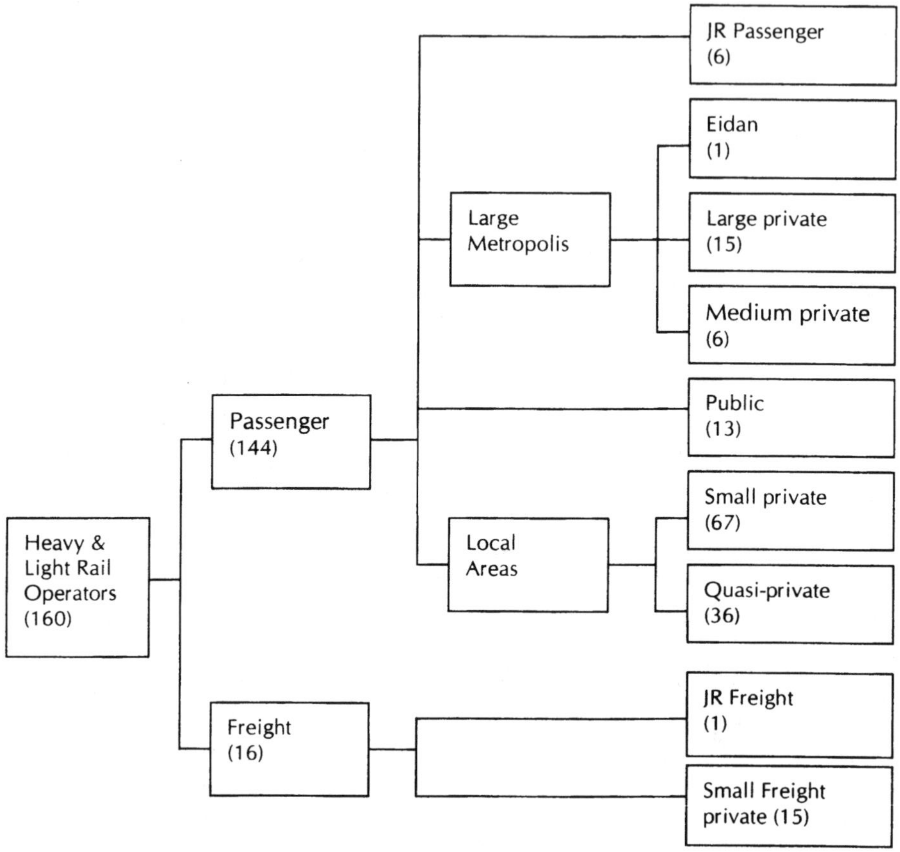

Figure 6.1 Classification and number of rail operators (Sept. 1996)

Source: based upon Mizutani (1994).

Passenger rail operators are classified in terms of four aspects, namely: legal classification; ownership; transport type; and main service areas. First, there are three kinds of legal classification: private corporations, special corporations, and public organisations. Private corporations are organisations legally considered to be private companies, including companies part of whose shares are held by the public sector. A public organisation is a department of the government such as the department of transportation of a local government. A special corporation is defined as an organisation which is settled and regulated by special law (Uekusa, 1991). JR and Eidan are considered special corporations. Second, as for ownership, there are three categories: private, public, and private-public joint ownership. Most Japanese rail operators are privately owned. Public ownership is limited to only 13 operators. Recently privatised JRs are not fully private sector because most of their shares are still held by the public sector. The most common transportation type is urban railways in large metropolitan areas. The major 15 private railways are classified into this group. However, JRs have both urban and intercity rail services.

Table 6.1 Classification of passenger rail operators

Operators	Legal Classification	Ownership	Service Type	Main Service Areas
Large private	Private Corporation	Private	Urban	Large Metropolitan areas (e.g. Tokyo, Osaka, etc.)
Medium private	Private Corporation	Private	Urban	Large Metropolitan areas (e.g. Tokyo, Osaka, etc.)
Small private	Private Corporation	Private	Urban	From large to small Urban areas
Quasi-private	Private Corporation	Private-Public	Urban	From large to small Urban areas
JR	Special Corporation	Public, partly private	IC and Urban	6 Regions in Japan
Eidan	Special Corporation	Public	Urban	Tokyo
Public	Public Organisation	Public (local government)	Urban	Tokyo, Osaka, Nagoya and 6 other large cities

Note: The author made this table based upon the classification by the Ministry of Transport, Rail Fact Book '96 (Suji de Miru Tetsudo '96) and Mizutani (1994).

Operators at the national level: passenger JRs

JNR reform

The national railway as a form of public corporation began after World War II in 1949 (Ministry of Transport 1992). Japan's rapid economic growth after the war spurred increased demand for transportation, with rail playing a vital role. However, JNR began to incur operating deficits, which continued to increase into the 1970s and 1980s. In 1980, the annual financial deficits amounted to about 1 008.4 billion yen (Mizutani and Nakamura, 1997a). The financial deficits accounted for 32.6 per cent of the variable component of operating cost (i.e. labour, energy, maintenance, material, service costs) or 25.4 per cent of the total operating cost.[3]

Although the causes of the financial trouble were partly the emergence of rival transportation modes such as auto and air transportation, the problems sprang largely from the public corporation system due to bureaucratic organisation, inefficient management, a tense management-labour union relationship, and political intervention (Kusano, 1989; Fukui, 1992; Fukui et. al. 1994). The crucial problem at JNR, according to policy makers, was the public corporation itself and the nation-wide control of a gigantic railway network under a single management system (Ministry of Transport, 1992).

The Provisional Committee, which was appointed under the Cabinet's jurisdiction in 1981, discussed how to achieve an effective, flexible administrative system and proposed privatisation with subdivision of the JNR (Kusano, 1989; Fukui et al. 1994). Over objections both within and outside JNR, it was decided to divide the mammoth corporation into smaller, more manageable parts, the six regional passenger companies, each a separate JR (Japan Railway) and the freight company called JR Freight. Two non-operator organisations were established at the same time, the JNR Settlement Corporation and the Shinkansen Holding Corporation. This happened in 1987.

Characteristics of the reform

By horizontal separation, the JNR was not only privatised but also separated into six regional passenger companies such as JR Hokkaido, JR East, JR Central, JR West, JR Shikoku, and JR Kyushu, and a freight company, JR Freight (see Table 6.2). There are two main reasons why horizontal separation was chosen:

[3] The costs of Japan National Railway were divided into the operating cost (3 964 billion yen) and the non-operating cost (44 billion yen) in 1980. The operating cost was divided into the operation cost (3 090 billion yen) and the capital cost (874 billion yen). The operation cost consists of i) labour (1 859 billion yen), ii) energy (223), iii) repair (678), iv) service(300), v) tax(30), and the capital cost consists of i) interest payment (476), ii) depreciation (342), iii) loss on retirement from fixed assets (26), iv) amortisation of deferred charges (31).

- the regional subdivision is to ensure that local needs for rail services were adequately attended to; and
- it was also presumed that the JRs would compete with each other to improve their performance.

Table 6.2 Profile of JR Companies at 'privatisation' (1987)

	JR Passenger						JR Freight
	Honshu Island JR's			Three-Islands JR's			
	East	Central	West	Hokkaido	Shikoku	Kyushu	
Route-km (km)	7 657	2 003	5 323	3 176	880	2 406	10 010
Pass.-km, ton-km (mln)	104 491	41 148	45 782	3 920	1 673	7 664	20 026
Train-km (mln)	227	78	151	34	16	46	75
Shinkansen operation	yes	yes	yes	no	no	no	no
Employees	82 469	21 410	51 538	12 719	4 455	14 589	12 005
Total assets (bln yen)	3 884.5	553.0	1 316.3	976.2	323.9	738.1	163.8
% stabil. fund/total assets	-	-	-	69.9%	64.3%	52.5%	-
Transf. LT debt (bln yen)	3 298.7	319.1	1 015.8	0	0	0	94.3
Capital (bln yen)	200	112	100	9	3.5	16	19

Source: Mizutani and Nakamura (1997a).

Other alternatives for dividing the JNR were discussed both officially and unofficially. For example, three alternatives were four regional subdivisions based on four main islands (Honshu, Hokkaido, Shikoku and Kyushu), about twenty regional subdivisions based upon branch offices of the JNR and division into trunk lines and branch lines. The last two were rejected firstly because there was great financial variation among the twenty subdivisions due to differing rail demand conditions, and secondly because branch lines could not be financially independent. As for the proposed four subdivisions, the Honshu region was considered to be too large compared with the other three, thus needing further subdivision. In addition to these alternatives, a division into urban rail operation and intercity rail operation was suggested, but was rejected as not feasible technically because both operations use the same tracks.

In order to ensure a sound managerial base, the subdivision into six regional passenger companies was adopted based on the geographical distribution of demand. In fact, 95 per cent of all trips were completed within the borders of these regions (Mizutani and Nakamura, 1997a). The six passenger JRs provide operation while owning their rail infrastructure, but JR Freight operates by borrowing rail track from these passenger JRs. JR Freight is a typical example of a vertically separated operator, paying a track user charge based on avoidable cost principle.

JNR privatisation

The privatisation of the JNR did not entail a complete conversion to the private sector from the beginning. The government was concerned that JNR's image had been so tarnished by years of deficits and inefficient operations that a stock offering would not interest enough investors, a debacle that would further add to JNR's public relations woes. Therefore, when JNR was privatised in 1987, the Japan National Railway Settlement Corporation (JNRSC) and the Shinkansen Holding Corporation (SHC) were also established.

The JNRSC was created as a temporary holding company, whose primary role was to repay the long-term debt held by JNR and to find employers for redundant JNR employees. The JNR related debts were 37.1 trillion yen in 1987. Of 37.1 trillion yen, 5.9 trillion yen was inherited by three passenger JRs (JR East, JR Central and JR West) and 5.7 trillion yen was inherited by SHC. The remaining 25.5 trillion yen went to JNRSC. The JNR debt held by JNRSC was expected to be repaid through the sales of JNR's assets such as land and the newly established JRs' shares. However, even if JNRSC sold all the land of the former JNR and all JR shares, making use of taxpayers' money would be inevitable.

SHC was established to lease the Shinkansen network to passenger JRs in 1987. SHC was the most typical case of infrastructure-operation separation in Japan. It was designed to equalise the economic impact of leaseholds among the JRs and to blend the costs of newly built Shinkansen lines and older lines. In 1987, the SHC leased the Tokaido Shinkansen to JR Central; Sanyo to JR West; and Tohoku and Joetsu to JR East. However, in 1991, the Shinkansen network was sold to these three passenger JRs and the SHC was closed.

In 1993, 62.5 per cent of JR East's stock was sold to the private sector. The subsequent recession delayed the issue of the JR companies' remaining stock, but with the recent recovery of the stock market, JR West and JR Central shares went on the market in 1996 and 1997 respectively. As of October 1997, 62.5 per cent of JR East's, 68.3 per cent of JR West's, and 67.0 per cent of JR Central's shares are held by the private sector. On the other hand, all shares of JR Hokkaido, Shikoku, Kyushu, and Freight are still held by the government (Mizutani and Nakamura, 1997b).

Regulatory and organisational differences between JNR and JR

In addition to the Railway Enterprise Law, JRs are also regulated by a special law commonly called the Japan Railway Law (*Ryokyaku Tetsudo Kabushiki Kaisya oyobi Nihon Kamotsu Tetsudo Kabushiki Kaisya ni Kansuru Horitsu*). Compared with the JNR era, there is much less intervention by the government in JR affairs. The chairman of the JNR used to be appointed by the cabinet and then this chairman, subject to approval by the Ministry of Transport, appointed the directors, including a vice-chairman. There are no regulations for JRs except the requirement that representative directors be approved by the Ministry of Transport, which also has to approve JRs' annual corporate plan. However, freedom of management of the JRs has become much greater than that for the former JNR.

The main differences in the relationship with the authorities can be summarised as follows (see also Table 6.3). Approval by the Diet (Parliament) is no longer necessary for changes in fare, diminishing the use of such changes for political purposes. With the division into regional companies, the government hoped to encourage competition and increase managerial efficiency. Several years after privatisation, there is still not much information about competition policy at the JRs, but in January, 1997 the government introduced an evaluation scheme called yardstick competition. It is no longer necessary for the Diet to approve the investment plans of rail networks, nor is there interference in the appointment of managing directors.

There have been many changes in the organisation of the companies (see also Table 6.3). The organisational form has been converted from a public corporation, which was one governmental body, to a special corporation, a commercialised body but still regulated by special laws. Service areas were changed from a single nationwide passenger service to several regionally based passenger services. Passenger and freight services were separated. Newly established JRs were allowed to operate non-rail service. Decision-making was simplified. Private company-type performance rating systems were introduced.

Table 6.3 Regulatory and organisational differences before and after privatisation

Items	Before privatisation (JNR)	After privatisation (JR)
Regulatory aspects		
(1) fare system	Approval by the Diet	Approval by Transport Ministry
(2) competition scheme	Lack of competition scheme	Conceptual installation of yardstick competition scheme effective after January 1997
(3) investment plan	Government investment in capital subject to approval by the Diet	Freedom by JR to invest without Diet approval but with Transport Ministry assessment
(4) appointment of directors	Chairman of the JNR was appointed by the cabinet Directors were appointed by the chairman subject to approval of the Transport Ministry	No regulations except that it is required that representative directors be approved by the Transport Ministry.
Organisational aspects		
(1) organisation form	Public corporation (national government)	Special corporation
(2) service areas	One corporation for all Japan	Six regional passenger corporations and one freight corporation for all Japan
(3) rail service	Mixed passenger and freight service	Separated passenger and freight services
(4) scope of business	Rail-related service only Non-rail business was not allowed	Non-rail business (e.g. real estate development, tourism) allowed
(5) management of organisation	Complex decision-making system Essentially government-type seniority system	Simplified organisation Introduction of private company-type performance rating system

Source: Mizutani and Nakamura (1997b).

Major operators at the regional level: major private railways and public subways

The fifteen major private railways provide urban rail service from the centre of the main city to the suburbs in large metropolitan areas such as Tokyo, Osaka, Nagoya, and Fukuoka. The relationship between major private railways and the JRs is competitive in certain cases of urban rail service. The ten public subways provide urban rail services whose main role is downtown distribution in the eight largest cities in Japan. Service areas by major private railways and those by public subways do not overlap so that the relationship between these two groups is considered not competitive but complementary.

The first private railway, *Nihon Tetsudo*, opened between Ueno (Tokyo) and Kumagaya in 1883.[4] This happened 11 years after the construction of the first Japanese railway. The evolution of private railways was coordinated with the modernisation policy of the government. Since the government itself did not have sufficient budgetary resources to establish a transportation network, it encouraged the private sector to invest in railways. By 1905, the total route length of private railways reached 70 per cent of its present level (private railways: 5 231km, national railways: 2 413km). However, a recession in the early 1900s decreased private railway construction significantly. Financial problems of private railways and pressure to nationalise for military reasons led to the passage of the Nationalisation of Railway Law (*Tetsudo Kokuyuka-ho*) in 1906. The Local Railway Law (*Chiho Tetsudo-ho*) in 1921, established a framework in which main intercity railways were operated by nationalised railways and private railways were limited to local and urban rail transportation only. During the Taisho era (1912-1926), the population grew rapidly in the central city and suburbs of large cities. Major lines had been opened in large cities. Buses also emerged as a short-distance competitor. Furthermore, the recession in the beginning of the Showa era (1926-1989) brought about the reorganisation of private railways. In pursuit of constant revenue, large private railways merged with small railways and participated in other businesses such as bus operation, real estate development, and tourism. In 1938, the Land Transportation Enterprise Law (*Rikujo Kotsu Jigyo Kyosei-ho*) was enacted in order to both avoid excess competition and support the war effort. In Tokyo, subways were consolidated into Eidan (Teito Rapid Transit Authority) and streetcars were consolidated under the Tokyo City Government. Private commuter rails were also reorganised as a regional monopoly. In principle, the policy emerged of one railway for each region, except in large metropolitan areas. After World War II, the transportation demand in large cities increased sharply. Private railways faced many difficulties such as cost increases, conflicts with labour unions, and serious accidents due to outdated rail facilities. Under these circumstances, a call was heard for the break-up of the larger private railways to achieve more efficient manage-

[4] This paragraph is a summary of Mizutani (1994).

ment. Consequently, at this time, the fourteen major railways came into being. With the end of rapid economic growth and the oil crisis of the mid-1970s, metropolitan population growth slowed. People also began using private automobiles. Light rails operated by local governments lost patronage in their competition with the private automobiles. New subway systems were opened by local governments from the 1970s to the beginning of the 1980s.

One distinguishing feature of private railways is that they also run non-rail businesses. The most typical non-rail businesses selected by private railways are real estate development, tourism, amusement and play facility development, and retail organisations such as department stores. Many researchers have pointed out the advantages of business diversification strategies (e.g. Saito, 1993; Killeen and Shoji, 1997). These are as follows:

- development of facilities such as housing and department stores along rail lines contributes to an increase in rail ridership in the long-run;
- more efficient labour employment can be attained. For example, if the rail service is in a slump, redundant employees can be moved to non-rail activities. The non-rail section can be used as a buffer section to avoid lay-offs, which are not common in the Japanese labour management; and
- the know-how achieved in the non-rail business could enhance the management of the rail service. For example, the information gathered in the course of running a travel business, such as travel behaviour, could be applied to making improvements in rail service.

The degree of the intervention by the Ministry of Transport appears to be lighter than in the case of JRs as these are still on the way to being fully privatised from a national railway. Railway regulations emanating from the Ministry of Transport seem purposely vague, stating that the authority can direct a railway operator to improve railway services when the authority judges improvement to be necessary. However, it is true that no private railways welcomes intervention from the authorities. For example, Hankyu, which is a major private railways based in Osaka, turned down a subsidy from the government to rebuild its rail track damaged by the Hanshin Great Earthquake in 1995. Hankyu chose to finance reconstruction of its rail track itself in order to avoid possible governmental strings attached to such a subsidy.

Competition between JRs and private railways

The relationship between major private railways and the JRs is competitive in certain rail markets. It is probably true that competition between JRs and private railways has been stimulated since the privatisation of JNR. Competitive performance and competition results vary among rail lines and rail operators (Nakamura and Mizutani, 1995). Clearly, the most important point, however, is that competition between JRs and private railways does exist, for example in suburban lines around large metropolitan areas whose JR services were inefficient. The type of competition seen in these cases has been line-base competition and service quality competition such as frequency between incumbent rail operators. Competition between JRs and private railways seems to be relatively more intense in Osaka and Nagoya than in the Tokyo area since these regions had several pre-existing parallel rail lines, and privatisation of the JRs became a trigger for competition between them.

New entrants

Many rail operators have been established since the enactment of the new Railway Enterprise Law in 1987 (see Table 6.4). Compared with statistics for 1986, the number of rail operators accounts for an increase of 32 (or about a 31 per cent increase) and total route length also increased by about 8 per cent.

Table 6.4 Transition in Number of Passenger Rail Operators and Total Route Length

Year	**1986**	**1987**	**1988**	**1989**	**1990**	**1991**	**1992**	**1993**	**1994**
Nr of operators	103	121	129	133	131	137	136	136	135
Total route-km	25 051	27 175	27 293	27 025	27 017	26 971	26 970	27 002	27 077

Source: Ministry of Transport (ed.) (1996), Rail Fact Book (Suji de Miru Tetsudo), p.67.

It is worth noting, however, that most of the rail operators that were established (or entered the rail market) are not totally private rail operators but quasi-private rail operators, which are jointly held by the private and public sector. In the late 1980s, several local branch lines of the JNR were established and revitalised as quasi-private railways. Since then, suburban commuter rail companies have also been built.

The main reason why a totally private rail operator has not entered the rail market is that the construction costs of rail track and rolling stock would be huge in large metropolitan areas so that no rail operator could sustain a rail business by rail fare revenues only. Most likely, quasi-private railways were established in order to avoid the business risk of the initial investment in rail infrastructure. In order to make it easier to enter the rail service market, the government established the class 2 license, for operation-only operators. However, the private sector still seems hesitant to introduce new rail services.

The planning of a Japanese railway occurs in general through private initiative. The Railway Enterprise Law states that it is possible for a private organisation to make a plan for a railway route and obtain a railway license. The most important point is that the planning of a railway project is not done by the Ministry of Transport, but by each individual rail enterprise. The Ministry of Transport assesses each individual railway's plan based on the opinions of Transport Policy Committees appointed by the Ministry. In general, the Transport Ministry itself does not generate plans for railway projects, but acts more as a director to the actors on the stage.

There are cases, however, in which the public sector gets involved in railway network planning. The first case is the planning of the Shinkansen network, for which the Ministry of Transport has responsibility. The second case is the planning of public subway networks, which are operated by local governments. In this case, local governments develop subway network systems. Finally, it is possible for the public sector to work together with the private sector, which occurs in railway projects in suburbs in large metropolitan areas. Because the budget of the railway projects in large metropolitan areas is tremendous due to high land prices, the private-public partnership is adopted in order to avoid project risk.

Rail operation providers and infrastructure providers

The class 2 rail enterprises, which provide rail operation borrowing another organisation's rail tracks, are few. The most typical case is the JR Freight company, which operates freight services by borrowing rail tracks from the six passenger JR companies. In addition to JR Freight, there are 11 such rail enterprises, accounting for a total of 111.3 route kilometres at the end of March 1995 (Ministry of Transport, 1995).

The class 2 rail enterprise's role is very different from operation-only railways in Europe. The existing class 2 enterprises own their own tracks on different lines. This means that these enterprises are in fact class 1 enterprises but provide rail services by borrowing other organisations' rail tracks partially among their total line hauls. Their roles involve extended operation to some specific facility or area such as an airport or a suburban new town, along with interconnection operations among different rail operators.

An example of a class 3 enterprise is the Housing and Urban Development Railway in Chiba Prefecture, owned by the Housing and Urban Development Corporation. The role of this line is to improve accessibility from the suburbs to the centre of Tokyo. Hokuso Kaihatsu operates rail services on this line by borrowing the HUD Corporation's track. Typical examples of existing rail infrastructure providers are shown in Table 6.5. Narita Airport Railway and Kansai Airport Railway are rail track providers holding airport-access rail lines extended from existing rail lines owned by companies such as JR and private railways. The main role of these rail lines is improving accessibility to airports. Kobe Kosoku Railway was established in order to connect four existing private railways. Its main role was to improve mobility among different rail organisations in downtown Kobe. Of four private railways, Hankyu, Hanshin and Sanyo provide direct rail services on their own tracks as well as having an agreement whereby they run trains on each other's tracks.

Conflict of operators and infrastructure providers

There are some disadvantages to operation and infrastructure separation based upon the existing operator's opinion. The most notable problem is scheduling of rail service. For example, JR Freight (operation) sometimes experiences conflict in rail operation with passenger JR companies (track provider). Problems occur in rail lines with large train volumes in large metropolitan areas. JR Freight cannot operate on its own optimal schedule, because passenger trains are priority. This schedule puts rail freight at a disadvantage against trucking, which can transport goods without such time restrictions.

Table 6.5 Major Infrastructure Providers

Name	HUD Corp. Railway	Narita Airport Railway	Kansai Airport Railway	Kobe Kosoku Railway
Date of operation	19 March 1984	19 March 1991	15 June 1994	7 April 1968
Major Stock Holders (%)	Public Agency	Public (2.1) Private (97.9)	Public (80.4) Private (19.6)	Public (40.0) Private (60.0)
Route-km (km)	8.7	10.8	6.9	7.6
Operators	Hokuso Kaihatsu	JR East Keisei	JR West Nankai	Hankyu Hanshin Kobe Dentetsu Sanyo
Track usage fee (million yen/km)	78	340	450	565
Major role	Commuter rail	Airport access	Airport access	Commuter rail
Metropolitan areas	Greater Tokyo (Chiba)	Greater Tokyo (Chiba)	Greater Osaka (Osaka)	Greater Osaka (Kobe)

Notes: (1) This table is modified by the author based on Ministry of Transport (ed.) (1995), *Railway Outline (Tetsudo Yoran)*.
(2) Track usage fees are calculated by dividing revenues from track usage by route-km.
(3) These numbers are for 1994.

6.4 Analytical framework: competition and ownership

Competitive environment and ownership

There are two important factors in increasing efficiency: a competitive environment (competition) and ownership. Parker (1994) shows a conceptual figure of the relationship between these factors and efficiency gain. Mizutani (1997) applies Parker's concept to the Japanese rail industry, taking competitive environment to be not open-access competition but yardstick competition. In Figure 6.2, the vertical axis shows the degree of competition. The movement from monopoly to competition shows gains in efficiency. The horizontal axis shows ownership difference. The movement from public to private ownership also creates an efficiency gain. Therefore, a change in both competitive environment and ownership structure from monopoly to competition and from public to private would bring about the biggest efficiency gain.

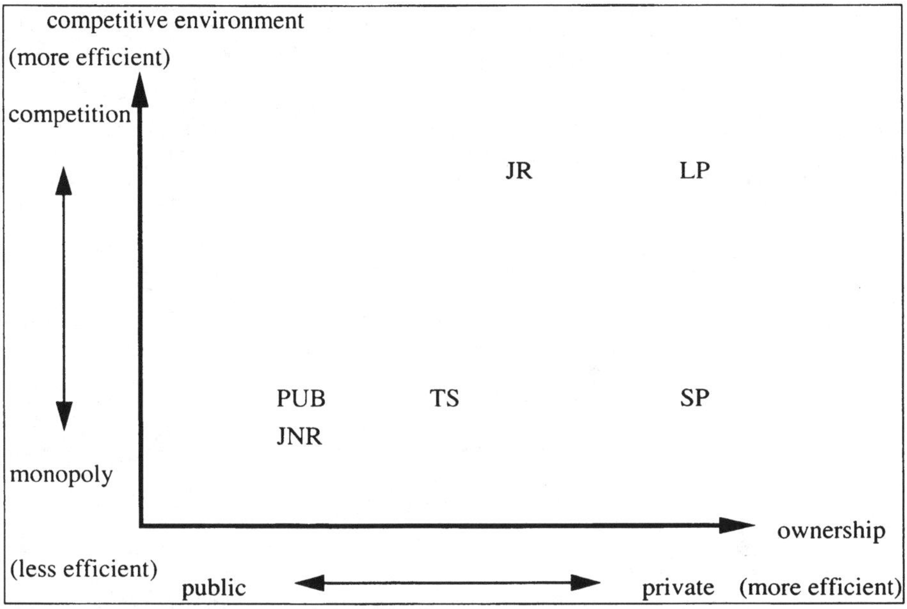

Note: LP: large private operators, SP: small private operators, PUB: public operators, JR: privatised JR railways, JNR: former Japan National Railways, TS: quasi-private rail operators (third sector): joint ownership

Figure 6.2 Competition and Ownership Effects and Efficiency

Source: Mizutani, 1997.

The main content of the Japanese regulatory reform in 1987 was to shift the ownership of the Former Japan National Railway (JNR). Another key regulatory change was that newly established JR companies were expected to compete with each other and/or with private railways. Whilst the competitive environment and ownership structure of most other rail operators have not changed significantly, it is likely that some large private railways are being affected by the privatisation and subsequent increased competition from the new JR companies.

Kinds of competition and competition factors

The railway industry in Japan seems less competitive because of its license system. However, it does not mean no competition. Based on the conceptual figure, there are two factors, which create efficiency: ownership and competitive environment. Furthermore, these factors can be divided into several kinds of competition and seen from several dimensions (see Figure 6.3). Of course these two main factors are mutually affected by each other.

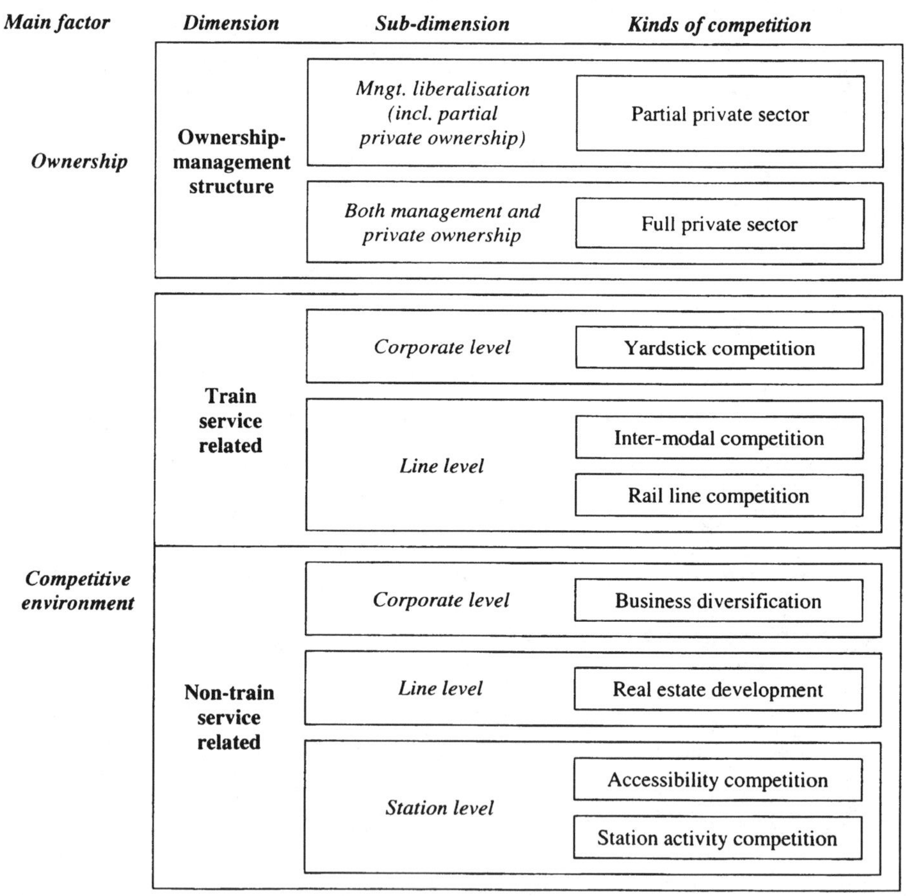

Figure 6.3 Kinds of Competition in the Japanese Rail Industry

Ownership factor is divided into two sub-categories:

- *full private sector*: The full private sector is run with the private sector's management style and the ownership is also purely private. Some argue that ownership difference does not matter but fully private railways feel pressure from stockholders to perform efficiently, and they are less likely to experience political intervention than fully public railways. This idea is borne out by empirical evidence from the Japanese rail industry (Miyajima and Lee, 1984; Mizutani, 1994); and
- *partial private sector*: As shares in the partial private sector are partially owned by the public sector, it is more likely to experience political intervention.

Competitive environment is divided into several kinds of competition from several dimensions. The first dimension was divided into two categories: train service and non-train service related. Furthermore, these categories are subdivided into corporate level, line level and station level.

First, the *train service related* level is divided into:

- *yardstick competition* (corporate level): Yardstick competition is competition among rail operators, generally in different markets, to improve certain performance measures such as productivity and costs. This has been applied for rail fare assessment in large private railways since the mid-seventies, according to Maeda (1979);
- *inter-modal competition* (line level): Inter-modal competition is competition with air transport for long-distance travel and with private car transportation for short- and middle-distance travel. This kind of competition is direct competition in the same market; and
- *rail line competition* (line level): Rail line competition is competition among lines served by different railways. Although the government regulates entry, there are several parallel rail lines connecting two major urban centres. There can be competition along these lines. The Osaka area has more parallel rail lines than Tokyo and privatisation has become a key to introducing this kind of competition.

Second, the *non-train service related* level is divided into:

- *business diversification* (corporation level): Business diversification occurs when a railway corporation provides non-rail services within a company or within group companies. Most typical non-rail businesses are bus operation, real estate development, tourism, and retail businesses such as department stores. Large private railways have taken business diversification strategies and have been competing with each other as whole corporations. Large private railways are said to be providing not only rail services but total community services, which include rail services (Saito, 1993);

- *real estate development* (line level): Real estate development is one business diversification strongly related to along-line characteristics. Real estate development, especially housing development, could contribute to an increase in rail ridership in the long run. Large private railways have long been involved in land development along their lines. They have competed in making communities attractive in order to affect residential location decision making;
- *accessibility competition* (station level): Accessibility competition and station activity competition are both examples of station level competition. Because walking distance to a rail station is limited, a key factor would be accessibility to a rail station by a non-walking mode, especially by bus. However, it is not clear how much accessibility competition really exists because the Ministry of Transport also regulates bus operation as a licensed system; and
- *station activity competition* (station level): Station activity competition means stations offering various activities to attract people. Private railways have many kinds of activities such as development of offices, shopping facilities, and cultural centres at station buildings.

Rail operators have several kinds of competitive pressures, although the degree of pressure varies by type and organisation (see Table 6.6):

- *Private ownership*: Public railways are indirectly held by many taxpayers and links of principal-agent spread into many stages so that incentives to run the organisation efficiently could be diluted. As a result, competitive pressure at public railways would be lower than at private railways.
- *Entrepreneurial behaviour*: A large private railway's behaviour is sometimes compared to an entrepreneur's behaviour. Although entrepreneurship has many meanings, here it means corporate manager behaviour which provides user-oriented services and/or creates new kinds of business both inside and outside the company without fear of risk. This kind of behaviour is rare in the transportation industry,

which is generally considered to be a very planned and standardised industry. The source of this behaviour is probably from competition among managers both inside and outside the company. Competitive pressure for managers might stem from the motivation to get higher positions or to head a leading company in the industry, or from a concern for creating new kinds of business to avert a decline in the railway industry. At any rate, at the corporate manager level, there is competition revealed as entrepreneurial behaviour.

- *Pressure from rail users*: Although, there is seemingly no competition on the supply side because the government regulates most transportation modes, rail users create pressure on the rail operator. For example, rail users can switch to auto or other rail operators in the short run. Even in a monopolistic market such as the commuter rail market in large cities, in the long run, rail users can relocate their residence to other areas.
- *Competitors*: Competition for both train-service related and non-train service related activities puts pressure on a rail operator to lure passengers.
- *Regulators*: There are pressures from regulators, notably yardstick regulation in fare and full cost principle without subsidies. First, yardstick regulation would certainly create competitive pressure because the Ministry of Transport assesses the large private railways' performance by using the yardstick regulation scheme when the revision of rail fare is necessary. Second, the full cost principle without subsidy scheme could be another pressure. Compared with public railways, there is no subsidy available for large private railways (Saito, 1993; Mizutani, 1994). The full cost principle as well as restriction of subsidy would cause pressure to attain higher efficiency.

Table 6.6 Competitive Pressures on Rail Operators

Pressure from	Type of pressure
Owner	Private ownership: pressure from stock holder
Managers	Entrepreneurial behaviour
Rail users	Need for better rail services
Competitors	Quality competition to capture demand
Regulator	Yardstick regulation in fare, full cost principle without subsidy scheme

6.5 Case study: The Osaka metropolis

6.5.1 Characteristics of the areas and services

The Kinki region was selected for case study. The Kinki region is in western Japan, and its main metropolitan area, the second largest in Japan after Tokyo's, is the Greater Osaka Metropolitan Area (which will be referred to as the Osaka metropolis) shown in Figure 6.4. Another important point is that there are many private rail operators in the Osaka metropolis.

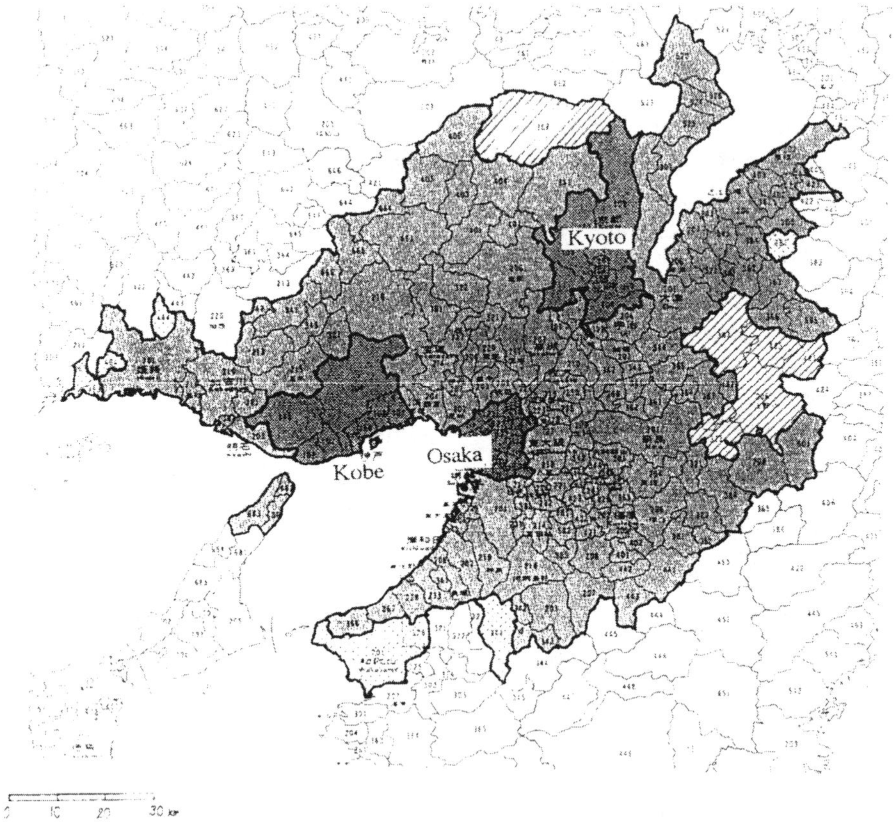

Figure 6.4 Osaka Metropolitan Area (Osaka, Kyoto, Kobe, Nara)

Source: Statistics Bureau (1994, p. 656)

Table 6.7 shows the basic characteristics of the area compared to the Netherlands. The main metropolitan area, the Osaka metropolis, consists of three core cities: Osaka, Kobe, and Kyoto. Osaka is the largest and is the economic and financial centre, with 2.5 million people. Kobe, with a population of 1.5 million, is famous for being one of East Asia's five biggest seaports. Kyoto, with a population of 1.4 million, was the capital of Japan and is now its cultural centre. It can be observed that the Osaka metropolis is about three times larger than the Randstad. The average population density for the area is larger than that of the Randstad. However, the population density in the core cities is rather similar. If we consider the suburbs of the Osaka metropolis, the densities become even more similar: 901(Otsu), 406 (Kameoka), 3 429 (Takatsuki), 1 681 (Nara), 439 (Sanda), 1 991 (Takarazuka). Table 6.8 illustrates the mode share in the Osaka Metropolitan Areas based on the number of trips, for the period 1970-1990.

Table 6.7 Kinki Region and Osaka Metropolitan Area: Characteristics

	Country / region		**Metropolitan areas**		**Municipalities**	
	The Nether-lands	**Kinki Region**	**Randstad**	**Osaka Metro-politan**	**Amsterdam Den Haag Rotterdam Utrecht**	**Osaka Kobe Kyoto Nara**
Area (km^2)	33 882	37 014b	5 514	10 522	502	1 588
Population (1000)	15 567	23 167b	6 325	18 431	1 981	5 681
Population density	459	626b	1 147	1 752	3 947	3 577
Income (US$/pers.)	19 050a	28 621c				
Route length (km)	2 795	1 773				
Passengers (million)	15 195c	13 685c				
Car ownership/person	0.362	0.300b				
Cars/km^2	137	188b				

Notes: Kinki region includes Osaka, Kyoto, Hyogo, Shiga, Nara, Wakayama, Mie and Fukui. The numbers in the table are based on 1995 (except (a)1994, (b)1992 (c)1991) and were obtained from several sources. Areas for the Netherlands and core cities are only for land areas.

Table 6.8 Mode Share (in %) in Osaka Metropolitan Areas

	Rail	Bus	Auto	2-wheel	Walk	Others
1970	19.5	6.7	15.3	9.1	49.1	0.3
1980	18.5	4.4	19.6	19.6	37.8	0.1
1990	19.9	3.3	25.9	21.7	29.1	0.1

Note: These numbers are based on Person Trip Survey.

6.5.2 Actors at the level of the case study

Authorities and transport companies

The Ministry of Transport regulates all railway transportation regardless of whether the operators are private or public. For this case study, the seven main operators were selected (see also their profiles in Table 6.9).

Kintetsu is a private railway with the longest railway network among Japanese private railways. Kintetsu's non-stop super express between Osaka and Nagoya is a strong competitor with the Shinkansen operated by JR Central. Kintetsu operates not only commuter but also super-express trains connecting several famous tourist spots such as Kyoto, Nara, and Ise-Shima, in addition to operating non-rail services such as housing development and amusement parks.

Hankyu is the only private railway connecting the three largest cities (Osaka, Kobe and Kyoto) in the Osaka metropolis. Hankyu is known for its entrepreneurial behaviour in the early urbanisation era, having engaged in housing development along with the construction of rail lines, as well as operating amusement parks and musical operas. Hankyu's main track rail lines between Osaka and Kobe and Osaka and Kyoto have suffered severe competition with JR West since privatisation in 1987.

Hanshin, a relatively small private railway among the fifteen major private railways, connects Osaka and Kobe along the coastline, which was urbanised early on. Hanshin has also faced competition with JR West.

JR West is one of the JR family railways. JR West' s service areas cover all the western part of Honshu Island, Japan' s largest. JR West operates urban rail services as well as local rail services and the Sanyo Shinkansen (between Osaka and Fukuoka). Of the JR West network, networks in the Osaka metropolis accounted for about 491km. JR West has been allowed to run non-rail business like other private railways since 1987, but the magnitude of its business diversification does not match that of other private railways so far.

Table 6.9 Profile of Transport Companies in the Case Study in 1995

	Kintetsu	Hankyu	Hanshin	JR West	Kyoto City	Osaka City	Kobe City
Year started operations	1914	1910	1905	1987	1981	1933	1977
Ownership	Private	Private	Private	Quasi-private	Public	Public	Public
Major service	Commuter	Commuter	Commuter	Commuter City centre Local	City centre	City centre	City centre
Route-km	594 (232)	146	45	5 070 (491)	11	106	23
Station spacing (km)	1.71 (1.49)	1.76	1.10	4.14 (2.40)	0.92	1.08	1.53
Passenger-km (million)	15 136 (10 377)	9 894	1 979	55 484	320	5 971	940
Train-km (million)	69.9	22.0	7.4	190.1	1.2	16.1	2.5
Employees in rail section	11 259	4 149	1 319	45 730	735	7 790	767
Rolling stock (vehicles)	2 133	1 338	314	6 463	102	1 170	168
Non-rail service revenue on total revenues (%)	19.2	48.4	59.1	2.0	67.9 (bus)	13.4 (bus)	45.9 (bus)

Note: (1) This table was revised by the author based on information from the Ministry of Transport, Railway Bureau (ed.) (1997) and Ministry of Transport, Transport Policy Bureau (ed.)vn (1997).
(2) Numbers in parentheses are for the Osaka metropolitan area only in 1994.

Kyoto, Osaka, and Kobe City run their own railway systems. The transport division of the city government runs these as well as bus services. Although these operators are considered as the typical counterparts of private railways when comparing service performance, there is a technological difference in that public railways are subway systems providing central city distribution but large private railways are surface railway systems serving as suburban commuter services. Direct competition between a public railway and a private railway seems unlikely because the areas and needs served are different.

Kobe Kosoku is a typical infrastructure-providing company with a class 3 license. Kobe Kosoku Railway was established in 1968 in order to connect four existing private railways. Its main role was to improve mobility among the different rail organisations in downtown Kobe. Of four private railways, Hankyu, Hanshin and Sanyo provide direct rail services on their own tracks as well as having an agreement whereby they run trains on each other' s tracks.

6.5.3 Railway services

Entry and exit

Although the organisation of the rail market in the Osaka area seems not to have changed much since the Railway Enterprise Law of 1987, as Table 6.10 shows, several interesting trends can be seen. First, under the new law, quasi-private operators have entered the railway market, and public subway systems continue to expand their lines. Second, no 'new' rail organisation seems to have been established since 1987: only rail line expansion can be seen. Third, there is no exit for public railways but several private railways have abandoned some parts of rail lines. It is worth noting that there is no case of an entire rail company exiting the rail market.

Expansion of existing rail lines might be seen as a threat by incumbent rail operators, whose share might be reduced by the expansion of the other rail line. The construction of a new rail line connecting existing rail lines could also be a threat. For example, JR West's newly established Katafuku-renraku Line was opened in 1997 to connect two existing suburban lines through central Osaka, making it easy for rail users of the two existing suburban lines to access the central city. This new line caused some rail users of private railways to shift to JR West, a very rare occurrence because the Ministry of Transport tightly controls rail licensing. In fact, although a private railway company had wanted to expand its line into central Osaka, the city subway's opposition halted the project. In conclusion, as long as a railway company operates without performing too badly, the licensing system protects it from potential entrants.

In Japan there is virtually no threat for an incumbent rail operator from a potential entrant, as long as the incumbent provides safe service within reasonable financial bounds. Although the Railway Enterprise Law does not clearly forbid granting a rail license to a potential entrant desiring to operate parallel to an incumbent's tracks, such a case could not happen as it would fail to satisfy the second or fifth criteria of article 5 of the law.

Instead of the threat of potential entrants, the yardstick competition scheme is applied to large private railways to avoid inefficiency.

Table 6.10 Number of entries and exits in the Osaka Area

		Before Enterprise Law			After Enterprise Law			Average
	Year	**81-83**	**84-86**	**Average**	**87-89**	**90-92**	**93-95**	
Entry	**Total**	**3**	**5**	**1.33**	**6**	**5**	**4**	**1.67**
	Private	2	3	0.83	3	4	1	0.89
	Public	1	2	0.50	3	1	3	0.78
Exit	**Total**	**3**	**1**	**0.67**	**1**	**2**	**2**	**0.56**
	Private	3	1	0.67	1	2	2	0.56
	Public	0	0	0.00	0	0	0	0.00

Note: (1) The definitions of entry and exit are newly obtained license (entry) and abandoned (exit) lines by an operator.
(2) These numbers are obtained from the Ministry of Transport, Railway Bureau (ed.), Annual Rail Statistics (Tetsudo Tokei Nenpo).
(3) Private operators include quasi-private operators.
(4) The 'average' means numbers of entries or exits per year for a given period.

Furthermore high construction costs of rail infrastructures and prohibitive land prices restrict entry into the rail market. Even if a need exists for rail services, for example to accommodate residents of new towns, it is not easy for the private sector to enter the market. A huge investment for a private railway company would be risky. As an example, Kobe Dentetsu which provides rail services for the north side of Kobe City, is a middle-sized private railway with old tracks that limit its capacity. It has been expected to modernise its facilities but modernisation has progressed very slowly, most likely due to its small budget. Its inertia can probably also be attributed to the lack of threat of new entrants into its market. The Railway Enterprise Law of 1987 tries to solve this problem by creating new types of rail licenses, one for rail service operation only (class 2) and one for rail track only (class 3). According to this provision, the private and public sector have recently started to establish new rail track companies to enter into new markets, leaving the operations to the private sector. For example, Kintetsu applied for this kind of rail license for a new town (Keihanna new town in the suburbs of Osaka and Kyoto).

Infrastructure-operation separation

The most notable case of infrastructure-operation separation is that of Kobe Kosoku. Kobe Kosoku is a track holding company, which is jointly held by the private and public sectors, and lets four private operators (Hankyu, Hanshin, Sanyo and Kobe Dentetsu) rent its tracks to run rail operations. Kobe Kosoku holds track facilities including electric and signalling systems, while the four operation companies hold their own rolling stock. Kobe Kosoku's main responsibility is the maintenance of tracks and stations and it charges infrastructure usage fees to four operation companies. The main revenue of the four operation companies (Hankyu, Hanshin, Sanyo, Kobe Dentetsu) is the fare collected by Kobe Kosoku, which divides rail fare among the four operation companies, allocated by their respective track mileage. For example, Hankyu, Hanshin and Sanyo make equal use of the East-West line of Kobe Kosoku, so that rail revenues are equally divided.

The general rule for determining an infrastructure charge is based on the recovery of the total investment cost in track facilities. However, if the track investment has already been sunk, the infrastructure charges would be calculated by the operating costs of track maintenance activities. The infrastructure charges to JR Freight were calculated based on avoidable costs of maintenance activities. As for Kobe Kosoku, infrastructure charges are based on maintenance costs of infrastructure. These maintenance costs include labour, material and service costs of both the maintenance and the administration division. If infrastructure charges have to be altered considerably, then there would be room for negotiating such charges between the infrastructure and operation companies involved. Kobe Kosoku has reported no conflict between the infrastructure and the operation companies. Presumably one reason is that Kobe Kosoku's ownership is shared equally by Kobe city (40 per cent) and four operation companies (40 per cent) so that the opinions of both sides (infrastructure and operation) can be equally represented.

Most private railways in this case study, including rail operators, are class 1 enterprise. Kobe Kosoku is a typical class 3 enterprise. However, it is worth noting that Hankyu, Hanshin, Sanyo and Kobe Dentetsu are also classified as class 2 on Kobe Kosoku' s track, as they use the lines owned by Kobe Kosoku. Rolling stock as well as employees and tracks is generally owned by each rail enterprise. In general, class 1 enterprises own these input factors, class 2 enterprises own operation employees and rolling stock, and class 3 enterprises own infrastructure and maintenance facilities.

Rolling stock leasing companies are not common in Japan. Small private railways, which are not financially strong, purchase second-hand rolling stock from large private railways instead of leasing.

Table 6.11 Infrastructure-operation separation in the case of Kobe Kosoku

Rail organisation	Track company	Rail operation company
Name of operator	Kobe Kosoku	Hankyu, Hanshin, Sanyo Kobe Dentetsu
Ownership	Kobe city (40.0%) Hankyu, Hanshin, Sanyo (each 10.7%), Kobe Dentetsu (7.9%), other private (20.0%)	Private (100%)
Rail license	Class 3	Class 2
Ownership of facilities	Track and stations	Rolling stock
Maintenance of tracks	By itself	-
Control of operation schedule	Contracting in from operation companies (Hankyu, Hanshin, Sanyo, Kobe Dentetsu)	Contracting out to a track company (Kobe Kosoku)
Management of station activity	Contracting in from operation companies (Hankyu, Hanshin, Sanyo, Kobe Dentetsu)	Contracting out to a track company (Kobe Kosoku)
Revenues	Infrastructure charges and contracting-in charges from operation companies (Hankyu, Hanshin, Sanyo, Kobe Dentetsu)	Rail fares from rail users

6.5.4 Business diversification and research and development (R&D) of private railways

Business diversification

Private railways were restricted to use of or creation of lines which did not interfere with the Japan National Railway's lines and thus travelled through less populated areas. While private railways were expected to be self-supporting, numerous bankruptcies and limited population bases forced private railways to generate a steady ridership for rail operation (Killeen and Shoji, 1997; Saito, 1993). This situation led to the utilisation of a business diversification strategy.

There are two type of business diversification strategies: within a railway company (a 'company-level' diversification) and within group companies ('group-level' diversification). Company-level diversification refers to a railway company operating non-rail business inside its rail company. Typical examples are bus and taxi services, real estate development, and retail ventures such as department stores and tourism. In 1995, revenues from non-rail business accounted for between 19 and 78 per cent of total revenue in 15 large private railways (Killeen and Shoji, 1997). As for group-level diversification, there are two sources available: booklets issued by private railways and the Securities Report issued by the Ministry of Finance. However, these sources do not cover all companies connected with the core rail company[5]. As an example, Table 6.12 shows Kintetsu's group company profile in 1995. The Kintetsu group had 152 companies and total sales revenues of 3,240,706 million yen. The sales revenue of the railway core company accounted for only about 9 per cent. Even though the railway company might garner less revenue, there is no doubt that Kintetsu's core business is its railway.

Typical diversification of private railways includes the following:

- transportation: bus, taxi, rental car, air transport;
- real estate development: housing development, business office rental;
- retail sales: department stores, supermarkets, concession stands;
- tourism: travel agencies, amusement parks, hotels;
- manufacturing: rail passenger cars, plant construction;
- information: cable TV, information processing, advertisement; and
- culture: movie theatres, musical theatres, professional sports.

[5] For example, a company is considered to be a part of the group company and is included in the Securities Report if the parent company directly or indirectly owns a majority of voting shares. However, if the profits of a company under question do not exceed 10 per cent of the parent company (railway company's) revenues, the company is not included (Killeen and Shoji, 1997).

Table 6.12 Business Diversification of the Kintetsu Group in 1995

Industry	Number of companies	Number of employees	Capital (million yen)	Annual revenue (million yen)
Railway	1	12 458	90 894	286 716
Bus	12	7 515	7 003	91 174
Tax and rent-a-car	23	5 860	953	38 272
Truck and air cargo	4	21 832	34 140	372 233
Ropeway	2	218	450	3 664
Private roads	2	140	500	2 341
Maritime	6	446	1 698	7 854
Tourism	6	7 128	5 050	787 129
Hotels and inns	29	6 242	22 104	101 673
Department stores	9	9 029	8 403	542 783
Restaurant and shops	8	2 648	902	66 483
Amusement parks, entertainment, etc.	10	1 540	6 307	50 676
Car dealers and car repairs	10	1 459	884	59 516
Real estate development	12	1 644	8 085	194 262
Manufacturing and construction	13	7 429	13 409	453 219
Advertisement, insurance etc.	5	1 782	4 170	182 711
Total	**152**	**87 370**	**205 042**	**3 240 706**

Source: Kintetsu (1995), p.23, pp.123-131.

Business diversification can contribute to both the revenue and cost sides. As for the revenue side, first, it is easy to see how real estate development such as housing development and office facility management could contribute to rail ridership in the long run. Access to bus operation also makes rail use easier. Second, activities such as amusement parks could ease demand imbalance between peak and off-peak rail services. Third, non-rail business operation could also contribute to acquiring the externality. A typical example is real estate development. Because the rail fare is regulated, the spill over effect often reveals itself as an increase of the land price. A railway company could secure improvement effects by purchasing the surrounding land.

As for the cost side, first, business diversification could make efficient use of idle financial resources. Redundant employees and land could be transferred to other business-input resources. Second, business diversification might stimulate rail business itself. For example, the know-how required for non-rail business might be useful in improving management at the core rail company. Last, there might be economies of scope between rail business and non-rail business. For example, the information obtained from the rail service on travel behaviour could reduce the cost of tourism operation. Therefore, it might be cheaper to operate both rail service and tourism rather than to operate them separately.

R&D and innovation

Private railways' R&D consists of that related to railway business and that related to non-rail business. First, rail related R&D consists of technology development in train scheduling, track maintenance and information systems. The main thrust of R&D at large private railways centres on how to reduce manpower. Some innovations in track maintenance activities could contribute to reducing maintenance costs. The introduction of more advanced computer-aided control systems could help increase train operation as well as the achievement of more train capacity.

An important characteristic of private railways' R&D is a desire for software rather than hardware technology development. Private railways display aggressiveness in developing new kinds of business one after another, with the railway business at the core. While the initial development of non-rail business at private railways mostly used know-how from the core railway business (i.e. manufacturing using rolling stock maintenance innovation, tourism using passenger information), recent development is surprisingly removed from the image of a typical railway company. For example, Keihan recently opened a bridal business by operating a special train containing its own chapel and reception room, with weddings taking place at off-peak times. This is but one example of 'development and innovation' using software technology in private railways.

6.5.5 Privatisation effects

Overall results

In this case study, the performance of JR West before (1985) and after privatisation (1995) is compared. Table 6.13 summarises the performance changes before and after privatisation.

Table 6.13 Comparison of performance before and after privatisation

Measure	Before (1985)	After (1995)	After/before and evaluation
Service quality			
• Peak interval (min)	3.3	3.2	0.970
• Average interval (min)	5.5	4.5	0.818
• Travel time for 20km (min)	25.9	25.4	0.981
• Variation of train service pattern	Many	Many	Few differences in urban services
• Service time (start, end)	4:54 0:50	4:50 0:59	Slightly longer after privatisation
• Peak load factor (%)	226	162	0.717
• Punctuality	Accurate	Accurate	Not much difference
• Accident rate	1.521	0.805	0.529
Finance			
• Fare level for 10km (yen)	156	170	1.090
• Fare level for 20km (yen)	267	290	1.086
• Av. Operating cost (per pass-km)	22.95	14.51	0.632
• Av. Operating cost less deprec.	15.50	12.04	0.777
• Subsidy (debts) (per passenger-km)	35.55	0.00	0.000
• Fare box recovery ratio	0.723	1.023	1.415
• Operating revenue recovery ratio	0.821	1.130	1.378
Salary			
• Standard monthly salary (yen)	261,884	323,115	1.234

Note: (1) Numbers in service quality and fare level are based on the most typical four lines for JR West and JNR: Kobe line, Osaka Kanjo line, Gakken Toshi line, Kansai line.
(2) Unit of measures : accident rate (accidents per million train-km), ave. operating cost (yen per passenger-km), ave. operating cost less depreciation (yen per passenger-km), subsidy (yen per passenger-km)
(3) (i) fare box recovery ratio = fare revenues / operating costs
(ii) operating revenue recovery ratio = operating revenues / operating costs where
fare revenues = total revenues from fares
operating revenues = fare rev. + sales rev. (e.g. parcel transport and sales at kiosks)
operating costs = labour costs + energy costs + material costs + maintenance costs (tracks and rolling stock) + depreciation + tax
Operating revenues do not include subsidies. Operating costs are considered as total costs of rail operation financially defined, which include both variable and fixed components of rail costs.
(4) All monetary terms are 1995 value.
(5) Figures in operating cost, subsidy, profitability and wage are obtained from JNR average (before privatisation) and JR West only (after privatisation).
(6) These numbers were calculated by the author based on several sources.

As for service quality, the overall service quality has not improved dramatically. Samples to assess service quality were selected from four typical lines (Kobe line, Osaka Kanjo line, Gakken Toshi line, Kansai line). Service quality was already good before privatisation but improvement can be shown in some areas, namely: average frequency, peak load factor and accident rate. As Mizutani and Nakamura (1997b) pointed out, performance improvement in service quality occurred in lines that were under-utilised suburban lines and which were competing with other operators.

A change in the financial situation proved to be the most remarkable result of privatisation. Profitability measured by fare box recovery ratio and operating revenue recovery ratio was 0.72 and 0.82 in 1985. These increased to 1.02 and 1.13 in 1995. These profitability measures improved by 42 per cent and 38 per cent. Such financial gains occurred on both the revenue and cost sides. On the cost side, productivity growth, especially labour productivity, brought about lower operating costs. For example, average operating cost less depreciation increased by about 22 per cent.

On the demand side, the increase in number of passengers was one factor which improved the financial situation. The higher fare level also helped. In fact, the real fare level increased by 9 per cent during this time period. However, the most important fact is that while fares had been increasing yearly before privatisation, the only fare revision in the nine years after privatisation occurred in April 1989, when it was necessary to accommodate the consumption tax introduced in Japan. As a result, JR West has received no subsidy since privatisation.

Wages increased after privatisation. According to statistics, compared with the JNR era, JR West's standard monthly salary improved by about 23 per cent over ten years. Salary was increased most likely to give incentives to improve efficiency, to compensate workers for their new, multi-faceted positions, or to recruit more capable workers who might otherwise be drawn to private railways. Another explanation was that before privatisation salaries consisted of many other fringe benefits but that after privatisation they were simplified and more transparent.

Reasons for performance improvement

There are several reasons for improved performance. First, JNR had been an unwieldy and bureaucratic organisation, sluggish to respond to external change. It was too large to be a single organisation and the system of decision-making was too centralised. As a result, there were several problems, such as the excessive length of time it took to make a decision and the inability of the organisation to meet local needs quickly. In order to approve a single initiative, it was necessary to circulate documents among twenty to thirty people who would stamp them with their personal seals (Ishii et al., 1994). JNR's reform therefore stipulated not only privatisation but also regional subdivision into organisations smaller than the JNR.

Second, the resulting JR companies have themselves become less centralised organisations. For example, branch offices have more freedom to use their own judgement when making a decision. As for organisational structure, hierarchy became more flat, evolving from four to three stages. This change shortened decision-making time (Kitani, 1997).

Third, a more private company-style performance rating system was introduced. At JNR, the wage system was based mostly on age and seniority, discouraging individual incentive to improve performance. The introduction of a more private-company style encouraged self-improvement among employees and made the organisation more active.

Fourth, improvement of rail services has occurred in rail operation, stations and facilities, and public relations exercises including the distribution of information have been used to enhance the JRs' corporate image. Typical options taken by JRs have been increasing frequency, varying train type, using clockface timetabling during off-peak hours, and increasing train speed.

Fifth, the most dramatic change in service quality has occurred in rail lines near large cities (Nakamura and Mizutani, 1995; Mizutani and Nakamura, 1997b). Stations were remodelled, elevators and escalators were added, and new stations were built. Telephone reservations and purchases were also introduced to attract more rail ridership. All of these changes indicated JRs' desire to polish their image among the public.

Sixth, according to Kitani's (1997) study, JR West has encountered no serious interference from the Ministry of Transport in the management of its company. Although the Japan Railway Law of 1987 rules that JR companies must have approval from the Ministry of Transport for the appointment of representative directors and for corporate management plans, the Ministry of Transport has offered no resistance to JR West's course of action. Management's independence could be one important factor in its improved performance.

However, unlike JR West, where political interference was light, some JR companies have been affected by politics. Most cases have involved the construction of new Shinkansen networks. Politicians hungry for votes in their home prefectures have used their influence to pressure JRs into Shinkansen construction in spite of the financial weakness of the new JRs to manage such large-scale projects.

Last, the management-labour relationship has certainly improved. At the end of the JNR era, massive strikes by labour unions often occurred and the relationship was at its worst, both sides viewing the other with great distrust. Since privatisation, management and labour unions seem to be working toward the same goals. At least there have been no massive strikes, and this improved relationship could well be a factor in the demonstrated better performance.

6.5.6 A private-public comparison

In this section, an evaluation will be made of the impact of ownership on performance. Operators selected here are Kintetsu, Hankyu and Hanshin as representatives of the private sector, and Kyoto City, Osaka City, and Kobe City for the public sector (see Table 6.14).

Overall results

As for service quality, in general private railways seem to be slightly better than public railways in many ways. Most notable is that private railways are more convenient than public railways. Both sectors have very high frequency but private railways operate many kinds of trains such as super-express, express, semi-express and regular trains. The combination of these kinds of trains ensures rail users a speedy arrival at their destination. On the other hand, public railways have a longer travel time, offering almost exclusively regular trains, but it is worth noting that public railways have some technological constraints that may prevent them from providing the wider variety of trains they would like to. Therefore, the ownership factor is not the cause for the difference in service quality. Nonetheless, the variety of trains offered by large private railways makes them superior in this area of service quality.

Public railways seem to be more attentive to the needs of the weak than private railways. For example, the percentage of stations with elevators and escalators or equipment for physically handicapped people is higher for public railways than for private railways. Again, it is necessary to note that there are non-ownership factors like that public railways are relatively newer than private railways, so that public railways might have a greater tendency to have installed new facilities than private railways.

Table 6.14 Performance Comparison in Selected Measures

Measure	Private	Public	Private/public and evaluation
Service quality			
• Peak interval (min)	2.3	3.0	0.767
• Average interval (min)	3.6	5.1	0.706
• Travel time for 10km (min)	14.1	16.9	0.834
• Variation of train	Many	Single	Private has more choice
• Service time (start, end)	4:49 0:44	5:15 0:28	Private starts slightly earlier
• Peak load factor (%)	159	165	0.964
• Punctuality	Accurate	Accurate	No difference
• Accident rate	0.268	0.308	0.870
• Consideration for the weak (index of facility installation)	0.662	0.773	0.856
Productivity			
• Passenger-km per employees (1000)	1 743	810	2.152
• Passenger-km per train-km	312	336	0.929
Finance			
• Fare level for 10km (yen)	247	267	0.925
• Fare level for 20km (yen)	313	360	0.869
• Av. Operating cost (per pass-km)	11.58	27.51	0.421
• Av. Operating cost less deprec.	8.81	16.94	0.520
• Subsidy (per passenger-km)	0.00	5.4	-
• Fare box recovery ratio	1.039	1.010	1.029
• Operating revenue recovery ratio	1.108	1.102	1.005
Salary			
• Standard monthly salary (yen)	314 294	358 108	0.878
• Work. Condition (overtime wage rate (%))	21.6	26.1	0.828

Note: (1) These numbers are a sample mean of selected operators: private operators (Kintetsu, Hankyu, Hanshin) and public operators (Kyoto City, Osaka City, Kobe City). Numbers in service quality and fare level are based on the most typical lines for each operator: Nara line (Kintetsu), Kyoto line (Hankyu), Hanshin line (Hanshin), Karasuma line (Kyoto City), Mido-suji (Osaka City), Seishin line (Kobe City).
(2) Units of measure and definitions: see previous table.
(3) Definition of measures: index of facility installation (average percentage of five facilities installation; escalator, elevator, passageway for wheelchair, ticket machine for blind people, toilet for handicapped people), overtime wage rate (overtime wage divided by the sum of standard salary and overtime wage)
(4) Subsidy for public railways is from the year 1990.
(5) These numbers were calculated by the author based on several sources.

As for reliability, measured in terms of punctuality and safety, there is no difference between the sectors. Both sectors have acquired reliable reputations among rail users. Last, as for train congestion, both sectors have an abominable record. However, the train congestion on private railways seems to be less.

Certainly private railways are superior to public railways financially. Even if we consider the technological difference, private railways are more efficient than public. As a result, the fare level of private railways is lower than that of public and operating subsidies are not necessary. On the other hand, it is necessary for public railways to make up operating deficits with operating subsidies.

The salary of public railway workers is certainly higher than for private railway workers. This is one important reason why public railways are more costly than private railways. Furthermore, as for overtime working ratio measured by overtime salary to standard salary, private railways have a smaller ratio than public railways. If we rely on these statistics, overtime working conditions for private railway workers are at most equal to or better than for public railway workers.

Possible reasons why private is better

User-oriented behaviour

Private railways are more user-oriented than public railways. The concept of 'user oriented behaviour' here is defined as behaviour indicating a willingness to understand passenger's needs and reflect those needs quickly. Although it is not easy to prove this concept, some cases seem to support the idea that private is better.

- First, some private railways use a monitoring system to assess rail passengers' needs (e.g. Keikyu, Tokyu, Kintetsu, Nishitetsu). Considering geographical variation and generation differences, rail operators select monitors from rail users and use these monitors' opinions to improve their rail services. Although some private railways do not have monitoring systems, they have feed-back gathering systems in each station to solicit suggestions from rail users. Hankyu is more aggressive. Although Hankyu does not have a monitoring system, it has been able to comprehend rail users' needs. Each individual employee at Hankyu is encouraged to share the corporate philosophy, which supposedly stimulates in employees the desire to provide not only rail services but also regional development and regional culture. Large private railways have also been upgrading new rolling stock, in spite of the fact that their rail business budgets are very limited.

- Second, the train scheduling of large private railways has much more variety than that of public railways. For example, Hanshin provides several kinds of train services such as regular, semi-express, express, and commuter express. Furthermore, large private railways have introduced several information systems for rail users. For example, private railways developed indicators for use above platforms informing rail users about the next train (i.e. type of train, destination, station stops). In order to get train information, facsimile telephones are provided for each station for deaf passengers unable to use regular telephones (Hankyu, Kintetsu).

Advertisement

Active advertisement by large private railways is a distinguishing characteristic which perhaps plays a part in attracting rail ridership. In the theory of industrial organisation, there are two kinds of advertisement activities: persuasive advertising and informative advertising. The former intends to enhance consumer tastes for a certain service or product while the latter provides basic service or product information such as prices and service characteristics. Large private railways are probably more active in persuasive advertising. Most public railways are limited to providing basic information on rail service, such as fare and operation schedule. On the other hand, large private railways are actively using advertisements to convince users how their services are superior to other modes or to other operators, and they are spending more money to get their message across. In fact, statistical data can reveal active advertisement strategies by large private operators, as Table 6.15 shows. This table shows, for example, that large private operators have spent about 18 to 37 per cent of total profits on advertisement, whereas for all Japanese railways the figure is only 4 per cent on average.

The main reason for large private railway's active advertisement is that the government regulates rail fare so that an increase in rail ridership is necessary in order to improve profit level. Large private railways have become active in advertisement to attract more ridership. For example, Kintetsu advertises its non-stop super-express service between Osaka and Nagoya, and its luxurious super-express services to tourist spots such as Kyoto, Nara and Ise-Shima. These services have strong competitors: the former service rivals the Shinkansen service by JR Central and the latter service rivals that of the private car.

Table 6.15 Magnitude of Advertisement Expenses in 1995

Operator	Total (million yen)	Yen per pass-km	Per rail service revenues (%)	Per rail service profits (%)
Kintetsu	6 308	0.417	3.2	24.7
Hankyu	2 631	0.266	2.5	18.7
Hanshin	301	0.152	1.1	36.7
JR West	6 806	0.123	0.7	5.2
All Japanese Rails	41 716	0.104	0.6	3.9

Notes: (1) rail service profits = rail operating revenues - rail operating costs
rail operating revenues = fare revenues + revenues from parcel transport, etc.
rail operating costs = variable costs (labor, energy , material, etc.) + fixed costs (maintenance of track and rolling stock, depreciation, etc.)
(2) This table is a summary by the author based on data from the Ministry of Transport, Railway Bureau (ed.) (1997).

Real estate development and passengers

Private railways are involved in real estate development to capture externalities by the improvement of rail facilities,[6] and to increase rail ridership in the long-run. Because the Ministry of Transport regulates rail fare, even if a rail company improves service quality for a given line, there is no guarantee that the rail company can get all increased value. For example, suppose a rail company invests in track and rolling stock in order to reduce travel time between suburban residential areas and the central city. Because full cost principle is adopted for the fare system, direct investment costs by the private rail operator would be counted in the rail fare increase. However, the time costs (opportunity costs) reduction is often larger than the fare increase. Therefore, it appears as an increase in land price in residential areas. The increase in land price is a transfer by rail service improvement. Therefore, the rail company has an incentive to capture the externality.

It is not easy to confirm empirically whether real estate development really contributes to an increase in rail ridership. However, most large private railways have a long history based on this belief. For example,

[6] If the rail service is improved, the increased value results in an increase in rail fare. However, if the fare is regulated and the operator cannot increase the rail fare, then the increased value would spill over to an increase in land value. Therefore, the rail operator has an incentive to capture the spilled-over value by purchasing land along rail lines.

Hankyu started out in a relatively less populated area. In order to increase the rail ridership, Hankyu became involved in housing development along the Kobe and Takarazuka lines in Osaka, areas which are now considered prime residential locations.

As a first approximation, a typical station with large scale housing development by railway companies was chosen and compared with a station of similar distance from the central city but without large scale housing development. Table 6.16 shows the results. Except for case-1, stations with large-scale housing development clearly have larger passenger volumes. Case 1 was most likely developed in the 1950s and has therefore already matured as a town, so that the passenger number has not changed dramatically. It is worth noting that public railways are also involved in housing development and rail service jointly. Kobe city developed both housing and rail service in the western regions of the city. These results show more rail ridership than in areas without housing development.

Table 6.16 Housing development and number of passengers

Case	Large scale housing development	Station	Operator	Distance from Osaka (km)	Travel time	Passengers at station	
						Per day	difference
Case 1	With	Gakuenmae	Kintetsu	25.2	24 min	28 735	(0.86)
	Without	Oji	JR	25.6	36 min	33 366	(1.00)
Case 2	With	Kuzuha	Keihan	27.7	31min	30 710	(3.29)
	Without	Nagao	JR	26.2	28 min	9 342	(1.00)
Case 3	With	Seishin Chuo	Kobe City	52.0	51 m. (1chg)	24 043	(1.84)
	Without	Okubo	JR	58.7	47 min	13 094	(1.00)

Note: These figures are estimated by the author based on several sources such as the Ministry of Transport, Transport Policy Bureau (1997) and JTB (1997).

The importance of housing development at the inception of project life should be stressed. Such real estate development could contribute to an increase in rail ridership from an early stage, easing the financial burden as the company recovers the initial investment costs of railways earlier. This does not however mean cross subsidisation but only that a company may attain more fare revenues through housing development.

Access services

Access service is also important in attracting rail ridership. Although public rail operators also provide bus services to stations, large private railways can be more adept at luring passengers. For example, although rail services along the Gakken Toshi line of JNR were improved dramatically in the early 1980s, the number of passengers did not increase much. Even residents close to the Nagao station of the Gakken Toshi line used the competitive Keihan line instead of JNR. According to Mizutani (1983), people chose Keihan rather than JNR because of the frequency of Keihan's bus access to Keihan's terminal station, Hirakata city station.[7]

Another example is shown in Table 6.17. Case-1 represents little variation in bus operation, while case-2 represents great variation in access of bus service to rail station. Clearly, the more bus services available, the more rail passengers there are. If there is not much difference in bus access service, then rail service such as travel time becomes important. Thus, the access service to a rail station is important. Bus services could be a critical factor in determining to what extent rail operators can attract rail passengers because the extent of attraction in the area within walking distance is limited.[8]

[7] This is an interesting issue related to the analysis of fair competition and the monopoly's vertical integration strategies. However, in this case study, I only explain the facts because the topic is too broad to discuss here.

[8] There is no doubt that population density is an important factor, but it is not a necessary or sufficient condition. For example, I assume that population density and walking distance to a station are 3,000 persons/km**2 and 1km. The total population of this walking residential area is 9,420 persons (=3,000x1x1x3.14). If we assume that the typical family type is two adults and two children and two persons per family use a train every day, then passengers per station per day becomes 4 710 people. This number is rather small compared with actual numbers at stations. Thus, accessibility is important in attracting more rail passengers.

Table 6.17 Effect of Access Bus Service

Case	Rail station	Operator	Travel time to Osaka	Bus per day	Bus operator	Passenger at station per day
Case 1	Takatsuki	JR	15 min	1 881	City and Keihan	61 825
	Takatsuki	Hankyu	25 min	1 230	City and Keihan	28 533
Case 2	Itami	JR	15 min	222	City and Hankyu	9 766
	Itami	Hankyu	17 min (1 chg)	1 288	City and Hankyu	23 777

Note: These figures are estimated by the author based on several sources such as the Ministry of Transport, Transport Policy Bureau (1997) and JTB (1997).

6.6 General evaluation and conclusions

Japanese railway regulation for entry is based upon the license system. As empirical results in the Osaka metropolis shows, there has not been much change in the entry and exit situation since the new Railway Enterprise Law in 1987. We cannot evaluate the effectiveness of the license system from the experience of the Japanese rail market because the system has remained virtually unchanged. Although Japanese railways generally have advantages such as urban density, many small private operators also make profits in smaller urban areas. Thus, so far the license system does not seem to cause financial problems. However, it is possible that the license system might engender passivity in rail operators to improve facilities. Although there might be budget constraints on a small operator to upgrade facilities, its inertia can probably also be attributed to the lack of threat of new entrants into its market.

The reform of the Japan National Railway, which is partial privatisation with liberalisation of management, has significantly improved efficiency. These improvements were achieved by the reform of several aspects such as organisational structure, management of the organisation, incentive scheme, rail service strategy and management-labour relations. However, the privatised JRs are not as efficient as large private railways, showing perhaps that full privatisation would be an important factor in attaining a higher efficiency level. Political interference has eased considerably but there is still room for political interference in the future, especially in the construction of the Shinkansen network.

Private railways clearly perform better than public railways in terms of productive efficiency. Although in overall service quality there is not much difference, large private railways provide a larger variety of rail services than public railways, as a result of private railways' entrepreneurial behaviour. Private railways operate non-rail businesses, the most typical of which are real estate development and tourism, which probably contribute to increased rail ridership. Private railways' advertisement activity and R&D in software also show active behaviour to attract more rail ridership, activities which on the whole maintain a stable rail market. By observing the behaviour of these large private railways, existing rail operators might improve their own performance.

The yardstick competition scheme might be one way to avoid productive inefficiency resulting from the license system. Although the scheme does not bring about a situation of perfect competition, some kind of competition does seem to exist. Empirical results based on Japanese railways' data set have shown that yardstick competition among large private railways works to some degree.

Acknowledgements

I would like to thank Professor Kenichi Shoji of Kobe University for his comments to the initial version of this paper.

References

Economic Planning Agency, Research Bureau (ed.) (1997) *Economic Statistics (Keizai Yoran),* Ministry of Finance, Printing Bureau, Tokyo, Japan.

Fukui, K (1992) *Japanese National Railways Privatisation Study: Japanese Experience and Lessons for Developing Countries,* World Bank Discussion Paper No.172, The World Bank, Washington, D.C., USA.

Fukui, K., K. Nakamura, T. Ozaki, H. Sakamaki, and F. Mizutani (1994) *Japanese National Railways Privatisation Study II: Institutionalising Major Policy Change and Examining Economic Implication,* CFS Discussion Paper No.107, The World Bank, Washington, D.C., USA.

Ishii, Y., K. Okada and T. Yada (1994) "Railway Management in the Age of Changes: Kyushu Railway Company" (Henkakuki no Tetsudo Keiei: Kyushu Ryokyaku Tetsudo Kabushiki Kaisya), *Transportation and Economy (Unyu to Keizai),* Vol.54, No.4, pp.5-40 (in Japanese).

Japan Society of Civil Engineers (ed.) (1990) *Transportation Improvement System (Kotsu Seibi Seido),* Japan Society of Civil Engineers, Tokyo, Japan (in Japanese).

JTB (1997) *JTB Timetable(Jikokuhyo),* August, JTB, Tokyo.

Killeen, B. J. and K. Shoji (1997) "Diversification Strategy and Urban Transportation: The Case of Japan", *Presented Paper at the 5th International Conference on Competition and Ownership in Land Passenger Transport,* Leeds, UK, 27-30 May.

Kintetsu (1995) *'95 Hand Book,* Kintetsu, Osaka, Japan (in Japanese).

Kitani, S. (1997) "Privatisation Progress and Its Effect in JR West" (JR Nishinihon ni Okeru Mineika no Shinten to Sono Kouka), In T. Imamura (ed.), *Effects and Reality of Privatisation: NTT and JR (Mineika no Kouka to Genjitsu),* Chuo Hoki, Tokyo, Japan (in Japanese).

Kusano, A. (1989) *Reform of the Japan National Railway (Kokutetsu Kaikaku),* Chuo Koronsya, Tokyo, Japan (in Japanese).

Maeda, Y. (1979) " Fare System of Private Railways: Focus of Large Private Railways" (Minei Tetsudo no Unchin Seido: Ote Shitetsu wo Chushin to Shite), *Annual Report on Transportation Economics 1979 (Kotsugaku Kenkyu 1979),* Vol.23, pp.139-155 (in Japanese).

Ministry of Transport, Regional Transport Bureau (ed.) (1990), *Annual Urban Transportation Statistics '89 (Toshi Kotsu Nenpo '89),* Transport Economic Research Center, Tokyo (in Japanese).

Ministry of Transport, Transport Policy Bureau (ed.) (1990) *Fare and Price System in Transportation Business (Unyujigyo no Unchin Ryokin Seido),* Transport Economic Research Center, Tokyo (in Japanese).

Ministry of Transport, Railway Bureau (ed.) (1992) *Issues and Achievements in the Five Years since the Japan National Railways Reform,* Japan Transport Economics Research Center, Tokyo.

Ministry of Transport, Railway Bureau (ed.) (1995) *Railway Outline (Tetsudo Yoran),* Denkisya Kenkyukai Tetsudo Tosyo Kankokai, Tokyo (in Japanese).

Ministry of Transport, Railway Bureau (ed.) (1996a) *Compendium of Railway Law (Chukai Tetsudo Roppou),* Daiichi Hoki, Tokyo (in Japanese).

Ministry of Transport, Railway Bureau (ed.) (1996b) *Rail Fact Book '96 (Suji de Miru Tetsudo '96),* Transport Economic Research Center, Tokyo (in Japanese).

Ministry of Transport, Railway Bureau (ed.) (1997) *Annual Railway Statistics '95 (Tetsudo Tokei Nenpo '95),* Seifu Shiryotou Fukyu Chosakai, Tokyo (in Japanese).

Ministry of Transport, Transport Policy Bureau (ed.) (1997) *Annual Urban Transportation Statistics '96 (Toshi Kotsu Nenpo '96),* Transport Economic Research Center, Tokyo (in Japanese).

Miyajima, M. and S. D. Lee (1984) "A Study Comparing the Efficiency of Local Public Enterprises and Private Enterprise: Railway Industry" (Chiho Koei Kigyo to Minkan Kigyo no Koritsusei no Hikaku ni Kansuru Kenkyu: Tetsudogyo wo Reitoshite), *Journal of Public Utility Economics (Koeki Jigyo Kenkyu),* Vol.36, No.1, pp.79-100 (in Japanese).

Mizutani, F. (1983) *Systems Analysis of Newly Improved Urban Rail Systems (Daitoshiken ni Okeru Tetsudo Shisetsu Seibi Keikaku Joho no Sakusei ni Kansuru Shisutemuronteki Kenkyu),* Master of Science Thesis, Kyoto University, Kyoto, Japan (in Japanese).

Mizutani, F. (1993) "A Private-Public Comparison of Labor Productivity and Utilization in Japanese Urban Railways", *Proceedings of the Third International Conference On Competition and Ownership In Surface Passenger Transport,* September 26-29, Toronto, Ontario, Canada, pp.421-437.

Mizutani, F. (1994) *Japanese Urban Railways: A Private-Public Comparison,* Avebury, Aldershot, UK.

Mizutani, F. (1997) "Empirical Analysis of Yardstick Competition in Japanese Rail Industry", *International Journal of Transport Economics,* Vo.24, No.3, pp.367-392.

Mizutani, F. and K. Nakamura (1997a) "Privatisation of the Japan National Railway: Overview of Performance Changes", *International Journal of Transport Economics,* Vol.24, No.1, pp.75-99.

Mizutani, F. and K. Nakamura (1997b) "Japan Railways Since Privatisation (2nd.ed.)", *Paper Prepared for Seminar on Privatisation and Regulation of Transport,* July 2-4, Regulatory Policy Research Centre, Hertford College, Oxford, UK.

Nakamura, K. and F, Mizutani (1995) "The Effects of Railway Privatisation on Competitive Performance: A Case Study of Japanese Railways", *Journal of the Eastern Asia Society for Transportation Studies,* Vol.1, No.1, pp.85-102.

Okabe, M. (1997) "New Passenger Railway Fare System: Outline and Features (Atarashii Ryokyaku Tetsudo Unchin Seido: Gaiyo to Tokusyoku)", *Transportation and Economy (Unyu to Keizai),* Vol.57, No.5, pp.12-23 (in Japanese).

Parker, D. (1994) "Nationalisation, Privatisation, and Agency Status with Government: Testing for the Importance of Ownership", in P. M. Jackson and C. M. Price (eds.) *Privatisation and Regulation,* Longman, London, UK.

Saito, T. (1993) *Private Rail Industry: Development of Japanese Style Railway Management (Shitetsu Sangyo: Nihongata Tetsudo Keiei no Tenkai),* Koyo Syobo, Kyoto (in Japanese).

Shleifer A.(1985), "A Theory of Yardstick Competition", *Rand Journal of Economics,* Vol.16, No.3, Autumn, pp.319-327.

Statistics Bureau (1994), *Population of Major Metropolitan Areas, 1990 Population Census of Japan,* Reference Report Series No.2, Management and Co-ordination Agency, Statistics Bureau, Tokyo.

Suga, T. (1997) "The Separation of Operations From Infrastructure in the Provision of Railway Services: Examples in Japan", In the European Conference of Ministers of Transport (ECMT) (ed.), *The Separation of Operations From Infrastructure in the Provision of Railway Services,* OECD, Paris, France, pp.155-176.

Uekusa, M (1991) *Economics of Public Regulation (Koteki Kisei no Keizaigaku),* Chikuma Syobo, Tokyo (in Japanese).

Van de Velde, D. M. (1993) "The Japanese Public Transport System," In D.M. van de Velde, J. D. M. Westeneng and E. A. M. van Hoek (eds.) *OV-regulering, Adequaat?,* Erasmus University, Rotterdam, The Netherlands.

Van de Velde, D. M. (1997) "Entrepreneurship and Tendering in Local Public Transport Services", *Paper Presented at the 5th International Conference on Competition and Ownership in Land Passenger Transport,* Leeds, UK, 27-30 May.

7 France

OLIVIER DOMENACH and PIERRIC TEURNIER
Jonction/Université de la Méditerranée, Aix-en-Provence

7.1 Introduction

The French railway reform, implementing the 91/440 EU directive in many ways does not go as far as the reforms implemented in many European countries. The most recent step in the reform has however been the creation of a separate infrastructure division (RFF *Réseau Ferré de France*). This has, for the time being, had no influence on the monopoly of the SNCF in terms of passenger services.

After a description of the legal and regulatory framework, and recent of its evolution towards a more regionalised approach, this chapter on France will present the position of the various actors in the new regime. Special attention will be paid in a following section on the regionalisation experiments currently undertaken in order to test a new, more decentralised, form of control on the regional passenger transport services provided by the SNCF. General conclusions will be drawn at the end of this report.

7.2 Legal and regulatory framework

Nineteen ninety-seven is year one of a new era for the French Railways. Up to this date and since its creation in 1938, SNCF operated on a basis which made it a 'State within the State', according to the French expression. A number of principles were determinant for its functioning until 1997: oneness of the company, 'public service' network, public enterprise monopoly, public service for passenger transport, cross-subsidisation in fares, monopoly of expertise, network planning and services monopoly, etc.

The SNCF was itself responsible for the services at the national level and therefore acted as such as a 'Transport Authority'. Its strategy gave, in agreement with the State, more importance to the high speed network, to the detriment of the traditional speed network.

As far as the regional services were concerned, partnership with regions was difficult. This was due to SNCF's overweight in terms of informational inequality in analysis and evaluation expertise, to the detriment of the regional-level partner. However, the regional services of SNCF were dependent upon the existence of a regional will to develop railway transport.

The revolution which the SNCF had to undergo in the recent past is twofold:

- *separation of network and production into two organisations:* both organisations – SNCF and the new RFF (see further) – will remain public enterprises and the network will remain a 'public utility network' but SNCF will loose its expertise monopoly on the infrastructure; and
- *regionalisation:* SNCF is going to become a service operator under contract from regional Transport Authorities. It will have to contractually commit itself to service performances, costs and revenues. SNCF will be fined should it not honour its contractual obligations. It will be possible for the Region to finance the network and the rolling stock. Consequently, regional financing will be linked to production performance, to ridership increase, to customer satisfaction, etc. These new components will enlarge the commercial dimension of the management of the services.

The two reforms will be presented separately in this section. At the end of this chapter, a section will be devoted to a closer analysis of the current experimental contracts of regionalisation.

7.2.1 Regionalisation of the French railways

Before 1972, the SNCF was a public monopoly, both for passenger and for freight services. All national and regional services were designed and operated in a centralised way from the national level. Since then, the legal and regulatory framework under which the French Railways have functioned has undergone several legislative and institutional phases which have led to an increasing regionalisation of the control of some of its passenger services.

For clarity's sake, these reforms will be presented here as three periods.

First period: 1972/1982: Introduction of service agreements for regional transport (without institutional power)

The 19 French Regions, each comprising several Departments, were created by the law of 5 July 1972 but did not receive any transport powers. It is only on 6 March 1974 that the concept of 'Regional Transport Guidelines' (*Schéma Regional de Transport* or SRT) for passengers was created by an inter-ministry committee, without however promulgating any official text. According to this decision, each Region's SRT had to include regional political choices regarding public transport, the description of a network of regional interest (including the improvements to be implemented to scheduled services and special transport, such as school transport) covering intercity relations within the Region, services to rural and labour areas and the principal relations with neighbouring towns and Regions.

With the Decree of 30 August 1977, as a further measure of decentralisation, the Regions were granted the power to negotiate agreements ('*conventions*') with existing transport operators, such as SNCF, for regional railway transport, purchase rolling equipment, finance lines together with other local authorities.

Second period: 1982/1995: Generalisation of the use of contracts

The Law on Interior Transport (called *LOTI – Loi d'Orientation des Transports Intérieurs*) from 31 December 1982[1] established important concepts in French public transport. It led to the generalisation of the usage of contracts (*conventionnement*) for the relationships between the Transport Authorities (created by the same law) and transport operators.

Right to transport and public service

The LOTI states the notion of the 'right to transport' and of 'public service' in transport.

- *Right to transport (art. 1 & 2)* means that any passenger has a basic right to move and choose a means of transport. The transport system should provide reasonable conditions concerning usage, quality and cost for the community, notably through public transport. It does not,

[1] And its implementation decree from 30 June 1983.

however, mean that each link should be serviced by the complete array of transport modes, but rather by at least one of those modes.

- The concept of *'service public'*[2] *in transport (art. 5)* includes the following assignments:
  - realisation, management, availability, maintenance and safety of transport infrastructure;
  - regulation and control on transport activities (including considerations related to national defence);
  - provision of information on the transport system; and
  - 'organisation' of public transport services.[3]
- The notion of *public service network (art. 22)* means that the investment appraisal for networks should include land-use effects and contributions to national development, national defence, exercising right to transport, ports servicing, environment protection and energy savings. Moreover, the appraisal should take into account the own profitability of the traffic on the network.

Organising Transport Authorities

The LOTI stipulates that 'organising regular public transport for passengers' is a 'public service' which may be handed over to 'territorial communities' such as Transport Authorities (called in French *AO* for *Autorité Organisatrice*, i.e. organising authority). This is true for (groupings of) municipalities for urban passenger transport (art. 27) and for departments for non-urban passenger transport (art.29). It has to be noted that the Regions[4] are *not* granted the competence of Transport Authority by the LOTI. Article 22 of the LOTI, however, stipulates that Regions that have established a SRT may establish contracts for the lines defined by those plans. Furthermore any changes in services of national interest have to be submitted to the Regions for consultation and, if requested by the Regions, an advisory committee has to be appointed by the SNCF regional management in order to deal with the questions raised. Territorial communities also draw up guidelines for the rail network in so far as their territorial competence is concerned. They are consulted by the State regarding national guidelines in

[2] This concept is essential in the French vision on public transport.

[3] The organisation task for authorities does not mean that a public enterprise should necessarily take care of the production of the transport services.

[4] These various authorities do not have a hierarchical relationship in France.

order to determine priorities in modernising, adapting and extending networks.

According to the law, network characteristics, service details and installations characteristics have to be defined by the Transport Authority in a 'schedule of specifications'. Other parameters, such as fares, financing and accounting procedures and potential subsidies have to be settled by contract. The transport services are then produced either by the authority through its own transport company or corporation, or by private firms to which the services are delegated. The law does not require to competitively tender these activities.

As new mode of governance, the LOTI also institutionalised the usage of contracts (*'conventions'*) to replace the former system of 'administrative authorisations'. Since then the Regions also have the possibility to make agreements 'on the margin' (i.e. take a commitment to compensate marginal additions to the supply of services by taking responsibility for the cost and revenue variations caused by these services).

SNCF

The LOTI establishes the French National Railway Company (*Société Nationale des Chemins de Fer Français* – SNCF) as a 'Commercial and Industrial Public Establishment (*EPIC*)', i.e. a self-managed public enterprise, which has the exclusive control over infrastructure and production:

- SNCF is thereby in charge of operating and developing the national railway network according to the 'principles of *service public*' (Art.18). According to this article, SNCF itself should be considered as a Transport Authority for national railway services. This network is State property (Art. 20);
- its own management, as well as that of the public sector, is autonomous, even financially. Its accounting is supposed to allow its controlling authority to appraise the real economic costs of the public service missions (Art. 25);
- its relationship with the State is stipulated in a 'schedule of specifications', which specifies reciprocal rights and obligations (e.g. management improvement, productivity and financial outcomes). Production planning is set through five-year performance contracts (Art. 24);
- state subsidies are granted according to its various assignments: right to transport, safety and national defence, energy conservation, infra-

structure network having an impact on the land-use planning (Art. 24); and

- the pre-existing specific status of its personnel is maintained (Art. 23).

The Decree of 13 September 1983 (Title III) approves the schedule of specifications of SNCF: the 'oneness' of SNCF is henceforth institutionalised and SNCF is in charge of both network management and railway services production according to the principles of the *service public*. In these two fields, SNCF is acting as Transport Authority for the national railway services. It is in particular incumbent upon SNCF to determine the services (Art. 1 & 6), the fares policy and the investment planning, which should then be approved by the State. SNCF is nevertheless supposed to keep an independent analytical account of those two activities (Art. 56). SNCF is also allowed lease a line or contract out services management to other railway operators.

SNCF and the regions

Articles 44 to 53 confirm the possibility of establishing service agreements by the Regions for regional services and other local trains. Those are considered as regional public utilities and the agreements concern only services chosen by the Regions due to their role in regional travel. Other territorial communities may also initiate agreements, e.g. for suburban services. An endorsement (*avenant*) to the contract has to be made for any amendment to contracted regional services. Regarding non-contracted regional services, SNCF has to inform the Region of any modifications and the services concerned may be incorporated into the contracted services. It should be noted that there is no separate regional infrastructure network as the whole network is State property.

As the contracts between SNCF and the Regions are 'on the margin', negotiations on contracted services are based on pre-existing local train services as defined by SNCF. The Region may only propose adjustments and is only financially responsible for those adjustments.[5] The Region defines fares for contracted services in line with the whole pricing policy adopted by SNCF.

For each Region, SNCF is in charge of establishing and managing (Art. 46) an annual regional account and a budget (both derived from its national

[5] All Regions established contracts in the 1980s, except for the Region *Poitou-Charentes*.

accounting) for its regional services. This account has to be submitted by SNCF to each Region annually. The accounting procedure has to be submitted to the State for approval. The regulation of these accounting procedures was approved by the State in the Decree of 14 August 1986 under the name '*account FC12K*'. This important regulation defines expense items (network, facilities, production, marketing, etc.) quantitatively assessed according to a number of 'units' which are then multiplied by the monetary value of each 'unit', itself appraised by SNCF. Revenues are also appraised and accounted for (notably revenues issued from regional fares paid on lines submitted to the national fares), including any kind of national or regional subsidy granted to contracted regional services, which are accounted as revenues. In case of a production cost decrease due to service changes, SNCF will be the direct beneficiary, since it manages the account.

Third period: 1995/2000: Experimental phase of further regionalisation

The Law of 4 February 1995 on Territory Planning and Development stipulates that a law should define the organisation and financing procedures related to regional transport and institutionalise the Regions as organising Transport Authorities for rail services, this in consultation with current municipal and departmental Transport Authorities (Article 67). This article determines that, prior to full implementation, experiments will have to be held in 6 Regions willing to contract the whole of their regional passenger rail services.

These contracts, starting in 1997, will run for 3 years, which means that this article of law will only be enforced in 2000 with the benefit of the lessons learned from the experiments. These three year experimental contracts in six Regions allow the Regions to negotiate service agreements for all regional services that they will have laid down beforehand. SNCF then becomes a (monopolistic) service operator and rolling stock manager, with a share in the financial risks, while the Regions have a majority share in rolling stock investments. The Decree of 5 May 1997 (Art. 15) stipulates that the 6 Regions concerned are entitled to be Transport Authorities, that the experimental phase will terminate on the 31 December 1999 but that it can be cancelled each year. During this process, the State subsidies previously granted to regional rail services will be paid directly to the Regions and no longer to SNCF.

Before agreeing to participate in the experiment, the Regions requested an independent audit on the regionalisation of the SNCF accounts so as to be able to determine their financial commitment and the costs and revenues of regional services to be contracted on their request (KPMG report in 1996). This audit dealt with a critical analysis of the accounting and invoicing system in place for regional services, an appraisal of the mechanisms of cost and revenue formation for regional services and their amount, proposals of amendment concerning the future relationship between SNCF and the Regions, specially during the experimental period.

According to this law, Regions will also have to adopt a regional planning scheme consistent with the national scheme, and including the regional choices in the field of transport network and services of regional interest (Art. 6 and following). According to this legislation, no French territory should be more than 50 km or 45 minutes away from a TGV railway station or a motorway. The State will have to introduce these accessibility targets in the performance contracts or public service agreements under its control. Any change in services which would conflict with these targets would be subject to an impact study and to a contradictory procedure at the appropriate ministerial level (Art. 25 and following).

7.2.2 Separation of infrastructure and operations

The reform process in order to conform to the 1991 European directive on the separation of infrastructure and production consists of two steps:

- *1995:* the oneness[6] of SNCF and the 'schedule of specifications' is reasserted and the separation relates to accounting only; and
- *1997:* the network and the granting of access right are entrusted to a separate public enterprise: *Réseau Ferré de France* (RFF). SNCF is still in charge of the production of services and keeps its monopoly. SNCF also continues to maintain and manage the network (which remains state property) in monopoly, but under contract with RFF. SNCF pays for track access to the network manager which is (also) SNCF. Access charges are determined by ministerial order after consultation with SNCF. SNCF attributes track slots, giving priority to national or regional passenger *public services* (Art. 18). The right of

[6] According to the 1995 decree, the SNCF kept its entire monopoly, both on infrastructure and operations. It is only the accounting separation that had to be implemented. The SNCF thus kept its 'oneness' and the State implemented the 91/400 directive in its minimal form.

international transit is reasserted, but not the right of cabotage. The right of access to the network by private or public firms, national or international, is subjected to financial, technical, human resources and organisational conditions that are under SNCF's supervision (Art. 2 to 16).

By creating RFF, the law of 13 February 1997 establishes the splitting of SNCF into two entities. RFF is a *Commercial and Industrial Public Establishment* (*EPIC*) responsible for the rail infrastructures that it manages on behalf of the State. RFF implements the 'National Railway Guidelines' (*Schéma Directeur Ferroviaire National*) whereby the consistency and the characteristics of the network are determined by the State. The operations and maintenance of the network are handed over to SNCF under the control of RFF as far as it relates to the technical conditions under which infrastructure services are produced and remunerated. RFF oversees all implementation of new work on the network but may delegate this to SNCF in return for financial supervision. RFF takes over from SNCF a debt of 132.4 billion FRF related to the network. RFF is submitted to private accounting rules and may call for public savings. The personnel has the status of railwaymen. Except for track usage fees, it has to receive all infrastructure-related subsidies granted by the State or other authorities.

The implementation decree of 5 May 1997 stipulates that:

- RFF defines the investment programmes, the network management and maintenance principles, as well as those which concern the traffic and running of trains;
- RFF grants the access and transit rights to operators according to the modalities which are to be defined by RFF itself. It also determines the access fees;
- in case of investments requested by an authority, the authority must provide its own financial support in order to balance this investment during its amortisation period;
- the operational management of the network for train operations is entrusted to SNCF;
- RFF fixes the maintenance program which SNCF has to implement. A contract with SNCF settles the technical and financial conditions for maintenance and operational management. The contract also settles the targets as regards levels of service produced by SNCF for these assignments and the control modalities laid down by RFF;

- payment for SNCF will be made on an inclusive basis for each assignment; and
- two local representatives (elected politicians) are to become member of the 18 member SNCF Board of Directors.

A second decree of 5 May 1997 fixes the accounting procedures for track fees. Fees have to take account of the infrastructure cost, the situation on transport markets, the requirements for optimal usage of the network and the harmonisation of inter-modal competition conditions. Four categories of lines are to be distinguished: suburban lines, interurban lines, high speed lines and other lines.[7] Those lines will be divided into elementary line sections to be subjected to track fees. Fees will include:

- *a basic payment* for access to the track;
- *a track booking payment* (even if the track is not used), which may be inflected according to the line, the timetable, the kind of train, the regularity in usage and the deadline of the request; and
- *a usage payment*, linked to tonnage, distance and train type.

Specific subscription rates (rebates) may be granted in return for usage commitment in order to finance specific pieces of infrastructure. Through this, RFF is allowed to use commercial rates in order to find sources of financing.

The access fees, the weighing and the modulation of the three payments will be determined by the State after consultation with RFF. Awaiting the determination of these fees, the payments are fixed globally at 5,85 billion FRF in 1997 and 6 billion FRF in 1998 based on the 1996 network.

7.2.3 Aims and considerations

Background to the reform processes

Debates and reflections have preceded the reform of SNCF. These were published in 1996, namely the "Martinand Report" on the future of the rail

[7] These are all lines which does not fall within the first three categories. They are local lines linking villages and towns in the rural areas and also the service tracks.

transport.[8] This report clearly questions the public service assignments of rail transport related to land use planning and calls for the reform recommended by European authorities:

- clarification of the competencies of State and Regions;
- separation between network and production of services;
- closing of non profitable national lines;
- real autonomy, modernisation and inducement of more dynamism for SNCF;
- regionalisation;
- establishment of regional and national public service requirements under contractual form; and
- granting of complete freedom for fares and commercial pricing.

Furthermore, the third period of the regionalisation, and thereby the current legislation, has been strongly influenced by a report on regionalisation from Senator Haenel. This report recommends the aggressive development of all rail transport in Regions where potential traffic development exists, the institutionalisation of the status of Transport Authority for the Regions and the administrative and accounting reorganisation of SNCF in order to deal with the regional dimension.[9] It suggests an experimentation phase for those Regions who are prepared to assume the role of Transport Authority status.

It is also important to focus on the French dogma of '*service public*' to understand the intervention of French authorities into public transport. In France the idea of '*service public*' has caught more attention from lawyers than in other countries. Since the 19th century, jurisprudence has gradually developed and defined the *service public*. This is the result of the trials conducted by administrative tribunals on matters of public service obligation (e.g. those of railway companies). At the political level, while it was not seriously debated, the State's rhetoric and actions have always consisted in referring to the *public service* dogma in economic philosophy and to its major principles: continuity, equality and mutability. Consequently, the rail transport's role as *public service* was never questioned until very

[8] Martinand, M. (1996), *Débat national sur l'avenir du transport ferroviaire,* Rapport introductif du groupe de travail présidé par M. Martinand, Ministère de l'équipement, du logement et des transports, 29 February 1996, Paris.

[9] This report also estimates the financing need for regional network improvement and services to be of up to 4 billion FRF per year.

recently in the Martinand report, and its role has drifted towards a 'socially desirable service for captive passengers'. The *public service* dogma was adopted by the State, as well as the locally elected representatives, the unions and the people. One may say that this dogma was the subject of an outdated national consensus.

The policy and strategy of SNCF towards the authorities has, up till 1997, always been to try to maintain the oneness of the company by avoiding a split in infrastructure and operations divisions. Behind this, SNCF is afraid that if it looses control on the network, especially the high-speed network, network development might be slowed down or stopped due to financial reasons. According to SNCF, it is the notion of *public service network*, written in the law, which could be put into question if the network falls under the management of a separate entity, especially if this organism charged with the evaluation of investments favours profitability criteria instead of land-use planning criteria. Furthermore, SNCF would loose much of its influence on the authorities. An other fear would be the end of its monopoly with the appearance of other operators and of other infrastructure maintenance companies.

The idea that the oneness of SNCF had to be preserved stems also from a belief in the applicability of the theory of natural monopoly to SNCF and from the idea that cross-subsidies linked to fares have to be preserved as contribution to land-use planning and national development. Since a few years, however, the fares implemented by SNCF are no longer uniform across the country (particularly since the implementation of the "*Socrate*" fares system). Even if these fares still partially respect the standardisation rules, they are largely shaded by commercial principles: peak hour fares, seasonal passes, fares for youth, etc. But the deficit of SNCF is thus legalised, as it runs an activity which is partly out of the merchant sphere, where general interest prevails over immediate financial viability, even if SNCF operates in a competitive transportation market.

Considerations and actions by the various actors

The considerations and actions by the various actors involved will be presented hereafter. Nothing yet can be said on RFF, being a relatively new actor.

The State

Despite the *service public* dogma, growing car ownership, declining rail services, the bad reputation of SNCF and drop in usage, together with financial constraints, made people's mind evolve noticeably and this led to specific action by the State. The State has firstly been led by financial considerations, without any deep thinking on the exact role that it wanted the enterprise to play. The second reason for the action of the State lies in maintaining social peace in an enterprise which is one of the union's last strongholds.[10]

The State's strategy was to dedicate itself to the national services, and more specifically to high speed structures, because of political reasons and budget savings. Under these conditions its main concern was to find a new institution to replace it in financing non-profitable local regional services. The closing of non-profitable lines, in accordance with SNCF, has always come up against pressure and objection from the locally elected representatives calling upon land-use planning arguments. The State's strategy was, therefore, to get the local and regional authorities to assume the financial consequences of their political choices in the field of transport. By limiting its subsidy to the currently granted amount, the State is assured to put an end to the inappropriate control of finances. The State has thereby ratified a two-speed SNCF: the high speed lines and the rest of the network, part of which will be entrusted to the Regions.

Regions

As the status of Region was created recently (1972), they had to assert their role in relation to authorities (municipalities and departments) which had a

[10] In the last ten years, 20% of work disruptions were due to railwaymen. In fact, a SNCF strike would be strongly disruptive, primarily due to the high rate train commuting in the Paris region. This concern with maintaining social peace has for a long time been the basis of the social policy of SNCF. The State has supported a slow decline of the personnel, so as to give reduce the discrepancy between the enterprise size and its traffics. From 1991 to 1997, the average staffs has gone from 200 500 railwaymen to 175 400. There has been no reaction on the union's side, since the pension system is on their advantage. This policy does not solve the financial problems, since the State largely supports the financing of the rail workers Pension Fund. The pension charges for the former 350 000 rail workers are amounting to 27 billion FRF, which is more than turnover. On this total figure the contribution from the State amounts to 18.5 billion FRF, that of the active workers amounts to 1.8 billion FRF, and that of SNCF amounts to 7 billion FRF. The railwaymen working on the trains retire at 50 years old, the others at 55.

long practice in the field of public transport networks. In 1977, the Region took the opportunity to deal with the local and regional train services (so-called *omnibus*) of SNCF and within 20 years, four fifth of the regional services have been submitted to negotiated agreements and renewed several times. Since 1985, the former *omnibus* services have disappeared, giving way to the new multimodal concept of 'Regional Express Transport' (*Transport Express Régional – TER*), including regional bus services.

Dialog between the Regions and the other transport authorities (AOs) was not easy, despite their complementary nature; while departments and districts are rather dedicated to roads, the Region is essentially dedicated to rail. Until 1997, the Region only had power to establish negotiated agreements. While originally the legal texts only covered services 'on the margin' (i.e. services adding to pre-existing regional services of SNCF), the legal texts evolved to the point that the agreements have become a means for the Regions to control all regional services and avoid unilateral downsizing of services by SNCF.

SNCF

SNCF, which was 'strongly requested' to lower its deficits in its 'schedule of specifications' and its performance contracts, sees the regionalisation as a way to either close lines and cancel non-profitable *omnibus* services,[11] or to have them supported by the Regions, who are politically closer to the users of those services.

The partnership of SNCF with the Region had some difficulties to settle. Due to its strong power (as a 'state in the State'), SNCF played a major role in settling these difficulties, since it often did not keep its financial and services commitments. Some of the contentious financial issues still exist and have aroused suspicion among the Regions, thus explaining their refusal to commit themselves any further unless they are entitled to the status of Organising Transport Authority and unless the past is audited. The bargaining power, which mostly favoured SNCF, is thus being brought back on the Region's behalf, given that the Region is now the payer and, consequently, the commissioner. SNCF is, henceforth, considered as a simple operator, responsible for its own contractual commitments as to production costs and revenues, services operation and their quality. It

[11] The deficits had increased sharply since 1990 and traffic had declined (except for the TGV and some TER).

assumes the financial risk along with the Region. In the coming years, it may have to assume it totally.

SNCF has no choice but to succeed since, except for the Regions, no other controlling power may be able to assume the costs of regional transport services.

Unions, personnel and company culture

Given the depressed market of SNCF (passengers and freight), the unions have adopted a retrenchment position on the rights acquired by the personnel. Their ability to mobilise and disrupt is formidable, despite the many unions which constitute their federations (at least 5 federations, including at least 10 unions).

Two major characteristics of the enterprise culture and the personnel mentality hamper a quick proper development:

- a primarily technical cultural imperialism created by engineers, who are mainly concerned about the network and its installations, safety and technical performance, and completely ignore commercial considerations; and
- the past resistance of the railway workers during World War II created the aura of a *public service* culture, which has long since been over. This culture is disconnected from the market place and competition by private operators. It relates more to a *public service* produced for captive users rather than as a service operated for paying customers. This rather corporatist culture tends to protect its own interests under the guise of public service.

7.2.4 Additional policy measures

Art. 14 and 15 of the law of 30 December 1996 have amended the 1982 LOTI law on passenger transport. This amendment pertains to the 'the air and the rational utilisation of energy'. This amendment determines that the urban transport plans, which have to be established by the organising urban transport authorities in a number of agglomerations of more than 100 000 inhabitants, have to be compatible with various other land-use planning measures and with regional plans on the quality of the air. The aims stated by the law are to reach a sustainable equilibrium between mobility and accessibility needs, and health and environmental protection and to reach a co-ordinated usage of all means of transport by an adequate usage of road space, a promotion of the least polluting modes and most economical modes in terms of energy consumption.

The law also determines more specific aims to be reached by the urban transport plans:

- reduce car traffic;
- develop public transport, other energy-saving and non-polluting modes (such as cycling and walking);
- manage the main urban road network such as to increase the efficiency of its usage, a.o. by informing the users on the traffic situation;
- develop a parking policy (type of parking usage and pricing), prioritising least polluting vehicles;
- develop a freight delivery system which limits its impacts on traffic and environment; and
- stimulate companies and public authorities to develop car-pooling and public transport usage amongst their employees.

It is to be expected that this recent amendment to law will generate additional policy measures in the near future.

7.3 Current organisation[12]

This section describes the current organisation as resulting from the legal and regulatory changes presented above. The role of each actor in the new organisational form will be summarised at the end of this section.

[12] It has to be noted that there has always been a gap in France between the texts and their implementation. E.g., despite the law, there exists no documents regarding strategic mandatory orientations with financial planning and the infrastructure plans are rather general orientation documents which do not (legally and financially) commit the Transport Authorities.

7.3.1 The State

The State keeps the national competence (in consultation with the Regions) on the definition of the broad options of the transport policy, in particular, its rail aspect through the High Speed Link Guidelines. The State decides on the organisation of the rail transport market: monopoly or competition. At the regional level, the State does not have competencies at the strategic level any longer, except through specific financial contributions. The State decides also on the status of SNCF and RFF personnel.

Infrastructure

Infrastructure is part of the national State property and constitutes a 'public service network'. The State has exclusive decision-making power in relation to infrastructures, even those of regional significance, since the Region can not oppose a decision to modify network characteristics, even if it is consulted.

The infrastructure management is entrusted to an autonomous public enterprise (RFF) although the State still approves the access fees that RFF establishes. Each contract between RFF and SNCF is also submitted to state approval. RFF submits its annual investment planning on the network to the State, which checks for conformity to the above-quoted High Speed Link Guidelines.

Services

The state keeps the control on the rail operator, SNCF, which is a public enterprise with self-management. The State entrusted SNCF with the production monopoly for rail services, which are considered to be public services.

The general framework for SNCF production activity was set up in 1983 once and for all in a schedule of specifications. SNCF production planning and the State financial commitments were drafted in the five-year contracts, which also included how annual subsidies granted to SNCF should be defined and negotiated on a contract basis. The State assumes all financial risks of SNCF production (as a public enterprise) since it grants finance for the whole production deficit related to national services. Performance contracts were cancelled in 1996 and replaced with an annual assignment letter issued by the State.

Fares

The State sets up and subsidises social fares at the national and regional levels. Through this it keeps its influence on the ridership of regional services (particularly for workers seasonal passes).

7.3.2 The Regions

The law will, after the year 2000 and on the basis of the results of the current experiments, define exactly the extent of the power of the Regions. This means that the powers of the Regions may be extended compared to the present overview.

Relationship with SNCF

The Regions are entitled to share risks related to costs, revenues and deficits with SNCF. They can also define incentives as bonuses and penalties, in order to induce better performances in quality of service. The Regions are dependent on the regional accounting of SNCF and thus remain dependent upon the financial expertise of SNCF. Some of the Regions have announced that they wish to charge costs and revenues of regional services on a Region-based accounting.

Infrastructure

The Region does not have the control on the regional network (especially for line closures), which is nationally managed by RFF. The Region may however influence decisions regarding lines of regional significance through co-financing with RFF.

Service definition and fares

The Region is entitled to define the consistency of the services basing itself on its Regional Transport Guidelines (SRT); but under the technical constraints of the available track capacity as granted by RFF. The Region selects the best list of services for the customer on the basis of the current ridership and on the basis of a normative approach of demand, the passengers' mobility needs, the meeting of demand and its evaluation. It regularly orders passenger surveys to be carried out by SNCF or private consultants.

Although the Region is responsible for the fare policy, the fare structure should be compatible with the national one designed by SNCF. The Region may define its own policy regarding social fares, in addition to those defined at the national level, provided it compensates for it.

Production

The Region has only one person to speak to, since SNCF has the monopoly. The Region may negotiate with SNCF and ask for a service to be sub-contracted to a private rail operator. Besides the service performances, the Region may define the quality requirements concerning these services and supervise them.

The Region may own the rolling stock in the case it supplies finance for it. It defines the technical characteristics of this stock, in consultation with the manufacturers. In the past the Regions have had a very active policy for purchasing rolling stock. Together with the manufacturers, they have now designed a new standard for regional trains, which they committed themselves to purchase (the first train will be circulating at the beginning of the year 1998).

7.3.3 RFF – *Réseau Ferré de France*

RFF is responsible for the infrastructure since May 1997, and is consequently responsible for the investment planing of the network, the work control and its financing. Since then RFF:

- determines the access fees requested to operators according to a 'frame', set up by decree; these fees have to be approved by the State;
- determines the track access procedures for operators, cabotage by other European operators remains forbidden as SNCF has the monopoly;
- influences rail transport costs with the fees and consequently the financial viability of regional services;
- is given State budgets and subsidies for network installations on the basis of its contribution to *public service*, land use planning and on the basis of the balancing of charges with other modes of transportation; and

- may also negotiate the co-financing of network with Regions which might be interested in improving the performances of regional services.

RFF is supposed to remain a relatively small entity, with a maximum of 200 members of staff. Its role should mainly be to conceive, evaluate and control the infrastructure construction and maintenance programmes, to define the rules relating to the granting of train paths ('slots') to operators, to define the infrastructure charges. The strategic action of RFF thus has a double frame: SNCF has the monopoly of services production, network management, operating and maintenance and the State has the control over the network, approves the access fees and grants capital and subsidies to RFF. The only real strategic power of RFF resides in the appraisal and expertise for all decisions concerning the network.

RFF budget is not balanced yet, as it may be seen below (deficit of 44% before exceptional contribution), even if nothing is planned to finance the new investments programmes.

- For 1997, the revenues of RFF are estimated to be 26.7 billion FRF:
  - State endowment: 11.8 billion FRF
  - Tolls: 5.9 billion FRF[13]
  - Patrimonial operations: 1 billion FRF
  - Exceptional contribution: 8 billion FRF.
- Its costs are estimated to be 31.1 billion FRF of which:
  - Paying off debt: 9 billion FRF
  - Paying off of other assets: 5.9 billion FRF
  - Network management: 16.8 billion FRF.

The institutional, financial and technical dependency of RFF upon the State, SNCF and the Regions does not allow for much autonomy. The risk lies in the fact that the former debt problems of SNCF might have been

[13] The "Council of Concurrence" (depending of Ministry of Finance) has officially given an Advice (N°97 A 09, 26 March 1997, published in "Official Journal", 7 May 1997) concerning the level of tracks fees. This Advice shows that railways will benefit lower fees than highway road transport, SNCF will take an advantage on future railway competitor whose traffic would be weaker than SNCF because the "basic fee for access to the track" is quite high and the level of fees has been artificially fixed at a low level (they do not take account of market transport and infrastructure costs but only the SNCF's weak capacity to pay). So RFF is a net subsidies provider for SNCF (supported finally by the French taxpayer) so as to permit it to present balanced accounts.

transferred to RFF as its own budget is likely to be insufficient to fulfil all its assignments. Debt has slipped from 134.2 to 148 billion FRF between 1997 and 1998.

The nature of the relationships and the balance of powers between RFF and SNCF (185 000 members of staff) will only become clear after some time and will be influenced by the personalities of their leaders and by financial considerations. RFF inherits of a substantial debt and its budget is not yet settled due to the ambitious investment programmes of the old SNCF.

Two scenarios can be envisaged for the future of RFF, where the State is the most important decision taker: either RFF becomes a SNCF debt settlement corporation, allowing the SNCF to start afresh, but reducing the investment programme of RFF due to its heavy debt burden, or RFF exerts all its powers given by law, even if this conflicts with the SNCF policy. The financial constraint will nevertheless remain, even if RFF as public corporation benefits from a State guarantee.

7.3.4 SNCF – *Société Nationale des Chemins de Fer Français*

The French Railways (*SNCF/ Société Nationale des Chemins de Fer Français*) operates on a total of 32 600 km of lines, out of which 13 500 km are electrified and 2 000 km are high-speed lines. Regional services make use of 23 000 km of this network. The regional rolling stock is made up of over 1 700 wagons, 1 400 rail cars, and 570 electric rail cars. A drop in ridership has been observed in the past years from 59.6 billion passenger-km to 55.5 for the total traffic in 10 years and from 7.8 billion passenger-km to 6.65 in 5 years for the regional traffic.

SNCF has the monopoly on all of service production (national and regional). It is the only one to have the technical and financial expertise to define national services. It owns its rolling stock on the national services, as well as its operational buildings, i.e. stations. It defines the fares after State agreement.[14] It doesn't assume any financial risk since its deficits – including contractual subsidies – are covered by the State. The performance

[14] Those fares are widely differentiated, particularly on the high speed lines, avoiding cross-subsidisation (*dépéréqués*).

contracts or the annual assignment letters issued from the State set up SNCF's deficit limits.

SNCF, considered to be an Organising Transport Authority, may enjoy its prerogatives at the national level regarding services production, fares structure and policy. In consultation with the Regions, SNCF takes care of the compatibility of its national services with regional services. At the regional level, SNCF suggests any improvement, optimisation of regional services, using its own expertise.

At the regional level, SNCF has become a rail service provider with monopoly right. It adheres to a schedule of technical and financial specifications regarding implementation of services according to the Regional Transport Guidelines drawn by each Region participating in the experimental process. It manages the rolling stock, which is partially subsidised by the Region and which, consequently, is partly owned by the Region itself. Its incentives are all subject to contracts, approved by the Regions or RFF. Since it has the expertise capacity, it collaborates and negotiates with the authority that has regional control, in order to work out the contract, as well as the schedule of specifications. Henceforth, it assumes a financial risks shared with the participating Regions as far as service production is concerned.

The situation in 1996 is worrisome. 1993 and 1994 led to a deficit of 8 billion FRF, and 1995 to a deficit of 16 billion FRF out of which 1.6 billion FRF for regional services and 11 billion FRF for the infrastructure. This situation at the end of 1996 has to be connected to the take-over of SNCF debts by the State (total debt: 208 billion FRF, which is 4 times the firm's turnover of 55 billion FRF, and debt interests: 15 billion FRF). In 1991, the State took over a debt of 38 billion FRF. In 1997, the French Railway Network (*RFF/ Réseau Ferré de France*) took on an additional infrastructure debt of 34.2 billion FRF. In July 1997, the State took over an additional 20 billion FRF, thus saving 1.3 billion FRF in interests to SNCF. The enterprise's debt was thus reduced to 50 billion FRF, an amount equivalent to its annual turnover.

The annual State subsidies are substantial. In 1996, 49 billion FRF were allocated as follows:

- equilibrium subsidy: 18.76 billion FRF, including 4.11 billion FRF for regional passenger services and 12.19 billion FRF for network charges;
- pension fund for railwaymen: 18.41 billion FRF; and

- interest paid on the 38 billion FRF debt (taken over in 1990): 4.35 billion FRF.

Infrastructure

At the national level, besides the production of services, SNCF has the monopoly of the provision of day-to-day management, maintenance, infrastructures operations and design of train circulation. These assignments are fulfilled according to a contract signed with RFF and according to the payment of those assignments on an inclusive basis (*forfaitaire*). SNCF pays access charges to RFF.

Since 1997 (Art. 6, decree of 5 May 1997), RFF has received the control on the infrastructure investment and maintenance. However, RFF is allowed to delegate the realisation of these tasks to SNCF who, due to historical reasons, has the expertise and the personnel necessary to conduct infrastructure works.

7.3.5 Potential entrants

CGEA and VIA-GTI, who will be presented here, are only potential operators. They have, however, the expertise to operate railway services as soon as, and if, the law (to be voted in 2000) allows them to do so. They will then be direct competitors of the SNCF. These groups, due to their experience in urban and interurban passenger transport, are used to negotiate passenger transport contracts with local authorities and to operate regional passenger services on the road.

CGEA

CGEA (*Compagnie Générale d'Entreprise Automobile*) is a subsidiary of CGE (*Compagnie Générale des Eaux*), one of the largest private French groups, with a turnover of 164 billion FRF and 220 000 employees. CGE is specialised in services provided to public authorities, such as hygiene, water treatment and transport. Its other activities lie in public works and telecommunications.

CGEA operates 40 urban transport networks in France, where it is the second largest operator with 13 000 employees. It also operates 1 150 km of local rail lines in France, which transport 1.2 million travellers in Southern (Nice-Digne line) and Western (Guingamp-Carhaix) France. CGEA has a 3.5 billion FRF turnover in passenger transport, 0.2 billion FRF of which is in the rail transport.

Its activity in rail transport has significantly increased since CGEA was granted 2 of the 25 passengers railway networks resulting from the privatisation of British Rail (Network South Central and South Eastern), thanks to its British subsidiary firm, Connex. Those two networks have a total of 1 500 km of lines, transporting 500 000 passengers/day with its 7 000 employees and 3 000 daily services. The two networks' turnover amount to 5.4 billion FRF.

VIA-GTI

This firm is a subsidiary of the Paribas group. It is the first group in urban transport of passengers in France. It operates 88 networks of urban transport in France including urban rail based (metro, tram) networks such as the ones in Lyon and Lille, and 4 networks in Germany and Spain as well. Moreover, it operates 47 inter-urban networks. Its turnover in transport amounts to 5 billion FRF and has 19 450 employees. Its rolling stock is made up of 8 300 vehicles.

VIA-GTI is not a railway operator in France yet but was granted a British railway network "Thameslink" through its subsidiary GOVIA, in which it detains 35% of the capital. It has recently (April 1997) built up a common firm (SODEF) together with the Cariane group which intends to become an operator of regional rail transport for passengers. The Cariane group is a private subsidiary of SNCF, operating road passenger transport services, particularly rail services transferred to road.

Its profit, in transport, amounts to 5 billion FRF, and to 19 450 employees. Its stock is made up of 8 300 vehicles.

7.3.6 Summary

The respective competencies and roles of the parties involved can be summarised as such:

The State:

- sets up consistency and main characteristics of the network, declares new projects as being of public utility and allows investments, grants a contribution and endowment in capital to RFF;
- elaborates and defines regulations regarding safety; and
- holds the control on 'industrial and commercial public establishments' such as RFF and SNCF.

Regions A law due to be voted in the year 2000 is supposed to institutionalise the 'organising authority' powers of the regions in terms of regional passenger transport services. This may have two consequences:

- the splitting up, in due course, of SNCF into regional companies as the contracts, and thus also the services, will differ from region to region acording to the degree of involvement of the regions in railway transport; and
- the organisation of tendering procedures for the railway services, allowing private operators to enter, similarly to what happens in urban and interurban passenger transport.

RFF (the French Railway Network):

- lays out, develops and valorises infrastructures of the national network (tracks, platforms and shunting yards) that it owns, is work master (choices, decisions and financing) of its own patrimony;
- entrusts infrastructure management to SNCF and covers costs; and
- suggests and perceives track fees for its network.

SNCF:

- makes use of the RFF network for services production with its own rolling stock and pays for corresponding track fees;
- operates the traffic management (tracks granting, train slots) as well as the circulation management on the network;
- is the only one which can be mandated by RFF to control work on the network and infrastructure investments; and
- controls the undertaking of investments (maintenance operations) on the operating network.

Private operators These do not play an active role at the moment (except for some small exceptions) but large French private groups await the opportunity to place bids for the operations of railways. They are members of the largest European transport groups and are both already involved in railway operations in Great Britain.

The new division of tasks for the services at the national and regional levels can be summarised as in Table 7.1 and Table 7.2. Further details on the powers of the State, the Regions, SNCF and RFF are given in Table 7.3 and in Table 7.4.

Table 7.1 Organisation of national service (since 1997)

Level of action	Decisions	State	RFF	SNCF
Strategic level:	Multimodal transport policy	X		
Determination of	Monopoly or competition	X		
general aims	Network	X	X	
	Personnel status	X		
	Budget fixing	X		X
	Public utility requirements	X		
Tactic level:	Design of services			X
Definition of	Appraisal of services			X
means	Stock			X
	Fares	X		X
Operational level:	Production of services			X
Production	Marketing of services			X

Table 7.2 Organisation of regional services (since 1997)

Level of action	Decisions	State	Region	RFF	SNCF
Strategic level:	Multimodal transport policy		X		
Determination of	Monopoly or competition	X			
general aims	Network	X		X	
	Personnel status	X			
	Budget fixing		X		
Tactic level:	Design of the lines		X		
Definition of	Design of services		X		
means	Appraisal of services		X		
	Stock		X		X
	Fares		X		
Operational level:	Production of services				X
Production	Marketing of services				X

Table 7.3 National network: Actors and their powers (since 1997)

	Region	SNCF		RFF		State	
	Con-sulta-tion	Deci-sion	Con-sulta-tion	Deci-sion	Con-sulta-tion	Deci-sion	Con-sulta-tion
Instutional aspects							
Definition of the multimodal transport policy						X	
Monopoly or competition for or on the market						X	
National guidelines for network	X					X	
Network							
Design and work mastering				X			
Toll fees			X	X			X
Creation of new lines	X			X			X
Improvement of existing lines	X			X			X
Closings of lines, single-track set up	X			X			X
Maintenance, operating and security of lines				X			X
Tracks granting			X	X			
Railway stations management and property							
Stock							
Property of the rolling stock		X					
Rolling stock financing		X					
Rolling stock maintenance and management		X					
Services production							
Consistency, changes and perform. of services	X	X					
Call for rail sub-contracting out		X					
Transfer on road	X	X					
Services marketing							
Fares policy and structure		X					
Marketing		X					
Information of the customers		X					
Services financing							
Property of the services production result		X					
Subsidy granting						X	
Personnel							
Personnel status and management						X	
Services appraisal							
Technical study appraisal of the services		X					
Financial appraisal of the services		X					
Appraisal & incent. to production perform.		X					
Appraisal & incent. to commercial perform.		X					

Note: When several columns are ticked off for the same parameter, this means that the concerned actors must decide or must be consulted together.

Table 7.4 Regional networks: Actors and their powers since 1997

	Region OA		SNCF Production		RFF Infrastructure		State	
	Decision	Consultation	Decision	Consultation	Decision	Consultation	Decision	Consultation
Institutional aspects								
Definition of the rail transport policy	X							
Possibility and freedom for out	X							
Competition for or on the market							X	
Transport Regional Guidelines	X							X
Network								
Creation and financing of new lines		X			X		X	
Improv. of existing lines, single tracks set up		X		X	X		X	
Closings of lines		X			X		X	
Maintenance, operating and security of lines		X			X			
Toll fees		X			X			X
Stock								
Property and investments in rolling stock	X		X					
Rolling stock maintenance			X					
Usage fees for the rolling stock	X							
Assignment of the rolling stock		X	X					
Services production								
Definition of the transport area	X		X					X
Design, changes and performances of services	X		X					
Call for rail sub-contracting out	X		X					
Transfer on road in case of service cancellation	X			X				
Services marketing								
Fares policy and structure	X	X	X					
Ticket integration	X							
Appraisal and marketing of the demand	X			X				
Information of the customers		X	X					
Services financing								
Sharing of the financial risks on prod. charges	X							
Sharing of the financial risks on revenues	X							
Property of the production result	X							
Property of the State production subsidies	X							
Personnel								
Personnel status and management							X	
Services appraisal								
Financial appraisal of services	X			X				
Technical study appraisal of services	X			X				
Appraisal and incent. to production perform	X							
Appraisal and incent. to commercial perform	X							

Note: When several columns are ticked off for the same parameter, this means that the concerned actors must decide or must be consulted together.

7.4 The regionalisation experiments

Several regionalisation experiments are currently being carried out in an attempt to better meet the needs of the customer by bringing the centre of decision closer to the area of concern. We are going to focus in this overview on the contracts signed in 1997 by the Regions willing to participate in an experiment for a duration of three years:

- Alsace;
- Centre;
- Nord-Pas-de-Calais;
- Pays-de-Loire;
- Provence-Alpes-Côtes d'Azur; and
- Rhône-Alpes.

At the end of this process, a Transport Act will institutionalise the role of the Regions as Transport Authorities, taking into account the conclusions of the experiment.

7.4.1 Principles

In short:

The Region:

- commits itself to improve and develop public transport in its area (by its entitlement of Transport Authority for and on behalf of the State);
- defines the policy for regional rail services;
- has control over the quality of service; and
- determines the fares policy at the regional level.

The State:

- transfers the credits to the Region (with an increase of the budget); and
- guarantees to preserve the quality of infrastructures and compensations in case of fare changes.

SNCF:

- implements the regional policy;
- is the permanent advisor for the Region and keeps the Region regularly informed about the conditions of its operation;
- commits itself to provide a better quality of service to the passengers in the frame of a safe management;
- manages the production, marketing and promotion of the regional (TER) services contracted according to the means that it defines in the frame of its self-management; and
- must provide the continuity of the regional public service whatever the circumstances are, excepting the case of *force majeure* or strike non relevant to its proper responsibility.

7.4.2 Contracts

There are three guiding principles for the contracting during this experiment:

- *transparency:* The Region is considered as Transport Authority whereas SNCF provides all information of technical, accounting and financial nature upon request by the Region and according to the clauses of the contract;
- *reversibility:* The contracts linked to the experiment may be cancelled every year; and
- *transfer of competencies without transfer of charges:* The State transfers to the Regions 4.3 billion FRF of subsidy for regional services which it used to grant directly to SNCF. Moreover, the State commits itself to granting each of the 6 Regions an exceptional contribution of 0.8 billion FRF per year.

The experiments are based on the establishment of three major contracts in each of the six Regions:

- *a State – Region contract* where the State delegates to the Region its competency of Transport Authority and a negotiation on the amount of endowment necessary to transfer the competencies without additional charges;

- *a SNCF – Region negotiated contract* which defines the relationship between the Region and SNCF; and
- *a 'schedule of specifications'* which details the modes of realisation of this service as well as the financial conditions for regional support.

The contracts signed between the 6 Regions and SNCF at the beginning of 1997 are more of a client/provider type than co-management contracts with responsibility and risks sharing. SNCF first establishes, then commits itself to specific cost levels (including fixed charges and renewal of the equipment). Some regions consider these calculations, based on the current operations and performances of the SNCF, to be sub-optimal, if not simply bad. This means that they consider the operational costs of the SNCF to be too high.[15] The budget constraints to which the Regions are submitted make them reluctant to increase their rate of participation in the deficits of regional services as they do not want to find themselves responsible for supporting SNCF deficit, even indirectly. The major stake is therefore to get SNCF to improve its own performances and services to the customer at constant costs.

The content of the contracts may be quite different from Region to Region, considering their freedom of contracting. The improvement of services from one Region to another will be dependent upon their involvement and interest in rail transport, as well as to the amount of funds they are willing to allocate. The contracts, which are the object of this study, are however very similar, sometimes word-for-word.[16] The obligations contracted by SNCF are the fruit of negotiations between two parties, as in every contract, however all strategic decisions are taken by the Region itself in the last instance.

The contracts elaborated by 5 Regions[17] were reviewed exhaustively for this study and the comparison of these experiments lead to the following overview.

[15] This could only be tackled in the future if a legal possibility was created to organise calls-for-tender, thereby suppressing the SNCF monopoly for regional services.

[16] The first contract, which was elaborated by the Rhône-Alpes Region, has been used as a basis for the following ones.

[17] Provence-Alpes-Côte d'Azur (PACA), Nord-Pas de Calais (NPC), Rhône-Alpes (RA), Haute Normandie (HN) and Pays de Loire (PL).

Network

The Region defines the lines subject to contracting. In addition to the lines included in its own area, the Region may also include the inter-regional lines, or even the trans-border lines (Region Rhône-Alpes), that it feels are necessary to extend.

Production of services

The Regions define the characteristics, quality and changes regarding services in the process of contracting. SNCF produces rail services in monopoly, it may appeal to sub-contractors with the prior approval of the Region but sub-contracting is forbidden. SNCF, compared to the Region, enjoys a large appraisal capacity (demand, financial, technical studies, etc.) Because of this, SNCF is the one to propose any action aimed at rationalising, improving and optimising services.

Infrastructure

The Region may participate in the financing of new infrastructures or in the improvement of existing lines, particularly in their planning by the Regional Transport Guidelines. The Regions may, in that case, negotiate a discount on track fees. RFF has to ensure the performances of the network as defined in the contract. SNCF is responsible for the actual maintenance of this network. Should that fail, the contract will be reviewed, specifically the items concerning finances if there are consequences on operating conditions.

Rolling stock management and maintenance

The Region can invest in rolling stock which it then owns. It supervises the assignment, maintenance and renewal of this rolling stock. During the contracting period, the Region can also control the contracted rolling stock provided by SNCF, for which the Region supports maintenance costs.

Fares

The Region defines fares, which should be in line with those established nationally by SNCF. The State is in charge of the subsidies for social fares. But the Region may set up other kinds of social or commercial fares. In that case, the Region is supposed to subsidise them. The Region defines the conditions of implementation for tariffs integration, so as to provide intermodality together with the other Transport Authorities.

Service marketing

The Region has control over customer information and modes of service promotion. It may modify them. It may also participate in marketing initiatives together with SNCF. The Region may also get SNCF or any other consultant to proceed to evaluation of customers satisfaction, demand and mobility evolution. SNCF commercialises the services and makes their promotion under the conditions defined by the Region.

Sharing financial risks

The Region shares the financial risks with SNCF. After services have been defined, the cost of the services will be appraised, firstly in accordance with SNCF accounting standards. SNCF commits itself to the charges contractually defined at the beginning of each year and will assume any overspending of this amount. Concerning revenues, the Region and SNCF contractually commit themselves on a forward-looking objective (subsidy included) which balances the costs. If the actual revenues are underestimated, the Region and SNCF share the deficit equally. If the actual revenues surpass the estimates, the Region and SNCF equally divide the excess. This excess will be considered to be profit sharing in order to make SNCF aware of its responsibilities (Région PACA).

Incentives for SNCF

The Region PACA added a minimal revenues clause (93% of the revenue objective) below which SNCF bears the entire deficit. The Region RA stipulated a maximum subsidy amount and no minimum for revenues, so as to limit the Region's risks. Regions HR and RA have introduced risk sharing in incremental percentages in order to increase SNCF's responsibility gradually: risk share of 10% in 1997, 25% in 1998, 50% in 1999.

The Region RA was the only one to precisely define the control procedures of indicators and the monetary amounts at stake. Meanwhile, the other Regions are planning measurements of customer services operated by SNCF; this will be combined with bonuses and penalties. The other Regions, due to time constraints[18] have postponed the defining of the practical modes of control until a later date; this will be subject to contract endorsement.

The Region defines the incentive modes, in addition to the results sharing described above:

- penalties in case of non-operation of contractual obligations;
- a bonus/penalty system in case it does (or does not) operate or improve the performances and the quality of its services; and
- issuing of exceptional penalties to SNCF for non-operation of contractual obligations, inadequacy in fraud control (Region PACA), and the non-transmission in time of the documents supposed to allow technical and financial control over the supply (Region RA), etc.

The indicators for quality measurements have been precisely defined in the Region RA and deal with:

- conformity with the train services (physical operation of the services, punctuality, train capacity, travelling conditions such as cleanliness and comfort, welcoming, information); and
- conformity with the station services (waiting time at ticket office, personnel at reception desk, opening hours, availability of ticketing equipment, information, station maintenance).

In case of serious fault on SNCF's side, the Region may cancel the contract in a unilateral way.

Monitoring

The Region defines all modes and procedures for technical, accounting and financial control of the operators' activity. It elaborates checklists which allow the follow-up of the conformity with the performance contract and which are indicator of the customer's satisfaction. It deals either with SNCF's study and expertise capacity in finance and accounting or with other consultants.

The Regions will have to develop their own transport departments, so as to be able to balance their bargaining power and their appraisal capacity with those of SNCF. This is an absolute requirement if the Regions do not

[18] The contract had to be signed at the beginning of the year 1997.

want to be placed in a position of information inequality as in costs and revenues appraisal.

7.4.3 The stakes of regionalisation

SNCF has no other choice but to succeed as the current finances of the enterprise are crippled and the excess labour force, that it may not eliminate, is great. The stake is so significant that the President of SNCF will meet with the association of the Presidents of Regional Councils twice a year from now on. SNCF hopes that the definition of supply by the Regions is going to result in an increase in train services and budgets, but this is not guaranteed. As an example, the contract signed between the Region Rhône-Alpes stipulates the creation of 91 new services in 1997-98, after that 85 services were already created during the last three years. These 91 services represent an 8% increase of the regional rail supply. The reference subsidy will go up from 860 million FRF in 1997 to 891 million FRF in 1998.

Some key data can be given for SNCF's regional services. The subsidy requirements for regional services are very significant, since the revenues do on average not cover more than half of the costs. SNCF's regional services represent 60% of its customers (500 000 passengers/day, 43% of those trips are work or school-related, average trip length is 15 km) and 40% of its supply in train-km (6 700 trains/year, out of which 6 000 are submitted to service agreements, 3 000 thousand buses, out of which 2 500 are submitted to service agreements). The regional services realise a turnover of 8 billion FRF in 1996. This is 36% of SNCF passenger-traffic turnover (out of the Paris region). The commercial revenues amount to 3.86 billion FRF, out of which 2.73 billion FRF come from traffic and 1.13 come from compensations for social fares. The State subsidy is over 4 billion FRF for operating these services, Regional subsidies amounts to 270 million FRF. The deficit of regional services amounts to 1.6 billion FRF.

Although it is considered as a taboo subject, SNCF is considering a splitting up into regional subsidiary companies as soon as the regional contracts have proved their efficiency over time. But the Regions might organise competition between those subsidiary companies through tendering (as for *London Buses*) or open tendering to private operators (such as CGEA, who does not comment publicly, but is only waiting for this to happen). Considering the Regions' growing role in the financing and maintenance of the rolling stock, the full acquisition of the rolling stock may actually constitute a first step towards tendering. The Region will simply have to entrust the stock to another operator after tendering; thus reducing considerably the entry costs on the market.

As far as RFF is concerned, it is hoping to find another financing source through the financial contributions that the Regions will accept to provide for the network. The total amount may evolve positively, depending upon the new Transport Authority competencies granted to the Regions.

7.5 General evaluation and conclusions

The future of SNCF will depend on the success of the reforms. Progress will be slow, given that the two principal actors in this growth (RFF and the Regions) must establish their new powers and have them recognised by the railway workers' unions and SNCF itself.

The French railway network was operating at 3 speeds: the high speed network, the national traditional speed network and the regional network, whose performance depended on regional political will. If these reforms are successful, the network could move towards a 2 level-network:

- at the regional level, SNCF would move both towards regional subsidiaries and regional networks, perhaps with competitive tendering and competition for the track; and
- at the national level, financing, design and costs of new lines will be more efficiently controlled by RFF, the maintenance of existing lines will be rationalised and the national services could become more efficient.

SNCF is clearly at a crossroad. It is condemned to succeed, but success is not guaranteed as the reform is incomplete. One may say that the State and SNCF entered this reform against their will. The State limited itself to reforming the railways with regard to SNCF's financial situation and according to the European directives while taking the personnel's reactions into consideration.

The regionalisation experiments currently being carried out differ from past and present contracts in other regions. In summary, the main changes are threefold. Firstly, the region becomes the true order-giver in terms of service supply, the regions defines the services to be provided and the fares, the region also finances the rolling stock and determines its technical specifications. Secondly, SNCF becomes a simple operator and bears both cost and revenue risks. Thirdly, SNCF promises to deliver a specific quality level as measured by specific indicators and bonus/malus financial penalties are established. However, the new power equilibrium between SNCF and the regions is not yet determined and only observation of the functioning of the contracts within the coming years will provide more information.

As far as the new legislation is concerned, the Regions are in their majority favourable to becoming Organising Transport Authority for the regional railway passenger services and wish to control networks and services for which they are financially responsible without having to face a powerful SNCF, as in the past. It is therefore to be expected that they develop their political and financial involvement into these services. The first contracts signed show that substantial improvements in terms of service supply have been agreed upon (see the Rhone-Alpes region). But the Regions also want to have all powers related to this financial involvement, according to the principle of 'the one who pays, decides'. The regions want to work together with the SNCF as they recognise its expertise, but they are afraid of being confronted with a monopoly without having themselves enough negotiation power. Discussions on further changes are essentially restricted to closed circles of experts and regional transport authorities and no public debate on these topics can currently be observed as this subject is extremely touchy from a political point of view. However, some Regions clearly state that they want to be able to call for tender under the new legislation.

All actors involved, State, Regions, SNCF and RFF are evolving towards a new equilibrium in their mutual relationships. The trade unions and the (potential) private operators are just waiting for things to happen. A failure of the reforms would be a sign of a continued, if not permanent, decline of the railways. Even though SNCF's social importance continues to be strong, its political weight is fading, given that its financial burden has become too heavy for the authorities.

8 Synthesis and general lessons

DIDIER VAN DE VELDE and PERAN VAN REEVEN
Erasmus University Rotterdam

This chapter starts with a synthesis from the analysis that has been carried out in this research. General lessons will be drawn at the end of this chapter. To facilitate comparisons between countries, a synthesis in tabular form will be presented in a number of sections.

- *8.1 Competition model chosen*: This section presents the general choice for a model of competition in each of the countries considered.
- *8.2 Policy choices behind model choice*: Three issues are addressed in this section for each country considered, in complement to the first section: the choice for competition, the reasons for the specific choice made and additional policy considerations.
- *8.3 State railway reform process*: This section presents in short the reform path followed and the transitional measures taken in each of the countries.
- *8.4 Infrastructure*: This section focuses on three aspects of the infrastructure: ownership, maintenance and track access.
- *8.5 Production inputs*: This section presents in very broad terms the access to the three vital production inputs (rolling stock, personnel and track).
- *8.6 Services*: This section summarises in broad lines the division of strategic, tactical and operational tasks between the actors in the country considered.
- *8.7 Experience with competition (a few tentative observations)*: This section gives only a few out of several points worth mentioning from of the findings of the case studies (the reader is referred to the country reports for more details).
- *8.8 General lessons*: This sections goes further into the discussion by comparing the observations and results from the various countries analysed.

This synthesis aims only at giving an overview of the main observations made during the research in the countries selected. The reform of railway regulation is a complex field and many details are of utmost importance both for the understanding of the functioning of the models and for the success of their implementation. The reader of this synthesis is therefore strongly encouraged to read the details mentioned in the country chapters and to consult the original legislation to prevent misunderstandings that could otherwise result from the superficial reading of only this synthesis.

8.1 Competition model chosen

GREAT BRITAIN: Tendering of networks

- Competition *for* the track where the tendering authority (OPRAF) specifies minimum service levels (to a large extent similar to former BR service levels) and further performance incentives (reliability, punctuality). Franchisees are then free to develop additional commercial services.
- Phased introduction of competition *on* the track under strict rules of *moderation of competition*: max. 0.2% of each flow until 1999, then 20% (currently under consultation), then perhaps free access. Today in practice: only incidental competition on the track, limited to overlapping franchises or competing routes.
- Intermodal competition with buses on short-distances, and with airlines and express buses on long-distance.

SWEDEN: Monopoly on national commercial network and regional services contracted/tendered by regional transport authorities

- No competition on the profitable national rail services, SJ operates these services without operational subsidies. Non-competitive entry may be allowed (no case yet).
- No competition on the track although it was planned for the long term but later postponed when the new government took power.
- Banverket can tender non-profitable national railway services.
- Transfer of regional lines to regional authorities and either contracting after negotiation (with *SJ*) or tendering.
- Co-ordination of tendering for several types of non-profitable services (national and regional rail services as well as other modes) by a new authority is being discussed.
- Some intermodal competition with airlines and express buses on long distance routes.

GERMANY: De facto national monopoly and regional services contracted/tendered by regional transport authorities

- No operational subsidy to long-distance services, open access in principle (but no clear rules for track slot allocation yet and no case yet) under legal preference for network-integration, clockface timetable and high-frequency local/regional services.
- Regionalisation of local railway lines with possibility of tendering (no obligation, additional legislation within each state).
- Some intermodal competition with airlines on long-distance routes.

SWITZERLAND: De facto national monopoly and regional services contracted by regional authorities to regional companies, with some elements of competitive threat/contestability

- Discussions on reform not yet finalised (1999).
- Regionalisation of regional services implemented (1996). Introduction of 'ordering of services' from incumbent operator, autonomous proposals by companies possible in the standard ordering procedures. Tendering possible but not compulsory (depends on Cantonal legislation). Efficiency evaluation method (*yardstick competition*) under development at ministry (*BAV*) for usage in the context of the service 'ordering' procedures.
- Open access for new/non-competing services possible in principle under legal preference for tariff-integration, network-integration and clockface timetable (no cases yet, further discussions going on).

JAPAN: Private railway companies with diversified activities

- No competition for or on the track (however intermodal competition rail/air on long-distance routes). JR companies and private companies have monopolistic regional positions (long-term licences).
- No or relatively small subsidies.
- Several forms of indirect competition: *yardstick competition* by Ministry through fares regulation, competition between companies (lines, urban areas, etc.) based on other activities along the tracks (diversified companies).

FRANCE: State monopoly and transfer of some powers to the regions

- No competition: monopoly rights to SNCF, however some intermodal competition with airlines on long-distance routes.
- Experimental contractualisation of some regional services without competition (SNCF monopoly), this may result in some indirect competition in the future.
- A few regional services historically under private operation will have to be tendered in the future.

8.2 Policy choices behind model choice

Choice for competition	Motivation behind model	Additional policy measures
	GREAT BRITAIN	
• (Dogmatic) position in favour of competition • Wider national privatisation policy	• Thorough implementation of economic incentives and contracts to steer individual actors resulting from splitting of BR • *Moderation of competition* as a first step to ease the road for privatisation	• Limited integrated transport policy (at least up to 1997).
	SWEDEN	
• Wider national deregulation policy • Increasing usage of tendering as competition instrument	• Gradual approach and belief in some economies of scale • Competition fosters efficiency improvements seen as necessary	• Co-ordination of public transport services by regional authorities (and SJ) • Environmental policy
	GERMANY	
• Reform choice not directly based on competition idea • Introduction of tendering as possible selection mechanism	• Efficiency improvement and need for solution to debt problem • (German re-unification played catalytic role) • Regionalisation policy in public transport	• Raise fuel taxes with explicit objective to finance the rail reform • Some local policies towards curbing of car use
	SWITZERLAND	
• Reform choice not based on competition idea but some competition accepted as instrument • Introduction of clearer selection procedures	• Standardisation of the conditions under which companies operate • Efficiency improvement and implementation of better possibilities for regional trade-offs	• Limited

Choice for competition	Motivation behind model	Additional policy measures
	JAPAN	
• Reform of national railways inspired by example of private railways • No direct competition	• Historically developed. • Streamlining of laws and regulations after restructuring and reform of JNR so that harmonised conditions exist.	• Car traffic restraint (only limited results) by parking policies and high usage costs
	FRANCE	
• Choice against competition • *'Service public'* tradition	• Give more autonomy and induce more dynamism at SNCF • Labour union pressure	• Law on 'the air and the rational utilisation of energy': urban transport plans (land-use integration) aiming at reduction of car traffic and development of public transport

8.3 State railway reform process

Reform	Transition
GREAT BRITAIN	
• Step by step • Creation of Train Operating Companies (TOCs) (subsidiaries) under BR-flag • Tendering (and privatisation) of TOC's by OPRAF (Office of Passenger Rail Franchising)	• Everybody starts with clean slate (equal conditions) • Reorganisation through privatisation of numerous activities
SWEDEN	
• Step by step • Since 1979 gradual regionalisation • Since 1985 gradual splitting of infrastructure and operations • Introduction of tendering after period of contracting (further extension expected)	• Company reform internally organised by SJ, with goals set by Government • Transfer of regional rolling stock to regional transport authorities

Reform	Transition
GERMANY	
• Step by step • Merger DB/DR, restructuring into DBAG with separate divisions (further reform of divisions in coming years) • Regionalisation 1996 (tendering not compulsory)	• Debt burden from the past and redundant personnel transferred to specific fund • Initial contract to maintain existing regional services in transitional period
SWITZERLAND	
• Step by step (continuous reform concept) • Review of existing legislation (initially for regional then for national transport), uniformisation of conditions	• Company reform internally to SBB, goals set by Government • Solution to debt burden required (modalities to be decided soon)
JAPAN	
• New uniform legislation for all railway companies • Reorganisation of JNR into the JR-Group (privatisation process not yet finalised)	• Settlement Corporation takes over most of debt burden from the past
FRANCE	
• SNCF split into SNCF (operations) and RFF (infrastructure) (not yet finalised)	• Not yet applicable.

8.4 Infrastructure

Ownership and investments	Maintenance	Traffic control	Access charges
GREAT BRITAIN			
• *Railtrack* privatised • Most stations and depots leased to TOCs • Investments programme monitored by *Rail Regulator*	• Subcontracted by *Railtrack*	• *Railtrack*	• Access charges to cover full infrastructure costs (substantial fixed charge plus additional variables charges) • Access charges determined by *Railtrack* but monitored by the *Rail Regulator*

Ownership and investments	Maintenance	Traffic control	Access charges
		SWEDEN	
• *Banverket* (not privatised) owns tracks and platforms, SJ owns ground and stations • Fringe network owned by SJ, private companies and municipalities • 10-year investment plan every 4 year by *Banverket*	• *Banverket*	• *Banverket* (since 1996)	• Variable track charges implemented to create similar conditions as for road traffic • Track charges based on wear and tear, accrue directly to the State, not to *Banverket*
		GERMANY	
• Separate division under DBAG (full separation planned, possibility of partial privatisation) • Investments planned Federal 'plan of demand' and by DB's infrastructure division • Regional authorities can take over tracks in some circumstances	• DB Track	• DB Track	• Access charges determined by DB's infrastructure division • Differentiated charges are applied (by routes, train categories and quantities) • Aims at covering infrastructure costs (not achieved)
		SWITZERLAND	
• No institutional separation, accounting separation for all companies, also organisational separation for larger companies (e.g. SBB, BLS) • Privates accept open access (for freight) but reject total separation	• Controlled by each railway company	• Controlled by each railway company	• All subsidised services have to take an infrastructure fee fixed by the Ministry into account (with exceptions) • Infrastructure deficit of Federal railways paid by the Confederation • Further reform under discussion

Ownership and investments	Maintenance	Traffic control	Access charges
JAPAN			
• Each railway company owns its infrastructure • Only a few minor separate infrastructure providers	• Controlled by each railway company	• Controlled by each railway company	• Internal to railway companies • Negotiations between companies in case of through operations (assessed by Ministry)
FRANCE			
• RFF (public company) • Annual investment plan to be submitted to the State	• SNCF, under contract with RFF	• SNCF	• Access charges determined by RFF within a framework set by decree

8.5 Production inputs

Rolling stock	Personnel	Infrastructure capacity
GREAT BRITAIN		
• Three privatised competing rolling stock leasing companies (ROSCOs) • TOCs can also order and own new rolling stock	• Complete transfer to winner of *franchise* then normal bargaining with trade-unions	• Planned by *Railtrack*
SWEDEN		
• No leasing company, SJ owns trains for national services • Regional transport authorities own regional trains (transferred to them)	• Various practices in the past, complete transfer (then normal bargaining) expected in the future	• Planned by *Banverket*

Rolling stock	Personnel	Infrastructure capacity
	GERMANY	
• No leasing company created by reorganisation. • Transport authorities subsidise the purchasing of regional rolling stock	• Redundant civil service personnel transferred to separate organisation, DB only pays personnel used • Transfer of personnel when tendered expected	• Planned by DB Track (unless track transferred to regional authority)
	SWITZERLAND	
• Railway companies own their rolling stock	• Personnel transfer organised in case of transfer of service	• Planned by each railway company (larger companies have infrastructure division) (general rules set by Ministry)
	JAPAN	
• Railway companies own their rolling stock	• (Stable position for existing companies)	• Planned by railway company (approval by Ministry of Transport in case of through operation)
	FRANCE	
• Owned by SNCF • Regional financing for regional rolling stock	• Status similar to civil servant	• RFF, but managed by SNCF

8.6 Services

Strategic level[1] **(main aims and service characteristics)**	**Tactical level (design of services)**	**Operational level (production of services)**
	GREAT BRITAIN	
• Franchising Director (OPRAF) and transport authorities in large metropolitan areas (PTA/PTE) • Additional entrepreneurial freedoms limited by general framework	• Train Operating Companies (franchisees) • Minimum level of service (PSR) imposed by *Franchising Director* (OPRAF)	• Train Operating Companies (franchisees) • Quality of operations (reliability, punctuality) submitted to incentive regime by OPRAF
	SWEDEN	
National (profitable)	*National (profitable)*	*National (profitable)*
• SJ (under specific regulation)	• SJ	• SJ
National (non-profit.)	*National (non-profit.)*	*National (non-profit.)*
• Banverket's tendering division	• Banverket's tendering division	• Operator
Regional	*Regional*	*Regional*
• Regional transport authority	• Regional transport authority and/or its planning company	• Operator

[1] The concepts of 'strategic', 'tactical' and 'operational' levels in passenger transport are further detailed in Van de Velde, D.M. (1997), "Entrepreneurship and tendering in local public transport services", paper presented at the 5th International Conference on Competition and Ownership in Land Passenger Transport, Leeds, UK (May 1997).

Strategic level[1] (main aims and service characteristics)	Tactical level (design of services)	Operational level (production of services)
	GERMANY	
National	*National*	*National*
• DBAG	• DBAG	• DBAG
• Governmental influence on infrastructure investments	• Legal emphasis on preservation of integrated services and clockface timetables	
Regional	*Regional*	*Regional*
• Regional authority (various legislation, transport plans)	• Regional authority (transport plan), its transport company and/or *Verkehrsverbund*	• Operator
	• (Operator)	
	SWITZERLAND	
National	*National*	*National*
• SBB, (private)	• SBB, (private)	• SBB, (private)
• Preservation of integrated system determined by legislation	• Ministry (*BAV*) has monitoring function, especially with regard to integration (clockface timetable, connections, ticketing)	
Regional	*Regional*	*Regional*
• Cantons order services (consultation with incumbent company, however spontaneous offers by other companies are possible)	• Railway companies	• Railway companies
	• Cantonal transport plan can limit the freedoms of the operators	
	JAPAN	
• Railway companies	• Railway companies	• Railway companies
	• Regulatory influence by Ministry (*yardstick* competition)	

Strategic level[1] **(main aims and service characteristics)**	**Tactical level (design of services)**	**Operational level (production of services)**
	FRANCE	
National	*National*	*National*
• State and SNCF	• SNCF	• SNCF
Regional	*Regional*	*Regional*
• *Région* in the experimental areas	• *Région* in the experimental areas	• SNCF

8.7 Experience with competition (a few tentative observations)

Results	**Problems**	**Remarks**
	GREAT BRITAIN	
• Large subsidies with commitments to subsidy reductions by franchisees • Productivity increases • Demand increase but largely related to economic upturn • Improvements in level of service, some autonomous commercial innovations, more fares differentiation, development of some bus/rail integration	• Regulation of Railtrack not optimal • No regulation of ROSCOs or provisions for capturing excessive profits on re-sale of ROSCOs	• Too early to judge consequences • Many of the current changes started under the intermediate BR-regime (TOU/TOC) • Change in accounting rules make comparison before/after extremely difficult

Results	Problems	Remarks
	SWEDEN	
National (profitable)	*National (profitable)*	*National (profitable)*
• (No competition)	• (No competition)	• (No competition)
National (non-profitable.)	*National (non-profitable)*	*National (non-profitable)*
• Savings by tendering	• No new entry yet	• Limited experience yet
Regional	*Regional*	*Regional*
• Production cost savings by tendering (15-20%) • Better integration of bus/train networks • Service (and demand) increase as a result of action by regional transport authority	• Barriers to entry • Questions about the fairness of bids by SJ • Future financial resources for regional authorities (transfer for central government) • Vertical separation make total financing non-transparent	• Many contracts still negotiated • The operators do not determine the services, the supply is ordered by the transport authorities
	GERMANY	
National	*National*	*National*
• (No competition yet)	• (No competition yet)	• (No competition yet)
Regional	*Regional*	*Regional*
• Savings by tendering • More services ordered by regional authorities	• Extensive negotiation rounds needed during tendering process • Fairness of position of entrants/small companies compared to DB (track charges, etc.) • Time needed to acquire new rolling stock	• Limited experience yet • No operations started in analysed case studies • Authorities subsidise substantially the purchase of new rolling stock

Results	Problems	Remarks
	Switzerland	
National	*National*	*National*
• (No competition yet)	• (No competition yet)	• Programme to increase the service frequency to 2 trains/hour
Regional	*Regional*	*Regional*
• More services for same level of subsidy	• Interrelationship with neighbouring services required substantial modification to winning concept	• Only one experiment yet (with vertical integration, infrastructure investments needed to realise winning concept) • Operations according to new concept not yet started (two years delay)
	Japan	
• (No competition *on* or *for* the track, but various forms of indirect competition exist traditionally) • Private sector more efficient	• Debt of former JNR not yet fully repaid	• Reform and privatisation (ongoing) of national railways besides pre-existing private railways
	France	
National	*National*	*National*
• (No competition)	• -	• -
Regional	*Regional*	*Regional*
• (No competition, only experiments with contractualisation)	• Appropriateness of accounting rules to avoid cross-subsidisation between regional services and other services	• Current regionalisation experiments expected to form an example • Some hope for some competition

8.8 General lessons

This section goes further into the discussion than the 'general evaluation and conclusions' included in each country chapter. It makes use of the comparison of the observations and results from the various countries analysed. Additional general knowledge and insights gained by the co-ordinating researchers in the context of the research are also used here.

This study was not meant to result in policy advice. It was rather meant to feed and stimulate discussion and reflection. A number of lessons, presented in a number of categories, will therefore deliberately be presented here in a rather 'telegraphic' style. These lessons are not and do not pretend to be scientific truths. They have to be interpreted as results of 'fact finding' research carried out in a short period of time in international co-operation. More time, additional theoretical research and, most importantly, more practical experience with the various competition models implemented in the various countries in the railway sector, are needed before being able to give more definitive conclusions.

Competition models

Competition plays a role as instrument in most railway reform processes in recent years. Great Britain has implemented this in the most extensive way. But numerous models of competition in the railway sector exist. To name a few:

- competition *off* (or *for*) the tracks (tendering/franchising);
- competition *on* the tracks (intramodal competition on the same tracks);
- competition *between* tracks (intramodal competition on different tracks – parallel lines serving the same main cities but other local markets);
- competition *besides and above* the tracks (intermodal competition with car, bus and plane);
- competition *between companies* on their own tracks (yardstick competition by the authority, competition for residents along the tracks, and/or profitability competition on the stock exchange); and
- competition *in the train* (competition between different quality of service on board within the same train, such as in night trains).

Competition *on* the track, for those countries who see this model as an aim, is usually seen as a long-term aim.

Pure models do not exist in reality and it is common to encounter different models on different markets within a same country. A difference between long distances and short distances is very common.

It would be wrong to think that there is one single better model that can be developed as a blueprint and then implemented once and for all. Each model will need adjustments in the future. Most countries therefore choose for a step-by-step approach where the future steps are often only sketched.

More models can be developed than can be observed in the real world. It will in all cases be necessary to take account of the specific local situation and aims to design an appropriate model.

Competition and regulation

Competition requires a substantial amount of regulation, often more than a single national railway monopoly. For a part, this is only an impression as national railways are often regulated by means of internal influence, i.e. an informal way. Competition has the advantage of requiring the intervention to become explicit; an associated advantage is that the correlated subsidy requirements also become explicit.

A 'referee' or 'regulating agent' is likely to be necessary to make the whole system 'work'. This is for a part resulting from the 'unknown', which is present in most reforms. The need for such an agent may diminish in the future when markets have settled (infrastructure, rolling stock, etc.)

Furthermore, the selection procedures (tendering) that can be observed in several countries are usually not mechanistic but require a substantial amount of negotiation, especially if service characteristics have to be determined by the tendering process.

The development of the required regulation and contracts necessitates specific skills, professional organisations and an appropriate amount of time. This can be quite costly (see Great Britain) but it is assumed to produce advantages in the longer run. A further condition for long term success in the tendering approach is the ability to avoid collusion and excessive concentration by using appropriate contracting conditions.

Integration

Many countries believe strongly in the integration of services (clockface timetables, connecting services, through ticketing, etc.) This is often more based on belief than on pure proof. The focus on integration often results in considerable efforts to guarantee integration by means of legislation and regulation (Switzerland, Germany and Great Britain).

Service design and regionalisation

A regionalisation trend of local railway services can be observed in most European countries. As these are often unprofitable and as the regional authorities do not have unlimited subsidisation budgets, contracting and tendering are often introduced by these authorities as instrument to guarantee value for money for the taxpayer.

The introduction of the competition instrument for services which do not cover their costs (i.e. 'competition for the subsidy') require from the subsidising authorities to become much clearer about their aims and/or required services than in previous state monopoly regimes.

This often results in the subsidising authorities defining exactly what services to produce (through their own planning departments or companies), leaving little freedom for the operators. In other words, many tendering models transform the authorities, perhaps unconsciously, into railway entrepreneurs, downgrading the railway companies to producers of train-km.

Many regional authorities have acquired their transport planning skills in the bus sector during a regionalisation phase (that often started in the 1970s, as in Sweden and Great Britain) and that came before the introduction of competitive regimes. Those that can not benefit from this experience but to which powers for the railway sector have recently been decentralised are faced with a substantial challenge. The authorities active in the bus sector were often disciplined by their duty to use local taxation to finance their actions. As far as the railway sector is concerned, subsidy transfers from the national level to the regional level mostly remains necessary in a transitional phase, if not longer.

The action of regional transport authorities often concentrates on better integration between regional train and bus services than under a national railway monopoly (Sweden, Germany) which pays more attention to long distances. This shift of focus can also be observed by the action of the

British franchisees and the Japanese railways (both introducing their own local feeder bus services).

The increased influence of regional authorities coupled with (the threat of) competition is seen to have led to changes in the attitudes of the state railway companies. Examples are given of requests by the regional authorities which were deemed 'impossible' and which suddenly could be discussed after the reform.

State railway reform

The reform of existing (monopolistic) national railway companies usually takes several steps and national legislation often dictates to the state companies the way to go. Several options exist, including various forms of unbundling (separation between passenger and freight, geographical separation, sectoral separation between Intercity and regional services, etc.), the selling-off of ancillary businesses and the contracting out of various functions (such as maintenance).

The creation of a level playing field is a requirement for fair competition. Access to rolling stock, personnel and especially infrastructure according to clear procedures may be required in the first steps of the reform.

In most countries examined (Great Britain, Germany, Japan, Switzerland and France), specific attention is paid to the burdens of the past for the state railway companies before submitting them to competition (such as transfer of debts and redundant personnel to specific temporary institutions).

Railway reform and entrepreneurship

Privatisation opens the door to entrepreneurs. However, as stated above, this is often limited to the 'production' of services. Still, new and existing companies have started developing, some of these operating at an international level.

Full entrepreneurship including service design is not widespread in the railway sector. It can only truly be observed in Japan where vertically integrated companies develop their markets and all related assets in a long-term perspective. Such a model would obviously be easier to introduce in Europe if services were truly profitable, but this could, in a first step, be achieved artificially by reshaping some subsidy streams into user subsidisation or revenue compensations.

A model stimulating true and full railway entrepreneurship in Europe remains to be developed. The British franchisees have only received some freedoms in this respect as they are submitted to a strict regulating framework and separation regime that do not allow the development of all synergies available to train operators in Japan. The British franchising regime should therefore be seen as only a first step towards a more truly entrepreneurial model. For that matter, only time will tell whether the franchisees will deliver the service improvements and subsidy reductions promised in their contracts.

Separation between infrastructure and operations

Some separation of infrastructure and operations is a common feature of most reform models, except Japan. The separation is often limited to accounting or organisational separation. Sweden and Great Britain being the exceptions with institutional separations.

If the implemented models, especially open-access competition in Great Britain, take off and traffic consequently grows then there will be conflicts in the access to the infrastructure and clear(er) allocation rules and/or price mechanisms will become indispensable.[2] Few countries appear to be fully ready for this pending regulatory challenge, not even Great Britain.

More entrepreneurial railway companies stress the importance of the integration between infrastructure, operations and – above all – side businesses (stations, real estate, etc.) This is very clear in Japan but can also be observed at a much smaller scale in Switzerland. The Japanese example shows how intense the interaction between infrastructure, operations and other businesses can be: private operators develop considerable mutually supportive business activities alongside the tracks (shops, offices, department stores, housing, touristic and recreational facilities, etc.) guaranteeing long-term commitments to the railway services. This encourages the 'railway mindedness' of those local communities.

[2] The Japanese railways show that substantially higher levels of capacity utilisation than European practice are feasible under specific conditions, such as double track lines with quadruple tracks at stations, limited freight traffic and, perhaps foremost, a high level of staff discipline resulting in extreme punctuality.

The effect of competition

The usage of the competition instrument in an attempt to reach more efficiency or greater customer-awareness seems to achieve at least some of its aims where it has been implemented. The introduction of a new framework of relationships between transport authorities and transport companies also appeared to allow breaking the conservative attitudes of some companies, showing that more things suddenly become possible.

It is however in most cases still too early to measure the full impact of the legal, regulatory and organisational changes, especially where reforms have been implemented in the past few years. The effects of railway reform will take many years to settle down as many of the related aspects (see, e.g., Japan as far as real estate is concerned) are long-term businesses.

Productive efficiency improvements are the most obvious and easily measurable consequence (unit production cost reductions of about 15% are not exceptional); with however accountancy changes making comparisons difficult. Increases in performances in terms of ridership and modal split are much more difficult to measure, as changes here often do not come alone and as time is needed to allow operators both to develop and implement new concepts.

Finally, it has to be remembered that the consequences produced by the implementation of a specific model always have to be interpreted on the basis of the starting situation in the region considered. In this respect it has to be remembered that the level of service and efficiency still varies widely from country to country. International comparisons can not be made on the basis of single percentage comparisons.